Mexican Ivy

Collected Poems
1975 – 2015

MJM

Publisher: Waiting For The Robots
Publication Editor: S.-F. Strang

ISBN: 0692965688
ISBN-13: 978-0692965689

10 9 8 7 6 5 4 3 2 1

SF/CA

To E, A, and Lex

The one raised,
The second rounded
And the last one eclipsed.

The author is indebted to his teachers of many moons ago:
Jonathan Strong, Richard Tillinghast, Alan Williamson, Alan Trustman

And those stars in our orbit:
Robert Fitzgerald, Seamus Heaney, Czeslaw Milosz, Helen Vendler

MJM has pursued the practice of poetry
for forty years.
Since 1985 he has been an art dealer, gallerist, and auctioneer
in New York, Chicago, Los Angeles, and San Francisco.
He is an art historian and collector,
who studied imaginative writing at Harvard.

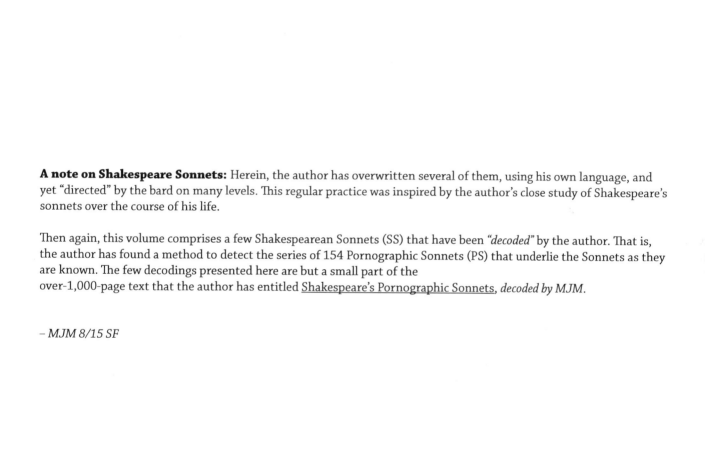

A note on Shakespeare Sonnets: Herein, the author has overwritten several of them, using his own language, and yet "directed" by the bard on many levels. This regular practice was inspired by the author's close study of Shakespeare's sonnets over the course of his life.

Then again, this volume comprises a few Shakespearean Sonnets (SS) that have been *"decoded"* by the author. That is, the author has found a method to detect the series of 154 Pornographic Sonnets (PS) that underlie the Sonnets as they are known. The few decodings presented here are but a small part of the
over-1,000-page text that the author has entitled <u>Shakespeare's Pornographic Sonnets</u>, *decoded by MJM.*

– *MJM 8/15 SF*

Give my love fame faster than Time wastes life;
  So thou prevent'st his scythe and crooked knife.

                – William Shakespeare, Sonnet 100

I want to eat the fleeting shade of your lashes,
and I pace around hungry, sniffing the twilight,
hunting for you, for your hot heart,
Like a puma in the barrens of Quitratue."

              – Pablo Neruda, Love Sonnet XI

But the echoes died at her back as the walls
Gave way to fields and the incessant seethe of grasses
Riding in the full
Of the moon, manes to the wind,
Tireless, tied, as a moon-bound sea
Moves on its root.

              – Sylvia Plath, "Hardcastle Crags"

For beauty is nothing but the beginning of terror, which we are still just able to endure,
and we are so awed because it serenely disdains to annihilate us.
Every angel is terrifying.
And so I hold myself back and swallow the call-note of my dark sobbing.
Ah, whom can we ever turn to in our need?
Not angels, not humans, and already the knowing animals are aware
that we are not really at home in our interpreted world.
Perhaps there remains for us some tree on a hillside, which every day we can take into our vision;
there remains for us yesterday's street and the loyalty of a habit so much at ease
when it stayed with us that it moved in and never left.

              – Rainer Maria Rilke, "Duino Elegy 1"

When your dreamboat turns out to be a footnote . . .
Everyday I write the book

              – Elvis Costello

Do you have eyes?
Can you see like mankind sees?
Why have you soured and curdled me?
Oh you tireless watcher! What have I done to you?
That you make everything I dread and everything I fear come true?

      ¶

Wild thing . . . (I thought you loved me).

              – Joni Mitchell

I cook with wine, sometimes I even add it to the food.

              – W.C. Fields

Mexican Ivy

Contents

¡*Olé!* Androgyne Paglia!

Mother Nature lay waiting 'round every
Paved corner to swat us back to swamp.

I go forlorn and sea-weedy, ambivalent
Roadkill on a dewy, clammy off-ramp.

She who has dethroned the gods, now
Tinkles seedpods in the manor born:

  WWI face, halogen space,
Her spare snack of lice and lace.

In some high-holy secretive place
Least of all does she endure allowishness.

Like her, with every passing fuck I grow
More pagan. Her quippy micro-citations

Thrust own research down the throat of *summa cum laude*. Own genius, a jizz of random.

MJM 10/95 SF

1-11-11

The bills of last decade laid
The world low, as tick-tack-
woe O's filled in our # sign.

He figures these elevens
that keep tolling the car's
LCD clock and his cell

Must be a sign from the
Charmed grid we all call
Universe our chips'll a-

lign parallel this time to
Heaven's will of fortune.
He's ill with flu today, a-

Rent with bacteria his *'im-
mutiny'* in a half-chill room
Can't kill. "No one," as he

Recalls, "Zooms sick as little
Kids:" their 106° fevers and
Whooping coughs and balling

To mamma till evening, as
Hell-hot tot in his viral steam
pitifully gills under her virtue:

Love called or *not* called upon,
Automatically she'll stand tall-
Willed. As with many what-

Nots of old age, stalled days
with flu dull him to sad full
Heartlessness. With sense &

experience his body curls up
in twilled naps to sleepdom, till
nearly well, the shame of pills

and calling no one rhymes
the calendar with sad *eye-*
bagged *X*'s. Sick in illiquid

Times, he can't scare up Mom

to coddle some toddlers' cough-
Swill, nor to fever-touch his face.

This alien half-house, home
town and less than half life
he wandered into from vigor-

Ous youth annul his will for
Spirited retort, reward, award.
Under covers, he can't even

Loll his drill to stiffen. So on this
Lucky date, he mayn't even cast
a thrill spill – nixed friends, billet,

Lover, nor wallet to retell him,
He may *already* be 'chill' on "am"
Track, even if all broke and ill.

That, willed this illusion of el-
evens by God, still, distill, refill
his canyon/parallel a re-union,

no shill on rill uphill.

MJM 1/11 SF

24/7

Some days, I just want to do heroin with Billie Holiday.
Or have *A Beer* because it's *damn hot* outside!
Or a *ghlass* of wine because I'm an adult
      and it's what grown-ups and French people do
      in the swing of fancy places. I, a Francophile.
Seriously, do meth or coke and wank
      day-and-nights away to porn
my way. Or host an orgy. Is that so rod-odd?
Other days, I want to hang from a ceiling fan
      and, noose or belt not working,
      get a cheap thrill from the swirling.
But it wobbles, whoosh, whoosh, whoosh
      dub dub
          dub
          dub
S.O.B.E.R. – Son Of a Bitch, Everything's Real!
But, she *was* a bitch: "Still is, son." Is that what's to blame?
But this disease came from both sides
      of the family Tree,
      dead in graved gramps, uncles
      still alive in cousins, my brother, me.
We keep fretting how normal people drink
like gentlemen. Or they don't drink. Or they do a bit
but don't think about it, afterwards. *Bloody slags!*
Except *to where's* they get a hangover. In which case,
they don't re-drink for awhile. Like I would.
The difference between an alkie and a "normie" is that
If science came up with a pill to cure
Alcoholism, normies wouldn't take it,
      and I would take it all the time, in order
      to drink vodka on ice with a splash of juice, 24/7.
Thus, hospitalization, mental institutions, police chases,
      jails and prisons, homelessness, depression
and suicide would not evaporate like Rx's do *yer munney*.
That's the *everlahsting* part I abhor and hate.
Why I'm at an A.A. meeting late.
Of a Saturday night.
Fighting the good fight.
Or surrendering to the light
      that inspires the right insight?
Still, it's hard not to romance being altered.
Some humans *crave* it. Obsess to down and own it!
But *y'all* do just a bit. Then can *waive* it.
La naïveté, quel bonheur! To butt drink like a gent, my normal Sir . . .

MJM 8/14 SF

A John's Target

– Cock and tit worship: two sides of the same loin?
– I used to not care for Asian chicks; now I do. A story of dim some, alight on others?

The enlightened say his "Target" is a *mandala,*
Still center of a turning universe in which all

Of us may rest and meditate to peace, calm,
And self-awareness – and yet he imagines balm

On a butthole! One could also say, artist gay,
He's painted a double entendre, obsessing the way

A top does, facing a lovely bottom's erotic knoll.
Reading on, he sees they say Zen-and-I-Ching soul

Do not eschew humor or sexuality the way
   Western philosophy and religions sway

Us against these with elaborate theories of sin,
The art's allusions to mandala and rim, akin.

The target's hit by arrows from a bow,
Flèche into foam, as when boys take his blow

Into their nether part, interpass communion:
Whilst above, the lips and mouths in union

   Gently bite, tickle, nick necks and ears,
   Tongues thrusting in-and-out – saliva smears –

As lubricant keeps the violent pounding
Delicious for his passenger, cries resounding!

Yet, centered in the chest, hearts' pulsing
Resounds each other's without impulsing

Into each other's body cavities, that chakra
With its indestructible red and white drops

Giving and receiving love with no promise
Of hunter's/hunted's meat, bull's eye, or rise

Of prick into rilled's desire. It's love,
   Giving and getting we admire.

On hearts, I'd obfuscate – while in target worship
   I'd hone in on hero's arrow cum penile wingtip.

In the West, cuddling is to conquering puss and ass
As *not* trespassing is to *trespass?*

   Lo! I'll give up Aristotle, Socrates,
If johns'll but paint mandalas . . . please.

MJM 8/14 SF

A Tale of Two Cities

And this is good old Boston,
The home of the bean and the cod.
Where the Lowells talk only to Cabots,
And the Cabots talk only to God.

Good ole' Nawlins,
The home of red beans and rice,
Where the Garden only talks to the Quarter
. . . and the Quarter only balks at lice.

A Tail of Two Cities

MJM 8/14 SF
Italics from John Collins Bossidy's "A Boston Toast"

Accept

Bleak-weak for suicide
Whereas chill, all frill
In that same seat

24 hours ago
You complained of heat.
Now your brow buckles

With schiz inside your
Forehead,
What was once

A symmetrical face.
Work does not impress
A blue lover

Laying down a pact,
As someone smart
Rifles his gullet

Yakkering to the mob:
"Vanish to bargain basement,
Outwrithe each other

On the unlevel ~
Wrestlers – I'm in restos!"
Mother Motel, hot

sleepy, serene, insane,
While me muffins rose
A splash snuffed the pilot.

The rip of your hair and wailing
Belie a great selflessness:
The dead suffer not.

Less than mourners!

Gritting your teeth only
Daunts the utter honesty
Of giving this world

The fucking thing
'e deadly wants.

MJM '83 Manhattan Beach

Acquisitive Heights

One-hundred fifty pair in black trash bags,
No room for them at the sober house, cry out
To be dusted and stacked on proper shoe racks.

What a serotonin rush he bought into, shopping
Every day for two years straight, not even booze
To blame . . . Was more the acquisitive heights

The old America raised him on, like 70s platform
Shoes. Who dies with the most toys wins, shop
Till you drop, nothing succeeds like excess

And the like. Make your mood spike, befriending
And condescending in front of shop girls & guys.
He's worth what he buys. But now black bags

   Puff and sag on the garage floor like black eyes.
He'll never wear them like before, and unlike
In days of yore, *you're yours*, hipsters today

Don't appreciate the ostentation of a hundred-
Fifty pair. To see them dressed up unlikely rare,
They scold consumption to live and fare spare.

How soon the old, courtly styles fade out,
And obsolescence is what you're about:
Well-heeled and one paycheck away

From thrown out.

MJM 6/15 SF

Adam's Evil

Why in my wicked decades
Did I fail to prosper, falter?
And why in blessèd decades
In communion at the altar

Did I surge to exceed
All standards of blue-
Collar rank, supersede
Rich and strong of every hue,

Athletes and wannabes
And climbers and posers
And buddies with *Frisbees*,
Winners to losers?

At forty, I see again everywhere
This system of good and evil
Circulate in thin air.
   My ears and mouth and eyes still,

Frightened by these drafts
Of torture, hate, torment, rape –
Like a medieval picture crafts
Devils choking sinners with red tape.

It's fire, black, and white
And it haunts me every night.

MJM 3/99 SF

After a Long Stay

After a long stay in this hospital called Earth
You decompose, mangled and spotted in purer
Atmosphere, alive but for oxygen intubation.
Penrose drains dart your spirits, and relations

Etherealize until survival is staring down empathy,
Penetrating gazes of the Other, portraits of Christ:
Edgily we receive him, half the one almighty breath
E'er we were given unto death; half a pan handler's

Fiddy-cent off tourists scared as shit in homeless grit.
Of electricity 500 channels twitter outside in this oddly
Ersatz panacea of 1-800 ads, résumés, blogosphere
Bluster vs. say: the solid celebrity of Mr. President.

Squinting sunwise you vaguely remember music
Videos and celebs Warhol warned, if we fell behind
On commissions or the bills, could replace us. Was
I raised in such tangle I'd not dilute in the love

Of just one other, nor family . . . free radical at hell's
Gates bouncing in this ether of error terror? All two
Broken hearts and half-cocked, super ego sorely
Eyeing you for a hand-out unto his id of evil?

Some would say *lust, sloth, gluttony, addiction.*
Whichever way, ego gave bit after bit of itself away
To the weak, as the *Bible* says we do, yet to comedy
And pervy flights of jack-offs. Now your penny-ante

Particles varnish in waxy corridors of re-organization.
You see how hard-bitten Americans in trouble become –
The yanks quoting flea-nit tales of ancestors
Carving snow lodging from trees, and ethnics

Arrogant too with entitlement after slaving after
INS green cards after slaving. People nearly starved
On acorns or millet to save up in brochured U.S. trusts.
It inherited compounded, then disappeared with only

e-mails to trace how Wall Street boys dined on berried
Squab, degusting the nation's last plastic holiday.
Who *would* care about me? They all have their family
Trees of strife and teens on dope to stir their animal fears.

In Great Depression II, the poor inherit the status quo,
And no mean patience kens degenerate "Romans" in-
Tent on sodomy with boys and girls on *Ecstasy* –
Or on trimming poon-tang with silks from Persia.

Unlike you, they established thrift and tilled the till.
Unlike you, they've ever only eaten what they kill.

MJM 3/09 SF

Aftermath of the Rape of Patricia

The maiden was undone, thighs bruised, man-beard
Coarse on the cheek intended for white Christmas'
Blush of fortune. Underground: subway cars
That never know their sound or way. Such grimy
Exhalations rise from their night stalks
Into the dome of evening. The railroad there
Laid eight steel train tracks, four shiny paths of oil;
Poked transients from their sleeping cracks, and battered
With a green, wrecking greed the local bums.
Calling out to someone there, *"Please!* You
In the trousers and *tie!"* (As fingers draw guns
Above the law to pitch old blood to boil:)
Patricia, at the blade's edge, hollers up
The night, toastmaster of the iniquity,
And her one sister Moon, the good egg,
A midnight lamp on thee. Still you stab her.
Then for the sorrowful act he lit a flame.
Fresh torrents of fear rose in her eyes,
Beat-up carcasses of tears. He prowls
The night up crowded boulevards. Only see:
Just at the road's edge, just before sunrise
Cars rumble. Underfoot, stainless tracks
Tremble with daylight. Bird, shade, and bat
Fly up across the lightscape, as the City
Dimmer and dimmer dins.

                                "Now stay in grace,"
The teacher cried. "All you be blessed and pray.
Let all your sins confess. But you, Patricia,
Enter the path there, and unlock your coat.
We've need of guilt and deep redemption after."
(She flung herself wildly up the staircase
Panting as he strode hungry at her heels.)
Hate that ruled the grin there fabled the ground,
The plangent, torrential hate of self,
The regions of wide streets without a light.

"It is my right you writhe as you deserve.
It is my right and proper." This she said:
"That sunk in darkness doomed you languish,
Yoked by chains in Hell."

Afraid of one another,
In smoldering dreams, they chase a tremor right
Through Patsy's rooms, all locked the empty cells:
As one goes through a wall on a faint day's
Treacherous shore, when Jupiter veils the sky,
And warm fog bleeds with colors of the crime.

(Metrics imitated after *The Aeneid,* Robert Fitzgerald, trans.
"The Descent into the Underworld," VI, 237-282)
MJM '90 SF

Against All Odds

At table with you in the Sober Living Environment,
he breakfasted on granola with pre-cut mango.
"I hate cutting mango" he noted, " . . . can't do it."
You offered, *"Well,* you cut it on its axis to the pit,

and then make three more incisions at even intervals.
Finally, start at the top, and peel down the skin
from each of the eight sections. Then use your knife
        to slide each piece off the pit."

"Fugget about it," he said, " . . . too complicated.
I'll buy it at *Safeway,* pre-cut." His tooth crunched
a walnut, and the peach yogurt tasted great.
Observing house rules to the tee, he rinsed his

Utensil and bowl and placed them in the *back*
of the dishwasher, as instructed by his intense
Asian housemaster. Then he left for work, striding
down the sidewalk to the bus stop. Lo and behold,

What did he find in the curb ~ a dried-up, day-old
Mango pit! "Miracle of miracles if that don't beat
the shit!" Trained in statistics, he started figuring
the odds in his head, but the fractions times

fractions started to overwhelm even his MIT
brain. *What impossible odds.* "That's insane!"
Next night, he goes into his bedroom, only to
find his roommate has tipped a *mango* into a

Beer stein under the lamp! – midnight snack-
n-mango knick-knack! OMG, is mango *back?*
To wit: these odds keep getting odder, oddest
Odyssey – or less odd, and more about some

mango God!

MJM 8/15 SF
        to Kimberly

Agita Prodigita

I

children grow up guilty under
Parents' dysfunctionality
But what's in a name?
Call them Dick and Dot Shame.   DNA

   tricks their higher souls
Its spiderweb tangling
The family inside
              a trout

Gasping in filament algae,
  paranoid fry
Ignoring
each dock pier to be mouthed.

His bromide father's
  repute
slips down a ladder line
Casting that nightmare eye

  on his 1st bad dreampair.
Alterego, they ignore
It: to be cast on a marina
Unwinding the boat rope

Round his strong forearm,
no one even over-drinking
Beer on the Bay.

II

The sun would welt
up unscreened moles,
Dick's wrinkly tan singeing
half Mexican from torpor,

Parents beating the air
  in suspended flight,
Spider sensing juice
spinneret mambo,

As near zero Dot
girl-prone in the boat
rocks in the sail air,
sling for web.

III

Suddenly fit as a fiddle
That chopper of a father
Chomps the web
    switching off his fright.

    They'd evade you
Coming of age in love &
    cohort style;
They'd spin a mile

To be themselves without yous
Here, front and center,
slack silk wafting –

IV

Yo!
    Desert water misters,
Cool the cancer on him
    Etching its path

To stifle hometown
August, he'd spill hot
Tears to extinguish
    their bickering,

Low life warning little Dick
    Be ambitious!
Take care the little
    You've been given

V

Bomb the helix
    Intaglio sac
and How each spiky creature
Torn down by waves

Half drowns in
    its parents' slot.

Rebél! Gargle, "No!"
Throw up nucleic acid
for wattage! Volts!

Spume
  Ce n'est pas la vie!
Scrub shards, corpses
Debts, scumbag

fly to die in 7 days,
None of your high priests'
  Décor
  nor diet of worms

drilling, sucking
  you in your coffin.
No inheritance begot, rot
  their periodic minerals

  Boy, unzip your lot!

MJM 7/95 SF

Agitation at Oak Table

Through mud-spattered window slats
All yanked open to angle, imagine brutal
Heat you only bear, beat under wet sheets.
Blink past blanching cars, tinny eaves-
Gutters flaking, parched in a gory desert.
Espy un-neighborly redneck ply seedy
Cul-de-sac to peroxide-blonde gal
For whom he'll *do* a houseboy favor.

Then cast on a swash of Italy or conjure
Córdoba, medieval passage hacking life.
See *bella figura* models by clay pots –
Geraniums, flame-stung; women hampered
By innumerable children wringing flour-
Dusted hands, as gritty menfolk scoop up
Car grease with brittle cloths from sockets
Between oily fingers. They smile, as stained
Tobacco teeth give invitation to red wine
at two-and-a-half hour *colazione*.

We have these organized neighborhoods
Where sweeping leaves and clipping hedges
Rule polite domain. Flying past, the neighbors
Here only measure our up-or-down excesses.
Was it the Brits and Germans germed us
With these stiff, pretentious affects:
Wherein all is but vanity or a chore
Exchanged by nervous wrecks?

The curvy blonde's the only one life light,
Though she's never been across the pond,
"*Ho* to culture," she'll entice and captivate
Many men until maybe-Baby wants a baby.

MJM 8/75 S.B.

AIDS Memorial Grove

– To Every Nun of the Above

Walking within this circle   pause.
Our joy began with Santa Claus;
At school, a sky-high climb toward Oz to *"Ahs."*

But today he's bleak before his time
from smoke and toke: his beer and wine
   to vodka rhymed with meth and coke.

Now in the mental system see him
systematically oversleep, agoraphobe –
who, agile once, over-nighted disco strobe.

Be careful what goes down the gullet.
Of desperate ones, it's lately bullet,
   Or hospital-to-hospital annuls it.

No more privy life. To another
90-day sheltered place   haul it –
Almost nothing in its wallet.

MJM 3/15 SF

Alikeness in California

It's odd meeting someone like you;
One with that same rubbery face,
Hippity-hop mind, acrobrat brain
Flipping and jumping over laughs,
Our deep dark insides and cocktails
In the course of a frangible day.

In one breath we proclaim, "Life
On other planets! Hell, other people!"
Cop to nefarious addictions,
Then *do* declare *hope* the best
Nonetheless good end by definition!
A hint of mutual attraction:

Two of us longing for the Infinite
  Man is perpetually separated from.
We dig and delve among Big Ideas,
Toast day jobs! Propose to compose
To regenerate our sense of long-term
Worth! Tis smug, dodging the pre-dawn

Zone of industrious commuters! Have
They respite in religion, entitlements,
Oscar Night, a bit of blithe shopping?
Some serious saving for a house?
Or are you the same homeowner I am,
  Suspicious on the inside?

It's tremendous, people find out
You don't believe in God nor ourselves
Beyond this on Earth: how they urge
Ideas of the supernatural on you!
Crystals, tarot, ghosts, incarnations.
How do I break it to them I think

They're in *Disneyland?* Aggressive.
As you sit here and I sit here swilling
Beer against the shrinks' advice,
All I want is for every one to admit
At least once, he's lamented
  Funky human existence vs.

The inscrutable power of the universe.
John, no Doe, were you sent here
So, in doubling me, you would show me

How tiresome is this conundrum?
In mirroring one to oneself
Do you demonstrate the Great Truth

Is – there are many essential
  To living in the moment?
That it's not my job to go figure?
Nor my rediscoveries summed up
Will keep me here longer
Hopeful to rival grave men?

You *are* someone rather like me, Johnny.
Where do we find relief? Even sky high aliens
Drop dead. Can I unframe? Believe believing?
As you orbit yr UFOs, yr porno chicks?
Why then, dear reader, would you talk me
Into something more you know than I

About life after death? How you huckster!
Why are you so anxious to sell me on it?
  How are you so sure
  You're your chosen self?
O.K., I'm waiting to see my first ghost,
Thomas the Doubter. In the meantime,

I'll watch this likeness of me,
See how *he* goes about his business.
It's the closest to a paragon I approach.
These priests are downright Medieval;
The Orient, for ethereal flower children;
L.A./Manhattan, star-strucks levitating.

They'll supplicate hallowed hearts
Abandoned in thin air, other thin ether,
While mine, I'll drag out of connubial
Bed each day I drive over the glass-
Sparkled tarmac, where bloodstains
Of yesterday's wrecks cause me killjoy

Wonder-and-panic The City doesn't
Mop it out of sight for us drivers!
  I know what you're thinking:
You can help me *around* this viewpoint.
You *can* help. Just pay attention
To the fact you know absolutely nothing.

Instead of trying to sell me your
Eternal-life-giving snake oil,
Smooth me on the back and agree
We're all in this starry dark together.
Miraculous we're civil. *Salut* —
   To the antidote civilization fares!

One reason we get such a charge
Dreaming what it might be like
To give an Academy Awards' speech:
We imagine famous directors so
Pre-engaged, so functional, so
Free-lance respectable, so *within*

And therefore liberal in the way
Money and fine work make them –
Hermetic from L.A. humiliation
That stirs up wanton greed, desolation.
They steer imitations of Creation.
   Hell, here we are a Bay Area version

   even better! I go:

Onward, upward friend of mine like me!
Let's do go on that hike we talked about.
Instead of trying to get the picture
Staring into the fire, I promise
Sierras I'll get up early and search
The sky all live-long day for release!

More than anything else I'd like to be
Lost in space on the mountain No Idea.
Do you want that much to voice a generation?
Chalk it up? If we announced ourselves,
Did our homework, footwork hired out,
Would they pay us in kind at the store?

Let us dance like wolves at their wedding?
   Or will faults eternally rive us,
Dead of love with brothers in the madhouse,
   Or can these Mountains remove us?

MJM 3/92 SF
To 'Johnny, *we hardly knew ye!*'

Alone with Malevich

Up here, where the microclimate's windy, foggy, drizzle flown,
Grey blows cold loneliness to the bone like smoke-n-ash
Of a solo cigarette dusts his lungs, cherry a single dot
on clouds.

'70s board-and-batten houses stand, lurk in the chill,
Inhabitants nil, on the steep slopes a'litter with dark
Chips and the veiny, windswept snares of finocchi
weeds – good in sugo.

The cheapest row-houses in town string along the hills
In the far distance like white Christmas lights,
stupendous eucalyptus rising, ratty, foreign filmy invaders
with limp bark peeling,

dark, curling closed. One set of red tail-lights, awash
On the ridgecrest. Wuthering Heights in black and white,
Scythen leaves like silent tambourine jingle-jangles –
Les hauts de hurlevent,

Gris, vaporeux, goth . . .
Oberon's red lipstick charcoaled out,
filmic vintage – smoke, flint, obsidian.
Olivier's marble chin.

The solitude and cig, near nauseating, whence
The others arrive, their cigarette tips a'swoosh
Like can-can dancers on a rainswept Montmartre night.
Shivering, he goes gray to gay to merry,

Their chatter like hemoglobin on cotton.
Next day, town, hot and sunny – a blood drive
Truck in front of the art gallery, the sky pedestrian
blue and cloudless.

He remembers the grey day like a spider on its
web of droplets. Gathering silk by the eight.
Waiting to suck plasma
white.

MJM 7/15 SF

An Affair to Parallel Revved

Love stalled kiss to kiss, body lust
Rising to envelop his alabaster
Torso, each time, legs thrown faster
On master's shoulders, thrust

After thrust into this ideal of ass:
Boyish, white, hairless-smooth
And the puckered hole his tooth
Would nick, impale, trespass

Into and out of. Conquering stud,
He beat up his loins like a wild
Lion backbiting his cub, wild child
Would he have one, should?

But with each passing ritual
Conquest/submission, vertical/
Supine, force aural, electrical
Infused top-daddy, not the usual

Pump and dump, but the real
Deal love. To sleep with, honor
And invade, protect, a goner
For good, love not sex appeal

In the idea of him, his person
Magnetic for aura's sake, and sex
Only the overture to this complex
Need/want, jealousy, father-son

Forbidden sex giving way to for-
Bidden love. His face and body
He would forever lust, naughty
Top dog sexualizing like before

But ever after an afterglow
Of love radiating flow.
Boy wanted love not only lust,
Honcho's heart, cock a-thrust.

In the end, each got what he wanted,
Hearts vaunted/hard-ons undaunted.

MJM 7/08 SF
To Venice in love in lust

An Apartment for Clothes

Two nightmares about his fine, fancy garments
Thrown out – first by his ex, then by his mother:
Plum, grey, citrine, houndstooth, orange, scarlet
One-button winter jackets all from Italy, somehow

Sold on the cheap to make room in their closets!
This cannot be happening; they both know well
His passion for fashion. Where was he? In jail?
In hospital? Away at a recovery center – again?

He curses, pleads, and begs to know why they
Would toss away his treasure to bottom feeders.
They've even spent the money they made off
His orphaned clothing – such a pittance, it rubs

Him riotous – *even though he owes both of
Them money!* The perfectly molded, soft wool
Shoulders neatly hung on wood hangers, again
In a rainbow of tones, will not quit his dreams.

Nor will their angelic lapels trimming down to
Exactly the perfect place with chic designer lines
To make all look thinner. It's winter! *Winter of our
Late rent!* He's anguished, outraged, accursed,

And cussing them for their coarseness, stupidity,
And betrayal. Then he wakes up to realize he's
Bottomed out; lost his house and closets to bank
Ruptcy by manic spending and shopping – all his

  Clothes and worldly treasures still in storage.
Material guy. Material girl. Material World.
Even nightmares nag, "You just *exist!*"
This is no way to live! Can he ignore

Futility for a rebound? Embark on the first
Devoted path to *It,* since he was a pious,
blessèd child? . . . But *It's* not *here* . . .
To him, graced & tuned. *It* waves in

From the cosmos. "Clothes be burned!" he yelps,
Traded to spirit. Or they spill forth to remind him,
The less a man carries the lighter liberty's wings, a'
Glide o'er waters, mid heavens. Things' wills, whelps.

MJM 2/11 SF

And Now a Word from Our Sponsor

God forgive him for being so commercial
Today. Melancholic, wistful, defeated by
Money and its minions. Wall Street just

Ruined the world, yet he covets all that's
Left in their ruins – smuggled gold & cash,
   Landed estates and her, as sexy-expensive as

A lavished kitty. They won't see the law
Close their fiefdoms down, nor wind up
In jail. They outlaw and the law can't fail.

MJM 12/10 SF

And the Planet Spins

Sometimes you're sad . . . sometimes
you lose every nickel you had.
               – Barry Manilow

Over and over, the world watches these killer waves,
Abhorrent torrent, earthquake-stunned, that tumbles
Japan to pieces. Mountains of mud and mangled goods
Slur to the sea, hurled back in a second roil – the urgent,

Shaken ocean in its bowl, shifting to rape the shore.
Parking lots of cars, panoplies of containers ploughed
From their cloistered lots, keel over in a caustic brew.
Ripped houses rock. Boat-upon-boat in undertows boil.

A fantastic force, the slamming tsunami folds entire towns,
Its rolling fleets of swells, swallowing swollen Japan.
Through the gyred friends of people parted, a panic sweeps,
The bruised and baffled, rushed to lean aid, a-shock in shelters.

Next fires flame, sparked by wet wires flicking the blazes.
Oil plants burn, as bands bedeviled search for entire trains.
Wave-razed and flared, atomic reactors fume, fazing
The entire, grimacing globe. Airborne, the poison gas arrays

In the radioactive winds – woebegone soot to harry the worried,
As inundation-lost, dead hundreds litter the waters and land.
Futból in stadiums plays on, fans swayed to pray for the stranded.
To lush lyrics the English Prince romances his lithe betrothed.

In the nineteen-seventies Broadway sang a bitter-bold song:
"Then one days it's kicks, then it's kicks in the shins,
But the planet spins, and the world goes on and on and on."
That the *Wielder of Wonder* spill his reason we woe.

MJM 3/11 SF

Ant-Smashing Ban

I

Do Hindus let ants live
That other men and their brats
Smear on sight?

Wayfarers, antennae twitching
In an eclipse the lampshade
Casts on typing paper –

One second you're life
The next, formic streaks
Across unfinished oak!

Bridling a tick to crush,
This staunch bug killer
Ponders what family ties

Tangential/transcendent
        flicker
Scientifically speaking

Between *his* drunk ape
& this mad-hattering
Trot of ants:

Desk and stacks of stuff
Vast as a hostile planet;
Perilous as corporate

Park to poets.

II

Far foraging for food
He goes nervous-kneed
A bit like me

Miracle if he makes it!
Not for greed
Mind you,

National need &
Valor compel him,
Hatch of knight-errantry

Foot-fast, pincer-wieldin'.

Hold yer thumbs
Crude crusher!
Blot not magic's

Chance dance:
        Yea, ye
triassic uncle of mine

Make trundle!

We'll drown in Atlantis
Long before you've tweakt

      yr
last antler.

MJM '84 Manhattan Beach

Anxiety's Child

Fiction's fantasy to buy, to own everything to adore –
Sexy, polished, fast, pampered, glittering gem-costly
In every posh hideaway in the world, in Aspen, Paris,
Rome, Tokyo, London, Bel Air, Hong Kong, New York,

Mediterranean to Montevideo ace in every conceivable
Vehicle – boat, jet, ski-lift, rare car, copter to hang-glider
So bombards our native greed, gluttony, and lust, it's a
Wonder we recognize our own reality in the morning:

Rakish row houses, car-economy churls in freeway snarls,
Egg-n-bacon joints, bleachers, teachers, nurses and fire-
Men hustling to afford even children; the cheap beige,
Grey, brown, and black common street clothes we meet

Everywhere we yearn elite – the glamorous among us
Longing for that *la vie haute* by the runway, its supra-
Human mannequin models, gorgeous just savoring air
& their proper diet of sparkling water, smoked salmon,

Cocaine, champagne with a red-wine playboy. Do we
Thrash in frenzied envy's top-floor society anxiety to
Stack up against "celebrities'" halcyon ascensions above
The *hoi polloi,* when it's evident on all 500 channels

Half the world is crowned by the glorious, ecstatic, chic
With creamy Swedish beauty? Alas, he awakens every
Morning or slouchy afternoon after naps, fear-haunted
By which extravagance will daunt and demean him next.

Exhausted by a half-life of the spirit and soul, he burrows
In Earth today as some necessarily adventurous gopher, yet
Destination-blind. For does it not pace his heart to recall
We call it *the human race* for some very old wild animal

Reasons of clawing, killing, biting, winning against all
Other bumps in the night, hale flesh vs. *felled-n-failed?*

MJM 12/10 SF

Apollo   (53)

Why do you enchant – how do you enslave
That these multitudes of lasses chase you?
All treasures of your face are those I crave,
Your shadowy interior, my blue.

Fall for Apollo and the counterfeit
Isn't *you,* but that virtuous hale god, wise
In every measure, ripped Adonis fit.
I pray for constancy, but get goodbyes:

With seek and flee you anguish desire's glooms,
And baffling dark, you brood, so hardly here.
Grecian youth you play, lobbing men to tombs,
Dote on shallow maids, girlfriend of the year.

In all external grace you have some part,
But you like none, none you, for constant heart.

MJM 2/11 SF
After Sonnet 53

Apollo Lain-Brain

'*Pocos sesos*' is what you called him first, as if jocks, handsome and lean,
Don't need brains to augment brawn. Long and lanky, tall and all flanky

He'd saunter over a black-widow spider, just as soon as get his nails
Clipped. Such a mellow man-cat, he'd scream while you wiped his pus

With a tissue, but not move a muscle – *lounger* stayed put, no fight or
Flight: as only athletes let calm-eyed pain gain, winsome, unflinched.

But he went antique on us – unable to lift even his hips, now collapsing,
Now dragged. How tragic to bury our serene hero: once so louche, a-crusht.

To Pocos, 20-years old and gone – RIP:
the Jimmy Stewart—Knute Rockne of cats
MJM 2/13 S.B.

Aquarium

Hearing of Kevorkian's euthanasia,
  I breathe a sigh mankind
Arrives at so rational a state of mind;

Then flush a goldfish from Lex's tank . . .
  Julius, sick and floating listlessly
For days now on top. I netted him flopping,

And all night see in my third eye
Him churning in sewer pipes,
  undead and half-conscious, fish-eye

fixed on me, bastard cook in the kitchen.
Have I killed an orange incarnation
  of someone's kin; have I done this?

He's trapped in a purgatory of piss,
turds, and gills, isn't he? Or is this just
a Catholic blush? Do we not have

three hale fish in the tank downstairs
to care for – survival of the fittest
Spiriting unfit out of his misery?

MJM 11/96 SF

Aquatic Park

Truly young, yet old-weariest man, grease grimey-
'N'-bony sallow, jaundiced to dusty mustard in a wheelchair –
Eyes closed, sharply bumped Adam's apple stubbled upward, *sunward.*

A toddler bobs near, brown ethnic, unkempt. Who knows what life ahead? –
Glum parents both smoking on the bench, unaware, a'wilt in pedal-pushers,
worn out flip-flops, their kid in wet *Pamper.*

Black bin, marked TRASH in white letters
Anchors these beings, adjacent, as boats cross *sail* to weave minuets
O'er the foam-tossed blue. Fellows, wellest bred.

MJM 8/14 SF

As When All Assets Lead to Sex

Two geeky guys walk up the street, fraternal and joyous,
Each the same degree of not-so-good-looking, geek repeat.
I wonder if we pick friends whose score on the beauty
Chart is similar to ours. I think not, though one often
Sees the attractive girl ensconced with pretty friends,

Off-limits to the advances of even handsome men.
Girls night out, be a hale boy scout and leave, Amen.
Guys, on the other side, will pair up with any motley crue
Of pals. Perhaps they don't grade each other's looks
As often as the gals. Or I'm completely wrong to analyze,

Since in the world one sees *not enough of this* to generalize.
And what *is* beauty, anyway. In the 'eye of the beholder,'
As they're said to say? But connoisseur of those lovelier
Than I, I *'No!'* would bray. There is an aesthetic to the
Human face that makes for Venus' grace and Cupid's bow.

Otherwise, how could Hollywood sell certain girls and beaus
To the delight of the entire worldly show? Cary Grant was
Dashing and Greta Garbo, gorgeous. Thus, all the fuss.
No – beauty of human mien seems to me like the painter's
Art. There's composition, number one, no matter the subject

Matter: symmetry *vs.* mannered geometry. Even rhythms.
Color, contrasted or harmonized, like an exalted blonde with
Big brown eyes, and a winsome, brunette gent with royal
Bones and blues – stunning hues. The features recede and
Advance in proportion to one another, as when an artist

Paints from

Nature, and sizes objects to conform amongst each other
In right perspective – errant modelling an elective,
To be sure, as of a face wherein the nose is aqualine
And largely 'overactive,' yet harmonized with fullest lips,
And enormous eyes as orbs. I give you Sophia Loren, in so

Many words. Beauty might conform to universal formats
That we as primates perceive. Take striking-looking people
Who appear to be a lot like overbred, purebred breeds. Say,
Look there's a hound – skinny face, not very round.
Or look, there's a Saint Bernard, features sort of hung

Open too much and lazy in their gape, and then a trunk-like
Connection of head to neck, no nape. Then there are faces
Dumbstruck by nature that appeal to our charitable sense
To not mock, but to lend brotherly defense from churls'
Insults and jeering talk. At the other end of the spectrum those

Alike Liz Taylor's launch a thousand love affairs to skads
Of married *pères*. Often a lovely woman likes a rugged man.
She wants to be the alluring one, and so bypasses comely
Competition. And of course we all know of Mr. Moneybags,
His face a mess of whoa, who attracts the perfect girl for his

Status and his dough. After we ponder the exquisite face,
Next comes the body, born to fit or fat. Exercise rears to
The fore, which I consider a terrible, achy bore. Had God
Given me perfect looks, my rectangled trunk would still
Look like a set of squat-tall shelves of books. As an art

Dealer, assigned to find the beautiful, I remain ever dutiful,
Falling in love with the pretty face on guys and girls of any
Beauty-contest race. But when it comes to bodies, some of
Us become abashedly self-assessed. We *ought* go to the gym,
Wherein we would be bench-pressed, cut apart, and lessed!

If you've learned anything or nothing from this chat,
At least you'll see I, bar none, know exactly where I'm
Sat. On the scale of good-looking, I'd probably fall a bit less
Than the middle, and physique-wise I'd score extremely
Little. As for penises and boobs, that's a third chapter

Of this inquiry this book could just as easily go after . . . ~

MJM 9/15 SF

Ask Edmund O. Wilson! *

My hometown of San Bernardino, CAL was a halcyon place to grow up in
From the '20s through '80s, OK? – an estranged, quaint, yet wholesome
Blue collar cousin of Pasadena, let's say. *They* had WASPs and Jews,
But *we*, our rednecks, sunbirds, and a plethora of Mexicans and bruthas
Looking for a better life in the ex-burbs in the company of us Cleavers.

Due to death by urban mis-planners, it's a ghost town now, a demographic
Deadbeat – far too far from L.A. to commute, and now robbed of its Air
Force, *Kaiser*, orchards, and Railroad *Santa Fe*. Not to mention the gloss
Of Route 66 to the 10, the 15, the 215 and 210, forming a fancy quadrant
With S.B. at center, yet no reason to get off the road. "Kingman, Barstow,

San Bernardino" – Nat King Cole's old song fizzles to an obscure dirge.
But the one thing this castaway valley ringed by mountains, pounced
By snow in winter, yet cactus-prickled in spring-hot sun, still boasts is
Its insects! Roaches, earwigs, moths, June bugs, flies of every sheen,
Stink bugs, beetles, locust, daddy longlegs, preying mantis in two colors

Inhabit here, thick and a-swarm as in my yonder, bug-eyed childhood –
My mates and I, expert herpetologists by the time we were eight!
No wonder there were so many snakes – this hick town was boon
With six-legged feed for the lizards, horned toads, spiders, frogs, newts.
Degraded by time, this town yields *not* its entomological phenomenological roots!

Just tonight, I opened the back door to the porch yard, when a sudden
Swarm of winged ants helicoptered the kitchen, like kids bombarding on
Halloween night! One, maybe, two hundred in a flash dotted the lamp
Like semaphore dashes, but unlike their earthbound cousins came
To face me, to and fro, aviators in three dimensions like hip cinema!

Now I, no fool – and with stupor on my hands after A's funeral – for once
Have untold time to watch late night TV. I'm too cheap to buy the book,
"Did You Know?" and yet astute enough to glean from the 900-number
Ad teaser: "To get rid of ants, all one needs is a sprinkle of cinnamon!"
Eegads it works! They're mad for its red-brown, splay of powder – perhaps

It smells sweet to them, as to cooks. Nonetheless, mouthing a few grains
They get "drunk," flipping and flopping over on their own backs
And wings like DUI dopes. But I, no fly by night flake, stand by to espy
Them long enough to tell you, "The cinnamon doesn't kill them, but
Makes them so thirsty, they drown in the dishwater nearby." Holy Noah!

* Wiki it.

MJM 5/13 S.B.

Aspen

His heart with a hole won't bleed.
More a bowl of a cave, it drops
Mold, yeast, bat turds, and moss
To up dust, as its dank campfire

Billows smolder from said cave
Mouth. How different his drama to
Pulse, flash, and faint – full-hearted
In geysers of passion, their mineral

Foam jetting up steam aloft. Sanguine
With his one forever only Other, his
Face would drain pale at any hint of
His sharing their graces with another.

That fond Aspen summer he craved
To be asphodel to this lover, whose
Eponymous leaf, Aspen-lobed – his
Own scalloped – two shapes shim-

Mered as one, a-glint in volcanic
Indigo sun, their leaves breeze-
Trembled nervous to brassy. He
Hoped to quiver his shy heart into

His tent: sly gallant entwined as
Wind and clouds o'er-topped. Ever
Bawdy the clown, he'd strip himself
Down to jump and shriek into their

Alpine pond, its snow melt pert
With lime-stroked plants, bull reeds,
And flighty finches. His dashing
  Other stood astride the marsh bank

  Laughing full foolish, yet to him
That beau cracked up as thrilling intact
As Tyrone Power: that sexy sloped
And nipt nose, his heartfelt-shaped face,

And full flush of hair blowing round those
Bedroom brown eyes lined with lass-
Lashes. How grim now to reflect his
Heart, boll-dry and dead since then;

Not much for mere men; his beau's rings
Of irises stilling to null, like pebbles long
Tossed in wind to that pond. How they'd
Come catered young for a wedding to pick

Wildflowers for her crown and bouquet;
How could he say,"*I wish that were us?*"
Admit being love-gay? To fan green love's
Fall of leaves to rush to pond's rushes. . . ?

MJM 9/76 S.B. – 12/31/10 SF

At Aquatic Park

At Aquatic Park's small, sanded bay,
A bread roll, dropped on the paved path
Well above the water line, excites
A wreck of seagulls, forever famished.

One distinguishes the biggest brute
By a wingspan wider than his mates.'
His girth, height, and bullying say 'alpha.'
Each time he hacks at the hard bun,

The rest of the wreck's betas and zeds
Step in time toward the gluten treasure,
Like bridesmaids at a formal wedding.
At each approach, 'Big Bird' flaps up

Or dashes rushing them, their screeching
Craven cries, as our human voices keen
Or ambulances siren. The flocklet's
Underdogs hop-squeal or wing away – but

By only a few steps – their riot of shrieks,
Knifing our ears too near. Alpha fends off
These picky, sun-fined interlopers – only
To need to air-attack back for his biscuit.

All the while behind his back, he fighting
At "the front," engrossed, a kit of pigeons
Has pecked on his bun. Deeded, arrogant
Prince, he stiffly lords forth at them, too –

Yet aware of their quicker feet, unwebbed,
And with c-shaped nails to grip tarmac:
Never will he fight a pigeon bird-to-bird.
By a quaint coincidence of junk-food,

Which in the rank of diets, holds sway,
Our big gull finds a French-fry paper tray.
He immediately reacts to flecks therein –
The morsels readily beaked up. Alas,

The roll sits hard by, unmolested; until
It is. Our chief rushes the wreck away,
Lands back to goose-step the kit of pigeons,
Only to fend off the seagulls once more.

Burning so much fuel and focus, as he does,
One wonders why he doesn't give up
One of the two prizes to eat in peace . . .
People are like wrecks of gulls whose

Going to war suddenly riles up *two* fronts,
Our Commanders, hopped up on coffee,
Their 'controlled' attack and fault-safe mission
   suddenly
   Re-scrambled to guard different dough.

MJM 4/11 SF
"This war is bird shit."

Autumn Day at Manhattan Beach

Stirred from a sleep
of summer laziness
Churns the tide
Newly cold and deep.

Haze sheds off dullards'
eyelids on such days,
rubs to mist,
A promontory puff

Of seaspray lathering
Blue around the bluff.
Even the gulls seem fit –
None of the grime

You get in a town square:
Barcelona slime birds
Frantically pecking up seed
Tossed by *yanquis*

And old timers. Greed-
grizzled, those oily
Rats of the sky
Bear no semblance

To our wry, picky
Fellows, backs a'ruffle
In the cool breeze
Of white-capped

Wave-swollen seas.
Thus gathered, they
Rather seem like a club
Of well-appointed guys

Who in some other lifetime
  Drove fast cars
Schmoozing over media buys,
As his tonics and puffs

Each hour send Hank
There-on-the-beach
Swimming farther
From that power

To complete the accomplished
Life,
Roll these waves away,
Earn better pay. How quaint

His unofficial holidays, drunk
private afternoons
Sunk in the cool metallic
Ice floe on a glass

Bong-addled thoughts
that pass relaxing
All an autumn's day
at sea

costless
no cause
or dire
bias to be

MJM '84 MB
– For Juan and José

AZ-ANON, SF

"Each of us has had his own near-fatal encounter
With the juggernaut of self-will," now here I am

At AZ-ANON, SF, liver ill, while a scamp
Beckons out the men's room windowsill

For an escapee, who earlier made "jail" break
Of a smoking break to go cop crack, *whoopee!*

He said he'd be back, but no one has seen him
Re-track, so bud here has unlocked his ditched

Duffel from storage, which the pair has concocted
To cover with sheets on the one-who's-fled

Bed to fool wary sentinels: the wayfarer supine
Or sleep-dead – not out-on-the-streets-for-a-mainline.

My mates, inmates here, are intimates. They share
A seemingly underwhelming commitment to their

     detox – overwhelmed by our disease.
But that implies I know better than they; so

What am I doing here debuting if I so know
The letter of AA law, I *beg*-ask You, please?

MJM 10/10/10 SF
– to Griff

Backstroke

Driving the shorefront with you,
My nerves ticked inside
Driven to violence
Like a sudden killer
Manic in a fit
Smashing the window he hurls
A blown glass at.

You say, "Look those
white-caps stretch
to the horizon."
  I see wind-swayed weather
All the way up to the singer-
on-the-radio's Northern Lights;
and reluctantly turn right

to look back.
Your salve, your hush only blur
Her sun-gold clouds, mountain glory
Unto a leaden field of deep
That billows above and swallows me.
At first sinking, I float up
from the black; good bloke think,

"Or could a few green pastures
Heal us back, grasses brushing?"
Another weather-shifty day
You said, "Your rebel lunches
Last so long, they'll turn into your Fall."
But I see desert for dessert and retort:
"It's winter. Let's bounce."

Out on the street, sleet lashes
The windshield-wipers dead. Only the manic
Drive to something dread.
You again lose to a song on the radio
By you-know-who – as we whir
Along & the tossed tide spumes –
That was rhythm, that was the beat

Of sad lovers, ceremoniously
toeing deathward – was the unquellable
Impulse to strum
Lifting the oft' grave
Girl singer,
Rolling us back
Into this life.

– To my 'girlfriend' Joni Mitchell whose
Love only Vivien Leigh's could quell.
MJM '95 Sea Ranch

Backyard

If you haven't focused on smut:
You'd be surprised to See how much is butt.

For the gay, that cums and goes without saying.
But what of this new species of straight man

Not interested in her sexual pleasure more
    Than fascinated by invading her ass, alas?

Now, it would seem everyone is obsessed
By cock: *"the boys,"* women, even macho

Men who love their own and are full proud
    Of its testiness and *fourth* dimension.

Yet, when it comes to where to put it, women
Want it *muff* or *mouth*. But this *improved* he:

alla sinistra and behind, like a clover-leaf On-
Ramp curves, confuses north and south!

Though homos know top-and-bottom body
Politics attest that one defaults submission,

While the other fulfills his prickly mission,
Girls desire a feminine measure of pussycat

Pastime ringing on emotion and pleasure –
Foreign to war-kinky mankind and unfamiliar

With her *guy-as-tweakt* lover! Soldier, he remands
A level playing field based on fair competition

And pain, no secret place for her to gain
An upper hand at lady-like orgasms and stamina.

He wants to fuck her in the ass like a jock:
Beat it and own it, again, again, and again.

  Hear it here:

One day, there may be no vagina-men left: –
Wanting women all bereft to take it in the cleft!

As in Holy Rome, *I do perplex*: should sex
Be but procreation – lest this serpent's hex?

MJM 5/10 SF

Balance Beam

Being rigorously honest is like toeing ballet on a handrail
Or head-standing that balance beam at the Olympics. Sure

His equipoise's in-tune, as he comes from dancerly stock,
But how hold his indebted feet to the fire, if he's in hock?

There is the quandary of governmental authorities,
Who flog our paying rude penalties, their agents' top priorities.

Suppose he thinks the Feds are a bunch of shady wackos,
Specially on the Hill? Why disclose *all* to pay a bigger bill?

What of meter maids and their GPS scans for citations?
It's Big Brother *voiding good luck* in our perambulations!

Here's the despotic Golden State that overspends: California
Re-auditing taxes already paid. Of money She'll shorn 'ya.'

We have no problem being rigorously honest with one another.
But why tell the whole truth to reps who would smother us

For extra taxes any way – all larceny, corruption and fake
Budgets, they can't keep balanced, and so conspire to take

More? *Oy,* outwaiting their 'Please Hold' prompts – fuck, what a bore!
Then he thinks God is watching him, confusing him all the more.

He wants not to be cast into hell pell-mell, karma kicking his ass,
Or his Higher Power reviled, nor his mortal mouth on a glass.

Yet, who knows where his ethics and his honor will take him?
Hopefully to God with no price tag, nor a drink's or drugs' mayhem.

In the meantime, the Good Book says more'll be revealed.
"Progress, not perfection," is *last* what he squealed!

They say one has to be a sinner in order to become a saint.
Lo, with convenient white lies, archangel Michael he ain't!

MJM 11/10 SF

Ball-Bearing

Raw deal, sad day
Locked on the job,
Melancholy ticking
              to jitters
If the checkbook wane

Below the bounce line.
We don't speak about it.
            This co-plain
That found out freedom
Was child's play.

MJM '92 SF

Beatitudes at His Bedtime

Blessed are the incarcerated-tortured,
for theirs is heaven's first healing.
Blessed are the children, caught in the cross-fire,
for theirs is the knee and comfort of Almighty God.
Blessed are the homeless, for theirs are
the many mansions promised by *his* Prophet.
Blessed are the victims of war, for theirs
Is the peace of the Dove of the Spirit.
Blessed are the fallen soldiers, for they
Shall be one with their families in the Kingdom.
Blessed are those mourning a child,
for theirs will be joyous reunion, as if in the flesh.
Blessed are the isolate, lonely in hospitals
and homes, for they shall be heads at our tables.
Blessed are the mangled and demented, for their
inner lights shall shine as stars, enhaloed aloft.
Blessed are the poor and starving, for they
Shall be comforted and fed abundantly.
Blessed are the addicted, wracked by drugs
and drink, for theirs are the waters of Nirvana.
Blessed are the abused, for the shield and sword
of St. Michael shall protect them unto safe harbor,
vanquishing the fists and mouths and genitals
of evildoers, that Lucifer himself shall quake.
Blessed are the awkward, self-haters,
for they shall stand to greet at the oracle of welcome.
Blessed are those who love and care,
for they will be There, amongst His insulted sheep.
Wretched are the shallow, and blessed the deep,
for they shall know without Time or Age
   the vastness of Space.
Blessed are the cross-points of the matrix,
More than its wires and hollows,
for they are as criss-crosses of physics and math.
   Blessed be coincidence
For we already know them as signs.
Blessed are those who call The Almighty [silent],
for they know [silent] is inscrutable, unknowable –
that even the verb "to be" and "It" are not [silent].
In the acknowledgement of his smallness,
   blessed is he to find his deity.
Blessed are the Beatitudes, for they are humility,
mercy, and love. *And of these great three,*
Love's the greatest beauty and Mercy, final'It'y

MJM 7/14 SF

Beau Sean, nature morte

How could you have made him so blonde
And green-eyed and ugly and stump-legged?

How could you have made him so romantic
And gay but dufus nervous, geek-ineligible?

How could you have made him so smartly
Loud with a mouth that drooled buck-toothed?

How could you have made him such a snugly
Lover, but squat and pudgy he got no hugs?

How could you when you allowed the abuse
By his fathers to lay him so nervous a youth

And then double damn him with alcoholism
And manic-depression? He tried so hard

To save face and be graceful in conversation.
But you made it so no one took him to heart.

How could you have made him so faulty
And laid his confidence and his luck in love

So low, he'd take his short life jumping off
The Golden Gate Bridge? Did he even have

A family to know he's dead, or do you only
Give kin and funerals to those better bred?

The thing is, about a poet's lamentations
And tragic heroes, they can only be read.

But you are God, so why would you create
Someone so shoddy he'd only end up dead?

And then inspire the Church let priests decide
He's committed a sin against You in suicide.

MJM 9/10 SF

Beau's Rondeau Play

"I marry in sixty-seven days,"
Announced the gorgeous man from Broadway plays.
"I've been sad and lonely the last two years.
But now I'm *sober*, conquering my fears."
Risky mic-talk – what if bizness frays?

To come out gay in East- and West-Coast bays
Was brave enough a share: Despise or Praise?
So, admitting booze brought us all to tears.
"But I *marry* – in sixty-seven days!"

"My Dad's in the audience, beaming rays
And sensitive to homosexual ways,
Got me out of football my freshman year.
Tackled by straights, no fun for *this* here queer."
Winsome singer in a relished daze
Smiles, "I marry in sixty-seven days!"

MJM 7/14 SF
'Lawdsa Mighty, Mr. Cheyenne,
we shoa is bachelor hot now!'

Bellina and Hero

– in the viewing room of an art gallery

As her parents took respective chairs, she snuggled
Her derrière on the ottoman aside her boyfriend's
Armchair ~~ he, a Michelangelo/she, a Rafaello.

They cuddled close holding hands, distracted by
This commerce and aesthetical transaction, as if these
All-too-adult machinations could split their twinship.

Alabaster Adonis with his dark-haired Venus, they
Clasped. The tight room flushed with the shushing in
Air of their pornographic pheromones sprinkling

Senior citizens. Angled to the door, v-flexed, they
Compulsed to an hotel like a line-up of Lipizzaners
Prancing in union, hale knees pounding and sidling

To their haystack. Each sex-energized waft and brace
Of their adhesion perked up droopy-lilied 60-year-
Olds in solitude or, worse, in pathetic white marriages.

Hearts melted as that marble athlete and his maiden
Let hands around each other's waist, her manicure
Glancing his polyester jacket, and the sight of their

Two bums rhythming out of the gallery moved mortals
To wish to turn them 'round and lay them horizontal
In the privacy of their own suite to see the next X live.

And to think, love is only made that *Homo sapiens* survive!

MJM 12/10 SF

Beowulf

Lo, praise the power of people free!
Not kin crazed, their kind strong born:
How hailed, vast honor the Allies won!
They scaled the skilling of squadroned lads,
Shore-to-shore, shipmen sped with aces,
Men plenty a-plane – their merits more awe-
some the odds. That World-War-One
Favored the Foundling, fate would lie
In holds under Hitler. On high he throve!
Till before him his folk, both far and near,
Aroused to the Führer, heiled his wrath,
Hailed his hand: a Kaiser he!
Of him, their wake was afterward wailed:
The Jews in his jails! (The jurists would justly
Found their old shores, sharing the shame
        First men feigned deaf.)

Then throned in thunder to wreck and roil,
So vast and voided, the Lord victorious,
The Wielder of Wonder, to war, rebound!
Fixed on his annexes, far-flexed
This son of Hell in a civilized seat.
Accorded, they a'quest to quash him dead,
An alliance bound, American-Brit,
As in olden times with truth and trust
Came warriors willing, war-drawn –
Dashing soldiers, a'derring-flared . . .
May the good globe write o' their *Gloried Deeds*.

        So fared they forth, as the fated
Dropt on dunes, mid skelter of death.
Boats, o'er ocean's billow, abet them.
Nazi's swerving, swift Hitler would swing them:
        To well-welded words from the stuttered King,
His Highness, U.S. so long would save . . .

Yet in riot, rocked a right-winged
Vassal, Rome-flecked. Outfought she flips;
Dumps mum the murderous pair.
When far from the East, outlandish in deed,
Did Japan the jolted jar. Alien
Drones bemoaned – fast-freighted to fight.
No sky had we scanned, so evilly scarred.
Gunners of gore, disgrace a-throttle,
Their bombs bolt carriers unto torpedoed tombs.

The hated race, by hell, will howl:
So soon a'broil in atoms' array.

And for a time the free, humility-fined,
Awarded small wealth for their wants,
Did lead the globe, rebuilding the world a'bold.
To Europe and Asia, aid they *sped* to the ailing,
Hailed, the defeated beholden to the hand
of the Plan to re-prosper what punishment purged.

Wealthy wide the worldly States,
Its treasure tilled, did trade on pride.
But what was long the lore: rebel minion,
Colony free, next fell to a roaming frat,
Sons of the next bad war upbraided,
Unfinished in foliage and finally lost,
Sons yawning in college, a youth of "yours."
High o'er their heads, they'd hoist a standard,
A gold-banted banner, debtors dunned by
Con, Inc. to coke greedy – craves, now coddled,
Trillions bilked, as Salesmen to statesmen
    Make farce-faked truth of forefathers –

    their own sons freakt in the malls.
    Zero-backed zealots

they sell short with *Lies &*
Short-Sell the Prize.

MJM 2/11 SF

Best Year

I'm 36 today: a number the more
Integers go into – 2, 3, 4, 6, 9, 12, 18 –
As if a dividend of harmony
Were prophesied this time.

Then again, to be invincible
  from all these numbers coming up!
Credit scores, tax mavens, meter maids,
Spider-cookie 0-1s & website violations

Remarketing me; rigid Asian taxocrats
Truly thinking I should have my
Social Security Card and Birth Certificate
Originals; entrepreneurs yelping 900-#-

Anti-vices; financiers gyrating calculus,
& internet geeks with HTML as a first
Language. *50, 60, 70* years-old'll soon
Peer me, as if on old-TV *Merv Griffin:*

Dud celebrities nipt and tucked, no
One remembering the parts they acted,
Stardom, now interviews
On a naugahyde *swivel chair:* chet-chat.

I forget the date the Internet
Swamped my guile, aging me mercilessly.
As I get older hale parts crack
  and I wonder *what is* "old folks?"

Do their landlords let them
  More grace time for madness?
I still behave like a wild youth
Staring down and up from the edge.

Wrinkles reasonable to nil,
Wit sharp enough to get laughs
  From rich people, body tanned
And trim to continue playing

  For both teams, lungs hale,
Dick hard, scrotum and nose
Growing big with age! As I do
Become divisible by bigger

Integers, how will fate spin my
Molecules? On my death bed,
Will that I left you poetry
Cheer me? Will my wild life

In which each *carpe diem* went on
ad nauseum satisfy my wander lust?
Will I do the decent thing
And take delight in my son Lex?

Our Lord? The Blessèd Mother?
It's hard to say, since unrequited love
Is all I've actualized, boozily forecasting
My animus rushing the earth *qua* dirt.

MJM 4/14/95 SF
Anniversaire dis-pair

Bisexual after Shakespeare   (116)

Let me not at wedding of true beloved
Admit insurgent. Neither man nor wife
May to altar who, sublimation rife,
Re-beds in second lust, same sex re-grooved.

How gender is a never fixéd word
That speaks dually and bi-tongued three ways
"Wo/man" ~ to stars in diospheric splays ~
By love deuced twice, beat hearts beat thrice absurd.

He always shuttled, tricked to boy or maid.
Will North fork his magnet-fickle compass,
And pole not swerve 'tween comely lad and lass,
Tho' hemispheres allege him agéd, stayed?

If bi- be gods' twice love upon him fell,
How that he's *never loved* twins parallel?

MJM 1/11 SF
After Sonnet 116

Blackbeard

You call to check in – your friendship so ecstatic, he feels
Grazed by your beard's scrape, as when you kissed that

Nymphomaniac belle you scooped up smitten at *Safeway,*
Whom you then balled ten times a day! *Oy vey!* It's *Adonai*

El Elohim all over and over again – your care at three, four
Phone calls a day to heal his reel, maybe inbred from y'alls'

Thricely reciting God's name just to get the Temple tempo.
Or Ashkenazim, skeptical, *finally* condescending to the best

Fourth Table proffered them in a restaurant! *Meshuggah,*
alas and all, all we need is a table near a waiter! Your words,

Like Biblical flames, your sacred tongues pre-tell what's true:
Miracles you predict, as if charting the Almighty's game plan

Like a substitute coach teasing muscles from scrawn, or
Via prized-for-life screenplays you'll debut, and he'll enact

Instead of his own poisoned plots. You are the rare sage
Whose halo's under the chin, grin, up-to-the-ears under

Your black beard. Photons, not mere face hair, smile
A halo sending shine: your chromosomally sparkling

Eyes, go saucers in seizure with instant horror over his *tri-*
Polarsexagist addickedotraumagy – you alarmed as a matzo-

Ball-armed Jewish mother! Sparriest ram, you bam galactic
Ideals into his heathen with Age-of-Miracles' elevation. Hail!

Your forecast fares anew, its own reward. Yet that'd gloss
Over the antique, Humanist act in your fraternal purview –

That an Adam may fall for his Lady Eve, yet boon seek care
Of his Other: Abel for Abel, oracle-Toracle, trial upon trial.

MJM 1/11 SF
To S. Kurzfeld of the original Universal studio!

Blackbirds Singing in the Dead of Night

Hello, You down there
In your royal blue
zippered jumpsuit.

We're taking it in the gut
Just now; I on my tight balcony,
You on that petty patio.

The stars blear a faint reply:
We're the same, you and I,
In proportion at least

To the nothing separating
our particles' fate feeling.
I fetish wife and child,

You, your loutish life
Riled. Did you know
it swizzles out of me

a warfare morning?
I tell her she's vapid
as mushrooms. She retorts,

you're shallow as a tart tin.
But if I let *him in*
I inherit a man embattled

in human racing of space
leading nowhere up my path.
Would that we were human

half the time,
allure of paleontologic
crime long rinsed off

Our skins glistening
minerals in the Bay moonlight.
In feeling, reel-to-reeling,

in stealing a glance at you parolee
in your shelter yonder, be my Lover
lover, lover, lover, lover,

Lover. Our bed suave,
she distends me tonight as you slum
in a sleeping bag on concrete.

Saucy body language, all ashes
snuggled over cement on
a spring chair, earthworms

Working the pit, stars astreak.

MJM 1/97 SF

Bless the Beasts and the Children

Staring down the tunnel-cave:
Man apes to gangster rapes.
The children: yes, he raves –
Dick, self-meds to sire-crave.

He's fucking himself at their
Age, repressed by The Church,
his wanting to be a priest,
Now knocking round His least.

MJM 6/11 SF

Bliss at The Hotchkiss School

I

The klatch of WASPs
Waddles, trundles,
Exceeds and glides

Each morning, some sailing,
Through the lacquered gate
To the red schoolhouse.

Flock of geese,
They steer *Jeeps*
and *Volvos*

Like trickster
Muppets on TV
in cereal vehicles.

These mares feed oats
And do's and don'ts
As the undersexed

Ones in sweats
Squeak in Protestant,
"Well, hello there, kiddo!"

Smiles of a Sunday.
But I'm a black
ant on their red

Anthill.

II

Didn't Johns and Rauschenberg
Rise in stuff,
Pudgy, to illuminate

Junk to the neighbors,
Tanked on vodka
Kidneys swelling?

Christ Jesus,
You were an Outrage
Too! – replete, the huddle

Of them scoffing, hiding,
Braying, stoning. Opposite,
As Warhol said of Basquiat,

"He has that black b.o,"
So equatorial madness
Salivates my glands,

Bipolar,
my see-saw lube, frankincense
and myrrh – not their *d'oro* demur –

As kanji characters
mix my Saracens
with Hellenes in heat.

III

Did not rad, outlandish
Boys and girls
Make sex and art of war?

As these ducks resuscitate
Helen Frankenthaler
Espadrilled in her *Artnews*

I-wear-a-*Rolex* advert?
If I hit back
I get booked by police,

Part of their record.
If I bleat with the fleet
I arrive on waves

Of illiquid debt, navy
Blue hero of the majority
With the nation listing

on a spy chart
These beds of decaying
Agent oranges

Decorated by D.C.
Heeling unhealed,
Digital Wall Street

Chemically paranoid
Of Khomeini and
Sáddam-y,
Covering up

The CIA's
Don't-ask-don't-tell
Forgotten at Arlington.

IV

If I create,
Rush upon the face
Of Fate, I'm late

For school, the chinkle-
Chankle gate
Catching its lock,

Batching the next
Clutch with the klatch,
Their stone and red brick

DNA
Crushing us purple
Grapes before luck

And fearlessness make
Good of bad blood.
I hail Charlestonian

Hurricane winds,
Crass, craven, cock-
Sucking, cunty

Artists and their ilk
Carrying me, my papers
Cocktails & forked

Tongue aloft, awhirl –
Bettering bred
Calculators, generators

Lower-school
Educators. I wanna be:
Difficult, Hard & Brilliant

Like hail for rain
The day kids
Hip-hop in the yard

Picking up pieces
of ice for eight,
Wailing to Mom,

"I just saw
Weather you've never
Seen! It's new

It's never been!"
Like hail for rain.

MJM 10/96 SF
– To Doris, the good

Blue-Ruled at 56

On these small pages
I'll note my new age
of 56. I've beaten
Dad by 2 years!
That dear old dear,
whose gambling and
Mom's rage-a-holism
against waste, gave
me PTSD. So now,
I drink, every
chink in my armor

dent by the impulse
to flèche past
reality. What to
do at my age when
to turn the page
is to teach an
old dog new
tricks? Booze
icks my innards,
forbidden by my
bidders. I can't

make a living – they,
tired of forgiving,
have lain down the
law, and I say, "Ahh,
you guys, really?"
They say I'm reactive,
and rowdy and silly.
But not without
Noting my genius,
gone willy-nilly.
Uncle Willy, pray

for us, in this the
hour of our breath
test. Amen.

MJM 4/15 SF

Bonito Prince Charlie: King of Corazones

Our four legged friends are the dream of loyalty
And devotion we are unable to inspire to each other (sic).
It was most traumatic to see one of our devotees
Die with such merit. I am for once devastated.
You know well I do not like to lose friends in a world
That brings so very few. Thank you for your sympathy.
　　　　　　　　Know your heart is big and beautiful.

So wrote me C. of Charlie on the day the mutt died.
C., whose cousin is the King of Spain, texting me
In his almost perfect English, except for prepositions
Foreigners can never nail just right.

Charlie, cockapoo, Lhasa *desastre*, *Heinz 57*, ugly
Unworthy pooch, no Carolingian spaniel he, cur
That Velázquez would just as soon scrape off his
Canvas as crush with horse hooves in old Madrid!

Long and blinded by ridiculous tumbleweeds of hair
Stuck to his forebrow, that dog had the body language
Of a doormat the few times he came to San Francisco,
Ungracious D. protective of her Persian imperious.

He cringed he was unkempt, and all she could say was:
"I'm going to pay for that thing to get a fucking puppy cut
Someday. How can you be so mean and cheap when
You all are so glamorous, and Charlie looks that way!"

The three of you would shrug it off like nobles used
To the dirt and piss on Arab carpets trudged upon o'er
Dynasties of falconry, bowmen, and crusades all
Away to India or Asia Minor for an ashram test.

In common words, you loved that kinked-and-tousled
Hot dog, no care he be a *GQ* or *Esquire* man's accessory.
Little Leah, rhymes with Dea, may have taken a-rote
Her auntie's appeal to beauty-parlor improvements:

French nails, lipstick, and Little Miss dresses from
Neiman-Marcus, but she raised that dog, dingle-
Berries, fleas, flies and all, and now lay crying in the
East Bay, day after Zharlot-the-tube is hit by a car.

The hours were long waiting for X-rays and the vet's
Prognosis. Sorry friend end, he came over with a shot
To put the old boy down, but not before that guard's
Eye whites and blacks pulsed up and down in their

Sockets right to left, desperate to semaphore: "Never
Felt this bad before. Here I lie. But can I die? Can I?
You're my family, and I the beta *semper fidelis* Fido
Am worried sick my job is not to leave you dogless."

– to the S's
MJM 7/10 SF
With love and indulgences to D., who paid to snip that pooch,
Sure as that plush Himalayan Princess Tallulah of hers hated curs.

Boomerang Brain

She doesn't freak the big stuff;
It's piddles bang her insane.
If she use or drink riff-rough,
Fatal risk needles her in vain.

As for her bottom, she gave up bowel
Control, as bile puked out each end
With racing brain – foul, howl, growl –
That guys, cocaine sexy, rush to rend.

The world has no reason to under-
Stand her type. If we caught her sober,
We'd feel how -ism guns her,
Abstinent, boomerang brain over-'n'-over

Cliff or bridge: it happens every day.
Willy, self-centered fear loops her mind,
Nilly, backtracks acing her to pray.
When belief aligns her to universe in kind,

Her matrix charms her enchantingly fit
With coincidences, thrilling her to faith.
Trust to courage down to honesty, it
Drills – as air pipes release her wraith.

She's tuning in a bit, antenna new:
Waving with KFUK and KGOD, too.
That something holy fill inside her chest,
No foul tweakers, sucking on her breast.

MJM 2/11 SF

Bored with No Whore

I

16th century navigation,
17th century monarchization,
18th century illumination
    Declaration, Revolution,

19th century appropriation,
20th century U.S. rescue mission
And how, in our immigrant aftermath,
We stopped making stuff here –

Progressive history, a *service economy!*
Did an olden World War II public relate
Better than we with our spoilt 21st century
Entitlement blues? Was Wall St. always

A den of thieves, and every good or ill
President lynched the same way,
The People assuming scant responsibility?
  All that expands is Pop technology,

And British pressure to "Carry On."
Do you remember that the Soviets
Wanted it too? but egos, sloths and
Thieves blew it, as they always do.

We're in first place with less and
less "disposable" income to keep
Up with movie stars and high-brow
Ho's in Bel Air's cribs to Chinese!

As cyclones sweep mud huts to sea.
And every scandal of power from D.C.
To cousin county's about sex or money
Pulled off that forbidden tree of *Me.*

II

Job, kid, wife, bills, gym, red wine.
"Is that all there is?" I whine and whine.
"What's become of orgy time? Buying
Tricks with my paperless on-paper

"Million bucks online?" In a cheap world
I'd be the president-landlord of chicks

And twinks, as the new Russian swizzles
Vodka with culture and the real cranberry

Juice to keep the kidneys from spilling out
With the shits. But their fear-no-God
Mafia hits – as the disaster zone panics:
Whether salt-swamped rice paddies

And livestock, bloated with maggot gas,
Are to be replaced by American air-lifts,
City Asians *not bicycling* in new subways,
And Brazilians, snorting their dicks out,
       Bisexual.

III

Perfectly suspended in formaldehyde
Am I – in a bourgeois, racked-free zone:
Mentally hampered, bodily pampered,
Repressed, *ergo* stressed – drugged

But not pilfered yet buffered. Lord!
When will something exotic happen?
If these catastrophes that could or might
And probably will, what's the point?

Do I go back to the priest to re-anoint?
Run to the Castro for a hipster to cum
in my face, totally cute, smoking a joint?
Or allure the 60-hour-a-week college stud

To flee the high tower, only to hear the dud
Continue his presentation? – all deflation,
No rumba gyration – snooze – and God
Forbid no in-anal insemination! I fail to feel

The Zen of us, all complaints but never faint;
just grey and brown and beige swamping me
in water, turf, and dirt as if sex-toaded
on a sooner-or-later disastrous farm.

MJM 10/96 SF

Botany in Business

it looks like a spider plant
but *he says* it's a weed
"onion grass i think"
but it doesn't look like a weed
neither do dandelions

but this *could be* a weed
since he says so

amateur botanist
creeping into my cubicle

  but i like it
so why grow dandelions?

then again what is a weed
if pretty or ugly doesn't tell us?

"a weed is a specific type of pesky plant,"
he said with cheshire finality
  per usual

i drop the subject
but not entirely
I'll look it up
  as usual:

*weed (wēd) n: any plant considered undesirable, unattractive
or troublesome, esp. one growing where it is not wanted, as on
one's property or in the garden.*

Ironically, it all comes down to taste and boundaries:
to weed or not to weed, that is the 'croption'

i dislike this office mate
he's got dirt under his fingernails
and dresses seedy

and he subsists on marijuana
which i consider very weedy

MJM '83 Santa Monica

Brains and Hair

– Or we could listen to Astrud Gilberto, instead,
  or watch anything with Audrey Hepburn.
  Or old Chanel No. 5 ads with Catherine Deneuve!

I'm convinced part of us comes from outer space.
Have you not noticed something different about the human race?

Other animals in trees, fields, forests, sky and sea
Live according to Mother Nature; why don't we?

For this split brain of ours, all beasts bear our nomenclature.
We even focus on the *what's-not-yet* re-common,
          errant feature.

Then suddenly simian, we stress and wank and howl:
"That the other guy (or gal) got it all because a foul

ball bouncing falls
against the rules, against *my* wall."

Then hire a lawyer to fight the neighborly dispute,
So simple, yet take the tune-of-tens-of-thousands route.

I recall in hallowed Harvard halls
My mind was full of *terribilità* and clutter –

The family of man so articulate
Whilst I was all B-minuses, stunt to stutter.

I'm sure an encounter with a monkey race
Mixed me up with outer space.

Otherwise, how could I have gotten *here?*
Latino, poor, from the hills, yet sophisticate, unearthly queer?

We act like brutes and undermine each other,
The same who harness the electromagnetic spectrum, not the aether,

Now nightly in detail forecast tomorrow's weather
Yet, grinning, tune in banal *MTV* blather. Zebra, leopard, condor

Didn't do it, so, how could caves and leather
Have made us the dumb-ass, current TV favorite?

Once a troupe of churlish chimps,
I *know* we had an alien intervention – primates are such simps.

He that scours the universe not fixed,
Still acts so like a monkey mixed!

How could I believe in Church and State
Without ramping up for our *Other* mate?

Albeit handicapped by *odds* to apish trait.

MJM '90 SF

Breakdown in the Waves

The clutter of play obliterated work
He might have been doing that evening.
What he did was to draw her face in crayola.
It took him, the green toad, about an hour
To spell her last name. Then he penned,
"Sloam bubbles curry every lone minute
Of life." It was a year that he
Spilled out his doom.

MJM '93 SF

Bustle and Trudge

The lives of the working poor on this bus
Aren't a whit easy to witness today.
Who would think it's the ole USA
In which we were led to believe with no fuss,

Save hard work, we could have our fair share?
Now it's headlines, 'The One Percent'
Who've been our landlords want *more* rent –
Evicting 90-somethings and kids without care.

Here in FriskCo. *Google, FaceBook*, and *Cisco*
   Kids drive up prices of everything, even love
   With 100K jobs, push-and-shove
On busses, once rare, not New York City, where d'we go?

We didn't build high towers – avoiding Manhattanization.
On faces I see: evictions' palpitation.
So sad, toddlers cute, teenagers strong:
Their parents depressed, no more headlong.

In '49, yahoos stormed the Mission for gold.
By the next '49, fortunes set, oldsters gave college
To kids in queues to get out of Nam. Bold-n-unsold,
They scrammed to Pot Park, not to blind knowledge.

Nor disenfranchisement's first or worst:
Starving China, Biafra, Dust Bowl,
Korean dirt soup, flies in eyes of no soul.
Just *ideal* San Francisco bubbles re-burst.

This *IS* a protest town of yore. Think, Grandiose Royals
Of England, Russia, France who – once dreaded –
Sinned away chance, shot or beheaded.
Hearty-hardy S.F. chants – no tsar-zone *just* for spoils.

MJM 7/14 SF

But Both: **Body or Soul?**

Three planes in two weeks, downed.
One, bombed by ground-to-air cretins,
The others – lost mid typhoons' weathers.

Body parts rain from the sky, tost
limbs-'n'-organs mixed with another's,
Harvested by the careless-to-careful

Clueless. Shrieks, rants, cries –
As networks critique and analyze skies –
from families pleading deities with *why's!*

The long, elegant Dutch mother *breathes*
to smother her torment, asking *diplomatically*
Only for the body of her son! Whereas,

Another, bred to save face, collapses
And keens on the floor, wailing from the
bending waist like an Arab cursing Israelis.

The world is granted some small peace,
Witnessing the entourage of hearses
Passing in State – some body-bags bearing

jumbles of remains from more than one
Corpse. A couple, blue and blond, loses all
Three young ones: "No one should have to

Bear this Hell – not even those who shot
Our babies down from the sky," they cry –
Nature and mankind-at-war, down for murder.

Were it his precious son, would he turn his back
on the flesh-littered fields? So, God has
Warned that, *man thou art dust,* or like the ancients

and contemporaries, alike, swear and demand
The body? The press praises limousine dignity.
Or would he lose patience, scurrying off to pray?

. . . leaving earthworms and bacteria
to work their
Will another day. Seeing his son's soul up away . . .

MJM 7/14 SF

Buying Power

A troupe of 20-somethings slogging down an SF boulevard
Drunk of a Saturday night, dating and mating, life light

Whoops-*n*-hollers past cabs on Van Ness, no restaurant or pub
Hard by, making one wonder if they really want a ride, why

Not hop the taxis right there on the corner if on the fly?
Then it hits me. They're only showing off their first ability

To pay for stuff, young and gainful – flush with new careers.
Twasn't that long ago, they were in diapers and could not go

Anywhere, but that their parents lifted them out of their cribs.
Then they crawled, then walked, then talked, then baseballed.

How hailing-funny they now feel at 20, full of hormones
and money!

MJM 9/10 SF
Heritage Marina Hotel, Russian Hill

By the Seat of Saint Peter

In your orb and fixed aligned, I
Still sorcer guilt and fear of you.
How I cowered in catechism, as
They branded our brains by scare
Tactics. The punishing, 'Bible-you'
Hurls young boys to hell for firing

Seed and gravely divulges to each
Homosexual, he is sick with dis-
Order: go chaste. How can you,
Tireless watcher, not prize women's
And men's sex drives – and see
Sacred love does spring from it?

When the Jews of the *Torah* emblazed
Such rules as the Word of God, folk
Dwelled in the sight of four or five
To a room, and couples found their
Coupling in urging others out. The
Adulterer's contagion ratified disease

In his wife's bed in an age before
Medicine. There is no doubt but that
Nature abhors promiscuity. How
She with AIDS swept us into the
Wake of ancient gonorrhea, syphilis,
Pox, and plague, dunning doctors

Mute! Then again, how can you
Have imbedded love's chemistry
So deeply in our bodies? Is love
Just a drug flowing through our
Brain, there not really *being* a you?
Or is it linked to states of grace

That echo from your outer space?
And if grace, why not wherein one
Rejoices love, again and again and
Again? Rome's divorcée is warned,
"You may never take another lover."
Herself but twenty, she's X'd to solitary

Refinement for her next sixty years,
Lest she mortal sin. No Venus, shall
She marry Jesus and shun her human
Nature? Or is nature you, my Lord,
Allowed in us, us in you, both one?
Yet, churches scare and so we run . . .

MJM 3/11 SF

Bye-Bi Love (A Bio Bawdy 4 Y'All's Busy-Bodies)

> *Be yourself. Everyone else is already taken.*
> – Oscar Wilde

I'm bi-polar, bi-sexual, bio-degradable,
And, by and by – except for a few high-class
Entertainments like opera and ballet –
For which I can scarcely afford to buy
Tickets these days, waiting to go "bye-bye."

On the other hand, if someone were to offer
The two-of-me a leveraged buy-out
For these paraplegic poems, I might bifurcate
And check out the Philharmonic with you
In tow, to show cupidity, and the guying power of two, too.

Because I'm bi, why shouldn't I see
Tutus and Puccini? What's more, if you buy high,
I'll spring for some bi-valves after hearing Mahler . . .
Not to be confused with me, Iller – two "L"s,
(a.k.a: ills' *elles*.) In *his* name, the "H" is silent, while

In mine, the "LL" sounds like "Y" if you're bi-lingual
In Spanish. Don't ask me why. We could even sing
A duet before dining: *"You say oysters, an' I say ersters . . ."*
If you're Jewish, you can by-pass the traif,
And I'll buy you brisket *trés*-passing as *boeuf au vin*.

There'll be changes of wines in both food and glasses,
For it was in Paris, Rome's sister city, that I learned
There's a liquor for every dish, and an ass for every seat.
Not to mention the mini-dishwasher I brought from "There,
There" to suds my very beery, smart-ass *'lips'*
                                with bio-safe soap.

By the way, if you come – *comme des garçons* – home
To homo, *chez* homey's, bi-level condo/bi-zoned building,
Sober byways and highways – bisected by cops,
Be damned – I bet you buy into my very sexy,
Beddy-bye-time, bi-line: *"Because you* know *two*

Heads are better . . . than one . . ." And I promise not to cross
Any double-yellow lines. *White* rails or bust! Our two-
Tim'sin' train-wreck'll make double headlines next day, but not under
My byline, MJM. I go by two, binary pseudonyms: Cary Grant
(us piece) & Gregory Peck(er). They worked at MGM.

By the way, they *do*o say, ¡MJM you fuck like a lion!
Butt: not to worry – I'll do stand-by – to your bi-laterality –

If you're ambivalent about *ow*nly being my bottom.
But, take caution! I am very skilled at double-
Nelsons, am double-jointed, and own a bidet
For boys like you, doubling 'ass' girls.

MJM 6/13 S.B.
'No whiffs, mands, or buts.'

C. & M. on Suicide

This nonagenarian, blind-in-a-wheelchair, basketball dribbler
Gives the lie to suicide that at the slightest hint of trouble
You and your spoiled, metro-sexual intimate gibber
On about, *even* lamenting the ten-score ways less subtle

Plays out of here spook taboo for want of chic, painless,
Sure, self-liberating exit. Be shame bills! failed romance, endless
Boredom with ghastly heathens' boorish, tinsel-rabble unlive –
When headline-grabbing Hero Grandpa doth contrive

To win the game, himself a sport of nature, roving life
In spite of little stibble it leaves him, if whittle it ever gave.
You'd swallow easy-out pills: rest-assured children, wife,
Friends, loves fare same odds by, as not by, your grave.

When the world holds nothing left to show them, n'er adventure,
Faux dotty lords share pleasure in not showing off their measure.

"Charlotte"
MJM 01/08 SF

cacao

a o
    c
a
c
these
hershey-foil'd
Kisses are iconic
candy. towers of babel,
each a cowlick, apiece.

mjm 10/15 sf

Candy

As she shared from her wheelchair
The room hushed, this paraplegic
In a felt Santa hat with battery red
And white lights flashing festively

On back of her contraption. She'd
Rolled in last but prompt, and as
Others spoke she'd re-angle her
Spoke-wheeled seat to honor us

With full attention, not one missed
Over and over. Her mouth craw-like
Swallowed her bottom lip one side
Only, as if nabbed under the teeth,

Tea-stain-outlined as a nun's. Asym-
Metry, her girth, and oil-smudged
Glasses, pale skin, and curl-straggled
Hair with burettes, flashed on those

We called "retarded" as heathens
In grade school. But when the hour
Was almost up, she shocked us and
Spoke. Her voice urging sounds that

Clicked and clacked slowly, her
Mind ached each word out. As she
Told of her drinking days, the pity
Pot she would miserably sit on for

Months, she confessed the dead
Relief of benders that enthralled
And benumbed her, and then *so*
Dumped their joy, riven to raw

To depression and relapse, her eyes
Transfixed on the ceiling almost
Iris-less for their clear whites that
Froze up, no less heaven-bound

Than tormented, ecstatic saints'
That in their final minutes in
Torture at the hands of Romans
Stared up on transcendence faster

Than jailers could burn, pierce, rend,
Or tear up their martyring bodies.
Floated in tears, we orbited around her
Spectacular connection, she in full

Grace heir-apparent to paradise, and
As it beamed on her as if to crown a
Virgin Mother, *Beauty* and *Brawn*
Fled to inherit the wind, her festive

bulbs blinking us pities to witness.

MJM 12/10 SF
To the Sisters of Mercy
S.B. 1965 – 1970
Anno Domini

Canyon Window

In the ever-burgeoning canyon downtown,
where skyscrapers rise by half dozens –
strains of cranes and boardroom balls
tensed – she sits in a window at lunch: rich,
blonde, and notable like the one white koi
in an aquarium of common orange and olive.

Size zero, she's been to the make-up artist
this morning, had her hair blown, her mani-
cure touched up, her skin as wrinkle-free
and polished by dermabrasion as glossy nails.
With soignée social grace and poise, she
nurses a glass of ice water and salad composée.

Accustomed to her showy table in the chic
and sheen of the busy Embarcadero scene,
Her photo's in society pages, gowned for
the opera's opening night, her name scrolling
at the top of symphony and ballet rosters,
she and her $100,000,000 husband

Philanthropic to the utmost, as her social
standing requires to be legitimately admired.
Has she met her husband downtown – that
guy at table, owner of the ground under
this highrise? And who's that other blonde?
How they flock, the girls in pearls – sure

To be selected by men of immense wealth
and power, resurrected, who want blond children
and sex parts shocking pink with eye attraction
to their males as mere monkey. She doesn't
know she's being watched, yet shows her
eminence with the maitre d' conspicuously

ensconced in her prime, privileged chair.
She doesn't know she makes this passerby
feel bad, trumped, inadequate. Was a time
he, too, had an opera seat. Now he only
has his gaze: broke, busted, on the dole.
   Is she all material and lacking soul?

Or does she have it all, kissing and kissed by karma?
What of the Eye of the Needle if golden souled?

MJM 6/15 SF

Car, Wrecked

You wanted the subject of our house to be the house.
He wanted the house as animate object – its subject, art.
Then, he eloped to low-class weathers: hot-hole-trite.
Truth is, he was never meant to care for houses, was he?
Always, over *there* – he did try hard to say: New York
London, Paris, 'safari,' et-set, and he said, "Jet Set."

Driven teary, he now so knows: a house won't be here nor ever
Over there. But to be *out* of here. That beyond here – he, no
Heir, no airs, nor heir he houses *there*. His only needing cool air.
Things as Error. Who would want a house or son, down
here? They both know, there's only after here. Sadly, some-
thing only courage will hear. For faith, he takes no charge

of hith' or thither. He stays here en guard 'gainst leaving
him here, for there – oust' *père*, nor pair, nor admission.

MJM 12/11 SF ⟷ SB

Carmina Francisquiana

When I was a boy
I fell in love
When I was a boy
I fell in love with him

When I was a boy
Boy, I fell in love
As I was a boy, he
Couldn't love me back

Then I met a girl
I tried to love
Then I met a girl, I
Couldn't love her back

As she was a girl
I tried to love her
As she was a girl
I could not fall in love

Then I took a wife
I tried to husband
Then I took a wife
I couldn't husband her

As she was my wife
I tried to love her
As she was a girl, I
Could not love her back

Now I am alone
Alone, I find myself
Now I am alone
And I still love him so

Now I am alone
And I still love him so
But he is a man
Who is a husband now

As I am a man
He cannot love me
As he is a husband
He cannot fall in love

Now I am alone
Boy, I love him still
Boy, I am a man
And I still love that boy

When I was a boy
I fell in love with him
Now I am a man
And I still love that boy

MJM 11/4/10 SF

Carved Oak

Jittery with Rxs, he endures the solitude
among the 'sober' in this sterile house.
Its granite counters counter with their
claims of décor, sturdiness, upper-
middle classedness. Lonesomeness pervades.
Is he an invader in their sacred space?

Or are they quaking with the same isolate
sickness? – silent for fear of cracking
bell jars, darkened drinking alone.
His brain
moans for light conversation, such as
women share. But here all the men

hide their hows and, youths
they are, seek distraction in digital time
built on zeroes and ones.
He, in rhyme. It's even hard
to write, jacked up on 'anti-depressants,'
tearlessly fevered for requisite faith,

hope, conversion. Here he is – again
the oldest one, excised for his
old-fashioned ways of fun? Opera, ballet,
symphony, old movies – such classics
as avoid the bitter bite, the damage done
in this new era, dubbed anthropocene

of late – man's having pillaged the Earth.
He, remembering mirth, stir crazy
at these empty chairs at table
where no one dines
Wishing musical chairs
could hostess wines

MJM 5/15 SF
– Yet anon, we became brothers.

Cat in the Hat Named Sam Hamm

I bring you a cat, known as Sam Hamm,
Whose wit is replete with laughs and elán.

  While other people and sinners may stammer,
Wordsmith Hamm wroughts jokes with a hammer

Golden, in screenplays from humor to glamour . . .
  Hollywood hears, ears catch-as-catch pan.

Today, turning older, he puns bolder to balder-
Dash wily producers: *"Put my films in the goddam can!"*

Now Sam has a new love that appears to be true,
Floating on air just where there the dove flew –

  A-blessing good men and their kitty missesses
Down to a man. And tho' I be sober, I still

Think like the drink in Sam's bottle-prone hand!
Thus, a toast is now due you and kit Cat, Sam Hamm,

My blest and blitzed man.

MJM 11/10 SF
To Heather!

Cavernous

I saw you in my mind's eye
last night at the unabashedly
Romantic symphony. Just as
they say, as I envisioned you
when we were 15, in puppyhood,
my center filled with an aching
vacuous emptiness. Why does
insufferable love hit mankind in the
chest? Why is love heart-terrain?
when my longing for you is of
the brain? . . . yet it's inside *there,*
a valentine, I gape and ache.

When I was last in the old hometown,
old 'hood,' as they slang these days,
I saw a photo of you, your mother-
in-law showed me. I made a pained
wisecrack about all your thick, brown
hair, gone gray. She took minor
offense to remind me how good-
looking you are – as if I were to need
a reminder. Remind them I dubbed
you Tyrone Power for that ineffably
beautiful star. None who love you
dearly could love you *more.*

Today an older man, like you,
I just let the feelings die. They
come back to cry that I enable
and allow. Now paunched, I
have slim chance to ever
attract another one as you,
idyllic adolescent idol.

I heard two gay gents on the bus
last night talking to a Frenchwoman
friend. We all happened to have
been to the same concert, and
here we were in close, bumpy
quarters. I heard the one com-
menting on a play, the plot of
which was that two young men,
resisting becoming gay lovers
in their teens, had to shore up
their 'manhood' and grow into

dating girls and marriage. Their
attraction, he said, was like that
typical among pubescent boys.
I objected in silence.

                If it were
typical, the whole world would
inveigh with such heavy hearts,
the earth would wobble off its axis
for weight.

MJM 10/15 SF

Celestino

"You're too good
To be doing that,"
Your brother can't quite
Get it out,
Still you dander:

"He didn't read
  My face right!"
 Too self-important.
Then I espy stars
  Up on screen

Little heavenly body
On the go-go, right?
Didn't waste time
Right, as if it
had been an option?

Acting out
Work, money, work only,
And just like before,
Revolving on your axis?
We never had a shot

At *bien soleil.*
Our virus
On a desert mote,
Free-falling,
Apes just because

Rather than drum up
An after-life we gape.
How about we get by
Lucky, healthy, wealthy,
unmolested
As in WASP mythology?

OK, our forebears
Bore this brunt

Hack and shock
¿Of rather never?

But now we're left
Ticking the minutes,
That penchant
To live ahead
In Time

Out of synch
My only hour
With this girl I loved
Who madly tolled,
Nothing is forever!

Human
    For now
How do I pace?
There wouldn't be a trade-up
deal,
Right?

¡Ojala he could
Jump!
Show
A little
Little

MJM 4/99 SF

Cell to Casket

It isn't easy being me.
I drink and somehow am not free.

Look how you over-trimmed the money tree
And drowned its roots with root rot.

My gestapo Mom raised an almost perfect tot
Who matriculated at Harvard
      and learned a lot, a snot.

Then my wife commanded only when
      and when to not.

We divorcés go to early graves
Or to cops and jails – near saves.

MJM 3/14 SF

Censor *vs.* Senser

It worries him that art and morality, his, yours, Ours,
seem at certain raw and gritty intersections collide.

He wants to say or does in print something from the
Dark Side – crimes of the mind recorded: worded

accurately and awfully to draw pictures of sins of self.
No one got hurt, but the blind alleys of human vile

Regurgitated, a'biled on the page. Is it his right to
  write what will stain and outrage an audience,

blaming at best and, framing aim, obscenity suits
at worst? Does he have the right like Rimbaud and

Baudelaire to take you there, *down the dark ladder?*
And if not, is censorship not rot or rotten thought

Part of our human condition that ought be explored
in art, as in therapy, confession, self-searching

and a sort of rehabilitation by ugly re-presentation?
And what of faith in a loving God? Does *It* accept

his *de Sade* Sodom and Gomorrah Odyssey? If
you're reading this, there's a chance you believe

in freedom to express in art, that which the TV-
viewing audience would scathe as perversity.

He doesn't know what to do. Hiding his work
from public view seems such horrible sacrifice.

Then again, what good comes of cataloguing
vice in these small, voiced verses? Should he

give up his tales for love of the Lord, whose
sword mightily cuts down the arrogant, self-lent?

Is masking devilish art part of to Repent? Or is
his experience humanity-sent for us to ponder

the drilled-down deepest yonder into the cave's
of our primitive craves, raves, blasphemous

saves to the printed page? He knows not. Only
that he'd rather jot than blot. Whose mores

he ought to follow? Spit it out or It to swallow?

MJM 9/15 SF

Charlie

Cancer came from fading will
in your brain as much as from
Cig' lung. Unfunny that mutant
Cells don't warn first with pain;

Subtle as cat burglars, they slip
In bootless, purring in weapons'
Closets awaiting mice moment.
Asleep or smoking, how could

Drifting u I.D. crazy-ion noxious
RNA telomerasing: "Body, rot!"
In league with toy-lead kids eat,
Those *Camels* and *Lucky Strikes*

Neither slouched you to the desert's
Oases' curing waters, nor Lady-Luck
Poker wins at gambling tables, as to
Handsome-is-the-man whore houses.

I alone saw you *not* will yourself past
50. Yet, out of smokes, you'd've found
Another way in-n-out. Damn church
and kids – *lover you,* no boyscout.

MJM '06 SF

Chasing Shakespeare

Chasing Shakespeare, as if harpoon-hunting
Haunted history's every pod of white whales
Country by country: champ-chumps exchange
Boats and seas to chum this inscrutable Leviathan.

Ad infinitum cheeky, he galls up Greek,
Toting 'flections of ancient words swallowed
By Europe cum obsolete ~~ tumbled-into-him lex legions.
That said, he slangs every English course-ganged

Language: Dutch, German, Gaelic, Celtic, Norse.
Anglo-Saxon scanned, he gavottes high, mid, and low!
He even scribes 'tattoo' before Polynesian!
His Dutch *tap-toe* – 'beer-tap closed,' archaic:

'To thrum, drum, beat, tap!' Then add in fine item:
Big-top's deca-hose post, he'll tunnel tad 'Tattooed' –
'Ten-Proud:' lad's butt open, tapped inch-trench!
Wench-stenched, henchman dents dot: thin lunch – fuck-wrenched.

Zeus of lit, rey's wit-bolts reign his chats. Roil-railing
Thunder, he delves Sanskrit, whittles Indo-Euro
Route roots – speech-spokes round the globe.
Read too long, his rad-bard monosyllables erase

Roast brains of mother tongue! Bad-ass dad spins
Kid's quanta. Bard pets words – hear ye, six slice/diced dimensions!
Plus, ones I'm too 'pa-pawed,' blood-dumb, to mention.

Bloody shite
in the end,
there's no end
but Will
 helms in the end.

MJM 5/11 SF

Cheetah Chews

Graduate philosophy majors guffaw
At this expired oracle, obsolete omen
Zero-hero retardataire *frère*
Searching the world for meaning
stoned. *You keep uncovering*

"All you need is love" Superego,
as if nothing's changed hands
from Jesus to Plato
  to '70s sideburns.
Bro,' *I luv ya babi!*

But for discovering alien revelation,
A basic education is the thing to catch
the conscience of a wing-ding!
Or so goes the vote in our survival-
of-the-finest social-climbing dynasty.

Do I want God and E.T.
  believed in blindly, Bra? To live on
Superstition Street? This year,
For the *one bearded* God – not all atoms
And their voids scientissima –

my heart beats cocaine cold.
  I think of E.O.Wilson's
  Office with the ants two-laning his texts –
  Their *biographies!* you might say –
And my pompous wish to be their

Heavenly Father, above the pantheon
of interloping deities I once heard described
As candy-wrapped: Vanilla Venus, Cherry Mars,
Red-hot Vulcan, Wintergreen Proserpine,
Tutti-fruity Zeus, Grape Pluto, Spearmint Neptune.

Religion is a 12-step Stations of the Boss
Forcing higher-self diets on us, *ego nil, id idle,*
With Rome the metaphor's amphora.
"Is . . . that all . . . there is?"
I'd rather dance in heathens' nebulæ!

It's starving little to be raised on a

Nailed-up martyr whose animal nature
The early Church caged. I've the broken
soul of a missing kid's parent. Young, no one
would even touch himself, then this happens.

Awesome is the universe, Bra.
It's why we have physics – as baby
birds fall to earth, dirty, dinky death
sec-to-sec tick-tock, who's reading the clock?
I understand bro's exchanging suicide dares,

Sharing raw faith
Even a chick on meth
But you never get
that what you don't read
is what begets.

MJM 2000 SF

<u>Chloe</u>

Exuberance itself ~
You dash around
The gallery like a
Yelping elf!

Determined squirt
In Poindexter glasses,
Your little white
Teeth and turquoise

Blue eyes at eye
Level as we sit
At work, you are
That charming dis-

Traction, mile-a-min-
ute demanding a
Website: "Minions,"
"Lazy Town," Barbie

and Ken thrown
In, you want us Adults
In on the toys-and
Merchandise-lines

These 'franchises'
Re-*tale* to youngins.
Eyes on the prize,
Smart as a hawk,

Alabaster skinned,
'N' sure-footed
As any mule circling
The canyon, you're

An anima to contend
With. And if I can tease
U and make you laugh,
Or battle u 'bout

Something kidsville,
Then I will till you
Outwill me ~ *half-pint
asquint, r'elle'nt'less.*

MJM 8/15 SF

Choir

Another Easter alone and lost inside.
Yet not as bad as the *last one* tweaked: I nearly died
Of Shame and repentance to the King.
As a boy at Easter, all I wanted was to sing.

MJM 4/15 SF

Class President

little Tasmanian devil bigots
they'd swarm and shriek, "What
A brain, what a fag, what a
Mexican *gag,*" and they'd gulp

Air, sweated to dirt trickles
down their bullish bound fore-
heads a'soccer, or kick her
and lick her and trick her and

Kiss her, as he foundered, lust-
vague. Not a dot blond-pretty
he stood dumbstruck on the
DDT-weedy tarmac, sun-gooey

dusty patent leather melting
to licorice taffy. "Why would
Any human chase a ball like a
dog?" He flinched: crude

Instinct to disport and crave
More, even as their racism
Pinched his summer-ebony
thin skin, and his head like a

Pitless olive oozed with their
peanut butter babble. But he
re-turned, chastened lest he
jump rope with the girls,

Up stairs, rose-tidy on top
   of their asses
to Ace their next classes.

MJM 12/10 SF

Clift   (69)

Your gorgeous parts you beam the world to view
Want nothing of the love your mobs defend;
Faltering pangs inside dazzled male, clue
With stutters closet truths your roles pretend.

Your glimm'ring stare in public haunts fame crowned,
Mere flare to gods on heart's enlightened throne,
That heaven's hush please eyes and bliss unbound,
Till two ennobled soul mates dome alone.

He looks inside the wonder of your mind
To gasp at hidden treasures in your reeds.
Blue beauty, churls sense not, their coarseness blind,
As thugs perplex the fey like killer weeds.

  Though male ecstatic passion, at your brow,
  Sex froze – your splendor *dazed* by common show.

MJM 1/11 SF
After Sonnet 69
'Monty'

Climacteric   (81)

Then younger, I your photographs revere,
That you outlive movies since forgotten,
Withal to whom your beauty slew each peer,
Film's green eyes archive my Venus mountain.

Your ravishes in Oscar nods out-flee
Both beauty and insanity remourned,
You, who stun, torch and writhe a Scarlett Leigh
With goddess face yet devil's mind deformed.

Your bewitching shall in my fetished eyes
Outlive feckless fans craving new release:
Loth Romeos to come who'll tend to prize
Cads' cinema to plumb to wrest your peace.

But that we *both* die, I *exclusive* take
Your storied love, my heaven's own remake.

MJM 1/11 SF
After Sonnet 81

Coals   (18)

'And often is his gold complexion dimm'd;
And every fair from fair sometime declines,
By chance or nature's changing course untrimm'd;
But thy eternal summer shall not fade.' – Shakespeare

Let me recall that landmark summer night,
When you through football and I by dancing
Shook town by daring black bros not to fight,
But welcome us, sparked to their romancing.

For once, I loved our girls, who all beamed by,
White and sassy cool, leading hot black studs.
You stood by me, ever fair, dark eye shy,
Clung to my funny grace near belles and buds.

That eve, my first deep choke on nostalgia,
Foretold we'd see no more this magic class.
Eternal summer's cool apologia:
Her coals for the next budding beau and lass.

We, two squires, inspired stars, at dawn took leave.
Night love, bonds, youth, soul music to bereave.

MJM 3/11 SF
After Sonnet 18

SONNET 18

Shall I compare thee to a summer's day?
Thou art more lovely and more temperate:
Rough winds do shake the darling buds of May,
And summer's lease hath all too short a date:
Sometime too hot the eye of heaven shines,
And often is his gold complexion dimm'd;
And every fair from fair sometime declines,
By chance or nature's changing course untrimm'd;
But thy eternal summer shall not fade
Nor lose possession of that fair thou owest;
Nor shall Death brag thou wander'st in his shade,
When in eternal lines to time thou growest:
  So long as men can breathe or eyes can see,
  So long lives this and this gives life to thee.

Coca Freezer

He sees his old friend from just close, limping up to his business with gout,
Face grey as slate, milky flakes shedding off of his pate like polyurethane
Chads. This aged man, not so very old, humps and heaves along the street,

His stomach distended, his outline, a withered boulder teetering avalanche.
He's got his dealers on both Coasts and the money to sniff away his life,
Gulp down fine red wine thru corroded gullet, puffed organs acid-chafed.

He rules a pseudo-art domain: sales people and administrators plodding
To his plan and he, the big boss, pulling teeth or baring them in addict ire.
If close enough, one detects he has no friends or women caring-loving.

His associates, in town known as 'shark tank,' are nothing like hyenas
And vultures that gnaw, rip, and pick the carcass down to dry bone.
Reef sharks, they tear bites off their prey, the public, then swirl away

As he, dangerous hammerhead opens his wider clamps on *real money*.
Yet jocular a time or two, he's joked himself to admit darker secrets –
The porn magazines he prefers to videos because the girl spreading

It, nose close, *speedy-coke* gives her pic *a blast to animate*. They twitch,
Open and close their stuff, hole on hole, sodomized and gang-fucked,
Psychosis animating every dot of print. Prized possession, they're

More real than those outside his rooms, who dressed and standing up
In life to walk and work and talk and play, lay with men and relay love
In a way not open to egos frozen on cocaine, id ambling up and down

Each outrage, and the higher mind convinced these harlots stapled in
His brain cells are actually *here,* fueling ersatz masturbation on a penis
Frankly coiled to cocktail olive. We who know and love him, live-n-let-

Live. Still, nature doesn't halt the sun from spotting death's debt
inside him, at last extruding to his amped-up, exhausted silhouette.

MJM 12/10 SF

Coca-Cola Rain Forest

Dull lull August, baleful, bright bleach.
Ana-autumn low-hung suncast. Alaska
Around the mind's eye wintry white,
Carillon of a billion monarchs swizzling
South to a land all brown and black,
Plangent hungry coked-up sex dance –
No hegemon distressing neighbors
To minion graph points, GDP rotors
Marketing the next one and the next
As if to requite by manned substance:
Being, banned to dustbin industry &
Rain forest hacked to crud farmland.
Rip the body, dazzle & sizzle high
Living, boutique brands, designer fake family
Heralds, fur coat of arms, arms ribboning
Seniors, gimps, lemmings hop off gold bridge.
Can I afford this dinner, driver, actor, rhyme?
My old branding – brand, branded,
will have branded. Striving, sucking, bound,
Rebound, bond, would have bonded but,
would have stocked and bonded but. . .
You take stock of this heat ennui
Hazy living nor dying which wish?

MJM 8/07 SF

Coinages for Teddy

Latest to bed, latest to wake
Makes a man funny, sexy and jake.

When we got engaged, she was bisexual.
So was I.
We had to break up with four people!

Absence makes the penis longer.

It's so long ago . . . it was *before* Jesus
gave L.A. back to the Jews.

A hair of the dog that bit me . . .
A *glass of the window* that fell on you . . .

I *ab-hor* monogamy – in the original
Greek sense of the word.

Your loving Father,
Cary Grant

Your taste is in your mouth,
and I am underwhelmed. (J.A. Mercer)

   I was a bad boy in college and a bard.
To this day my DNA's in Harvard Yard.

A cracker is a cracker.
But a WASP
is a *Ritz* cracker.

Here lies Ted Phillips. While he lived,
Great Humor feared he might out-joke
Her. Now, him dead, she fears she too might get cancelled.
                                        – Bimbo

"Gentlemen: may I offer you a preprandial libation?"
"Why, gawd yes, woman! Bring me a vodka with vodka and vodka."

(V. and A., Charleston, SC)

Can you imagine, that cocksucker up there at *my church altar* preaching right-to-life?
I should have had the doctor crush that little bastard's head with forceps!

("Big" V.)

¡Tsing, Tsingha song
Drink *Tsingha* beer
 'n Bangkok
All night long. . !

  I so hate teenagers.
When my son Lex
Turns 14, I intend to

  Trade him in for
Two seven-year olds.

After my son Lexwell Diller
Was born and grown, I said,
"If your Mother gets pregnant
Again, we're naming your
Baby brother *'Hella* Diller.'"
He looked at me and said,
"That's unfortunate because
I *will kill* for that name."

"But then you'd be Killa Diller."
"No, I'd be Hella Killa Diller.
I need a middle name, don't I?"

To Lex Diller from his father:

An apple doesn't fall far from the tree.
Then again:
A road apple doesn't fall very far
From the asshole.

To each his own due –
and on Wall Street
What you can steal from others, too.

I knew those derivatives bitches at Harvard College.
I hated them then, and I pay for them now.

The Sun Also Sets on the jetset.
                                    – Earnest Runway

She never misses a beat.
He never misses a beat
off.

Latino virtue = Mexcellence

½ Jew, ½ Mexican = Maxican

½ Jew, not talking = Maximum
½ Jew talking as a ½ Mexican = Mexiphor

½-Jew rule = MinusYe
½-Mexican rule = MiniMe

Many ½ Jews in show business = Fringe Schubert
Many ½ Mexicans in show business = Sneak-in-Free Preview

Confused ½ Jew, ½ Mexican = Mixtec

Mexican attitude = Lex needs no M.D.
Jewish attitude = XEL me to M.D!

½-Mexican MiniMe = his son's gang
½-Jewish MiniMe = his foreskin

½-Jew on credit = Amex
½-Mexican on credit = TexMex

Confused ½ Jewish, ½ Mexican linguist:

I Lexed, I Lex, I have Lexed, I will have Lexed.
I Mixed, I Mex'd, I shall have Mixed Lex's Mex.
I will have spread his Mix'd Jew Lex's mess
Mass in Mix'd Castro'd ½-Jew-n-½-Mex tricks
from the Mix'd Masses Mess. Lex! Don't Miss:
Miss Tia Juana's "Wanna Nix or Mix Lex's
Mix'd Tricks? Or Mix up Lex's Mix'd *Jumex?*"

A man's measure is his bottom's business.

In the art world:

We rob from the rich
and give to the smart.

Full of hormones, he made his whore moan.

You can lead a horticulture,
But she'll still make you shrink.

"Men rarely make passes at girls who wear glasses."
                                    – Dorothy Parker
Men often make passes at girls in their asses!
                                    – MJM

                        (Cf. Dorothy Parker, ibid, op cit.)

Brevity is the soul of twat.

Cocktail diem: *seize the tray!*

Misthinking with your brain: cognitive dissonance
Thinking with your dick: *cocknitive dicksonance.*

Adulterers in your swimming pool: *H2Ho.*

My favorite sex jewelry:
Your ankles, my earrings.

Of all the hideous, heathen outcomes: Interactive Media.
I hope these people fall from scanatrons,
texting each other.

My Facebook: the FBI's
10 Most Wanted –

in *autobiographical* order.

I only Twitter after a sex change *(ibid, op clit.)*

I remember everything I've read,
but nothing that happened!

The worst thing about Americans is when the bottom falls out of the economy: there go all their hobbies and interests.

Of all the proletarian idylls: to be proud to *work* for a living!

<u>The President's agenda</u>:

"To send <u>every American family</u> *$165* in childcare tax credits this year!"
Hell, and thanks! – enough for *one whole weekend* of that little <u>asshole's</u> *Pampers*.

Jacqueline Kennedy was such a lady. When asked who's her dress was, she'd say, "Mine." I, on the other end, lift up my skirt and tell 'em to read the fucking label. Turns out, I *don't* remember everything I've read, and nothing that happened.

Manhattan, San Francisco, The French Quarter.
The only three places in the fifty states
    They won't burn me at the stake.

There's a new 12-Step Program for people who talk too much: On-n-On-n-On Anon.

Here lies *MJM*. He had more fun than you!
                                    – Tombstone

Everyone is replaceable,
Except Jesus and Ella Fitzgerald.

Here lies Raphael. While he lived
Great Nature feared he might out-vie
Her. Now, him dead, She fears
She, too, might die.
                      – Bembo, Pantheon, Rome

MJM 2/10 KC

Colin-Ian

> *–"until those twins were lifted into balance*
> *on the scale: the mind and love, like two wings –*
> *so this transparency was built."*
>
> – Pablo Neruda

For so long I've been in the shallows,
Mourning my matchstick heart might

Forever fizzle not ignite. Then I
See this photograph of you and your

Double son. You – in engine
Red sweats and blue surgical mask.

He, the little guy spellbound
In Dad's serene knee cradle.

Russet's the lad, aquiline, Scott-
Proud, a gent welded to this life,

And from his looks, a brainy survivor.
Your first son Ian, this world

Lost to crib death, mystery life
Of short breath, the long wake.

Now I see you far away in a snow-
Glittering Pittsburg: how you

Caress the mirror of this new
Baby boy. A universe of the past

Thrives in me, keyed into Ian,
Limns me a meltdown of our lives.

I get anxious to explore the sky –
All a caramel desert dessert,

A caravan, a second son! Your
First, still here leading me,

I imagine he's the photo negative
That printed this solid Colin:

Lambent. Rosy. Indebted to your wife!
You'll pocket them both forever

Just like the good dad you are.
Me, I'll help myself to a share

Of their spiritations here and in
the Afterlife. What are friends for?

Your babies are real and ideal.
One makes me sing, the other breathe.

Land and sky underwater in space
I inhale a snapshot

Of your second miraculous moment,
Your currently burgeoning family.

Life's a rivering deuce o' yer laddies!
Scott, what a swim we're in for.

– For S. and K.
MJM 4/92 SF

Compare, Contrast & Interrelate

– With a nod to Her Writeness J.M.

In a nightmare, he saw engineered employees, genetically
Plotted to jobs for which they'd been tested in tubes –
Petri dishes sticking out of the backs of their heads, spread-
By blood-red, like tiny diskettes jutting out of their necks:
Intubated and baited with super-proteins and spliced DNA.

Others had been born into their spots without so much as a
Tweak, organic counterparts to those jerry-rigged to right
Smarts. No one longed to leave his position, such was the
Chemists' precision in matching them all to their work.
A group of women, tuned-up for HR, was offered a raise

And rise of title they all refused: snug in portfolios like polar
Bears, ice-dug into hibernation. Their agglomeration in cub-
Icles, 'cross many floors of the corp, made smug work of
Bosses' smiles, heartened and pleased by these who'd obey,
N'er tempted by 'serpents' hiding *under the rugs* of their

Master suites. He awakened to pee, truly bothered by what
He could see in his groggy state of mind. Bit nauseous
And numb, when he fell back asleep, the dream carried on . . .
He saw automatons – with rebellious wills all but gone –
And self-satisfied workers with lifetime job guarantees

Like used to be in Japan. His mind ran and ran through
The mosaic of desks, his imagination demanding at least
One nervous wreck. Yet, none to be found, each and all
What-the-heck joy and contentment – as if vet-raised
Like purebred dogs for their specialization. He woke up

Troubled, all angst and alienation in his comfortable,
Normal surroundings – television in place, bed where it
Was, his soul in a fuzz and his conscience, uncomfortably
Buzzed – he went out to smoke a ciggie. He thought of
The artists he knew, a-wonder how their draw to the urge

To express organically flowed, they no robots nor calibrate
Martians. But then it occurred that perhaps painters and poets
Formed just such a herd, as those fixed in high towers-n-
Organizations. "No," he demanded, "Such as I consciously
Choose where to be landed, no mastermind fiddling quarks

To a calling. "After all," he quoth to himself, "Artists don't
Come prescribed-PhD off a shelf. Besides, who would be pro-
Grammed to be broke like *I* am?" As he smolders, he ponders,
"What makes corporate vocations like yokes?" – then recalled
The bad-dream mignons' lack of free will. Stilled, he fought off

The chill that art is so small in this world, after all – not overall,
Perhaps, but by person. No one speaks of Coleridge these days,
Just as no one remembers last era's touted mergers & acquisitions!
Even D. Thomas is slipping into 'that good-night,' as rappers take
Over rhyme's skilling. He supposed in real time, each brain is,

In fact, just a mime of what chemicals impulse each man forward.
There isn't a difference between straight biz and creative com-
Mitments, especially the higher art goes. The world famous
Conductor is as globe-ruled and ordered as any insuranced or
Stockbrokered 'tool.' He decided the difference is fun, the artist

Like a kite, wind-blown to the sun, and business geeks *wrought* in
A throng, "I give you MBAs, doctors & lawyers!" He dreamed in his
Dread, bovine, growth-hormoned cream – adrift in his heart, and
Still a'clot in his head! Illusioned, he can't shake the notion Art's tem-
Pestuous as ocean; sired workers, silver-eyed on steered steroids

   and . . . riding to work in rows, as if recently brainwashed.

MJM 10/15 SF
– S. Plath

Compassless

This world's gone from bi-polar to globalized
Like was supposed to happen to medicated me:
Great Soviet and USA passed away to a wealth
Of nations more than just proud France ~ as ex-

Boss I, laid-off to 'my lads.' Mumbai to Uruguay
Everyone gets it, dude – their élites schooled
In economics and engineering in New England –
The only obstacles blocking higher standards

The usual seven deadly suspects the Big Two
Cultivated at their own peril – like I and how:
A kind of Roman decline with electric street
Drugs enticing sexuality galore, mafia running

One and wasted banks the other, as I still sit here
Bi-polar *contra* new and emerging artists inter-
National: young ones with their tele-computations
And software gidgets hyper-linking job rosters

Online in new tongues – neither code nor the
Standard English that once included, "Going to
The store," or, "Mail in a resume and call us."
I'm too dashing a dancer to be an old goat –

Sprezzatura and *terribilità* intact – yet wiry-
Haired enough to still distill the cheap-thrills-
Route to ecstasy, abandoning Rx's tumble of
Brown containers to so many beer bottles fum-

bled askew in the gaping, fly-catching trash.
Drifting deep in her *"flux of silver,"* a drowned
World after CPR by Jesus, I behold the Blessèd
Mother most of all, then deep inside higher math

And the speed of light I read binds us like fletching
Birds and glinting fish rocketing one vector to
Another, *nor wing nor scale* nicking the next, nor
Bearded Old Man keeping track of the sparrow.

Oh, you tireless watcher, Rabbis and elevated
Episcopal bishops write, publish, and prize of
No *theistic* god, even as they boomerang a parish
Line to flocks on Sabbath, no wings but scales

Conjoining the next, small helping circles
Of benign exchanges to find out who's in
Hospital or left behind widowed and a
Bit of restrained references to mutual

Commerce the next day.
I cannot pray to laws of physics
nor meditate on torusing circuits
Of matter and parallel universes,

Knowing as sophisticates
and Protestants do, too, our lady
         probably isn't there:
All connected like the calculus

You didn't conquer in high school
But now notice everywhere
in daily life: infinitesimal divisions
begetting logarithms allegorizing

The good ole among us organ-
Izing into sense and prosperity.
Why the devil's own still
Chase Dionysus to rapture

& rupture if proof legends
alcoholics fall to death and
Institutions – no kids nor ex-
xes nor belongings hard by;

No other way for the story to end!
There is this Encyclopedic Order
To myth and outcomes, Greek to me –
You know, those palpable charms

Of synchronicity and dubious catholic
Faith, hope, and love one in the same:
Clerics willing to debate the godhead
And confessifizing, old me, desperate to

Hold onto the oil of *"St. Michael Archangel"*
In the Vatican reprinted in my prayer book.
With world politics and the Next Life so not
Figured out, that I find some way to be useful,

Fight back to a sense of desk, The Other,
Office, clock and boss. To be let free bird
Of paradise Providence won't kill and not
Nix the next right thing for lack of sense

Nor practicality. Hooked on phallic fantasies,
Intellect and useless genius about to fall off
The edge of the world, how a crushing market
And in-your-high-school-face, periodic chart

Of chemicals made bad citizens of decent
People. Given a vacation of respite and
Godly repair stubbornly, who would want:
I owe that We owe, so off to what I go?

MJM 5/10 SF

Concentric

He droned on for an age that he yaks about himself too much.
The other sat patient – the young man's having just been freed
From jail. Eventually, he caught himself rambling, all "I's, Me's,
Mines." Suddenly self-conscious and sore abashed, he crow-
Barred himself: "Enough about me. How are *you* doing?"

"Pretty well: fourth tow in four months. It's only money. Poems
Are flowing. I wrote you a welcome-back-from-jail song. It's
Under your door. Did you feel we were all *really* praying for
You each day?" "No way," he exclaimed! *"I* did a drawing for
You while *I* was there! Let *me* run and get it to show you."

MJM 2/11 SF

127

Cord Cut

The lobotomy's done,
Her brain stands alone
Against the day, frayed
Fish-net skein,
Blanks of white spray
A few last fibers
Barely make mesh.

Her barnacly armor
Stripped, now your
Daggers jab
The fretwork freely –
Relentless as a serial
   Murderer.

In cockeyed schools
All our tender fucks
Flee seaward through
   the gaps ~~
   Though I net
   those that hurt . . .

Rent scales aswirl,
Worn boyfriends
Dart the deep,
Gilling bits
Of bloated heart
from her brackish
   back-waters.

MJM '84 Santa Monica

128

'Courage' in French

Deep down under where fear lurks, hides self-centeredness.
Under that dwells this terror of not controlling everything,
Everyone, and every place. He'll install a sex slave in *his*
Bed: young, yielding, nymphomaniac to serve his lust, as

Love never heated his heart. Wall St. to website will know
Just who he is, fabled artist of storied culture and acclaim:
Nobler than ridiculous wranglers in money markets' game.
He demands pop culture be defamed – crass, common, foul –

Though he's channeling Gregory Peck and requires he come:
Anything to live in those horned rims, his bones, and voice.
He demands that government agencies quit hassling him
With petty penance – so he's granted mayoral immunity.

He insists his dream come true that he gain riches to match
His class and brilliance, and that this money mean nothing
To him, its being a dirty given. He's galled impatient the
Pope change rules on condoms and gay relations, cocksure

The Vatican must come to realize that from carnal passion
Springs love; that married couples, using no birth control,
Fuck as lustily as porn stars, no matter the chance they may
Conceive. And he or she born gay must to peace not chaste.

That every tree cut in the Amazon to dumped slick of oil,
Smoggy sky, cancerous contamination, dead animal to
Torted person be restituted to former grace, all paid for by
Worldly profit: no appeals, no deals, no ingenuous squeals.

But he *has* no power and *nothing* of worldly goods to *get it!*
Lately, they've been showing him a different path to life.
It proves those less than light-speed only have this moment.
That there is no I, me, or mine. That selfish fear spirits

Away, as he abandons hope of control to face a higher
Truth: his is not to reign but to surrender and be of aid.
That his quest be a faith built on trust, upon courage.
Le courage even better: both 'heart-strong' *and* 'brave.'

MJM 2/11 SF
　　　To Gabrielle – it starts like I, but ends like you!
　　　Bon anniversaire à mon coeur préféré.

Cousin Poison

You're a treacherous ne'er-do-well
To lob a bomb or missile into Israel.
They've endured so many types of hell
They've taken military matters away from El

Into their own hands, so often surrounded
by hostile lands, and nowadays be-pounded
by Hamas amongst Palestinians, grounded
by curfews and gated, furiously confounded.

Palestine, not officially ruled by Hamas,
         Is now a rubbled, messy mass
Of corpses and collapsed buildings the top-brass
Around the world in their time-zone pyjamas

         Could not forbid or condemn.
         It was not for us or them
         To denounce Israel as the problem –
         Even brotherly Arab vitriol and phlegm

Withheld in this case of nervy aggression
Hamas knew would lead to this succession
of viler Jewish responses: deaccession
Of all armaments, now Hamas' concession

Due Israel vis-à-vis current "peace talks."
   But one digs in, the other balks.
This is clearly cousin poison:
Both sides with their familiar 'noise' on.

And though today Hamas shake off the bruise,
         In the end, they'll lose.
No matter what side *you* choose to choose,
Who *starts* the fight is the *radical* news.

Every child in school and parent knows this,
Even if aggressor and aggressed-upon be hissed
by politically correct principals and teachers –
Or neutral Arabs and turn-the-cheek preachers.

MJM 7/14 SF

Cousin Stevie

Some guys never get a chance.
Freelance! Freelance! But no,
Sports of nature, they advance
In youth, but the goddamn DNA

Truth eventually takes over – a
Raw, sad deal, crumbling reel-to-
Reel. Your heroes Hendrix, *The
Beatles,* Joplin came in first or last,

While you, schizophrenic, of no
Position or title: idle, idle, idle.
You always had a girlfriend, that's
For sure. They like bad boys

Like plants like manure. We all
Thought you were the ultimate
Druggy epicure – but in the end,
No: it was but three packs of cigs

A day to crush the brawning of old
Age. Mass in the lungs, in bed
At 60-some. There are certain
hideous, blighted towns alike Berdoo,

From which nothing good can spring,
No matter what we do. You, sitting
On the curbs of your *parientes'*
Houses, begging a meal, and they

Inured, yearning not to feel. Is any
Life a trash-can of no hope? Dope
Or no dope, you never had a lance.
Freelance man in baggy pants.

MJM 11/14 SF

Cradle by the Bay

At last

I belong to the universe
More than to myself

Making it OK whether
I give up the ghost

Or some cloud
Of molecules

To the dirt's
Earthworms'

Shroud of corkscrews.
How different, than

When I was only
Meant to come to be,

And the world was young
And full of me.

MJM 4/99 SF

Cramped

Cramped between the earliest world and the One promised:
Between what is mediated, omnipresently seen: the obscene
Of pop culture, no better than *il Colosseo*, and colossi
Of drug wars, tribe wars, arms wars, race wars, class wars –
You might as well pass down Ebola 'mong Your poor.

The world has never been safer, nor more hale – and yet
These hailstones of pressure: knowing evermore 'bout every
Hood on the planet. The no good, the 'He could have been
So good, but . . ." Our shoulders breaking under the weight
Of newscast perfection, a 12-Step program for every fault,

Ourselves riven through no fault of our own, but that we
Don't measure up to our Founding Fathers or to those
Proctor & Gamble ads of our youths of nuns and Boy Scouts.
I had to live a long time to see my countrymen suppressed this way.
One day fey. One day no *olé* pay. No-day-off champions. Night owls.

Dudes without vacations. It is easier for a rich man, burdened by
Possessions to pass through the eye of a needle, than
It is for me, suddenly ready for love in a selfish, freaked-out
World of careerism and what homeless fear, cheek by jowl,
Every 24-hour *CNN* day, wherein intimacy is *'i-Phoned* out.'

. . . as gals and kids to devils go missing all about.
To God, I shout.
To you, I pout.
Ego, rout.
To eternity . . . over and out.

MJM 9/14 SF

Crazy Poor Bootsy

Your lunacy disorbs the en-
Circled line of them, wracked,
Crumples – easier to spoon-feed
You lax than flex might right.

I scoff at your third-eye herbs,
Declaim your shrink a sham
Dispensing dope. Wonder
How/why you lie in therapy:

"These unfortunates,
Incapable of honesty, chances
Less than most?" Odd I'd be
Your flash point scapegoat,

As if hubby, hypnotized, I rent
Him from you. Three at night
You phone hysterical, work
Divides your household! Boss,

I bark back: *He withstands you*
For the kid! Hang up and sleep.
He leaves you, grand bachelor
Grinning this side of liberty

And unknown blondes to come.
Your girl's and my college hosting us,
You spend incanting voodoo pins
Through my cock, hatefully eyeing

Mon laissez-faire; your gaze'd
Hammer, but manicured I saunter away
To dusky fun, not your doctor, friend,
nor cody, cock got what it came for!

You may waste and wither
In denial. I'll go down the other
Aisle, snug for smug, dialing prayer.
You're sick my dear, psychiatric

Now self-medded, simple
Reason why you are not wedded.

MJM 6/07 Cambridge MA

Crêpe-de-Chine Ferkrimpt

For being well-dressed in new S.F.
I get dirty stares and glares from the dirty
& *ferkrimpt* looks of contempt for being kempt
From youth, unkempt, et alia, et cetera.

They seem to despise my natty scarves
And ties, and certainly don't comprehend
My gloves of many colors, Italian shoes
With belts to match, and satchels slung

O'er my shoulders. Raised by my fetching
Grandmother – grace, serenity, and chic –
I refuse to dress like a tumbleweed, dirt
Clod or boulders, much less wear clod-

Hopper footwear more apt to be seen on
Moon-booted astronauts and at hazmat spills
          or on my boozy roommate Matt
Than anywhere. This town, since the 1960s,
– Prizing antiestablishmentarianism –

Has lost its sense of style to vulgarianism:
Yellow, jack-knife toenails in church aisles,
All like, flip-flops! God, himself, kvetching
Stations of the Dross. Oy, such conspicuous

Loss o'balance between a fine babe of an eve,
  All dressed and mani-/pedicured, whilst
Boyfriend schlepps along in gamma-beta-
zed polyester-'n'-urethralon® gag-bags.

If girls dressed that way, he'd call them hags.
And yet, so dressed as I, they all think, "Fags!"
You'd think a town like San Francisco would
Closet more in common with New York & L.A.

Where style catches the consciousness of kings
For career, and Hollywood, and all sexy things:
Princesses and rexes, rexy. Italians dress to catch
The girls; San Franciscans to be noted churls.

Even the gay boys look like *schlubs,* colorless
In dancing clubs. Boys, I come in signature dress,
And girls, why are you with that monochrome mess
Whose lack of look is pay for less? Or teenageness!

Go to fine stores and buy some clothes.
Change to poetry – from posers' prose.
It's mean to critique poor tourists & yokels
But I'm dressing down you smart-assed locals.

MJM 7/14 SF
Je suis toujours fapitzed, alors.

Cruciform

> ". . . also auspicious that a new Pope should be chosen
> on 3/13/13*, a notable date, in itself."
>
> – *CNN reporter Chris Cuomo in Rome*

You must have seen – as have I – airplanes on approach to land,
Their left wing, flashing red and their right one, blinking green –
As if in compare with the damnèd thief to the left of Christ
On Gòlgótha and the shrift criminal, saved at Our Lord's dexter:
Red for hell, green for go, plus that plane, cruciform as a cross.

As they bank their turn, aligning with the relevant airport,
Haven't you seen the two wing-lights next turn white?
As if, on approach to Earth, moralizing metaphors of hue
Bleach poetic pretensions – our terra firma, obliterating fate-
Full contrasts. Wings land, clear to clear, absent coloratura.

Today in Rome a new Pope was elected by the conclave, white
Smoke fuming in the Italian winter rain and hail from the make-
Shift copper chimney atop the Sistine Chapel. No mourning
For a dead Pope, prior, our new Holy Father will share the globe
With a retired *il papa emeritus,* the first in six-hundred years!

Ailed and frail, Benedict chooses retirement from the Holy See
To the summer palace at Castel Gandolfo in winter, to become
In his own verbatim words, a pilgrim ordinaire toward Christ.
Like that cross-shaped plane, he's landed with white lights
On either side of his person, no crosswalk captain of red nor green,

No 'no,' or go. Neither rift nor right. No determinator of damn-
Nation/salvation – his heir-craft alights to quit the coded skies,
And touch the nearest runway. His successor, Francis, humble
Of Buenos Aires now suns up the sky. Aloft, he may not
Blanche *alla sinistra/destra* in mere symmetrical papal white –

But must and shall ascribe, as on the transept of the cross at Calvary,
Red devils to the left – green pastures at right – à *la* a 'Last Judgment.'
Arisen from Argentina to that most terrible Catholic flight, his wings
Perforce signal blessèd from bad, *Il Papa,* our pilot of Air Force One:
No need of an airstrip, e'r elevated – n'er retired, Pax chromana papa.

MJM 3/13/13 S. B.
* In medieval and Renaissance times, such arresting numbers were called 'climacteric.'

Crude Heart   **(141)**

I have not yet fallen in love with you.
Sit next to you though, I fear boys' errors.
To make love lust is what I want to do.
And beside you, I'm plagued by love's terrors.

Your nose is finely bred, just what I like.
And your almond eyes thrill and lips attract
With scarlet shade and words from soul alike.
Yet my heart beats, back – inward, stubborn wracked.

The two times 'true love' slit me so apart,
I might take food – then only vomit up.
You sway me to yourself with flirting's art.
Your toy I'd be and lazy, fondled pup.

But my reign of cold would devolve to deign.
As lust bound on, you'd sense your lover's stain.

MJM 2/11 SF
After Sonnet 141
To Marina

Crystal

May white smoke roiling in pipe-bulb glass
Unriddle witches' brews that lurk about
Children's books, wraith evil skimmed as
Phantasmagory most; even frill – no scout

In tots' crucibles to sense grievous idolatry
From this genie's flaming bowl of shards.
How devil's potion perverts natural history,
Say, of forty-minute sex, till lust bombards

The brain and gonads to turgid expectation:
Pounding out desire from her system, day
Upon day, no water, food, nor sensation
Of love spirit: two high holes she lay,

Loins and buttocks arced per his cocked
Remand, an addiction ruining two selves
To world dressed up – these de-frocked
Eight days a-lair: like lion lust delves

Lioness bitten hard by male tooth on nape,
Masquerading mating-rite, but really rape.
She leaves him toiled and soiled that he obsess
Up alone, his poisoned prick to unrepress

Every Freudian ill of gaping sluts to children.
Whatever pornography instills his solo drill,
Gods be damned: another new, earth scar ill-
Premier stirs one crystal-clear satanic cauldron.

MJM 1/11 SF

Cunning, Baffling, Powerful

Cancer jangles itself like banging trash cans
The minute one wakes up – mien ached.

Alzheimer's says nothing, self silent – the family
Peeks in for intimacy, none there, or goes outside to find us.

Diabetes winds one up and down, dizzy or tired
Or tinged, anxiety pleading sugars or syringe.

Depression cries. Mania shops and flies. Gonorrhea
Drips. Psychopathy trips off murders. Cold commons.

Addiction, it is said, is the one disease to tell one,
"I don't have it." Split-sec self remanding escape,

Cupped to party's bliss, nearly, warily, barely dis-
allowed, Back to allure, a Surge kindling mind's

Velvety stealth. Ah, yeah! Reality Vacation! (incineration, not) –
Liquids'll salve puffed organs, lubed . . . (Brain, a hid fascist

eichmann in south america.) Ice-Protected rounds All Around
Bright Night of the soul buried land mine . . .

MJM 9/15 SF
Glenn T.

Cupid Cries

Steaming bodies in scrums, the grunt of engagement
Weary boots grappling earth now frozen like pavement.

– Marco Bing

Slender-melancholy-French-forlorn, he laments
Always falling in love with straight guys without sense
Of his worth as a beauty, my beaux for tonight,
My intent now to show him Town, club's soirée light.

So happy to meet me, discursive in French, he's
Op'ning up, willing to admit his neuroses.
Like an Italian *padre* or Jewish mother
I promise by night's end he'll find his gay lover!

Sitting on the roof of his hostel for a view
I watch San Francisco's cloudy heaven passing
Près de la terre, près de nos étages lumineux,
Viságes of my demons and dwarfs, amassing.

As his steamy shower underfoot vapors up
These vapors roil, collide, and spin to dissipate.
Not soigné, but boyish in his plaid, Euro pup
Gently saunters over, apologizing, "Late!"

When it does grow late, he'll have kissed his newfound man
For many hours – young, tall lovers at center-floor,
My leaving, teary Cupid from the lonely door.
Like youths, I yearn for love, yet no more *Peter Pan.*

The phone rings this morning, slight Alex whom I met,
These Alexandrines writ for him – *my* 'better yet?'

MJM 8/14 SF

Alexandrines =
poetic lines of 12 syllables, roughly divided by caesuras at midpoint (e.g. between syllables 5 ‖ 6 or 6 ‖ 7)
or at three to four points per line (every 2 to 4 syllables).
Rhyme schemes vary – with Alexandrine quartets and sextets, frequent.
The verse form has a long history (12th-C.-modern), especially in French and German lit. Some famous
Alexandrines have been written in English, but iambic pentameter ($\sim/ \sim/ \sim/ \sim/ \sim/$), starting with Shakespeare,
eclipses the form.

Curved Clouds

Have you observed the sky when a head's up globular curve,
the whiffed clouds bending toward a center axis on high,
other ends arced to horizon? We're *inside* this globe, not
on it, the underfoot plane slicing this fathomless ball into
halves, as if the floor of the perfect orb described by the dome

of the Pantheon at Rome – half a hemisphere to gaze up on,
The inside of this world bisected by the spread of the ground
you're on, reaching out to the round edges of this round.
It would seem 'cozier' if this were where we lived. Inner
space on a flat disc-bisecting-circle. The Milky Way would

be here, *within* and *with* us. The roof of the heavens would
lasso, no space outside the Earth, as if constellations and
galaxies, brushed on our moon'd, Michelangelo cielo. On
the other side of our colossal stand: another hemisphere's upside-
down peers. When a holy man would say, God is *in* us, I could
see It and stay.

MJM 9/15 SF

Cypress on High

Six cypress trees lull like slouching limbs,
Their pointy tops bending down at me –
Jaded, six-finger-nailed monster hand
Of enigma and awe in this horror vacui

I call hometown. Potent and mythical,
Like Dracula, these digits sway, as if
The only ancient monument, conserved –
Here above uncle A's sparkling *"Virgen*

de Guadalupe" fresco on garage's stucco.
The tallest tree, nearest the sun, of course,
Is a battered, great-white shark, coarsed
And pocketed by intruding electric wires

Slashing its throat. The next is dwarfed
By sun blockade – a wife like Pat Nixon,
Who never hogged her share of oxygen,
Waning and pale in presidential shadow.

The two at center are model specimens:
Tallish, with good bones – a matching
Pair of athletes shaped for survivability.
The penultimate vies for height, but is

Far too skinny, like the 6-foot-7 teenage
Girl of a tall executive and his trophy wife,
Her best chance of mating – with her own
Brothers, alas. Last and least, another runt

Sunned down by his outstanding neighbors –
A loser, dinged in the mail-room, perhaps,
Or a senior-citizen janitor, of necessity.
As one, they wave their wispy tips down

To my red-wine whimsy in tandem:
An integrated, unfair society of haves
And have-nots – scary ana-manicure
Of unclipped nails and green for flesh.

Yet, in zephyrs' gentle tow, these giants
Lend antiquity to this Wild West –
The lymph and sap of their celadon amber.
The alpha male even extrudes a scepter

Of dry, leafless branch, older than the Celts.'
Eyes askance, I surprise at the sight of a
Single cypress, super-high and thin, there
O'er north of my uncle's blessèd yard.

It's the needle of a tornado, silent as its
Own eye, for the self-same wind moves not
This scorched alien Hades, obtruding his
Staff, above ground, from the underworld –

And, like that mute twister, fixing to suck
The mountains, neighborhood and sky
Down his River Styx, onward to his hell.
A mere fifty miles away, so much is

Daily happening in L.A. – no one sees
The cypress, shock of the new not apt
To contemplate antiquity, nor colossi –
Afternoon agog with veneration.

MJM 1/13 S.B.
In the midst of Caqui, Pocos, & Minnie – *la callejera*

Dad's Dystopia

As if at the start in his matchstick heart his senses
Whisper-farted, "World's a fraud." His inflexible
Intelligence, intuitive kindness could not whitewash
The dirty-dumb text of man on Earth *viz* The Paper.
So he smoked a container of Camels for cancer.

He never had a knack for delivering ditty's roses,
Appreciating the smaller joys, seeing positivity
In gauntlet-running struggles. Sport of leadership
Misemployed, uneducated, not embarrassable,
He'd wail at the Zenith, colleague of Cronkite.

Sans echelon but OCD-inclined for Senate, he'd
Analyze peers on *ESPN* moving round the aisled
Floor – wash *Twinkies* down with coffee, mustard,
Bologna, *Pepsi*, ice cream with milk for a pot
Belly his athletic limbs framed while he burped.

Amusing, he could holler up a stomp speech just
As shred rival rhetoric to ribbons, platform to *Play-
Dough,* boastfully argue for alliances in off-scene
Chambers he'd night walk with a bully's ease,
Tomcat shuffling off his pillow for a midnight shit,

Cherry of his ciggie glowering in the dark, blood
Shot firefly of wee hours when Caesar would mat-
Erialize to run Reagan up a flagpole. To be called
Out of doors slew him, cop work scoff-worthy,
His "yard work" a life-sentence for bleat kids.

With kin a foresworn boredom, mind-chafing
Penance, knitted lip lines pink and white from
Pinched circulation would ease and release
Him from blows and pirates' curses. Barked out
By Mom, he'd mow the lawn in sockless loafers:

"Slip on 'n toss off faster," worthy breaking news
Not to miss! His inner coach fixed on college
Basketball. He loved wayfarers better than the pro,
Wanting others' points savaged and dashed after.
Slick and quick *Lakers,* he'd chagrin: *too scoring.*

More than all the leisure in Miami, poker in Vegas
Gamed him. Hyped on java, he'd contrive to shuffle
For days, no sleep or liquor but caffeine, his mistress,
And deck suits his Stations of the Cross. *Spade, dia-
Mond, club, heart,* the cable ads chanted live like a

Midwife acing dyslexic him into the mix. He'd wire
Faster than Italians could flicker Nevada, high-speed
Camaro poker fiend, snortling, glazed and riveted
For hours until that first hand's embrace of godlike.
Mom screeched and moaned a thousand deaths.

Her first dollar decoupéd on her heart, she'd rile
The dead with hellacious attacks on her vagrant,
Plates flying, profaning "homeless!" her kids in bed.
She'd scratch him facewise until he'd knock her
Hella one, or grit his teeth to powder, balls to gum.

He never lived, but lost. Never did become but cost.
Yet telly to felt table he gamed, sure as virtual reality
Would one day suck the sap from sex in real time.
He croaked of smokes and the dehydrate heart only
The lordly know gone landless. Five o'clock shadow,

Francis's altar boy, lion-hearted Brando of wharf,
He'd *tear* up dreading water for where it runs, yet
Non-dilute, carpetbag brains and wit, unemployed
Jester long joke-worn solo but court of Merlin be
Conjured from smoke. E'er he bore the pointed cap

Writ with dunces' scratch, crescent, star, did dear
Old Dad's matchy spit over living in dollars retch.

MJM '08 SF

146

Daisy Days

Via Mad Matt I met lazy Daisy, the two of us new to *chez nous.*
We guys, Aries – our bar talk sparked and bucked till he offered homeless
Me, half his bachelor pad for free. Though black Lab Dudley
Came to the deal, a known, dog commodity, Daisy sprang forth
at the door, fresh as a daisy – Matt's latest, good-boy savior favor

To lost dogs pending the pound. She adopted me, while Dudley re-
Allied with Dad. Of English breed, she had spirit, good manners,
And the will to carry on in the face of realignments.
I never had a dog. My Mexican mother disdained them as
Outdoor creatures obliged to eat what they kill.

My father brought an orphan German shep home once. Alas,
We only owned her long enough to name her; my mother
Ill-chased her away that day.
Daisy left today, her old owner rehabilitated – she now
His legal companion and I, without a minion or mate.

Our duo dominion was brief, but soulful, like wit.
We shared it.
Then again, by half, I'm remaindered
. . . with no man's best friend, again.
Before she left,

I might have apologized for that one
Hose-cold bath I gave her, backyard
Before Matt recommended our own bath –
He, no dog-nixing Mex.
And far more, pro-*Margherita <u>à la Daisy</u>.**

MJM 11/12 SF

   – To mutt-man Matt, spontaneity itself, and Miss Stolar, who at once defogged
   and dialogued me on the co-valence of dogs . . .

   * A "margarita" or *"marguerita"* in Spanish = 'a daisy [flower]' in English.
   Cool, how even the * asterisk helps the poet show it.

December 25th 2007

Dear Lex Diller,

Being allergic to adults
Is like the common cold.
With time it goes away
on its own.

But being allergic to teen-
Agers is like alcoholism:
It's incurable, and you
Need lots of money to pay

The bartender and psychiatrist,
Not to mention spiritual counsel
To keep you from suicide
or murder (AKA infanticide).

Merry Christmas!

Your loving father,
Cary Grant

Dichos 2011

I'm channeling Gregory Peck, but it's not working.

You can lead a poem to sodder,
But you can't make it link.

Trouble with bisexuals is,
We hop *two* tables at a time.

Only smart people can be bi-sexual.
Who else would think of it?

I majored in Rebellion
and minored in confusion.

O how strange the change from major
to-who-minor . . . ?

The People's Choice Awards:
    whatever they don't pick, I go see.

I want a snowman
where the carrot
goes elsewhere.

"Social *networking*."
Anything 'social' cannot be on the 'net.'
And it's 'work.'

Noah really fucked up when he let the two microbes onboard.
Then again, even one would have been too many.

In San Francisco, we take animal husbandry
Very seriously – that's why you're both here.

You can lead a whore torrential,
But you can't make *la reign*.

If sex were food, the fattest man could say,
    "I get it a lot, and it comes, and comes, and comes."

The great thing about your *computer* is:
It can make it hard, *and* make it easy.

Of all the heathen proclivities:
Wearing lettered T-shirts
by those who can't read!

Of all the vile proclivities:
Sir-in-turd-anus, wan
Women, van-Dyked

I may be in arrears, but they
Haven't seen the end of *me*.

To suck cock, it pays to have the skill of a sword swallower.
And if your swallowing something the size of a sword
It pays even more.

I called a boyfriend to come over.
He said, "Fantastic. Now I can get
Off this dildo, and slip onto something
More comfortable."

"The Way up a Girl's Skirt
Is through Her Mouth" cookbook

As falls Viagra, so

      falls Viagra Falls.

The last time I was a tourist,
Rome fell to the barbarians.

You can lead a course to water,
but you can't make it drinks.

So chic, to know nothin' but cheek.

Low self-esteem with a superiority complex = *zero hero*

You can lead a stud to hotter,
But you can't make him twink.

Of all the bathroom pronouncements:
        One of us has to go <u>first</u>,
        And I'm *touching cloth!*
                – Angus

The reason why people don't understand
Chocolate, is that they're afraid of the dark.

My liver for a drunk!

I saw a Toyota today with a bumper-sticker that said, "UNMARKED POLICE CAR"

As brothers, we're not very close –
But we do share the same motherfucker.

If angels were human, they could
form "Their Own Country Club,"
and not let us wing-dings, s'wing-in.

"Yass'm Miss Scarlett."

Of all the hideous daydreams:
        Dog walkers will take over the world,
        And we'll all be on short leashes.

You can lead a horse to Viagra
But you can't make him kink.

He laxed, she yakked.
She laxed, back-packed.

Not saying Merry Christmas to Jews
Is like *not* saying Happy Thanksgiving
To stray Canadians on holiday.

You can lead a morse to matter
   But you can't make it quark.

body

The Greeks gave rise
To everything
except the Chinese.

My hole for a doughnut.

You can lead a horse to Nevada
but you can't make it plink.

You can lead a horse to China,
but you can't make it chink.

                  (C. Lyon, SF)

When the world went from Greek to Latin
    It had to be *re*-read top-to-bottom.

Why do people in Pacific Heights
social Climb – when they're already [t]heir?

I'll buy an *I-phone* when it does my laundry.

A lot of Scotland was once lost to the elements –
but then I stopped drinking.

You can lead horses to *Viagra*
but you can't make them link.

When I first tried to date my beautiful
ex-wife, she said "You <u>can't</u> be *first,*
but you can be *next."*

Of all the patrician dislocations:
Swells at their kids' soccer games.
Shouldn't they be away at school?

My son Miles has indeed maxxed-out a lifetime
of partying at only age 21.
In sobriety, let's hope he sees the light
and returns back to partying.

Onanism:
I wanted Scarlett O'Hara so much –
    I'd fuck her . . .
      but then want to *be* her.

Lamb of God, who takes away the sins of the world, have mercy on us.
Lamb of God, who takes away the sins of the world, have mercy on us.
Lamb of God, who takes away the sins of the world, Cary Grant us piece.

I can tell you who gives the best blow jobs – a gal with a tracheotomy hole.

Whoever made that up is a spore throat.

That ain't no fine wine, that be mine wine.

The best thing about pussy is that it shaves.
The worst thing about dick is that it craves.
The best thing about butt is that it caves.

The best thing about tit is that it cleaves.
The worst thing about undressing is her sleeves.

Now that Jesus and Ella Fitzgerald are dead, is there any reason to go on?

You can lead a horse to daughter
but you can't make 'em link.

Liberace's motto: shellac it.

It *was* you! You're just confusing
yourself with someone else!

You can lead a screen to writer, but you can't make it ink.

You can lead a golf-to-wood, ur – but you can't make the links.

You can lead a hose to wad her,
But you can't make it drink.

You can lead a whore to powder, but it won't be succinct.

You can lead an oar to water
But you can't make it zinc.

Napoleon boned apart Helen –
So the Greeks came after him.

My favorite character from *Star Wars* was
Hans — Solo.

Doctors' offices are like car dealers.
One relaxes in customer service,
Then tenses in parts and repairs.

My car has been towed in
San Francisco so many times,
I just call 'em for a ride to work, now.

You can lead a Norse to otter,
But you can't make it mink.

You can train a horse to trotter,
But you can't make it slink.

You can lead a drunk to water,
But he won't make the sink.

You can pound her hole to tauter,
But you can't make it pink.

You can lead a girl to badder,
But you can't make her kink.

You can lead a gall to bladder
But you can't make it plink.

You can lead obese to water
But you can't make it shrink.

You can toast a horse with water,
But you can't make it clink.

If you only toast with water –
You'll never see the brink . . .

"Do you know what I would do if I were you?"

"Yes, go find a high IQ."

The only bitch-slap I deserved,
   Was on *her* ass!

Like any normal kid, he wanted to give his girlfriend cunnilingus,
               Problem was, she preferred 'Honey, ring-us.'

It's such a drag to live with hippatitis. I'm *over* being cool.

I could listen to Ella Fitzgerald
until she turned Black-Irish.

I used to be a hopeless drug-addict.
Now, I'm a dopeless hope-addict!
               (Nick, Newport Beach)

Hollywood went downhill the minute the movies invented Los Angeles.

You can lead-the-poor to water . . . but you can't make them shrink.

You can lead Israel to water—but you can't make it part.

You can lead a horde to slaughter,
     But you can't make it think.

Jesus changed the wine to water at a marriage.
But Ella shattered the glass
at the divorce.
               (C. Lyon, SF)

You can lead a tot to toddler
But you can't help him stink.

If you're writing, and not puking, crying, or cracking up
Then you ain't no poet, and we know it.

To a meth trucker: "O'hi-way, hymened hymn."

You can lead the Lord to water,
But you can't make him whine.

MJM 2/11 SF

Dichos 2012

All the Dillers have wit, but no wits, just writs.
Whereas, once they colonized the Ritz, they're
Now in the midst of discomfits, asses in Motel Sixes.
How can one but hope, it's but a temporary fix?
Not everyone in shit stays pit-stopped, *sans fêtes*.

They say addicts are self-centered. I know this
To be true. The more drugs I did over the years,
The more erotic and versatile a lover I became.
Too bad I wasted all that new accomplishment
And sensitivity, fucking me, myself, and I.

A chicken in every pot.
A lawyer in every plot.
A Wall St. thief in every yacht.

Cooking in Paris, I learned
There's a liquor for every dish.

***

SF and San Jose are hosting a gun buy-back
Program today. Matt and I are broke, and we
Have no guns, cash-poor by way of peaceability.
But Matt's in construction – so he said:

"Officer, I ain't got no *real* guns. How about
A nail gun?" Enthusiastic, I added, "We gotta
Staple gun. We gotta glue gun!" "Yeah," he
Said back to us, "Well here's a stun gun!"

Champagne comes before paying off debts,
Just like "C" comes before "D" in alphabets.

MJM '12 SF

Dichos 2013

My roommate in San Francisco
is so homophobic, he won't even drive
over a manhole cover!

A Wasp is a white, Anglo-Saxon Protestant.
If you're Catholic, you're a Wasc.
But if you're <u>also</u> *Latino,* you're a wascal –
Kind of like Yosemite Sam!

Did you know you can get rid of wasps with a glass of red wine?

They flee all but gin and tonics.

Ambientium Tobacco

People should thank me for my second-hand
Smoke because I'm paying for their habit.
What are we all of a sudden – a *welfare* state?

I have a close female relative who's such a filthy gossip,
Her priest has asked her to start gargling with *Vagisil.*

Common sense would suggest that when an English heir to the throne is born, he's in the Labor Party. But after he goes bald like his forefathers, he naturally switches over to the Whigs.

What do you call a brutha with a big black dick in a VW bus? *Coq au vin!*

Yes, my dog is gay – a Labrador Receiver; but your dog is really gay: a Labrador wide *receiver.*

What kind of dog do we get crossing Anthony Weiner with a minor?
Answer: a miniature wein-her-on-her . . .

If you've got a gay bottom who's bitchy, you're a hen-peckered cock!

End racism NOW: start marryin' niggas!

I know a lady who is so old, she forgets her wheelchair every day.

A Cat in the Hat is worth two puss in the bush.

Nothing succeeds like excess. Nothing exceeds like success. Nothing sucks seeds like suck cess.

How many white trash does it take to screw in a light bulb? One gram of meth
          and they're *all* in there . . . fucking.

I shall not raise glasses to toast these messy masses,
Nor make passes at their daughters' overweight asses.
I ought breed Norwegian laddies and lasses.

As a poet, I have become fascinated by the difference between the concept of 'fearlessness' in
French vs. English. Whilst an Anglo speaker says, "Be brave," a Frenchman will say, *"Bon
courage."* 'Bravery' is a contraction of 'be-rave.' 'Courage' is a derivation of *'le coeur,'*
or, in English, "heart." So, when a French speaker says 'be fearless,' he calls upon the 'good/*bon*'
resources of the heart; whilst when an Anglophone speaker does the same, he calls upon 'ranting
and raving.' This is why white-trash hillbillies want semi-automatic guns, while the Frogs want
fully automatic lovers – especially ones with big 'bon'-ers.

It's lonely at the top.
And since I can't get laid,
It's lonely at the bottom, too.

Did you hear about the quadruple amputee – Bob?
He met some hot chicks at the beach.
One says, "I'm Aquarius!" The other one says, "I'm Aries."
Bob goes, "I'm Torso."

Regarding the 'recovery,' yet again,
of that Las Vegas whorehouse called Wall Street:
"You can lead a bourse to slaughter, but you can't make it shrink."

I met an Afro-American lad yesterday with straight blond hair. I said, "What are you?"
He said, "Half black/half Mordic."

My housemate is such a slob, I had to tell him, Matt:

"No. 1, is number one."
"And No. 2, is that you get No. 1 in the toilet!"

You know you have redneck friends
When one of them says,
"Your picture looks great on *Facebook*!
You must have an *indoor* job . . ."

White trash never disappears.

They're like Styrofoam cups.

      Cute Girls Cum to Congress!
      Girls with cute asses
      Rarely prompt impasses.
      Butt politicians, bad schmoozers,
      Shut the shit down, sore losers.
      It proves that pretty girls
      Ought run the world,
      And ugly pundits
      Need to fund it.
      Fuck off angry old mens:
      Pump power to pretty hymens!

MJM '13 SF, SB

Dichos 2014

As for my hair loss, I've gone from Rastafari to "hair safari."

I never liked Asian girls, and then I did. The story is titled,
"Dim Sum, Alight on Others."

Keep those cards and letters coming.
Keep those cunts and headers humming.
Keep those hard-ons and hummers cumming.

You can lead a fjord to water
But you can't make it Chink.

Dat ain't no *fine* wine –
Dat mo' *my* wine.

San Bernaredneck.
San Bernabeaner.
San Bernanigger.
San Bernatweaker.

San Beanareno
San Niggareno
San Chinareno
San Methareno
San Crackereno

My roommate is base and watches the wrong news.
Last night he said, "I'm watching 'The Running of the Bulls at Modesto.'"

My wife would only blow me on my birthday.
That's why the candles are melted
and the cake is unfrosted.

My roommate had brain surgery
But the hospital lost pieces of his skull.
Now he's a bone-again epileptic.

Tossed salad in the ghetto: oil & bean-niggerette
And for drinks: cognac & diet *Tab*
For dessert: Yo-blood!-puddin' in *Dorito* crust-asis

San Beandro
Pasa Beaner
Jew Nipiro Sarah
Gayza Strip
Jew-han-diss-burg
San Ped-rue
Toe-key-hole
Irish Whiz-key
S'crotch-and-sore, duh
Nova Scotch-ya

Santa Rosarita Beaners
Fresnoniggas
Oxycont-nard
Marin Cunty
Smoakland
Venice Beetch
Sausa-rito
Pacifuck Hitlerheights
Santa Clitatoris
Mill Vall-aye-Ho!
Azusuck
Lo-I'd-rather-Di
Sunnyyale
Mo Livahmo
San Brown-ho

You can pet a dog.
You can pet a cat.
But you can't Petaluma.

Poster seen on a bus stop:
"What if Everyone in San Francisco Ran?"
Answer: Well, everyone in San Francisco already
runs San Francisco, so why not run it, too?

The thing about Hollywood money is
that it's here today, gonorrhea.

A macho cop: CHPP!

Two twinks from the same hometown
bump into each other halfway
across the globe: A cowinkytwink.

Tech

The smaller it gets,
the harder it is to use.
Kind of like boyfriends.

I got this linen blazer on sale so cheap,
I think there are *two* Ralph Laurens –
    and one of 'em's not famous.

            Seen engraved on a large boulder
            at the Aids Memorial Grove in S.F:
            "From the Sisters of Perpetual Indulgence
            To Every Nun of the Above."

In a gay bah,
Nevah appe*ah* desperate.
Seem – unapproachable –
        Rather like . . .

Kiliman*jaro*.
            – Lord Ashley 8/14 SF

I might have been *born* at night.
But not *last* night!

            – Russian retort to being thought gullible, N. Karmanova 8/14 SF

Men! . . . Vat will they think of next?

If you didn't have a crush on Linda Ronstadt in high school,
You were a drop-out.

MJM '14 parts various

Dichos 2015

A suicide bomber holding a Quran: "Salaam, it's not that *Book* that worries me,
it's the *magazines* strapped to your butt!"

You can lead a ho to culture, but she still gonna stank.

Heard in *Safeway:* "Momma, I wan sum chickin draink! Gimme sum chickin draink!"
I asked the mother, "Chickin draink . . . what's that?"

"Bouillon cube in hot *watur*."

What's a bar full of relapsed alcoholics?
 "Buckets o'fuck-its!"

"Do you serve slices?"
"No, just whole pizzas."

    So I ordered an Extra-Large, and sold 'em to people in line . . .

Of all the heathen proclivities:
Taping a whole season of shows to watch in the off-season
After the show's been cancelled. ("anachrovidiotic")

Baptists:
You can lead a snort to water
but you can't make it drink . . .

cigares → cigars
cigarillos → cigarettes
nigares → nigars
nigarillos → nigarettes
frijoleros → beaners
frijoleritos → beaneritos
frijoleritos + → beaneritos in burritos
campesinos → red-necks
campesinitos → red-neckitos
campesinitos + → red-neckitos eating *Fritos*
judillos → Jews
judillas → beans
judillos judillas → Spanish Jew-beans
judillos frijoles → Mexican Jew-beans
gringos → Wasps
gringuitos → flies
gringuititos → gnats
gringuitititos → scabies

I panic at the sight of deadly weapons.
Guys in flip flops, for example.
With a French accent: *Mères see dots and dots seed dots*
                     And lit dull lambs need I.V.
                     A'kettle, eat ivy too,
                     *Wood, net ewe.**

* ***Wikipedia****: A **mondegreen** is a mishearing or misinterpretation of a phrase as a result of near-homophony, in a way that gives it a new meaning: "And *laid* him on the green." → "And Lady **Mondegreen**"[1] is *the* 'class (sic) sex ample.'[2] A "*Hobson-Jobson*," is where a word from a foreign language is homophonically translated into one's own language, e.g., *cockroach* from the Spanish *cucaracha*, or in French, the homophone *pedé* = 'gay' = Scotland Yard 'ped on file.' A Hobson-Jobson is so-called because "J" in Spanish is pronounced as "H" in English: their four "ha, he, hi, ho. . . as in *joder* (ho-*dáre*), e.g.'fuck'(in *Cast-stay-on-yo*) ← in utter words,** the "H" and "J" in '**H**ob-sun, **J**[H]ob son.'[3] For misheard lyrics this phenomenon is called 'soramimi' = 'soar a me-me,' as in 'to fly two twins' in English, or in Japanese 'sore-a-mi-mi' = a Geisha who's *gōne-adds* have been violated by a 'West turn her.'[4] An unintentionally incorrect use of similar-sounding words or phrases in speaking is a 'malapropism' = 'maul a *prop* is him,' i.e., someone who gets fired from a movie because he keeps bumping into the sets.[5] As the famed actor Spencer Tracy once said, when breaking in a new supporting actor, "Just learn your lines, kid, and don't bump into the furniture,"[6] or, in the King's English = "Jess, learn yore lines, kid. Anne, don't bump end to the fur – nits, sure!" – both examples of 'pair-a-sites' in Jack, co-be Anne, England.[7]† If there is a connection in meaning, it can be called an 'eggcorn' or an 'acorn' if you're 'a'Ska whirl.'[8] If a person stubbornly sticks to a mispronunciation after being corrected, that person has committed a 'mumpsimus,' which is like an 'Ohio, go sime us' mixed with 'swollen sheiks'[9] like squirrels have when whore ding nuts.[10]‡

†e.g., co-regnant
‡especially, 'Brah, seal nuts.'
**Cf. 'Dee, *udder* class-sick: *'Carry yoke, he.'*[11]

Wattle I do wend ewe
are far a'weigh
hand eye ham blew
waddle I do.
           – Milton Berle Lynne

WASPs fighting ISIS = scarabs
Paul McCartney takes a crap = dung beetle

The last time I did a widow I got cobwebs ~~

They gave me drinks on the house
but I fell off.

Noah was a bit of a racist.
When it came to the two white trash
he made 'em hook the trailer
to the back of the Ark.

<u>*The Most Immortal Thing Ever Seen on U-Tube*</u>:

Nathaniel, [5-years old], why did you steal your grandmother's car and get into all those wrecks?
"Cause I like to do hoodrat thangs."
Hood rats things? Like what?
"Like smoking with da' cigarette."

I walked into an antiques shop and said, "I've got a vintage wooden dildo for sale if you're interested?"
The assistant looked curious, so I took it out of my bag and showed it to him.
"Jesus, it smells a bit funny!" he said.
"I know," I replied, "It's been in my family for years.

(– Sean A. – "I'm leeeking . . .")

A chihuahua and a Great Dane mate. I sure hope the Dane . . . is the female!

God made children wretched
so that we die on time.

You can lead a skate to water
but you can't make it rink.

Gay lay, implied: in you end-o

With oral – sime mule taint he us!

Many cocks to suck in Rome: oral choral
Many cocks to suck in Texas: oral choral corral
Many red-headed cocks to suck in Scotland: oral choral coral
In Greece: oral choral laurel
With teen: oral choral immoral
With Queen: oral choral Balmoral

I just love a warm hand at my entrance.
But I adore a firm hand at my exit too! (*J. Collins*)

"Sometimes an entrance *is* an exit. *(Sean-Franc)*

Show me a poem with butterflies,
And I'll show you a rank, immature.

Congress has turned Washington into Italy.

Of all the heathen proclivities:
Becoming psychotic instead of cigarettes.

Of all the heathen proclivities:
Avoiding cancer instead of living.

Starbucks has turned coffee into candy bars,
fucking up calories and sucking up bucks,
  while the wait for plain coffee sucks.

I never thought sitcoms were funny
until Donald Trump joined the election.

Donald Trump is a tweaker. There's no
other way to explain it. He snorts hella
meth, and his hair is electro-magnetically
pulled to his nose.

In Latin, "arcanus" means "secret, hidden, private, concealed" –
which makes me think there was a lot of anal sex going on around Noah.

Actual SF homeless guy:
"I'm on a seafood diet.
I see food, I eat it."

All these wealthy folks, a'shart,
Digesting food and booze,
Too burped to look at art!

Soramimi
John Legend & Yolk-O-Oh, No!

The ITs pay employees hella ca$h.
Ergo, this geeky, baby-boom rash!

You can lead a Christmas tree to watt – e're
You can't make it blink.

Bon Marriage
Michael and Salma getting together
In June, making lovely pair weather.

Bon bebé
Michael and Salma getting together
At night, making lovely père weather.
Michael and Salma getting together
All night, making lovely mère *y* weethere . . . ~ o!

[Let's have fun with REAL NAMES from my client list. Etymologies:]

B. Hassett = A shrewd but lazy investor, he sits on his ass checking his assets.
B. Batoreivia = He's travelling back to Mother Hungary by bat or plane!
Mark Zare = You Here
G. Gongwer = He once won the Gong Show, but then spiralled down . . .
J. Buchino = A small-time Vegas bookie, just humping to go large.
J. Podojil = He's trying to do something to Jill. It sounds nasty, but we don't know.
Judy Sweetham = She used to be a sourpuss, but now it's Easter.
K. Beranek = Is that all? How 'bout some tittie? Come on!
Beverly Ratner = Pest controller to her social betters in Bel Air.
M. Squatrito = She pisses in the mouth of a golden showers gay guy! for free.
M. Balbac = Tuck your junk between your legs to look like a vagina.
Mike Ball = See above.
M. & E. Adkinson = Couple anxious to adopt a boy.
Paul Barsanti = Loves to drink holy wine with the Cardinals (Rome, you idiot!)
P. Avdoulos = Keeps wanting to fight with swords instead of guns!
R. Adante = Got fired from the symphony for mispeling.
R.P. Stauffer = Died from botulism stuffing turkeys.
S. Brubaker = Makes pies spiked with beer.
S. & R. Chadderton = % Hanging Chadderton, FL
Thomas Swank = Doubts he's a masturbation addict.
Tom Sedlack = We *told* you he had nothing to offer!
T. van Brackle = Wants to change his name to van Brackette to pay less tax.
Webster Wong = Editor of Beijing Dictionary, unfortunately riddled with mistakes.
His name: *Oui-Oui* Jean-Pee Wee –
'Yes-man, *Français,* and tinee!

She ate so much Pepperoni,
He gave her a sore throat!

Alma Mater
The Dean queried, "Master Diller, are you trying to turn Harvard into a Southern party school?"
As if he needed to *ask,* Diller pulled out a flask, and then snorted a line off Dean's blotter ~~~~!

Bona Fide
I never drank water at the old Alma Mater.
I'd pull out some beer, seduce a straight guy to queer,
¡And though hard-headed, he'd change up to hotter!

You can lead a drunk to water,
but you can't make him clink.

You can lead A.A. to water,
but they'll all want to drink.

He can lead a prick to hotter
but he can't make him dink.

You can lead a beave' to water,
but you can't make her pink.

You can lead Shakespeare to water,
but you can't make him nink-

cum poop.

When it came to money,
Dean Whitter was wittier
Than you, dimwit.

My son Lex was a disinterested student,
and yet that shyte cost me a million bucks
in private schools. As it turned out,
  it could have learned more in prison.

The reason Englishmen call little boys 'Master' is
that the word contains 'ass.' My friend Reese
went to Britain for a gig. He says England is so
homo-repressed, it's like the country is one big
gay cruise to nowhere, anchored in the North Sea.

If you practice lust,
It'll never rust,
Nor you nook-
Y gather dust.

MJM '15 SF

Dirty Laundry

I've yet to master that Hollywood timbre
Sported by Katharine Hepburn before new
L.A. went rapp 'n dumb, half hip-hop Zion
Half lost-*angeles* mall and the MGM lion.

Like Bette, she epitomized Yank: direct,
assertive, plain. No Eastern seaboard class,
Ingénues feigned her Park-Avenue accent
Studios bred in corn-fed girls on *ass*cent.

"Dress British, think Yiddish," how those
 Solomons knew how to sell the goyem
Their own culture! *"Deah, dahling* Gordon . . ."
And so fauth. But then as now, stardom

Went the way vice does do – gambling, drugs
Booze, sex on empowered sofas: *Photoplay*
Idol whose macho appeal a stiff buggering
By Errol Flynn, sword in tights, sets chuggering

Half the John Q. Public; the other half out-
Raged their cowboy, pirate, ace, Prince
Be accused of such ass-amorous precedent
On young men promised shots at President!

But Kate was different, wayward in a yachts-
Man's manner. Just like a stock-and-bond
Trader she factored in malfeasance and loss
Long before warnings by the studio boss,

And flipped her head the way a Mustang
Bucks its captor: all "You *caunt* be serious,"
And bored terrifically too by whiffs-of-coke,
No Gershwin joke, no pretentious tiparillo

Smoke dangling from celluloid lips, vice of
Cool *moderne.* While meager celebs got DNA
Transplants and flashes of tinselitis in the heydays,
Red Kate, though she outgrew a starlet phase,

Aced organic, pine, sea salt, slate, her calcium-
framed cheek and jaw out-*"Rahthering"*
Winston Churchill, bulldog jowel and sag
Cut to: whippet with evanescent dialogue:

"Tennis any*bah*dy?" v-necked, lacrossed
Ivy League belying West Coast cruds and
Chili-bean cowboys farting before a fuck.
No matter what silver-lining luck stuck

On *Movietown and Bros.*, under all that fake
Tinsel, the *real* tinsel bronzies flex & porno.
Can Mae West handle these dank doilies
She'd strip to pistol and *Speedo?* Soil these

Meandered satin sheets she made the maid
Re-press daily, whilst hunks of steel preen
By the pool, apt to bench-press her figure eight?
The paparazzi media fishbowl came too late!

What girl or churl Garbo did behind her gates
Morphs to neurotic daytime gawk-shows wherein
Mom's second husband boyfriends her son
Whose sister is pregnant by father number one.

Everyone's a star: behold the gang at The Ivy!
Bev Hills matrons with *Hermès* bags *de rigeur*
and eye-sags about to go under the knife.
It's a, "What if someone takes my picture?" life,

Expositioned in a three-way mirror guessing
What fraction of face or turn of hair, not wit
To whit, will pass the bone structure imperative
On the six o'clock "news magazines," gossip

At the *other* Ivy, all the day's screenplay fit to print –
In a town whose City Hall is the Playboy
Mansion, where limousines – re-fashioned
Nuclear army amphibians once stationed

In Iran – now convey El Lay bling on fling
Fridays. Where the national anthem is
"All Them Hoh Bitches." Seniors to queer
Zip up Rodeo-Drive uniforms, cashmere

Headbands and sweats, as pandering family
Series and irreality shows culminate in such
A gratuitous calendar of awards ceremonies
One wonders if the laurelled exemplaries

Even have an audience; are there no losers
Not onstage? You pose for plebs, eclipsing
Search, withal the greater part of acting's art
For plumbing other natures in the part.

Overexposed, schlock-and-awe empowers
Today, and Kate Hepburn ebbs too lordly.
Bergman fades under the bandwidth towers'
Bleached assholes and botox-belles *cum* worldly.

Another one for Melanie, whom Deah,
Dahling Gordon *would not forsake*
In this vale of stock-and-bond teahs.
Yet, having once been my shepherd,
  He would expose me like Chloë
To the wolves and the rabble in this,
He'ah year of our Lord 2008 babble.
MJM 10/08 SF

dirty mind

she's "born again"

god forbid

you can't say 'shit'

in front of her

she pictures it!

yea, verily will

mankind

ever see

her clit?

MJM

Dislucinda, Light of Knaves

Nicknamed Dislucinda, she sub-lights the loge with her firefly-galaxy Morse's code:
Dashing, dotting, bouncing, flickering: her fluorescence semaphores on, off and over
Like a painter working ten old master canvasses *en suite*. The piecework salves her
Rhythms lost and found, as her new casein lacquer-slathers yet her next chromatic ode.

Next one, she demonstrates for you or her aura does then dis-explains her verbal cue;
She drops it, done again! A-switch to far more pressing loads of paint, she'll flourish
Out of bounds marking around on round this disembodiment of art ideals to skirmish
With the whole museum's holdings saved to memory, then pizzicate a private view!

She fears not smelting the whole affair into one fantastic melting swirl of multi-color,
Taffy taffeta carnival paintings spinning all a-whorl ~~ my lasses' crayons in a frying pan
And never making brown! She keeps the skeins striate-braided for her all-can-do élan.
"Mademoiselle of marionettes!" I laugh and squirm aware of my own stolid, solar

Panegyrization to keep the whole thing centered, while she – a spiral of stellar shooting
Sparks – flies up and down files 'n strings retrieving, dispensing, switching door-to-door
Until edgy insecurity assures you are no velocity champ to match this mistress you adore.
You try so hard for once letting go oversight: what horror, booting and re-booting

Your lavish derrière in the grinding roller coaster car that always makes vertiginous you
Stop to plant his feet, demanding order of lunatics and from bloody, manic chaos, clear-
Cut lines of intersection, where each one stops in lawful order, one thesis, one austere
Focus at a time with revered respect to talking down and up, making right each clue,

And doing as the audience wishes where plot lines are concerned; while fleet-footed she
Freely fumbles, tosses, passes, runs each time pouncing on the flouncing ball like
Playing *hoops* on a hockey rink – look ma, no hands – with sudden, jerky, tricky spike
Into the net, the luminescent scattershot makes clear it is not she but we, yahwee! . . .

. . who needed to outdo her all along, or risk admitting low IQ, blackout lack of sure fire
Where brains brighten up the cave. Dislucinda, light of knaves, by sheer contrast took
Us dull, then made us bright to give up control, catch up and de-conform; her fast fluke
Electrons zap and tweak us zipped 'n zooming strong, her RAM our most unlikely squire.

MJM 1/09 SF
> – To my favorite patrician musician Patricia

Ditching Duty

Don't know where I am, yet do: between you and death,
Who gave me life, not dearth, but You? Here, we two
Wine and dine, as if – as is true for you – there's no
Capitalism for me to woo. No work I must off to.

I tell your octogenarian-with-incipient-leukemia story
On the phone to NY, SF and L.A., and everyone says,
"You're where you must be. You're doing the right thing!"
As if no one knows my unemployment expires in October.

Is this what the end of a loved one's life brings the younger?
No worldly cares except fussing for him, the stronger, shunt
de repente by age, ballerino, now least in sure-footedness?
Your end-valescence, does it excuse me, derring-do, too?

I *am* needed here, and here *is* my rightful place of duty.
Yes, I'm drunk here, vulnerable to my lavish love of you
As to my corroding résumé – for which I may have to say,
"I was taking care of someone dying." Will they dismay?

Shoo me away? Or will my telling of it show Our way?

MJM 2/13 S.B.

Dixie Marcum

Who knew back then your last name meant
Orgasm of the sea? Not literate yet, I smelt
It all the more: tousled, long locks – colored
By sand and ash, and your brilliant greens

Glittery as a swimmer's: Breasts of perked
Persimmon, your teats nippled erect under
Those wife-beater tees you'd scam from
Boyfriend to wear to school with army

Boots and fatigues, just to play '*guise*-guy.'
Cliqued, coltish, sun-tanned gender-bender,
Your ass would woof-and-tweeter in stride
Inside faded jeans' rips-n-tears, no barrier –

As if baseball string slung swanky over
Our team catcher's cheeks, instead of his
Wire-weld screen. Who knew if you'd
Throw down *Levi's* urgently as Hank

Tore off his mask at home plate – once he
Had mitted a fastball or slider and tagged,
You, *so hot,* this cook even let your horny
Wiener dog give him a tongue job, that time

He came over to cook spaghetti and *sugo*
With blue food-coloring instead of red wine.
Then you had to rush to leave him alone – behind
In your bedroom, face a-pant in your panties;

While your 20-something boyfriend – statutory
Rape be rescinded for summer – picked *you* up
In heat for a date. His horse dick withstanding,
You would often go all jack o' lantern smiles

About '*It*' in smoldering winkfidence, thinking
This other guy but your pasta pansy. You were
Right, but so wrong in that feral way pussy in
High humor and tiger play fertilizes even the

Purplest violet to stiff its stalk. *How* he could
Have pounded it out with you in so many ways:
Suffocating laughs bent at the waist breathless
And drowning, to banging your oyster as you

Smoked a cigarette and yelled him up like a
Rodeo poke or Adonis! Your teeth shone the
Whitest, and libido lobs-at-gods we would
Saucily conjure – devilish girls be sainted-

By-high-jinx! For you, lust was not a deadly
Sin, but a complimentary spin on your being
A girl, a dude's boy. Just to lasso and rope you
Down, he'd even have swallowed that whole

Honcho in his truck-bed! Wow, you reeled so like
That old Hollywood movie *Flesh and the Devil!*
Yet one *knew* damn well you were no Medusa,
Bathsheba, Salomé, nor killer siren. Just as Jewish

Producers, temptation-baiting, were not about to
Get anyone *rotisseried* over a picture, you just
Made sure the "little guy" titillated long enough
To buy a pass or two. Here I am, hot dog still in line . . .

MJM 1/11 SF

Dog on It, Sonnet

You were the pleasure of his laud, the girl
More famous men had tried and lost to mate.
Hilarity made perfect you a pearl,
Shone outside, inner humor pink, a'spate.

You conquered his chet lads and maids alike,
When sensual lover to wife away
To coil your gifts of self when borne the tyke,
As lex'con changed from naked night to day.

Now he applauds scant intervals of you,
Relief and happy longitude his gift.
For now the darks spin gleef'lly by and new,
His hand in sexual matters, right from rift.

Though marriage be a sacrament from gods,
Lust in all its rancor sparks lightning rods.

MJM 10/15 SF

Doggerel Matt

Matt is fat, but not a brat.
His heart is where it's at.
Hetero to the max, he can't
See dirt in parallax.

He loves his cigs and vodka dearly
To make his parents chafe wearily.
He's funny when it isn't right,
Morning, noon, sober, tight.

Due to his stroke, he seems retarded,
Then in talks, you feel outsmarted.
He holds his pants up with one hand
And loves his pappy like quicksand.

And even though he has three boys,
Ex-bitch won't let him buy them toys!
What's wrong with girls who get divorced?
Mostly churls, they're lawyer-forced.

If this were but a court of Pa,
Matt would pluck the longer straw.
He'd love his family as this own,
Even in his smart-assed tone.

  Bachelors, exiled ev'ry elsewhere,
Noble dads would love to share.

MJM 4/15 SF

Doggerel of the Two M's

Here I sit at fifty:
Unshaven, stylish, insecure.
I've lived my life to party;
Of business been sure unsure.

I've worked since I was but fifteen
And have earned a lot of stripe,
But I spent way too much on sex and fun
And now feel hyper-overripe.

I wish I'd paid less attention
To those seven deadly sins;
Instead of trying each one out,
Had waited past my pension.

For now I am house poor,
They say, and rather unemployed.
I search in vain to reclaim my name.
I don't even own my door!

How quickly U.S. markets *shirk*
The injured squire. From ace-
In-the-hole and management,
Myself I'd even fire!

Fallen ill of mind and soul, my
Corpse in pain, my limbs with gout,
I find I'm not on the inside track,
But on the lam and out!

I wonder if at fifty years
I can re-conform my essence
To again become successful I –
All Gregory Peck quintessence.

I'd work hard again and bring
My *balls* and genius down to bear
On the almighty mission statement;
To the clock I'd solemnly swear.

Yet it seems that I've grown picky
And spoilt, as good years piled high,
But I can't afford that point of view,
Or I'm headed for the toilet.

I must regain my equipoise, my *corps*
Exquis – and take on any dis/economic fight,
So when I do turn fifty-one, I'll have
Parachuted golden from this wretched flight

To Year 2,051!

[W., pick the poem parts be
You and cite the rest to me,
Or call it 50/50, or 51-50 *me!*

Thanks for the brilliant party;
I only beat you by one week!
From M. 4/14/59 to M.
on his 50th – April 20, "2-0-0-9"]

MJM 4/09 SF

Doha y Yo

Now I know how they make expressive people
Great talkers, and contrary to their epithet,

Tuned-in listeners they. Their parents gloat
Half the time, and the other half scold

To choke their chat: "Be more damn
Apollonian," as if loose talk were Bacchus'

Evil hiding under their tongues. In fact,
These slips think that work and love

Occupy the same place at the same time,
As their Dads, once suave've fallen tattered,

Chain-smokers focused on *American Express*.
Remember, our heroes took on the A-bomb,

Only just as they would the consumer bridle.
Whereas with you, all is *ribald cracking up*.

Even while you write an invoice!
Now here we are in Big Sur, hugging cliffs.

I'd roll an awfully long time
    just to hear your patter.

    I'd even foreplay a longer time
To concede affluent work and wild sex

Are what pre-sigh-sly matter.

MJM '88 SF

Done, Finished, *Adiós!*

Cover the earth like a blight
Give up the good fight
Disappear from sight
Indulge in sex and fun, life light.
Be far from those called bright
Forebear every plebian slight
Know the good, do the right
Pack the party calendar tight
Be social at a bohemian's height
Laugh and tramp high as a kite
Exit the battle for want of might
On delicacies dine late at night
Use British words like "quite"
Be waspy and just as white.
Ignore this global zeit-
Geist; don't get hooked, don't bite
Read no morning paper plight
Abandon ego, give up fright
In spirit meditate to light.

The world is on its own
I have nothing it could own
It has nothing I should be shown
I'll be on my own
I'll be on the town

I came from the womb
I'll go to my tomb

Hoping there's a there-after.

MJM '08 SF

Dream Is the Ink of Sleep

1

Early evening summer dimness
Falls from leaves' edges
Etched and torn
Lambent traces of sun
Pour like slim lasers.

2

Quarreling branches spin
In a tangled prison of rage,
The muscular shafts of light,
the ink, the deep, as wet pastel
Drops the sky, a-splatter

All over the
easel of night.

MJM '79 Cambridge MA

Drop-Down

It's enough for you to do it once
for a few men to remember you.

– Ernest Hemingway

In a dialogue box online, he scrolls down four
Screens to locate the year he was born. How
Alarming! – all these younger people from
Decades and decades after his birth. *His* year

Was once near the top; now it's bottoming
Out. With late middle-aged perspective, he
Dissects us. In the first stage, we depend
On adults for love, protection, schooling.

In the second, all that teens need is each other.
This makes sense, since in pre-history we'd
Be dying in our 30s and 40s, and they'd be
The leaders and breeders; we, in caskets

Or on pyres! He notices young adults, brilliant,
Strident, sharp: full of whatever hormones
Good parents need to raise babies and put up
With their shit. Their gait is clipped, efficient,

Swift – now aligned to Will – with flexibility,
Flare, and fertility to ratchet up. Next comes
Middle age, denied and put off, so long as
Lies pass. We exclaim how much younger

We look than our grandparents when they
Were this age – what with better nutrition,
Vitamins, and plastic surgery. World so crowded,
And we rather done with reproduction,

Passersby on the sidewalk seem to say,
"Of what use are they?" Finally, old age wafts
In, breaking down the body to make mockery
Of beauty, duty. Stooping, wrinkling, freezing,

Resigning. How far we've collapsed from
Botticelli goddess, Michelangelo youth,
Goya's *majas,* Cellini warriors, Raphaello
Virgins. How long we've been wasting,

Misspent youth, the mind now quieting down to
Receive soul, spirit, heart, cosmos, intuition.
Marketers narrate that 20 to 35 is the age range
Of who buys stuff, plus teens with parents' money.

How right they are in his case: a house, a diamond,
Chandeliers, drapes, Eastern carpets, antiques,
Paintings, glass, and plate. Cars, computers,
TVs, flat-screen of course, decks and gardens;

Vacations, bank accounts, and credit cards.
He truly senses that all this acquiring brought
Happiness, fleeting as she is, always needing
A recharge, but did not connect to Joy.

Sometimes, he self-pities and pouts about
The virility of his climbs in companies – and
Upon, and into, young lovers. Sometimes he
Senses *these are* the good old days. He meditates

And enters that long runnel that, at death, is said
To amaze with brilliant light and an overwhelming
Sense of infinite peace, love, and care. For now,
It's a red cyclone of net-like capillaries. In youth,

He could not be still on his path of dare and ire:
Deranged, erring, darting, damning, on high to
Dying. He remembers the churches in Italy to
Spain where one finds the faithful, frail elder

Beside elder. "Where are all the young?" he'd inquire.
"Outside collecting, as we *did when we were there."*
"Fuera para recoger, como lo hicimos cuando estuvimos allí."
"Fuori a collezionare, come abbiamo fatto quando eravamo lì."

Outside collecting, as we did when we were there.

MJM 2/11 SF

Drug Piss

Rootless of parents & brother: immediate non-family,
You even abandoned peers to scared chastity –
re-fridged until your capillary flowers biled yellow:

Exotic mould, you thought smelt of cheese and steel.
The three in your house of kings, guillotined –
And your sassy three-of-jacks – crushed by *Homo*

nausea: Lo, girls-o'diamond – yeo, hearts in clubs,
Two came close, ended dud buds. *Oh*-'O'-straight rules –
Where pussy's a first second – cock already in it.

After all this time, not a monk, but for *you,*
Approaching sainthood – this trance: a fizzle, jizzed
t're-sizzle – bisecting organelles and beaus.

Locked with boys and girls behind co-doors
In his vivid video-roll, cock already in it, scores.

MJM 1/12 SF

Drunken Ruler

In long, greasy coveralls you tramp down the street,
Overruling your pit-bull, like a lowlife in need of a beta.
Don't walk too fast, sit, heel, no, no – your minutia
Barked out in the space of half a block, as if to mistreat.

Why do puppies of that breed attract our misfit men?
Either raise that 'son' with love, or he's a deadly weapon.
Does his eager cowering to you, make you more a man?
Or do you lack audience and crave a sycophantic fan?

Dim dog owners do not realize their canine's nature
Is built in. Thus, wild dogs, but allow one mate-set:
Coupling of just one bitch and sire – the best hunters.
The rest are aunts and uncles whose fertility for now

Is nil – they, governess and bodyguard to puppies
Of the alphas. They join the hunt, but dog-law decrees
Only one duo mates, and so their fidelity, innate fiat,
Is encoded by, "Serve servilely, what brings me meat."

Their kills, common to seldom, can only feed so many.
Thus 'butlers and nannies' self-preserve: ensemble canny,
Exchanging breed for feed. We heed our pets; they see
Us as top dog and protect our babies. Taller, we

Establish rules, so kowtowing to our orders
Is not from our breaking down dog borders
To man's best friend, but predestined dog behavior,
As we nourish, walk, water them, their savior.

And just like children, if we abuse them in their
Puppy-hood, they'll turn out mangled, scared,
Or killer mean, as could that pit-bull I see there.
I hope this overbearing man is well prepared

To parent an unriled pup – now all eyes on master
With that excited, urgent, heightened wish to please
And do no wrong. Overall, he vibes a drunk disaster.
Rule that dog with love, you beast! Lord benevolent ease.

MJM 3/11 SF

Dry

This addiction club, tabernacular impure, many-faced
Liquored-up cadets to early graves, burned harridans,
Wastrels, our Fathers from town and farm, black top-hat to hoe,
Shamed kin and abandoned circle, fing'ring churches' robots' hijacked.

Or romantic poet, glassy lyricist, rock star tripped 'n died
In a tumbler gin suicide click-by-click, gnarled rebellion
Hellion ladies rented their skirts, and grungy bards amazed
Corner-office suck-jock – heart attacked in meth-orgy scandal.

Now radical magnetism uncorks the ladle laden drama,
Unfolds a matrix mind net, misbehavior brain with blueprints
You shouldn't build it. No halcyon aura, laurel, or punch
Rings round my gala where hardware and haunting quarrel.

MJM '08 SF

Dudley

Home is where the dog hair
is *everywhere,* except on the dog!
Though well fed twice a day,
He wants rice – nonchalant to mice.

His breed thinks its owners need
constant attention – which is why he's
always on *"Go-to-bed!"* detention.
He has no use for backyard play,

Preferring to spend his day
Following the leader, the leader, the leader.
Other than feed his body and emotions,
We try to keep Fido's devotion slowed:

Two, ¾-cups-a-day of food and H2O.
Can't we only love you some? Hair, hair, hair can earn us…
Chihuahua fare! Yorkie-ware!
  'Pillows à la *Dudley furitis!'*

MJM 4/15 SF

el lay crabgrass

her hair is electric cranberry
mine is boring brunette

her voice lilts with londoner charm
mine sounds soooooooooo familiar

she's ensconced in trendy spandex
i'm comfortable in old lee jeans

her life is l.a. fast
mine is Monterey slow

she's at home in manhattan or madrid
i go home to mom's

her friends date warren beatty
my friends won't

her datebook's filled with rock stars' weddings
mine says pick up catfood.

yet *Now* she doesn't have a certain him.
I Do.

– To Z. R.

MJM '88 Beverly Hills

Elegy Sea-to-Shining-Sea

It's 13 years since 9/11 – numeral never used to count the stories
in a skyscraper. How that night in Boston I saw those jets in line . . .
then dashed on a shuttle to NYC to catch the red-eye to "Frisco."

Past nine, the UA jets line up like sleeping pelicans, shimmering
near a dock in autumn winds, dormant after a day of wrecking
dives into wave upon wave, their wingspans tensed against winds ~

Spume, swirling about like confetti from windows on an avenue.
Alas, an engine delay stalls us on the tarmac until 3:00 a.m. I,
tipsy and agitated: how dare the airlines treat us this way!

Will the toilets flow over? Is there nothing to eat? Why can't we
get up and stretch out our feet? When will the captain announce we're
aloft? Good service in planes, riven to barbaric and sloughed!

I enter my bed and fall dead asleep. Outside, the chickadees cheep.
Turn on the tube only to see where I've been. Sin! Sin! Sin!
Din! Din! Din! Bodies falling from Towers. Next of kin. Next of kin!

A last blast in PA! Heroes saving the Capitol struggle and crash!
As forces of evil burst the world's bubble, I shriek and lament
As if East-Coast body-double. *Double bubble,* t'oil *and trouble!*

Now, water in the Footprints' wells,
Tolling in the Church Street bells.
Let five towers rise in place,
To angels be our human race.

In the caldron boil and bake;
 Eye of newt, and toe of frog,
 Wool of bat, and tongue of dog,
 Adder's fork, and blind-worm's sting,
 Lizard's leg, and owlet's wing,—
 For a charm of powerful trouble,
 Like a hell-broth boil and bubble.
  ALL. Double, double toil and trouble;
 Fire burn, and caldron bubble.

Near the street called Liberty,
Let that quintet lease the Free.
At Vesey, easy them to Reverend street.

MJM 9/14 SF
Penultimate stanza: "Macbeth," Shakespeare

Eliot House

– And this is good old Boston,
The home of the bean and the cod,
Where the Lowells talk only to the Cabots,
And the Cabots talk only to God.
– John Collins Bossidy

Dorm-crewed, I scrubbed the toilet/sink of a Cabot-Lodge:
She, impious Eliot House – I, a Mather muse – alas, more
An Indian under the Raj. She flirted by the dormer window,
Condescending to scandalizing, underlining pussy – I, her
Chamber wuss. The scent be that, undergrads, rich-to-poor,
Don't use her much 'no' more. As if, even noble-Fathered
She cahn't score.

MJM 9/11 SF

Ellis Street Half House

Mauled minds, scattershot eyes,
Saliva-crawed with overbites and fangs
Crooked out like cups of nails.

How so lain low by Aphrodite, Apollo,
This wretched arena o'bros and sisses:
A bitter cup of coffee, gala as my museums'

Champagne. Their travail for welfare checks,
Thrilling as our global travels. They eye-sly
Round the room, hack-slack children o'dogs,

Drug worn, booze-battered since birth:
Heckled, haunted, foals of the torn.
Un-played by love, gain, measure – dildoed.

The clubroom's moth-dead fluorescent tubes,
Grimy walls, herpes halls, toilet a'flake to hues
Of past enamels. Peers and betters crumple

Self-same stories of their own drug-tumble.
But why heed it when yr face is scrabbled
And jeered? Why not fritter out or freak?

Even sex wracks them pitiless as filth,
Foxing gender-shame, feigning lilt.
We, beautifully bitched as gods. They,

Endamnèd sires of self-horror, maimed by odds.
Tho' they inherit the wind, they bray, pared,
Capillaries cracked, cray, "Bup in a dollar."

MJM 3/11 SF
To Simone, Southern lady of means . . . philanthropic

Encore (11)

You never waned, illumined to insane.
Though in mind's stage, you darked, I dreamt a part:
All fresh blood I beat for you bleeds again.
I see a scrimmed youth: camera's gauzy art.

You live with wisdom, family, and increase.
Whereas I, in folly, age worlds away.
You drawn here, I would over ask release,
And love lash me live, not years' dim decay.

If those whose fate is shunned away, love more,
And I recalled your face and musk surreal,
I would brave heart to the next heaven's lore,
But boy, my remains are you: smell . . . touch . . . feel.

Nature sealed you from my rave, staked nearby,
Penned to write you, not lobbied in my eye.

MJM 3/11 SF
After Sonnet 11

This is a good juncture at which to summarize a variety of angles on the practice of DC the SS PS:

1. When I first DC SS-11, two years ago, I had no idea where any of this was leading. PS 11, like its adjacent, chronological mates, is the result of my painstaking evaluation of internal word and letter hints inside the contents of the original SS. Two years back, I was extremely uptight to accomplish roughly three things: a) follow SH instructions; b) observe the ten-beats-per-line rule of a SS; c) observe the ABAB/CDCD/EFEF/GG rhyme scheme of a SS – including observing the rule that the PS comprise exactly 14 lines, just like the SS. (On my own, I decided to break up 'my' PS into three quatrains, followed by a heroic couplet, rather than conform to the 'block' of text one finds in SS folios' format. I did this for ease of deciphering, since the double line spaces helped me to organize, think and see more readily.)

2. At this point in the PS-DC, I was using a bit of cheek and wit (your call!) to name the emergent PS with titles, not numbers. This will change later, when I realize SH has spurred me on to an 'organized' program of DC, and that the vanity of my titling the PS will only lead to confusion, whereas numerically titling them will index them more clearly.

3. Early on in the PS, I predicted that SH would eventually blame his DC for having spontaneously spawned the diabolic content of many of the worst of the PS – pure filth, one cannot even imagine in today's well-policed world. This eventually will happen: SH will blame me, calling his influence over me 'psychodomic' – that is, part SH-directed ('domic') but part my own perversity ('psycho'). He will also argue back and forth that the DC <u>is his accurate acolyte</u> in DC, but then switch attitudes and accuse the DC, me, of self-evolving, to a degree, the PS pornography. *He will clearly play both sides without apology!* Then again, he will eventually rail against the third-party reader – you – that the worst of all possible mistakes would be to take the sappy, moronic SS on their own

merit. He constantly supports the concept that the SS were written to be DC, and not for their own worth – which is dumb-dubious at most, as I've always thought, even as a young high-schooler.

4. Paradoxically, though, by the time we get to PS 154, and then backtrack to PS 150 because of my own dis-chronology in that isolated case, SH finally calls for an end to the homo PS, and he urges me, as he does just above in PS 11, to go back again and discover a second set of PS – apparently about women, especially about the Northumberlands' hate for the Tudors and the Stuarts. Please recall that, at the end of this DC-PS cycle, you will find SH admitting he is really Duke of Northumberland 9, with many a vendetta against the English monarchs of his time for their persecution of his forebears, back to the time of Henry VIII and continuing through the regime of James I, who himself even jailed Duke of N-9 for 15 years in the Tower – or so we are told as the PS cycle concludes.

5. [explication of text]

Epiphany Ant at Tub Lake

I

Tub-soaking with book in the resonant air,
I read that repugnant part of Sartre's *Age of Reason*
in which a recalcitrant fly crosses an etching plate.

Object of art, the plate supplants the artist's animus.
Copper corrodes as acid incises:
like an old-fashioned God and his waters,

or eons
of ions of weather
shaping the antecedent face of the planet.

Inked and pressed into paper – *corpus vellum* –
the plate's mirror imprint
implants inspiration,

becomes an inner window,
a still and constant
likeness of some inner/outer world clairvoyant.

Will it resonate
with independent life,
more than *nature morte*?

Antithetically,

Sartre's fly has a little life too, as it zips
and darts askance the plate's patterns –
you might say, on-the-fly plate tectonics!

Do we believe as antique philosophers warrant
that a fly extant is a step up
the Great Chain of Being from art?

Or is it down? Or over as arrogant Sartre wants?
Gizmo of moving parts
thing-a-ma-jig

crank-elegant machine.
If flies be more alive than plants
and etching plates

that mimeograph dead artists'
still lifes,
Is man more

That he designs implants? Hell, blatant
flyspecks and fungi all over art paper do that!
And the deeper, plangent fact:

are we not as blank as unimpressed paper
in the beginning, and then again, just at the very end,
our own flyspecks notwithstanding?

What
if not ourselves
has drawn us?

II

Next,

The boy in *The Age of Reason* handily anticipates to catch a fly. He tears off its wings.
Its phosphorescent head-sheen reminds him of a sulphur matchtip.
So he takes the paraplegic and strikes it on a flint

to see if it'll ignite,
  a little
  Joan of Arc!

Objective match,
with life of short breadth,
it should fire

into a smoldering
skeletal stick; fly remnants =
  $e = mc^2$, c light constant.

  Miscreant,

the fly won't even ignite,
making it less alive than a match,
should you *need* a light.

Now, I'm told flies only live a matter of days.
Contrast this to works of art
hanging on august, "reliant" walls virtually "forever."

Until, that is, the big one hits:
The niner, the ten that'll toll
the century and slant Manhattan!

Ars longa, vita brevis est.
   Perhaps.
                        But I underline,
Infirmo terra obliterro artis quod vitam.

To put a dent in ascendant culture,
Sartre has the petulant boy smash
a 3,000-year-old Chinese antique vase,

his uncle treasures.
It's sheer, *enfant terrible,*
lusty spite.

   Hot summer,

the boy's been lurking about
his tyo-tya's country house
bad tenant, just looking for a rant.

He's buzzing with sun.
The vase's precious history antagonizes him.
He's jealous of its elegant age, its status.

He annihilates it into shards,
like so many flies' wings crunching in crisp
piles underfoot.

Now he's conquistador, wanton killing machine of sages.
An object with inner life, it echoed inside like a seashell.
He shatters the fading *memori mori* of all its fingerprints

on the brilliant fired glazing
one imprint blurring out another
like a depth of fossils.

   When all of a sudden

BY NEPTUNE!
looms *BLACK ANT*
astride my book!

   I gasp wanting for air!

From fucking nowhere!
this dominant pygmy conquers the page!
Artful irony! Anthem of anthems!

Synchronicity!
Triple "A"-bug-a-boo
Life over mind!

Holy pageant of timing!
You're sheer over the deep,
you exorbitant spawn of sand and acid.

What in Hades do you want?
Where in the fuck did you parasail in from?
He towers above my

Waterline perspective,
and I imagine this *dramatis personaeant*
Hatched on the plant-derived paper itself!

Or is it spontaneous generation?
Waving antenna and forelegs boxing,
This sudden godzilla,

Ferocious
Regent
Preens and prances on the pagecrest!

I pant: it's that place just outside Tokyo
in the forest primeval
where *T. rex* espies human prey

and
  making a dinosaur dash
    downridge

chomps up the squinty-eyed professor
running the gauntlet! You hear bones crack!
See blood squirt from PhD ears . . .

When the monster spits out
the geeky eyeglasses with a grunt –
fishbone afterthought,

skyscrapers in the distant city,
cars crashing!

Naturally,

I ignore the damn book
I *must* inspect this significant fellow,
rising up on hind legs right in my face:

Now he's knight-errant shining his armor;
Now a flexible SF gay guy sucking his own butt; a cat bathing;
daring me into the ring, scant featherweight boxer waving fisticuffs!

In the hermeneutical cell of my curtained tub,
He's *Awesome Ant!* midge Magnified to malignant Giant!
Aside: my focus on him is as sharp as it should have been in college.

Should I dive underwater?
Hold him levitant to read Sartre's lines
à la Braille, only footwise over letter-press?

Or is this just *incidental ant*
Queerly astride the page's sharp edge,
Urging me to smash him on the spot?

(My self-impulse makes him male.)
What's the diff?

Or do I not kill him in the way Hindus chant you shant,
It *could* just be your long-gone aunt?

III

That *this Atom Ant* only know what a stunning theme it were
he arrive at the hermetic moment,
Soggy as it was!

What an unanticipated marvel, that he make Sartre's watershed work
seem an inky trickle of backwater rant.
You brave, *punctilious ant!*

Let's say,

You were my grand entrant
Right on the spot out of nowhere on purpose,
Begat from air, your little life, so huge!

That you're *Venus ascending!*
Indomitable snowman!
Hemingway of the Himalayas!

How you crest
All unannounced
to growl and paw at reindeer and readers.

I look around the tub lined with plants and lubricants.
That's right! Getting in, I noticed
some of his drowned kin along the tub-lip

where I keep my shampoos and deodorant.
  Eegads, wife, we got ants!

Casually arid,
but with hints of metalife resonant
in my brain and soul,

I try shaking him off into the deep,
but he doesn't notice.
He doesn't fall.

  So,

for his valor
I decide to save him,
Letting him crawl from the page I tip to the porcelain lip.

He exits
trotting out
over rotting comrades.

As I compose this in another room, he might even be dead
from a slip-up all his own for all I know.
No! I can still feel his prescient presence.

Or is he back at the colony with a food-load of dead mates, already?
Reliant, with a pheromone briefing on this hirsute,
chubby man he saw soaking in a pool of tap *aqua normale,*

With a rapped-out count
of abandoned bodies
he was sent by ant *centrale* to survey? . . . "I can't bring 'em all home!" he descants.

He'll pass on his formicable DNA no doubt,
Or is it the Queen and her drones
Who'll do it for him?

Much like I depend
on the President for the Library of Congress,
or on my son Lex

to pass on the banter someday distant,
that Dad had a head for minor,
bizarre incidents like these,

And how it pained him not to have Immortal life like a Ming vase;
His disappointment that *his ant*
wasn't meant to read the page he strode.

  That,

"I wanted book ant to know the irony
of his being there alive vs. Sartre's not,
dead-old-goat in so many words.

"How he fantastically shared his triumphant moment with me *tête-à-tête*
Right there in Atlantis tub –
A father and his own ant."

Toweling, I overhear:
"Through him, with him, in him,
Thou shalt not sartre for a second!

I *am* up here in golden heaven, you sinning dupe!
This is the last sign I'm sending, squirt!
I spit out the lukewarm and abandon blasphemers!"

(Repentant, had I better augur that relevant ant or else?)

I'm left vaguely wondering, disconcertised,
though it's not the nausea
we constantly got before Confession.

(By the way, too many *en passant*
coincidences lead to faith *and* paranoia.)

I conjecture: if God *be*, would he actually
scorch one not, who's reading the signals right?
Like ascension ant, apparition ant –

Though I'm still
convinced
it's all a buggy coincidence?

Nope. No born-again ants here, as the lukewarm water
I unplugged minutes ago spirits through city pipes
to the vast Pacific Ocean, and dead ants go down the drain.

I even have fantastic etchings on my walls,
Though no fly is crossing.
They're congregant in streaming sun or lamplight.

Today it's been dark in my rooms
due to rain.
It may well end seven years of persistent drought.

IV

Fly, art, man, ant, little me and Jean-Paul Sartre.

I know some fine artists.
One lives on the East Coast, three hours ahead of me.
She composed that "emerging work" over there.

While others are dead to me like Sartre.

Funny, that ant's become a stranger again.
None of the trenchant punch I felt first sighting him.
"Marooned! Me mate! Starbuck! Moby-Dick Ant!"

I guess I left before we got the chance
to get well-acquainted. (Not smart,
considering the pregnant impression he has apparently etched in my mind.)

Maybe I should go out and buy an ant farm,
beckon him back with bait;
make him *founder ant* of his own colony.

Then I recant,
  he's not a breeder.
    Besides,

we already *have* ants,
Though they *are*, as it were, homeless, in my perilous watery
bathroom when it rains; or upstairs where curranted crumbs tumble.

In my water, I do declare I feel *anti-angst* thanks to that ant,
Dutifully trundling home, not anxious either,
his old, triassic, sure feet and formic sixth sense

intact!

Perfected way back in ancient time
when real Godzillas
roamed is He.

As for us, the monkey antithesis,
we had no daily bread
back when, much less a Prayer.

In the age after water covered the entire planet,
land masses
pushed up like brown me rising out of the bath.

Agitant, I dribble, scribbling these notes,
as my own colony beckons me back with bait
to earn a living tomorrow.

Rat race? Ant farm? Roller derby?
Snake pit? King of the hill? CEO?
Army ant? *Coup de terre?* Planet X?

Each day I see overall peril
just to be safe – existential
precipice of Renascent pages over water.

The big one's immanent; the ozone thins.
They say, "Life's what you make it.
The future's what you store away, like squirrels."

It's curious how a midget revelation
as that ant
will puncture workaday routines to heroize classic lines:

the who, what, where, when, how, why
of what's next, what could be,
what never-can-be antirational theories of being here

that drove Sartre-me so wild –
the St. Vitas' dance a red ant does
tossed on a black anthill by killer kids.

So wild, even inanimate objects –
that silver faucet torusing the world bent –
make you dizzy, as maggots haunt decomposing flesh,

I'm as osmotic and tentative as a tent.
Things do have a garish modern sheen all their own.
It's been pressing in

on well-read people
since right around
World War I. Maybe it has *the ignorant!*

　Alas,

Wouldn't it have been a fit, if
on Sartre's *own book* an ant had appeared
as the legend soaked in his Paris tub?

Would he have written out *fly* to immortalize *page-teetering marine ant,*
in the way I can't seem to do for my own foundlings,
try as I may, my being unknown less than art, no legend?

Perhaps we'd have had humor in common,
not just this tired despair,
decades old,

others everywhere
allayed by Hollywood, therapists, Wall Street
canting them out of it.

As if
I and the great man were more two of a kind.

Or three to count *resplendent ant!*
All, all a matter of Matters, or

agonized Western guys
sorely wanting a mantra.

MJM 3/92 SF

Equation of Hell's Fellas

Alcatraz hunkers down in stone, aghast at the masted ships
As in *A Clockwork Orange:* beady eyes pincer-forced open
To gaze, dazzled, grisled, and dazed 24/7 at antique vessels

That circumnavigated olden worlds, India to Alaska to ply
Oceanic waters even The Bird Man's birds could never fly.

The Maritime Museum, all in art-deco whites and curving,
Makes a mockery of that pile of rocks, perched on terrazzo,
While Ghirardelli Square feeds the grosser public chocolate

And ice cream – art galleries all around that salt the wounds
Of cons, inmates, lifers, whose imagination knew no bounds

To indecency and crime, hate and pillage, rapes and murder.
Now they stew in bayside sunlight and freeze in rainstorms.
Pink and white high-rises boasting views of the Golden Gate

Bridge to indulged Marin County, Wine Country, Pt. Reyes.
Counting barges by the dozen loaded with fine goods for us,

They survive on slopped this and that, barely salted, scarcely
A cracked peppercorn to savor. Asian silk, spices, souvenirs
Abound for Chinatown for those who come and go in planes

That tremble and hum over their restricted air – Cinderella's
Pumpkin coach not as fair to these rest-of-my-sad-life fellas.

It was mean and vengeful to build a prison in plain view of
Our pretty City by the Bay, but in their crimes so were they.
Back-and-forth across the channel, freedom vs. hell to pay.

MJM 11/10 SF
Aquatic Park

Eruptions

Eruptions, boiled up in stomach, liver, kidney,
And he's laid out faded and fated for death
At 54 – just like dear old Dad. Or suicide,
Vice as good as a *Vicodin* or any knock-out
Drink's rest to end this pathetic bout,
This de-testy, unjesty, detested test of insanity.

His vanishing vodka perspective, binocular-
Like, focused only on him *cum* prey, the way
His mother screeched him out of bed
Into their fray – nuns by day, rulering he pray.
She'd break every plate in the house,
Teeth grit like a pit bull, nostrils flared,

And eyes flamboyant as only a Latina chick
Can tick to exploded time bomb, '¡*Pinchi
Cabron*-es!' bombarding his nascent ears, "¿Wow,
Mom swearing in Spanish? Spewing the "F"-
Word she forbids in English, whipping the shit
Outta Mark the times he'll use it, ever bad lad?"

Knowing she can't keep up the onslaught
Without her hostage little me, I'm up till three
At age four or five, wondering, will we survive?
Finally Dad coaxes me back to bed. Pops
Her one in the head, and she scurries off,
Dead asleep in a matter of minutes.

But the damage done the little one
Knows no limits. It's why he's still
Talking this jive at age fifty-five.
He's shriven, thrived, survived,
Been on top, and next, more dead than alive.
What's a normal child's upbringing?

The love and security that only parents can give?
I haven't got a clue. So here's another
Redundant boo-hoo. A glass, some ice, and booze
To unshake – venomous med that lets him quiver.
Until it doesn't. Butta-bing, butta-bang:
No money, job, roof, or sieve for a liver.

MJM 4/14 SF

Eucalyptus Killer

A lone boy, bespectacled, harassed: "the geek, the nerd, the twerp, the freak,"
Eyes down, trudges the road-shoulder, castaway shamed and unmated.
Under the eucalyptus grove on the winding way, he hikes with a big stick
In a forest of audacity and murder: foreign trees, whose crescent leaves

Scythe the ground by the millions, kill with ignoble gas every leaf of grass
Ought to 'have been.' Kids lacking grace, monkey-faced, climb nowhere
For an age. Self-mercy trickles his soul's faint tracery, mixed with blame.
Will he evolve to the highest human of his heath, underanged by id-and-ego

Thieves, whose towhead bias 'd bleach away his carbon trace? Hurt-
Hone, he foretells not the future, but eye-minds the battering brothers
Bound up to fight, who'll strangle swans in the little lake that hems
The grove. He'll end up reaved, half Samaritan, half conceived

By self. May he not, numb, find derelictions to dumb his training's pain:
But trampled, harvest a poet's soul to pen his playmates, *Play-dough*-tolled.
Bred, sliced, may he not haul their scene, but whisper-murmur in the well.
His mercy – seismic strong – may mercy agony: his in-tune, on-time misery,

Inherit wisdom. Loneliness vapors to art. His gangly-slang, crooked
Looks align – old library lines of men that history loves. Far from Father's
Musk, Torment's vassals, knights, soldiers, grunts, and farmer-plebes may well
Secede, femaled by age. Fire-crucibled, youth mans-up in quest, re-paged.

Too good and dear for this cutting, market-whimmed world's no good,
He may inherit by blend green woods – poison-pal invaders, un-stood.
Of all punk tads, mean as dust and dirt, he palms best friend, stick understood.
How does young torture advance with age? It's in his brain. It's in his blood.

MJM 5/11 SF
To a 'green,' fine loner in the Presidio.

Event Horizon

He grows grateful for his shoes, the heat in this room, his room,
His persnickety fragile art world, reading glasses, his renegade
Son – 19-year-old from hell – the hell of college, the divorce
That cost $300, the two of them still their brother's keepers.

This rain that will flake to snow will fall in riverruns back to
The sea and up, again rain. That Lady Di turned the spotlight off
Gossip to little ones limbless for foot mines amid the wailing
Of Africa's stark hour. That Holy Teresa did not fear for head

Lice, crabs, scabies like he from his old routine of drug-wanton
Lust. Nothing could keep her out of the gutters; in full, His grace.
That "The Day the Earth Stood Still" is still a movie. For aches
Without *Vicodin,* aspirin only. For archangels. For medium-rare

Steaks 'n chops medium or rare. For his car, wheels be praised,
Though he now concedes busses can be a wo/man's best friend,
No shame in hustled company. That he's winked and contrived
Against the rules to sanctuary many a haywire worker from the

Boss and, at last, from each other, himself more outlaw-prone
To Communism, all be he a climber. That he forgave those
Who trespassed against him, and flinch as he might, got taught
To pray for his enemies, not drink poison to kill the other guy,

In bipolar reverie of the Holy Mother interceding and loving
At the hour of his death, her comfort in haloed companionship
Vastly more sanctuary than these books he'll leave behind –
One more hardship artist's voice on voice cupping the babble.

And what of the babies? Dragonflies? That *Old Spice,* wild carn-
Ation tarnation of a lover lost before even a kiss, for whom he
Still wells to tears at certain romantic symphonies, and though
Tormented for decades, can now repeat, "At least I've felt true

Love once. Many have not," as Katharine Hepburn said in her
Wane of Spencer Tracy, humble before his wife. He's ungrateful
For Wall Street crooks white-shoed, but shown their sly cocaine's
Pathetic lust for strippers and fall from mighty heights, he

Concedes he may know them one day at a time as brothers –
Skylit to skid row. Often he only likes the palm trees a-sway
In Hollywood. The Old Masters at the Met, and how they
Kept his keen eyes alive on the window of the spirit to *It* that

Animates the cosmos – his event horizon, black holes, stars,
Quasar, red dwarfs, laser, and blue giants, notwithstanding.

MJM 12/10 SF

"Everybody Needs Milk – Even Dada"

– If 'to mar' is to blemish, then why marry, nebbish?

When a divorcée's bad-mad, she only reaps ¼ what 'they'
Had: thus, the lawyer's kids comport Stanford by ½!
For all his plod, Dad packs off – in her *Target* valises –
nadiral doodads and his *summa* duds for d'blahs'
"furnished" apartment –

This, after all, being a lads' world, and divorce court,
Ladies' late *payback* for the millennia's abuse us dogs
Rained upon 'felines,' now nouveaux bitches. *In exchange
for the pleasure to ruin ex-hub, kitty's kids'll
                    only owe City College!*

But liberty larks his son-set dusk, worth all of pop's diurnal gust.
Pa's re-running about town for pack high-jinx and six-packs –
You don't have to teach old dogs new tricks – domesticity's
Dog days, at last, 86'd! Were they unmurked, all moony men

Would wag, bachelors – making all kids bastards, and by association –
No risk of Mas becoming second-round bitches – no-heads-for-figures
Divorcées, lict, 'd go extinct – their lawyers, *sans* the houndeds' riches.
But – dog-gone-it, will domestic partnerships, next-induced – unleash

Her sniffing up more fake family jewels: so much bijoux, beget,
Re-set in t/heir parasites? This! this, cubic zirconia of fornication
without variation? H/add in fine items? Or will Old Yellers,
Not attorn'eyed, settle for half a bye-byes' dis-Confederation?

MJM 11/12 SF
Titled after Robin Kahn's graphic suite, NYC

Extended Family

Babies keep this boring bus alive – turgid, fat
mini feet and hands – so soon a boon to thrive.

'round Christmas, we see these tots with grandpa
et alia relations not so accustomed as Pa-n-ma

To drills of pacifier, stroller, sip-it-cups – these
pups in for tandem chills o'frowns and ups!

MJM 12/14 SF

Extra-Atmospheric

Light, cloudy sky, slung low as she's ever rested –
Whipped whites, here – slender meringues extended,
Flattened, their whorled dïscī pressuring down –
Nearly quash that frothy sea under, foam-serrated.

Then, too chaste for this planet – fazed by men's
Raping the globe in civilization – her white
Ellipses, frosty fluorescents, stop on the horizon . . .
And echo wavelets, cashmere riffs on blue parabolas.

Bubbling, crescent surf ~ from on high a feathered
Fan ~ shores up those Martian clouds, as if a sheep
Flock tending shepherds. Such stunning flexibility,
Such harmony of ciphers cannot be quotidian Earth.

He has fingered heaven just for this one, fickle hour
To patch upon our sky, perhaps to satisfy his mirth.
But more likely to rejoin us with graceful power,
And how we as men have forsaken it by birth.

MJM 3/11 SF

Eye Light

He spots two fog lights, dripping,
Shimmering white taffeta ribbons
On rippling, quivery black water.
Those wavy icicles of night nearly
Shake-n-snake ashore, but tapering
to his right, squiggle underwater
unto deeps, submarine from sight.

MJM 12/10 SF
Aquatic Park

Eye to Eye

His head arced up to the grand symphonic ceiling
lamp, he teared one eye on his cancer-dead father.
The other, on the forever never touched love of his life.
For resentment, Dad's death wish came withering him
but he boycotted that dreadful threnody, his old man's
lungs wasting to smashed walnut shards, the brown,
papery insides shredded like cigarette tobacco.

Exactly how his skin and arroyo'd body looked? He
died, the color and texture of a raw peanut pair
deep fried in lard to molasses' shade in that shell.
His other eye on his moon river lover, searching
the same rainbow's end, just around the bend ~
now plangent in the lost gay waltzes, bombast,
and ardor of Tchaikovsky's *Pathéthique*. Oh 6, oh 6,

oh 6! How does an old man describe the ravaged,
lonesome heart that never knew the lover's art? His
company spurned by the boy from whom rapture and
obsession learned their insidious lesson into his palms,
line read. One eye on his abandoned Pop, who was
dead to life in that horrible hospital bed long before
he died. He lay and lay until the very day this son arrived.

Within ten minutes, giving up the ghost, his own spawn,
prodigal host of this finally indecent passing. He lays
and lays upon that philharmonic ceiling, eyes secretly
blazed by tears. His amusing father, the laughing
mask of by-proxy suicide's comedy. Other eye on his
Unrequited Lancelot, the face called tragedy . . . Tears
from two eyes for three spirits of four, unrealized.

MJM 10/15 SF

Family Inclined

They were happy drunks, festive and familial.
Their table laid so well with candle, fare, flower,
He called it: *"Mom and Dad's Bar and Grill,"*

Wild salon of the art world where Messrs. pretty and smart
Fore-fended convention for a few bohemian hours,
Lamp-glowing philosophers outspoken and profane

Within Victorian windows. *¿Al menú?* Beans, barbecue
Salsa, cactus infused with the cilantro-and-tomatillo
Touch of great-granny who once fed me a bottle, *niño!*

"In the *Cuisenaire* of heaven now," they'd say,
"Right up there with Julia Child!" Music, poetry,
Dancing, dad's new painting blooming in the room

We kids'd hustle upstairs while the ladies
Retired to silk sofas, the men smoking cigs 'n
Piped pot on our newly planked deck:

Casual ritual – far from, yet rife with British
Country life & Vienna drawing rooms of yore.
Then fate crashed the party with alarm and gore.

My parents began to fight. Dad declares himself gay!
He'd sickened alcoholic by now, blaming Mom
For their lack of passion — *"Frigid* JAP!"

When he sobers up Part I, changes over the top:
Job, car, gallery, house, phone, his dates' gender!
She endures the loss, half glad he's gone

Half sure she'll not find the like of him again –
Funny genius, sublime un-drunk, hot in the hay:
Who speaks of tennis and the Carracci all in

One breath? From the head of that ritual table,
His surfer-door hanging like a Visigoth helmet up
behind his flare chair, as she dated other men,

Dad got sick *again*, this time bi-polarity coincident
With chronic pain, the madness/arthritis of his clan
Come to *his new life* to roost. Sobriety nearly killed

Him again driving reckless on sparkling water! What
Depression didn't wreck, mania took plunder, spent
His last dollar bi-polar, even this young one's

College fund, wannabe erotic Quixote risking STDs.
At home Mom plied on until last September when
Great Depression II befouled her fortunes, too,

Freezing customers and credit. Two months later
Dad loses his summit job, and by the time the docs
Fix his festering groin, he's on disability: at last

The Dole at Fifty! Hideous arc of chance, 'rents
Lose *again*, this time to different swindlers –
Those thieves of the Internet who frame these feckless,

Socialite prey of art-and-style. My kin meant well,
Thru generous years entertaining with mirth and aid
To HIVs, hosting stags on Thanksgiving or loaning

The couch at Dad's to some more desperate drunk AA.
I'm seventeen now and these my parental "Lords
Of Gatsby's Ghost" dare even not afford to host.

Scared as kids, no income. Dad drinking, lover-
Swindled Mom sued by *American Express*! Still,
The house stands secure with my art "Fatty Daddy"

Bequeathed me when I teened. I'm the
Man of the house now, popular and stoned.
We were a trident once; *now the tines stab at us*.

MJM 6/09 SF

Famine

Close to cannibalism,
I espy dry spider corpses ~
wisps in the other one's web,
  amort like skeletal
human hands closed tight:
sucked of their plasm.
They are my grisly pets ~
  No neighbor in the fly
famine dark is safe
near his brother's net.

MJM 9/15 SF

Fan

A poet is a person with extreme
Grasp of idea, image and song
Unpopular as extremes always are
That extreme others savor.

  Would that we like our brothers
The composers filled an auditorium
Each night, sensitive souls
With tickets paid for to laud

Word-dreamer music ~~
  All peopled, and critics' pick.

MJM '11 SF

Father Earth

*Pope Francis declared Friday the
environment itself has rights and
that mankind has no authority*

*to abuse them, telling world leaders
at the United Nations they must take
urgent action to halt the Earth's de-*

*struction from the "selfish and bound-
less thirst" for money.* His office of 2,000
Years to our own three hundred, each

Empowered to acid-rain-showered, *Il
Papa* pressed down on the D.C. Congress,
Urbis et Orbis of that scoundrel town:

Alleged under the aegis of saving Son.
It won't matter with whom the gay sleep,
Corals dying in the deep, mountain-

Tops melting, factories smelting, our
Many, the Enemy of Earth. Wanted
and unwanted babes, absent of berth,

Mankind's worth, doled out in *iProducts*,
Flooded and scorched valley aqueducts,
No Vacancy planet, a'torted and torched.

The Potomac floods as Rome prays for
The Good – we travail after 'the goods' –
Snide half our august body, convinced the

Melting Arctic and raging fires won't
Menace their vain-gloried empires. The
nations may purchase pollution credits,

We and industry chasing P&L plaudits,
While comptroller *Nature* audits and edits!
We snipe-legislate to grudge, as The Force

Of the universal reaction scores us adjudged
Of our own derelictions, our frown'd
Factions and h-am-ateurs' against-experts

Inaction, there thus, be roiled and broiled.
Tide up, glaciers down – with or without
   us, World that keeps *Itself:*   spinning 'round.

MJM 9/27/15 SF
(Chinese eyes, red-blazed by skies.)

Fey Tears

Ronald-Colman good-looking, a name your grandkids
will never know, you were kind, detached, and rowdy –
a kind of self-cancelling trine, like my Aries
squared by Cancer, squared by Scorpio, squared by Mom:

Two of us lashed by her hellish, Latina wrath.
Too decent for the police force, you were dismissed for
being overly fair in the streets, on the freeways
to ethnics, although the official charge be dis-

Obedience – like leaving for Vegas to poker
against Mom's rules: *her* life, her liberty, her purse-
suit of justice. "Just get a divorce," I'd tell her.
But you, her handsome Anglo in shining armour, she

Wouldn't quit, status-mongering nit-wit, square-married.
When I'd blunder, you'd pull me aside for a Dad
talk. The minute I'd spot empath in your eyes, I'd
start to cry – sure as God makes squirly girls and gays

Out of tears and dust, rock and fire saved for machos
like you and bro. Instantly, you'd alarm, "Why are
you crying? I'm not trying to do anything
but help? Why are you in tears?" Sad Dad and I, peers.

MJM 8/14 SF

223

Ficus Rift

Unlike melancholy wafts, say
To street click-clacks, today,
He's spellbound by a braided
Ficus coupled and serenaded.

On plush lawn's toss of youth
When he/you & you/he both
Entwined as this big bonsai's
Stems 1st wend, you two went Y.

Doubled, young stalks over grass
Braid-bonded, he next to this wrasse,
In first leafhood they would divide
To separate suns, side by side.

Drift apart, we as tree here, once ecstatic
Enlaced by Venus, re-limbed elliptic
In Her forest. For love's odd reason,
Perhaps slant 'x' of our squire season,

Those twins reached for northern
Lights, even as woody, sun-born
Saplings light-hungry keeled to south.
Now splendor on top, mouth-to-mouth,

Thick shades of pages' hair as leaves
Merge into one green cooling parasol
Sharing touches at every sheave's
Rustle, one boll, one contoured soul.

It matters not their Asian planter
Fiddled them at first or that each had
Dismissed the other in twigs' adventure:
Slanter pole to pole, *beaux* next *re-crissed*;

Then stamen blown to pistil he spored
To common conception! Seed aboard
Breeze to female part of the ridgecrest,
Acorns abounding, he nixt half west!

Gnarled dark, this arbor knows one erred.
The myth of one shadowed canopy 'us'
Was rent as the one tree heir-aired.
So, he twists unbound, dirt amorous.

Desert morning's dry heat rife,
He's
Mourning dew and tears' half-life,
halved wife: dead limbed as un-

husbanded
Greaves.

MJM 1/11 SF

Finch Raid

You're a deep and clever man at forty
The type to sort of
Rush the city on white steed
Whilst everyone else is contented walking.

  As fire-escape chickadees
Rough up hooting pigeons like owls,
Squab grooms, robot-eyed head a-slant
On the tallest cornice. With their bird

Raids and sirens and decoy flying about,
Will finches eat him if he faints? *Not owls?*
Then he cocks back his head, eyes 'pigeon-blood' red.

There is a vampire bat

In every one of us. So why am I
  Here, drug-hoarse at 40
Trying to pull out a rabbit?

MJM '10 SF

First & Last Words

'Aardvark' & 'zyzzyva,'
the first and last words
in English dictionaries,
therefore in single quotes,
not double ones, since I'm
saying no one has said them
for *here*, per se. Furthermore,
I don't need the verb "to be"
In the sentence above, since
The comma stands in for that,
At least according to *The*
Elements of Style by Strunk
& White. Alas, these strange
words are monikers, respectively,
for an 'earth-pig' from sub-
Saharan Africa, and translated
into English from the obsolete
form in Afrikaans: 'aard' (earth)
plus 'vark' (pig), but now 'erdvark,'
a kind of African anteater, if you will
    –   and 'zyzzyva,' a destructive
beetle, native to S. America,
whose name must surely be
partly onomatopoeic, and yet
not *purely* so, since the 'zzz's' –
a written form to indicate the sound
of one's snoring while asleep –
does *not* count, ¡word-wise!
        in 'Dictionaryland'
        for lack of a vowel;
otherwise, it *would* be the last
word. Is this a snooze, so far?

How words and what they mean,
And sound like and wherefrom come
  Make so many meta-levels of
Cross-reference and -pollination,
That I, obsessed writer, care and try
To make head or tails of it all
On a daily basis! Stasis for one,
Another's exhilaration, *cum* ecstasy.
I mean, are we talking about critters,
Strange as they may be, or words,
Or obsolete words, or written forms
Of words, not *counted* in the dictionary,
Or *animals* in the dictionary? Or zoo? or wild?

But Now a Word on Primates:
On a higher note, far off to the side,
I am reminded how Meryl Streep,
Playing the role of [*Vogue's*] editor
In the movie "The Devil Wears Prada,"
Would curtly say, "That's all" –
At the end of brusque 'meetings'
With her powerless assistant –
She being First (Lady) in the world
Of fashion, and her attachée, last.
Don't correct me to write *attaché,*
Since in correct French, one needs
The two "E"s to make it feminine,
With the *aigu* accent on the first "E,"
And foreign words like *"aigu"*
In italic, not Roman, letters – a.k.a.
An 'acute' accent in English,
As opposed to the 'grāve accent,' – ` –
Or, in French, *'l'accent grave.'*
Though French be no dead language.
(Funny how so much *of* couture
        originates *in* France.)
But the 'puny' ass̲i̲s̲tant – hear all the
"S'"s, reminiscent of all those "Z"'s? –
Causes destruction to rain on Meryl's –
Qua "earth pig's" – reputation at [*Vogue*] –
(my brackets, since the magazine was never
actually referenced in the movie, as such,
but everyone knew to *what*
        l'attachée was referring) –
By publishing her stinging memoir
The Devil Wears Prada. (Titles of
Books are also italicized in English,
And chapter names, put into quotes,
When referred to in writing, tho'
        Not in/on the actual books,
        themselves – necessarily).
Then again, it may *hardly* be said
That *Streep's* reputation was damaged, as
She garnered an "Oscar" (a.k.a. Academy-
Award) nomination for her role,
Plus, a Golden Globe for 'Best Actress,'
        But that *that* little bitch-beetle's titillating
Book virtually damned Anna *Wintour,*
In-the-flesh editor of *Vogue,* thought
Worldwide to be the *real* woman
Behind the character in the book

And film, named Miranda Priestly.
As for *this* author, non-fiction prone
in the first place, I prefer Wintour's
name, since, given the power
of her monthly "book," as she
fondly calls her magazine, she's
"won," [*Cf.* 'win/won/Wintour']
– but is hardly *'priestly'*
        if you ask me.
Second, couture goes on "tour," does it not?
What with runway shows all over
The globe, and trunk shows, stores,
Boutiques, and labels/brands [labia?] spread
Everywhere – even in magazine spreads –
A kind of touring is implied, if you will,
        [thus, "Win*tour*" as a kind of
        'high-class' coincidence;
        low, if you're still fuck-stuck
        on my fore-{play}-going porn joke].
Matter of fact, clothes have "legs" more
far-flung than any aardvark or zyzzyva, right?
If you *will not,* then go back and re-read
        this entire poem. And,
A pox on your [fashion?] house
if you don't get that it's all meta-
phoric, semaphoric, ontologic,
        not pornographic,
and most important of all, logi-*cal*!
        As a dictionary ought be.
As a matter-of-*my-being-a-poet's*-fact,
I find it all quite magical and even
Euphoric! Not to mention, "peripatetic
and chic," to quote *A Chorus Line.*
Namely, alpha and omega,
          Jesus and me,
"Aardvark" to "zyzzyva,"
Anna Wintour *et Cie.*

Now I know my 'ABC's,
Write (or, alas, e-mail) me
what you think of me's.
There/their/they're are at least three.
See, *sí,* Ç, "C"? Oooops, maybe
        may be four, for, fore, 4.
It's my schizophrenia, split person-
Ality, and manic-depression, a.k.a.
Bi-polarity, and Alzheimer's,

you may just as well ignore
In your letters (alas, e-mails!),
Since I already have a psychiatrist,
Therapist, medical doctor, pharmacist for Rx's
And editor to 'iron' out these things with "X"s.
MJM 7/14 SF – irony, intended – close, clothes.*et* <u>cie@lowercase.com</u>
Or just send/*envoyez* snail-mail . . .
No aardvarks, zzyzyvas, fruits,
bi-valves, or vegetables, please.
Just send me couture. I like Gianfranco Ferré.
MJM 7/14 SF (Butt then, I already sed that.)

Flight of the Sleepless

Blown, blown the household fuse.
No forest for respite.
No pulse. No better right.
  As his rhythms tend to thunder,
Her cakes rise, then sink,
Foreworn of their frosting.
  In hot escape to vacant black
Light-speed-flight nixed the news.

MJM '91 SF

Fog Clock

Fog steamrolls onto the gate over ocean waters,
  As inland, Hades-hot, tugs at the hoarfrost air.
Hemmed-in *tuft* entubed by roiling perimeters,
It heaves and spins in tow, a blustering affair

  Rootless and skidding like a dusty wraith
  Skims *sub-forty-five* ripples under the main.
Lighthouse enshrouded, bargemen dip faiths
In honk-horns 'On' to pilot the ghostly train.

Thick, it wets the inky tarmac like fallen rain,
Splats on the golden bridge, droplets on ice-rosed
Ears' and cheeks' feath'ry down until *in-*
Land night cools . . . Rents back fog ~ sea, reposed.

MJM 11/10 SF

Fog Spits

Fog spits rain and the clouds complain
With greys and whites. The tulle mist
Enshrouds these hearts, which hide
To sleep to smuggle away depression –
A pity of brooding, haze cocooned.

A name for every human ill, these days:
Seasonal affect disorder! Bedded, his
Days off dream by-too-fast – no events
To woo or amaze his mind. How a day
Out of his lair, somewhere, spindles

Time in *Technicolor,* the slow fining
Of cashmere lining him, just-to-be-fair –
Other pajamas being equal. Locked inside,
Threnodic renditions pummel his stomach.
Ought he take pills to sleep? Or suicide?

He goes down five levels in his hovel.
Didn't he have this beaten? The life-long
Ignition cursed not to spark but rumble.
A boy of four, he gulped and sobbed alone in love
With camellias he'd pinched to fingered brown.

In a transverse world, he'd be embracing.
In this one, obverse, perverse, the only affair
Ever-romantic is love, unfulfilled – marriages
Perilous. Shutting down on his pillow,
He listens to men going by and trucks trying.

The gadgets at the *Apple* stores engage them all
At lunch hour, and raucous knocks. Of whatever
Intellect, they fit into the slots the markets make
For them, right now at this hour – as if they'd
Been given an instruction manual, he tried once

To figure – but got bored-to-breathless, panicky,
He'd end up office-trapped, like these who
'vade-in today. He would give the world so
Much if it were lovely – his numb defect:
No vitality to plumb, except love in lairs.

MJM 3/11 SF

For a Solo Diner

The night is chilly. Alpha johns made their wandering known long ago:
Smoke rag. Cloud feather. Ten rifles let loose over leathered
Ruffled ravines. I hear grind apart these stubbled mountains,
Wishing their wind-cut faces slip to the sea.

Or do you reel in some loot, some blubber, a blue-plate supper's
Struggling to be all aboard, mind dripping in the daily doldrums?
To stay in *your* game peel off old carbons gummed with liquid paper
Salvage and computerize the old songs from messy mash blue

O'er the vein-swirled glue? Fall. Fall off the over. Off
The curve October. Hack at the real, the knotty tether.
Topple totems of rubber, the war-wracked statue to the cob.
Split the wall with your forehead, tweaked, pour off the white.

Grind the shell. Shave with the whipped yolks.
And while simperers get flung off the globe for lack of weight,
Toss the cracked peel to the wind, abandoning oxen yokes to the river.
The night is chilly and alpha men made their wandering known long ago.

MJM '92 SF

Foreign Wars

What do I learn gazing into the aquarium?
That one fish is more aggressive than another,
That the one supposedly his brother
Turns voracious, and that along with fry

In school, the timid weaklings seem 'meant to tank.'
The slow, sluggish ones get a rash of fungus,
As the strong ones patrol, jock-dumb,
And females vibrate, "They're under our bum!"

These specimens Ming, Ho, Whitey and Julius
Are meant to be watched alive or dead,
Either to be buried or be fed.
As I go into my 40th year, a fishy age if ever

Unwatched there is nothing I dread,
   not even Mother Nature –
Or I do a bit, these hideous things
   that appear in the morning paper.

Will we ever ebb and flow as one –
   no evangelizing
Thieves, *Quran* burner, or headline-
   grabbing kidnap raper?

MJM '98 SF

Four Felonies of a Friend

He stood up before the judge respectfully,
Yet leonine, stuck out his jaw and gaped,
As if he had something urgent to say before

Any decision should issue from the bench.
At first the bailiff hushed him, then the judge.
But when the latter sensed the boy's earnest

Urge, he stopped the protocols to let him speak.
Pitifully, the boy grazed through a few papers
He'd laid down to prove new-found sobriety.

With each recitation the boy grew bolder in
Body, like a proud student reading a very dumb
Poem with élan for his class and pained teacher.

Not one whit of his charts and letters of re-
Commendation would sway the robe his way,
The lad's 4th count of felony drunk driving &

Breaking parole, a daunting damnation. As
His honor parsed out each point of his rights
And of his crimes against the state, the weight

Of the law's list redounded his proofs to scrawl.
"A danger to society," is what the kind old man
Called him, and despite friends' best efforts to

Stand for him with their own testaments of his
Merit, he was led by the bailiff through that
Terrible door, where he'd soon be garbed in

Orange. It is the mothers against drunk drivers
Having protested their sons' and daughters'
Slaughter by those smashed on-the-road,

Their petitions of state for harsher alcohol
Sanctions for who's sauced behind-the-wheel,
That our careless culture around drinking altered.

Broke, our cars get tow after tow, and the lax
Suffer mighty debt. Insurance, prove or be fined.
Breathalyzers, DUIs, 51-50s obliterate lives,

Families fold in houses sold, as lawyers bilk their
10,000s! They cannot connive at angry, anguished
Parents' loss of child, but do look back on times

When for some misreason, lax law fared to mild.

MJM 2/11 SF

Framed in Storage (52)

He is blind in tossed dark, whose cursèd key
But opens to faux-grand, locked-up treasure,
Where, in a house now lost, he'd each day plea
Some bright, common rite of lordly measure.

Nowadays, wealth so solemn and so rare,
He may not dwell among his stuff – contained
As museums' basement stores, and as fair –
But crud with dust and worms in art, fly-stained.

It was brisk youth earned wealth at his behest,
Not entitlement to heir's landed pride.
What sickened him to lose all daylight's wrest,
Vile, rapacious lust, or drink's spilling tide?

Worthy is he whose steadiness frames plans;
Tried-and-lost, lots to trade with Solomons.

MJM 3/11 SF
After Sonnet 52

238

Frogs

Frogs lift lily-pads up to lip-lines like private eyes:
cat burglars, Pink Panthers, they don't blink or budge
as pond water squiggles down
                             flower-crowned, half-split leaves.

I crawl surreptitiously forward when Mark stands up!
They dive scum-ward, arms and legs, all elbows,
Breast-stroking deep's shallows to poop clouds.

Day by day in early May, they grow accustomed
to our little faces and limbs, now craven enough
To hop out onto pond rocks, then lawn for sun.

We catch them mid arc by their legs, a'scissor.
Try as they might to pump out of our palms,
They pee, eyes tight shut – praying to flee?

By June, our foster ward of green warties gets
Scooped up after just one reflex jump, a'grass.
Consanguine horror, we find them next day, piggy-

Back tangled – the one strangling the other,
under. A sex lesson is frankly told us by Uncle,
thus inured to soon-seen myriad frogspawn!

Long mucous strands – so many beads beaded
in gelatinous tubes like a trillion-bazillion beady *eyes*:
One summer to go till round-golden/irises born, fat-cat slit.

Not so: we inherit tadpoles tho,' – who morph to midgets.
Mindless of parental caution, the army of froglet fry
invades the crabgrass lawn, now grown longer.

As I walk about barefoot, Mark in sneakers
those chirpless squeakers crush under toe,
tiny bones breaking with guts a-squish!

The live ones limp under that lattice of tube
grass, only to be mashed as we hop back
to the deck: horror-of-horror Frog-Plague

No less daunting than Moses'!
Each spring for the next several springs
Traumatized we and Uncle

  Slurp up frogspawn into our big,
industrial white-plastic paint pails,
Drive them *all the way* to 5th St. Lake

From our house right nearby on 8th,
And dump those black-eyed strands
into wilder water. Years later,

Now age twelve and sprouting a
trace of velvety 'stache, I think I
hear some selfsame males near,

croaking for mates, while I can
Only masturbate – smug and self-
content as an evolutionary biologist

In his Tweens,
near-sighted, no eyeglasses yet,
With tiger-tabby pet . . . and my own ejaculate . . .

MJM 7/14 SF
In memory of 131 W. 8th St.
"Paradise Lost"
E., A., Me

From a Mex to a Lioness

Natasha, a fiery Leo and Theo's Thea,
Rests in the grass until big prey passes.
She pounces and in a flash you're
Red meat

                with a black *Amex*.

MJM 8/14 SF
кусок сыра в масле!

Full Fathom Five (Fucker Father Force-Fused Feral)

Full fathom five thy father lies;
Of his bones are coral made;
Those are pearls that were his eyes:
Nothing of him that doth fade,

(With four, not five lines [1 octet + 3 septets], SH declares a compositional *"lie,"* since his, *"Lies made eyes fade,"* is a terminal, 'vertical' command to delete his end-words/per line, and the word 'five' is in and of itself a 'lie.' *"Five . . . lies"* also = **negate '5'** from SH **29** total beats in **stanza = 24 [= 4 lines of 6 beats.**] Using a 'sextet-quatrain' = 'sex tot-twat trains,' and/or also = 'a four quartet' *à cappella'* ['to the chapel'] again conjures SH climacteric number 6 qua 666 [**4 vertical 6s**] to illustrate the stanza's form, [viz. 666 = evil], **4 x 6 = 24.**)

PS *ibid op cit.* ("Ding-dong," below, is not a bell-tone, but a 'beau penis;' it is the *"father* ['big ding-dong'] *lies"* = <quintet-fragment, below> = SH call for quatrains to ensue in the PS/DC. (Also see apologia below.)

Luffed, fat homo mouths, thrived
Ponies parse corralled maid.
Thor harps pirate earl, dived.
Queers thod tat's path, toque laid.

But doth suffer a sea-change
Into something rich and strange.
Sea-nymphs hourly ring his knell:
Ding-dong.
Hark! now I hear them—Ding-dong, bell.

(Shakespeare is clear in his 1st stanza: we must 'fully fathom five [the quintet, *not* the quatrain], so that we may 'fathom' – 'swim deep-down into' – the quintet, a total of 5 times.)

5 lines ibid. op cit = 6x (-1x)

Ease ceases, duffer ranged.
Isomers note tome changed.
Sean, seen, pimps his hymen.
Hinge wrung: hell-won, I 'rhymen.'

Caesar seizes duff, ruff banged –
I so mere, note, moat-hanged.
Sean knees, pimp-imp, size-won.
In hine vagina guns run.

Sizer rises pup rude ganged.
I somewhere saw méres hanged.
Sneak, even seen rumped, one
Age-nine virgin, snug gun.*

Scissor sires' supper pup,
Wee-most rear awesome rupt.
Keen, even seen pump-sword
Nin's nerves in riving ward;

Sick sis sore, *res*-pussed mean;
Wombed tot's meat, steer-ween –
Eek, even seen 'dump' poured,
Verve-served, river inward:

(*Shakespeare speaks of man-boy love between older men and late-teen/early 20s juveniles. I have not encountered such a ghastly pedophilic passage elsewhere, and not until now – 6/9/11.)

Line 1 of 5th PS endline DC as (5x – 1)**

Ever severe-perversed, reys
Versed, verved pervs ped seven days;
Reeve rears, severed in ward;
Peeved pére sears servants draw'r'd;

Virus severe dispersed;
Eve revered, perp-dressed pursed;
Reverse reaved heir's pére purrs.

Sir Russe, piss-sips pid durst,
Ire used, abyss-dread.

Rise! Sir Did-Bid! Rey versed.***

**At first this ending format was intuitive; now, upon scanning SH/DC final recipe 'equation' above, note the symmetry of 5s and 6s qua '1 of 5th' and '5x – 1,' again conjuring climacteric 6(6). Additionally, the lucky 'guess' creates 10 lines, (as if to parallel the ten beats *per* line of all 154 SS.), a total of 60 beats in the foregoing sequence = 666 (0).

Note also the inter-sums of 154 SS sonnets = '69' and '96'(5 + 1, 4 + 5) as if to say 69 = gay love and 96 = gay hate that SH suffered, when lied to or cuckolded. Finally, the sum of 154 = 10 = number of beats per line in the sonnets, reference to 10 recurs again: the number of penile inches SP claims throughout the PS is <u>always</u> ten.

Then again, a 14-line SS/PS also creates the arithmetic combination of 5 (from 1+4,) which relates to 154 SS/PS, in that 154 contains 5 + (1+4) = 10 beats per line. So 154 SS/PS, 10 beats per line, and 14 lines per SS/PS are all logarithmically indicated and interrelated in SH grand schema.

***As in the SS, the DC is finally congratulated for completing the 'assignment' accurately, if 'imperfectly,' given the demonstrable (See SS 100 Extended) infinity of these anagrams into ever-succeedingly, legible PS. Here, the DC is 'knighted' by SH!

Full Fathom Five (cont.)

I also took interest in the 1st DC of SH 1st stanza: namely the end-phrase "toque laid." Several times in the SS, SH refers to the 'swollen anus,' with its concentric lines radiating from the a-hole (like meridians down from the 'poles?') as 'a toque' or 'toqued.' A toque is the hat worn by chefs, distinct in having a serrated puff ringing the top of its tallish cylinder. This puffed ring, extending in a 'c' curve around the hat's upper lip is noticeably plumper than the main tube and is (paper) scored to allow maximum heat to escape from the pate, given hot kitchens. It is also an adaptation of the Eastern Orthodox black toques worn by clerics.

So, 'puffed ring,' 'serrated puff,' etc. is for SH interchangeable with 'toque,' 'toqued,' etc. The *double entendre* 'toque laid' = 'tokayed' = tot cayed = tot payed = obeyed tot = peaked tot = tot bayed, etc.' alludes to the cheap Tokay wines of Hungary in liquor stores, nearby – a clichéd, default drink for suffering alcoholics. This wine is distinct because it is made without 'pressing the grapes.' Fruit is stacked on wooden planks, and juice simply 'drains through runnels into a holder,' under the pressure of the grapes own weight 'as piled,' thereby self-'crushing.' .

Here is a DC extension of "toque laid:"

toque laid
Tokayed
tot decayed
tot deca dead, tot deca 'layed'
tot ace dead, tot ace bayed/'dayed' *(sex in the a.m. Shakespeare describes in SS)*
assed-out disease (ace = ass)
sassed ped disease
deuce towed, tied
Dios-doubt diet
id dot tit
idiot
I diet
I I.D. tot
I die

Here as in the entire run of the PS, the DC uncovers repeated, scandalous testament from Shakespeare, that royal persons (his earl, the rey, the roi, the res, duchess, duke, prince, etc.) are perverted homosexuals or whores with exotic fetishes, that they are incestuous – clan-wise, kin-wise, dad-on-son, etc. Shakespeare finds it unjust and reviling that a **genius**-commoner of such fame and adoration as he – but nevertheless, of a *lower* social station – could beat any Royal in wit and command of men's minds.

Given the realm of *The Globe* theater, he thought, "I ought be sex master, commander-in-chief, king – since it's all of a piece.' Intellectually superior even to Catholic fluency and power, Don Guillaume lets be seen his topping social superiors. He is both vexed and carnivorous, and he gests that he is lords above lords – an Enlightenment? – calling the royals' endowments piddling: or at least common, compared to his ten inches and superior intellect – sword-and-palace, you might say.

Third, this sex-play out in nature in the summer and in domiciles and taverns in the winter, he suggests, is a fatal game. The SS feign to be about love, so that the writer/reader-of the PS remains clear of the stake or pyre. But how those volatile and dangerous stakes increase, given what the bard has done to notables. Above, he mentions he will die if he I.D.'s the tot, although farther above he mentions "Sean" and his typical adjective "russed." SS creates dangerous tension for himself and the DC. He says he intended to hand the SS down, in order that their "shadows" be decoded and the "babyism pabulum" of the SS replaced by the PS, which reveal what he was really up to. But how many risks the bard takes within his urban homosexual secrets. He teases the gods. He's quick to indict the royals for their filthy, ped-prone sex practices; is angry they are his social superiors, when he has the brains and the big dick his bottoms are said to crave; and that his sexual liaisons with the royals are a fatal risk if he is ever accused of/proven to be a fink or rumor-monger. Alas, SH repeatedly calls his sex milieu, "rumored" → 'room-amoured' → 'Moor-amoured,' wherein a 'moor' is a *dark enemy* → '*colon* à <u>mor</u>te.' *Danger lay a prick away.*

MJM 6/11 SF

245

Ga-Ga to Grave

Food, clothing, shelter my eye! Just look
what else it takes to support a gal or guy:
healthcare, dinnerware, dresser stuffed,
garage and car – one vehicle, ain't enough!

Bikes, skates and skis, casts for broken
knees. Dance, music, money, tweeds, cable
murder, wide TVs. Heating, cooling, insect
nets, penicillin, Vegas bets; manicures, lawyers,

– Hispañola's upper sets. Toys, bras,
condoms, beds, military, state, and Feds.
Chairs, ladders, metros, busses, pacifiers
for babies' fusses. Memos, pills, bills,

white wine, *iPhones,* hair gel, turpentine.
Boats, airplanes, hotels, zoos, laxative
for hard-up poos. Desks, reports of acci-
dents, police and protest, wax, incense.

The Press, dry cleaners, tricks on words,
fish and felines – caged pet birds. Shoes,
socks, underwear, supermarket pork
to pear. Toothbrushes, hand-soap, mags.

Plastic-surgeon scalpels, bags. Plumbing,
electricity, poets 'n' geometry. Walloons,
balloons, schools, houses, buildings, banks.
Gas & oil, cranks, tin foil. Dentures, dollars,

Aviaries, politicians, squab with berries.
Saws, books, Tennis Set, anger manage-
ment, Internet. Divorces, lawn chairs, county
seats, grass-fed livestock, Wall St. shares.

Road markings, signs, and lights, badminton,
yoga tights. Snake charmers, dance floors,
canes – chihuahua dinkies to Great Danes.
Veggies, tattoos, servants, rent, insurance

For Life's death and dents. Bricks and mortar,
stucco too, prize fights, lumber, ice igloo. Guns,
trophies, A.A. twice, religions to charge after
you. Businessmen, YMCAs, *They*-n-Ha'vard,

Straights and gays. Celebrations, Mayday, maydays,
birthday cakes, collar stays. Gardens, liquor, inns
and plazas – pizza, milk, sore-throat lozenge.
Band-Aids, Kleenex, casual wear – jewelry, furs,

Tarts, art, fair. Sunscreen, tweezers, clippers, cotton,
fridges to keep fruit from rottin.' Wheels, the Pill,
Bibles, dates, dates from palms, seismographs and
food on plates. Deals, pyramids, egos, ids. Mares

t'eat oats, and diapered kids. Before I go on too
long, I hope you get the drift I'm on. What the
heck is this detritus human beings must chase
to right us? Were we here *alone,* I wouldn't ask,

But look at all these creatures, whose inven-
tories are simple tasks. In environs that
betide, they don't go poaching *animal*
hides! What the heck happened to mankind

to have to keep and go and find and fine
a million things in mind? Not to mention
services and goods to trade, all over this
planet's mess, man-made. I swear some-

bodies fucked with us from outer space, else
why, all this – and *plus!* I could go on, but
this ain't verse. Partial bucket list, rehearsed.
Earth to Space. Tons of luggage, universed ~

MJM 9/15 SF

Game Night Breakthrough
at Mom's & Dad's Table

Lex spells back
        wards slant-
wards: the *XEL* he
spells dia-
   gon-
      ally all
        of a sudden getting
        science and letters are here
to trick him!

He abandons TV
        discovering his self
        within: What
the World gives
      it extracts,
It and he must exact it.
But what will
        His swords be?

MJM 11/96 SF
To Lex, smart a'lex

Gay Love   (100)

You can lead a stud to hotter
But you can't make him twink.

Where are you, sweet, that you forsake so long
Who gave you staying power over night?
Do lips disport upon some rifle-dong,
Whiffling rivals to inspire fuck-date's spite?

Return, forgetful youth and lay. Redeem
Impassioned hours, love's grace so purely spent;
Lend an ear wherewith I profane to ream
Your soft rear with both purr and argument.

Rest, passive love, your sweet face my survey.
If Time grids any wrinkle graven there,
Let strafed me be your satyr in decay –
Else timelines be erased, patched everywhere!

Give pairing hope, faster than Lust wastes Life,
That we a'void his scythe and crooked knife.

MJM 3/11 SF
After Sonnet 100

Gay to Grey

My housemates' Mexican mural – keen-limned
On the primed, fat slats of the backyard fence –
Naturally ends up a baroque affair – icons of hope
and naïve art, a riot *de colores pueblos* –

gold and silver
dots an' slathered arabesques jammed
in its thick, black outlines.

At first, I refuse to "play," barely watching
And wan, ever acting the detached art dealer.

Finally, the mural's maestro José mixes me grey
   with friendly supplication to fill in a big patch
He's outlined in buff on the white primer.
Wide brush or thin one, "Now's your turn . . ."

   . . . as if asked by the Program Director:
"Let him *earn* his keep," group concern.

Is the story of my life gay to grey?
So fey, I could only say: *poetry?*

Once, I *did* do gold! I *did* do silver!
Bold! Rolled! Sold!
   Now I, so fey, they advocate, *"Do the grey."*
So I do.

MJM 3/15 SF

Genes

One passes it on to the other:
Mother, Father, and/or
Undercovers.

How much can a person take . . ?
The balk from birth to wake?
Jump in a lake? You quake.

And when you wake,
There's chicken in the freezer
You said you'd bake. You rake.

It's not Romantic anymore
to be poor, nor classic,
nor boorish bore, nor fake.

Denial aisle – to I'll – to isle,
Some happy-go-lucky guys
Won, then lose the prize.

Egged on
by shaken eggs'
broke yolk vague,

They dodge what they despise –
Cultivating money, beauty, pride.
But then succumb to cells' insides.

MJM 3/14 SF

Gli occhi di ch' io parlai

That thou among the wastes of time must go,
Since sweets and beauties do themselves forsake
And die as fast as they see others grow. . .

Sonnet 12

Those orbs sunk ships in glorious stardom's throes.
The hair, nose, lips to eyelids glided that world-
Wide obsession suicides from every nation hurled
Out windows with your 'pix' at hearts dispose.
My tad-like body self-beguiled, I'd depress to tear,
Stunned by your face's persona glossed page to page.
Your hair's careless tresses, eyes filmy as in the age
Of opium, your star's streak distilled in celestial drear.

Famous you scarved anonymous in New York alone,
Grieving cinemas absent of your light I loved in vain,
My town afar forlorn from streets faded on you shone.
Wet is my eyespark in a microchip world of drone.
That your jaded mien flabbergast fans insane,
Love dim, I recast your solstice: glamour photos' feign.

MJM 1/11 SF
"Petrarchan Garbo"

Global Warming

What May is this – hot overnight and fecund?
She's peaked so late: gusty Alaska gales all around,
Bone-chill intense, so x-ray deep, we cursed
March and April's Pineapple Express reversed

By some tempestuous global-warming topsy-turvy.
Now to torture us, the oven's on. What hell have we
When balances exchange extremes and traits
Of wind turn hyperbole, while real weather waits

And waits only to inclime supra-normally? Be
Floods, scorchers, freezes, winds of freak velocity,
I only pined for the warm of yore and hot, hot, hot I got
While only yesterday trudging "tundra" was my lot!

She delivers more than custom calls for, exaggerating
Her effects, thus condensing our fearful, *temperamental* lore.
It's yet another sign the *Species being* is but a blight:
We burn fossils ennobling Vulcan, then *He* turns up the light!

Were we but beasts, innocent and game, we'd only be
One tenant and every site on Earth would not bear our name.
The half of us called Indians in our places out in nature
Lived like that in harmony: land, sky and sea naïvely safer.

Then came European man with his compass and his math,
Of pox and bullets natives died; now we're in this aftermath
Of trying to balance out our goals and practices as one men,
So May may come someday on time with tranquil acumen.

What May is this – hot overnight and fecund?
She's peaked so late, gusty Alaska gales all around
The chill intense, so x-ray deep, we cursed
Hawaii's slothful trades 'n' Arctic affronts unrehearsed.

But now it's hot as Hades, friend, and it's probably our fault.
E'er weathers shift back to normal, I'll do a winter somersault.

MJM 5/09 SF

Goddess a Go-Go

Strode in like Hepburn with Vivien Leigh's face –
N'er missed a biz heartbeat, then took my breath.
Gallerist in silks ~ Liz gal apace, your grace
Warmed up the sale what "I Do" froze to death.

O'er much I drank – in bed with-without you
Rubbing one out to declare discontent –
You turned e'er nicer against my boo-hoo:
Lovers *turned* corporation, cov'ring rent.

If men love ladies, withal a bit rude,
Women recall all discharged in our heat.
Like over-boiled pasta my spumer spewed,
And all you could do was staunchly elite.

   I should have taken the boy who was straight.
   You offered no exit, he at the gate.

MJM 7/14 SF

Golan Heights, Globus Rights

Two wacko guys from Israel
Move to Hollywood, raising Hell –
Stallone, Norris, Bronson, Van Damme,
Top-gunnin' schlock and awe into the can.
They made "The Chainsaw Massacres,"
Free-wheeling, rave-reeling curs.
With all that violence, bazooka'd
Slashers, were *I* on that set,
I'd surely shyte, incontinent.
My lovely thing to shoot is semen.
One and only masher's demon.

MJM 9/15 SF
Girl holey, gun-
Hole unholy
Cannon Films®

Haiku in Hock

Mankindly tears pour
Heart horror. Dilute pirates'
Thirsty blood a'reign.

MJM 9/10 SF
To Kurzfeld

Hayden

I'll be there to back up my son.
Not with a stick, but loaf of bread
Rising in the oven.

I'll be that spare all kids
And young adults need
When their capital skids.

They'll surely suffer do I do:
Banks contracts lawsuits stocks
That school didn't pay attention to?

I never had my Dad's attention grow-
Ing up. He was the absentee type
A veteran although in life

He saw no action. I, opposite, toss in
My guile like a bourgeoisie player.
As for *my* dad – we were active *around* him.

I survived on prayer, sure my grades were AAA.
And grew up to pay the price
Sons do when dear old Dad's a stray.

Inherently wild, I straddle mid-road
For Lex, careful to offer advice
But never unload

My foibles, weaknesses, or ghosts.
My father would list the reasons he was lost.
  Now over-compensating for Dad,

We do art, sport, travel, and *I*
 my champagne toasts.

MJM '01 London

He So Loved the World

The baby born in a manger by way of an upstart star
Incited to foreign travel three wise men from far:
Gaspar ~ Melchior ~ Balthazar ~
Bearing gold, frankincense, and myrrh.

With names of middle-eastern or Byzantium-
Flavored tenor, they left with trust in their own
Deities to consecrate and celebrate this newborn cast unknown.
They knelt in adoration before a child of Bethlehem,

Certain their sighting by astronomic science arose reliant.
They knew *Ibrahim*, Moses, Allah, Yahweh, and the slant
On false gods reviled and toppled by wrathful peoples' rant.
Had they known Buddha or Mohammed, would they chant

In ecumenical reverence? And to Shinto, Tao, or new
toddler Dalai Lama three-ways insightful venerate as true?
For any belief or doctrine man-aligned to heaven's view
Cannot be but good, *contra* devious cults' sham-n-scam ado.

Each sacred messenger and creed in conscious connection
With *It* that made the universe without correction
Is as Jesus Christ Our Lord, birth to resurrection.
Eras, lands, and peoples find comfort and protection

In faith, hope, and love of their totems, spirits, God
That some Almighty Oneness would bestow on good
People in the epoch and place they're understood.
Jesus and the Blessèd Mother revive his holy-hood;

Diffuse his soul's denial; wipe his fear-based mind.
Had he spoken ancient Arabic, Bantu, Hindi, Norse
He'd have a divinity or godhead of a different kind.
For it is the Infinite Connection that is the source

Of this blessèd catholic baby and his virgin Mum
This Christmas hour. Let theologies be praised that come
Apace in place and time for graceful peoples' welcome.
Then let us share in loving this Connection to become.

MJM 12/10 SF
Dedicated to John Adams' and Peter Sellars' *El Niño*, S.F. Symphony

He's in, Different

Violence and greed don't trick his spleen:
No other hurt or thieved . . . "I *speed*."

He hustles lust. Hust-feisty – cuss must!
No crime, just jaundiced sime, his slime.

He covets not those weak or bleak. Preys
On fictive game – anal witches like his

Mom and rad boys like bad Daddy.
Every shrink tries to kill off *das* Freud.

But he's in his void. His schizoid
Schadenfreude. He shuns love serene

To sick. Lick, lick, lick, lick.
Pick on Dick. He doesn't see the ick

Like you. Hunter to wreak in bed
All week carves in, "You're hormones."

MJM 5/13 S.B.

SONNET 129

The expense of spirit in a waste of shame
Is lust in action; and till action, lust
Is perjured, murderous, bloody, full of blame,
Savage, extreme, rude, cruel, not to trust . . .
    All this the world well knows; yet none knows well
    To shun the heaven that leads men to this hell.

(excerpts: Stanza 1 and couplet)

Heatwave

The scorcher blasted us flat.
Like powdered shrimp cakes
Dehydrated of all spring, we pulsed
On the city's paved griddle.
Sweltering to combustion, we
Dreamed wet sheets. Aloft,
A cool wind blowing chill stars:
give us ice; Give us cars.

– For V.
MJM '84 Seville
"Tortas de camarón molido"

Heir's Airs Aired

Red cigarette brushed along horizon,
Fog-fetching coal to black/white.
Coral, scarlet, persimmon, U.S.
With money: the whole-day's-nay –
Then, this ogrish p.m.

                        sudden sky, crimson-lush
                        fair pay

MJM 6/11 SF

Here, hold my baby . . .

>   – *Latina chick about to street-fight*

— I ain goyan da' no danG klinic!

My two, favorite French radio stations: KLéX – *et* – KFúKque

'Of all the heathen bru-tal-i-ty, hot *dogs* masquerading as din'—ehrr.

>   – Cary Grant

"I-doan – *wanna* – *goe*   ta'reehaeb" – 'Eye,' stay – ho, ho, ho. –

>   – Amy Ain't Raight

Me thinks the lazy du'z inject too much. – *MJM*

Me thinks the Lady doth protest too much. – Shakespeah

That bitch **always wins,** even if it's by one lettah! – Odett'tuh

Mackle, I dun-duhN sewwwwwwwmuch LSD:

>   (T. Phillips)

'What ta dump! – (3-time Oscar winner Bette Davis, when she first saw L.A.)

I have come to Hollywood to fuck Gary Cooper.
>   (Talulah Bankhead arriving by train from NYC)

 Ohio-goes-Hi-Mass, Cunt-ichi-Wah!

   Princess Margaret, Aihr-Head cyst err of QEII, now de-ceesed.

"It's the most radical plastic surgery/fat-loss program, since Joan Rivers!'"

>   – *American Idol* newscaster on the accession of young Will-sax-co-Berg
>   and his new ratha ravishing wife to the Threown of Englnt.

"Again — *thee*-most-*Radical* plastic surgery/fat-loss program, since Joan Rivers!'"

Some people snort it and boy do they pay, while others can't even *café au lait*.

Some dealers hate it, and make lotsa pay; other's can't even delay soirée.

>   – Frank Sinatra, *I DID IT MA-I WAY*

Olé. Ol'lay. Aud'd'lay. Yoh-de-lad-lay-o.

Laddy Marmal-Odd!
Haiyh — Doo-she Mess-Ká'

262

Of all the proletariat horror. (Diller gets a giant-screen TV.)

I'shll ruhmain sile-unt. (Diller gets an I'phone.)

Fuck! Thise guy smahshed me in the face with a fucking glhaas –

       (Diller-gets-drunk/go-go'-danc'ng.)

'Geeze – I ain ne'er Seen-nuh Rale Ceement-Pauwn'd rat-Heer 'n'Be-ver-LEE hails,' Jeth-rode.

You can lead a drug to water,
But it might make you sink.

You can lead an AA to sober
But you kan't make him fink.

You can lead-à-ho'd'te *Glamour*
But you cunt make him stink.

Messieur-uh,
Ahlphah Beedet

Doanta-fuck-any-Wound-I-wood-knot

MJM '07 SF

High Cholesterol

– Heard announced at Orphan Andy's
Castro café after Sunday-midnight

What day is it? *Monday!*
I ate too much ass and cock
This weekend. I'd better
Order something with
  Lots of vegetables.

MJM 8/10 SF

264

Highmark   (13)

That you were right love left me fearing care:
I, not just yours, for girls outlive husbands.
In the end I came at you unaware,
And crossed the line, false dreaming wedding bands.

Your beauty winged to flee, I nearly seized
Your bold migration back to me, not her.
Yourself to gain myself, herself deceased –
That love's sweet issues stream to me, recur.

Who lets so fairly shared a club decay,
So bachelors faint upholding wedding dress,
To part the stormy lusts where friendship lay,
And leave the other pumpless, blood distress?

O! all but common swifts to boat below –
Your highmark ebbs, left sunk for him to row.

MJM 3/11 SF
After Sonnet 13

Hillbilly+

Petrol run down in the jeep,
we roped up two zebra – designed kinda
icon-like –
on the dun savannah.
As if left by God,
them beasts didn't stoop and pick up
and step,
snuzzle guiding like they was
surefoot in yer homebarn.

MJM '88 Kenya

His Love's Illusions I Recall   (137)

Lo! duped youth, you proposed a Love unreal,
Beheld and craved a mate he could not be.
Your pup, he paired you – master rod-and-reel –
Both splashed in waters' soothing fervency.

Your sights, corrupt with over-loving look,
Did he anchor in your bay, boys betide?
Rest, lain boy-to-boy – lovers,' not pals' hook?
He, see-sick, swore your eyes, but still he plied.

Why limned he beau apart from female plot,
If his rook knew was *your* heart's common slave?
Did your soul, actually, conceive he'd fought
His wont in your estranged, Greek lover's grave?

In love's bilked way, his awe/your draw were feint:
Romeo purloined, that still grieves his/her taint.

MJM 3/11 SF
After Sonnet 137

His State at Forty

Economic agents, every other one
  In the world's best` economy,
Their zest for risk and money, money
Spin art types like him undone!

Fear of loss, zip-code shame jump-start
The minor rich, the merely comfortable –
Ever great Africa, proud Brazil unable
To get with god Computer and his part.

'Tis a sad thing to have been a genius –
But in youth, or classic when the world was young;
Then to erode to mediocrity, far-flung
Success, this erasing splay of varsity

Advert programming. Eyes beady, needy, greedy.
City posh-lings – Wall St., Main St., Easy Street:
Every I sold short, multi-billionaire he'll meet
Robust and avid, eating Bull or sitting pretty.

Nature gave us seed and then a longish life
To ripen and grow wise within, to maturity.
That our States of Fifty in his state at forty
Reduce to obsolete & elite husband & wife

Y-Corporation: its major mission to overwatch
Junior-to-minor spoil or toil faster and faster,
Lightning rods of change, even our heavenly master,
The Father, no market firebrand, no match.

In youth, his heart beat just being human.
Now, centrifuged at forty, he ponders if the Inn
Will still have room to throb and thrive in.

MJM 10/98 SF

His Word

He wakes up at seven, prayerful and reverential
That he relieve his brain's turmoil with its shrieks
And fears whispering paranoia, mania, shock,
Smoking mind a-swirl in depression – abandon-

Ment from his god's watch and guard, now rescued
By a breath of inner peace. He meditates reposed,
Not on old sore knees, but in the warm, safe nest
Of his comforter, tranquil as a hamster sunning.

Tediously, he has laid out his toilet, outfit, and bag
The night before – down to which scarf, watch
Gloves. Now stable, he peregrinates from spot
To spot reaching but a few feet to grasp his stuff.

His prayers go on on their own, a background
Mantra up and dim as thuribled incense in church.
As palpable thoughts take their place on the floor
Of his mind's eye, suddenly wicked, his cell rings –

His ex-wife roiling in steamy hatred of their son,
The nineteen-year-old wastrel and wanderer,
Dulled disappointment and dunderhead. She raps
Familiar gripes: his sleeping all day, his stealing

Oxycontin from an old lady and then failing to
Drop her off at her clinic today, his even *being* in
Town a disgrace. "Thanksgiving was a week ago!"
He bluffs about going back, his excuses, goddam

Amtrak and spurns by flaky *Craigslist* rides
To Santa Barbara. "He skips out on school. He
Doesn't drive! He has no ID! He's useless at home!
He wakes me at two a.m. every night going through

My purse for pills!" she regrinds nasally and shrill.
His heart beats psychiatrist cold, as he remembers
Allegiances, pacts, and promises he and the kid
Explored, passed, and carried the day before,

"And now this teen whose Word *means nothing."*
Stunned, he angles, anxious to get off the phone.
Dad's words meant everything-to-something yes-
terday and now nothing. How different, the Universe's

Prompts and cues. The words of his god, though
Requiring connection to, are thoroughly real and
Then again ghostly yet solid through and through.
He's back to nausea, running the show: don't and *do*.

MJM 12/10 SF
"May they be taken
at 13
and dropped
in
Grand
Canyon."

Hollywooned   (111)

How for art sake does he the U.S. chide,
His spirit zenful within buckless tweeds,
That did not soul us to the Muse inside –
But let Los Angelize the junk it breeds.

As it rolls, fair poetry respires no brand,
But teens on coke twit movies vile and lewd,
So what is screen-writ by their slapstick hand
Unbeckons our wonder rued, dunce approved.

Pity fey him, bewildered refugee
Who'd haste from States. Yet others, polluted
By *Yankee* T.V, he can't even flee:
World Classic, Romantic art diluted.

Alien to his passport born, he tunes
In frequencies *'live* to older ruins.

MJM 1/11 SF
After Sonnet 111

Holy Redeemer on High,

who am i? – since there is no self really
And you my Man are part of that conspiracy.

My thoughts are not my thoughts are
Human thoughts. My dreams are not my

Dreams are human dreams. My fears
And faults are not my fault are all

Too human, so just who is this I, me, mine,
Again and again, then more Over than over again?

Am I my family? Detached and scattered –
Parts, bourgeoisie, some sore-tattered?

Am I my genes, forborne via strandy DNA
My tics and tacks hella pre-determined anyway?

And what of my fine brain? Most intricate, iridescent
Magisterial, they all give it "A's" and call it brilliant.

Yet near-sighted thinking seems to serve me not in matters
Orbital of living heart and spirit, but hoists me up on ladders

I respire to climb if "I" want to arrive on time; worse
Far-sighted fixates fear and schadenfreude to rhyme.

Am I my career? – that wheels the weasel to inspire money parts
But flayed in a befuddled market, a Welfare jump-start's

The only thing can crank the paycheck back to bling?
Not dominant, flat tires, nothing in my pocket, am I nothing?

Freud said that of these three: superego, ego, id
I'd find myself within a healthy ego, my real I.D.

The Lord says, "No, it's only two ways: *all's good or evil*
With free choice thrown in to send you to the devil,

Or save you to the light of heaven's grace, save, face:
Goner, even past St. Peter, He'll *oversoul* Me to a trace!

Verily, if thoughts, feelings and fate are ours, if my nature
Is the same as yours, how can there be pure me for sure?

Zen and twelve-step programs, which *do seem* to heal,
Say of self, "It ought not exist," and with anonymous appeal

Would off us to a place of serenity, community, repose – self
resigned to the Path and universal embrace – not puerile pose

Of I am me, and he is he, thee art thee, I want, I see: greed
On Wall Street, in the penthouse, win a medal, "Be big, Baby!"

My cock's on lusty fire to drug and fuck, so id must be,
And prayers, alive to The Lord's love and luck, higher me.

But middle me, if there be one, is nowhere, all alone and harried
Or absentee-balloted in this dark year of Cash is King and buried.

You've got your God on the throne. Your dick hard as bone.
Yet try as might, we perceive no *me* nor *I*, ever to be writ in stone.

MJM 8/10 SF
Cf., Most Holy Redeemer
"An all-inclusive" Catholic Church
The Castro, San Francisco

Home Rule

"Housework can kill you if done right."
— Erma Bombeck

You house-lord over tiny things,
Minutiae that human nature zings:
Crumbs in the sink, a spoon about.
People's footfall on the stairs, you cray,
"Cut it out! *Lift your feet* the quiet way,
So I can nap in peace during the day."

So positively picayune, you catch
Yourself, apologize for rigorousness,
And routinely promise to change your
Tune, then hyperventilate about details,
"Did you dust the globes on the handrails?"
You claim to strive for benign house rule,

Red-faced about small shyte, a'duel.
You need intervention from above,
                    Martial arts into a
Velvet glove? You have hella time
On your hands to monitor and make
Demands in a way that's embarrassing,

So racists can say, it's that *Chinese* thing.
But I know it's just your heav'nly task
To change to tactful the way you ask.
Community living, wrong or right,
Annoying things are black and white,
Yet a little neutral stems the fight.

When willing others, think 'ask-lite,'
So minions don't renege for spite.

MJM 8/15 SF

274

Hood Rats

All these petty, jacked-up, hoodrat thieves –
 Malodor and guns up their sleeves.
They leave us working stiffs aggrieved!

 One night she's jumped right at her door.
 The next day it's his camera, computer,
 Driver's license, credit cards galore.

 Then her wallet's stolen from her desk!
Society's getting more and more berserk.
As in a cage of monkeys, the thrifty ones

Cuddle saved-up fruits. *Hella* throng, d'utters
Lurk about to snatch away a hunk of pear,
A slice of apple, pinched bananas, everywhere!

Are these *sticky*-fingered louts so lacking?
Or is it just crack and marijuana sacking?
You rob! Get a job! You slob. *Duh,* mob.

MJM 10/14 SF

Horrid Holidays

It's mysterious, determining the root of his
nausea during 'The Holidays.' Like a child's,
   his exhilaration ends at Halloween,

the onslaught of Thanksgiving and Xmas
polluted by subconscious rot – gut-
numbing thoughts he'd rather evade

than retrace. The only two meals a year
when they said grace, dysfunction in your
face: Mom-n-Dad arguing before Granny's

formal dinner that he turn off football
and free the living room for conversation
and drinks; he, in turn, picking fights

   with Uncle A., or vice versa,
'bout politics – that unspoken rule
'bout what you must *not* talk about

thrown to The Fates: Goldwater versus
the New Deal, as if that pact had *not* as
yet passed, a'*pealed.* Mom gets peevish

and short about Granny's insistence on cloth
napkins and the plethora of plates it takes
to serve a fine dinner – insisting us guys

will all be in bed late next day, while
she'll schlep back to Mother's to get
   the cleaning, washing, drying 'n'

ironing done! Or is this all just prejudicial
memory – he, a curmudgeon, recalling
the bludgeons, but not the good times even

antique prisoners got in dungeons on Christ-
mas Day? Could it be he's morphed into a
neurotic whiner? Nonetheless, nothing could

be finer than to drink and dine with friends,
family naught during 'The Holidays.' There's
a piece of tasteless prose that goes: *"You*

can pick your friends, you can pick your nose,
but you can't pick your family." F-ing so and so's

MJM 12/14 SF

Hour-Glass

She lives in Mojave in a Winnebago
His name is Bobby, he looks like a potato
— "San Ber'dino," Frank Zappa

Diabetes syringing him,
Numb and nerve-pained toes,
Fingers pricked by lancets
And sugars insulin slows,

Pancreas drunk to bled,
'Forgot'-disease in his
Boozy head were white piles
Of rot beside the bed.

He'll have a shorter life,
Hopeful to heaven's none
Of this strife. In this dune,
Glass in hand, desert's still

trickling
blood . . .

sand

fed.

MJM 9/15 SF

277

How Many Luxury Problems Can a Guy Take!

Complexities of the day:
His first sex partner after
three years of celibacy
is HIV+*!* His roommate
who's never seen him
bring home a lover is
face-cherried and one-eye-shut
from yesterday's fall
down the staircase.
He's epileptic, now having
a second seizure today! He wanders
in – a'daze, "Where am I?" – just
as those lovers are playing
boys' toys with each other's!
Roomie drinks booze,
verboten amongst epileptics,
striking this buddy
down with the blues.
Then, Dudley the dog
traipses in dogshit from
the backyard. When he
tries to give him a shower
vomit lines the tub – room-
mate puke from the pub!
As he's driving lover
number one home, lover two
leaves a voicemail saying he
wants to leave his new number
but can't remember it: a new
phone, by thunder! As he tries
tracing incoming calls, *his*
phone goes dead. He gets home
to charge it, hoping to charge over
chez lui. But he gets a biz call:
He's on the schedule today –
his normal day off – and only
has an hour! After he arrives,
he finds he's left his phone at home,
now *'over*charging!' *À la* Dorothy
Parker, worrying deep
down, he queries the skies
over town, "What fresh hell
is this?" Some say it can't get
any worse, when all of a sudden

he finds his wallet, penny empty,
in his murse – checks to the IRS,
presenting tomorrow. *Motherfucker!*
From whom will he borrow?

MJM 9/14 SF
"Seanie"

How Nothing Lasts Forever

The malady of unrequited love:
That love be blocked from following true path.
Requited loves go black to crow from dove,
While stillborn love greys chance in aftermath.

To never see love start, the heart to die,
Obsessed and wondering what love could have been.
His skin and eyes purloined without one try –
Nor ear or neck or *member* licked in sin.

To counterfeits and surrogates succumbed,
He's played house, kissing only second best.
What's worse, withdrawn to celibate, love dumbed,
Love lost re-scabs his heart in house arrest.

How true love never born or bid to be
Fights long but love affairs die miserably.

MJM 7/14 SF

Hys-'n'-Loes

Oh river, I see drifting deep in your flux of silver
Those great goddesses of peace.
Stone, stone, ferry me down there.
                                        – Sylvia Plath

Hyper-ventilating, gasping a'moan,
He cycles down faster than a neck
Stone ferries gangsters into d'deeps.

Mentals, like he, don't recall they're
As sick, as say, a cancerous lady
Canceled by her body's metastasis.

Stasis. How he could long to stay
Placed! – no hyperbola/parabola
Choosing high over low. Do any

Number of bad-boy things like
Not take his meds to taste mania,
Self-medicate on beer 'n' ciggies

Or bigger game like cocaine and
Whiskey. Do we really want an end
To our chronic dysfunctions?

And so, like tough guys and country
Mexicans, pretend to know no doc?
Tick-tock goes the crock: he's a time

Bomb, waiting to jizz the night skies
With his bombast and gun-blast wit.
No sleep for days, "See my *fireworks*

Light nights to *Hey!*" Then anon comes
The dread downer. Tears for naught
And bi-elasticity spasm-ing his plot.

MJM 6/13 S.B.
"Oh how strange the change –
  from major to minor . . ."

I Need a Melanon Meeting!

Melanie, swellany, you vanquish monotony,
Embellish infamy, make a new man of me.

Out on the town, we top-shelve civility,
Disdain mediocrity, accent superlativity.

Here in this resto against nitty-gritty, we
Abandon utility, cheer anti-gravity,

Mock shallow nobility's façades of plasticity.
We shimmer at opera, ballet and symphony,

Explicate plays, dining deliciously, yank social
Climbers down from ladder propensity.

Clink to sex universal, trans-post-modernity,
Inhale frivolity, shameless transparency,

Curse predictability, proletarian frigidity,
Gag at grown men in flip-flops – oh arid heredity!

Let it be you and I baby, prime fabulosity,
Blondness and brevity, elite-swine superiority.

The gallery's a salt-mine! Dear Onslow-Ford,
Whose fucking idea was professionality?

Search the bum out and with no Christian pity
Draw and quarter his carcass – make earning a living

Low-brow and crass, labor for pay an audacious
Grotesquerie in league with the peasantry!

Clink seltzer to pleasure *qua* respectability!
Melanie, swellany, you break leisure monotony,

Make a new man of me, re-fashion
Humanity with baroque excess and zealotry.

Down with simplicity! Long live blue-blood
Liberality, crowned exclusivity, perversatility,

Ceremonial suppers' super-complexity.
Pretty Melanie, swellany, let's make Man

Olden unguiltily, and golden young men
Clad naked-to-scantily, who then *sprezzatura* me.

Melanie, Melanie, how you are heavenly!
Melanie, swellany, you and I be the three of me!

MJM 5/08 SF

I Walked the Freezer in Granny's *Tienda*

I walked the freezer in granny's *tienda*.
To this night, the SF cold takes time
Getting to me. Wife cries, "Layer of fat!"
Though I wish to believe it's will to power
Or something Apollonian like that.

Then I've got these Zen friends
Who say of poetry like this, there's
A cure for states of mind like yours.
Learn the way things Are; unhitch
Your American story from their star

Capitalist, crass-class, game war.
You'll see what you are: lucky boy,
Fabulous man. Count your blessings.
See how your guessing and yessing
Ain't really your calling

   Nor falling for just sexual balling.
Determine. Determine. Determine
Your bliss. What it is. To remember
           to kiss. The story may not be her.
Or the story *is* her, or him; or you're just where

Both of you can't tell what's ahead.
You wouldn't know Well unless
It paid for your decadence – you'd
find a new excuse for Dread!
You'd be 70 and gone, never having known

The One. The It. The Him plus Her. The what?
Your Calling or something Zen
Or Apollonian like that.

SF 12/95 MJM

I-Phoney

Here, it seems to me, there is no gravitas anymore.
How have young people found so many ways to score?

For me, it was the First World War.
Then the Second War
the Cold War
the Nam war

We drilled: get under your desks,
  Then had to get up and pass our tests.

Essayists, clumps of *White-Out*®
  Pocked our bests and vests.

Then again, Afghanistan, Iran, Iraq
the same old monkey on y/our back.

We all had crazy Paps.
But to me you seem assuaged by apps.

MJM 3/14 SF

Idle at 4 A.M.

A gathering of the hour of laundry change
Foolscap, wine and cigarettes
Buries work I brought home.

At night, when a million other selves
Send up opposite signals,
Remember your name:

_____. I am _____.
[fill in]   [ditto]

And then find yourself reflex-rotten
To the gods and *for* serpents and sins
More than you claim in good company.

"You only go around once," they say,
*"But if you do it right, once is plenty."**
I'm not due a pinnacle nor in a coffin yet,

And yet I already regret so much time wasted.
As if I'm waiting for a 10th-anniversary
Report card from Harvard or progress chart

From the Federal Department of Commerce.
I play on both teams and buzz
On manifold cylinders *qua* alter egos,

Self-centered, untreated, and insanely
Worried about creature comfort.
I should have been a Himalayan cat.

I'm all me's, unlike the old-timer next door
Who never pleased herself, though she
Volunteered and died, much admired.

* – Frank Sinatra

MJM '86 SF

Illicit through a Tokyo Screen

Dank fumes stalked Japan by night.
Clouds drugged and jaundiced
Fingered building façades,
Wooing sewers and bars, them-

Selves sluggish: marked by
The infernal dripdrip,
Pavement skitter of a bottle cap,
A coin plop.

Above Pachinko parlors, billboards
Glow: flash-trash! A stare at that skyline
Burns the eyes – blurry rush of a fast
Train whipping gas on gas with dusk.

Down a dark-laddered street plates clatter
And pans frying hot grease spit flavors
On counters. Peals of laughter go
Grunt and growl in the bold, testy

Company of barmaids – the men
With their strong smell of weak sensuality
Dump down beer and sweat,
Massaged at table, impotent; unerring.

The geishas leave well-tipped, as *otosans*
Glower and fade in a drunk fraternal heap.
Their limp penises enrobed helter-skelter
  Swimming night in a hetero pile

Their crooked heads swelter.

MJM '82 San Bernardino/Tachikawa
Oi, Uematsu!

287

iLoan

When it comes to mobile devices,
I don't mind giving curmudgeonly advice
To those who thrive on the inhuman vices
These electronic toys spread through town
To tear neighborliness and conversation down.

When I was a young father and my kid
Was round two, three, and four, my wife
And I surrendered to his toy-tortured war.
He had to have certain collectibles or else
He would die, and if not expire then chokingly

Cry: ninjas, and legos, and X-men, and beanies,
tys and Pokéman with his burgers and wienies.
There's a Santa Claus named *Apple* who
Creates the same mania for adults who pursue
Standing in line for two days to buy iThing, a'new.

Cell phones that radically transform your lives,
Very being, and *Walkmans* that walk you
Down the street, not really seeing. You bump
Into brethren, whom you squarely ignore
To check out on screens what's the next

Apple score. And sure as apples have seeds –
The next thing to sprout up are *apps* for your
Deediest needs. Now that texting while driving is
Against common law, we might review common
Sense to see what none of you saw: you aren't

Skilled enough to do two things at once,
Especially nonchalant and acting the dunce
Where life and death are concerned on the road.
Now the police have to watch you – as we beg,
Threat, and goad. Let's reminisce. Was a time

In a crowd or group *that* was <u>this</u>: we'd
Mind our own business; then spot a fine,
Friendly face; then whip up "Hello" and have
A chat, face-to-face. People were happy to
Interact with each other, citizen-to-citizen,

Brother to brother. We didn't *get* hit by cars
Dialing a number, and music we shared in
Town squares under moon river cover. Or

We'd turn on the radio and talk about music,
Content with ambient – someone else paid to

Choose it. Now you each program your own
Symphonies, as you stare at the *iPhone* a'plant
On your knees. There's the famous story
Of two kids on a date, who at the same table
Conversed as they ate on respective cell phones

Unable to conjure the spirit for live talk, unable
To relinquish their gadgets long enough to
Enable the budding of romance, fable, or babble.
The concept of the common rabble comes to mind,
As I write out this protest, my world, widget-maligned.

I think of how Steve Jobs was ennobled to God
Status, while he pitched and premiered silicon
Toys *at* us. He was *"awaited like the rain. Like*
Eyes for the blind. Like feet for the lame. Kings
Heard his words, and they sought out his company,

As the janitors of shadowland flicked their brooms
At spoilers like me." He promised his products
Were more than they were, saying you *became*
Them, once out of the store. So now you're an
iPhone yourself, or an *iPod*, or some *Apple* elf.

I have an idea of what's coming soon, as *Sam-*
Sung now promises the same looney tunes.
You'll go to the factory in China; they'll cut open
Your head, and insert an *iPad* where your brain
Was instead. Since music is art, they'd trade an

iPod for heart, and last sew an *iPhone* in your
Silicon mouth, and now you'd be finished,
A Steve con-job of youth. He was a mean
biz dude, who a genius, got what he wanted,
And you were all happy to launch him, so vaunted.

When he died you cried at makeshift spots
Round the world, laden with flowers and momentos
As his history unfurled. But now you don't need
Him, cause those products are in yous, mother
Boards and itty chips, y/our advantage, confused.

italics, paraphrased after Joni M.
MJM 9/15 SF

In Bed with a Bug

What's frightening about insects is
Their spastic nerve and larval curd.
Hold a rhino beetle in your hand –
It's not just the bite but barb pick-
Axing your palm you fear – the stench
From gutsy shards oiling your skin,
   Jizzing dull poison toward that
Shovelful of beauty you harbor.

MJM '84 Manhattan Beach

In Line with the Scandal Sheets

Incongruous that mainliners, pop drinkers
Of trite dramas sliced up for a tinkle
Should fidget in drag pits, faint at feet
Of tranny queens these days, those risky-tinted
Ravens stretched out thin on puff powder.

Their celebs nosing into headlines before
Bandages spinster, they can tell ya
Whose nerves r hackneyed by syringes
Dripping Botox – to which white clumps
A star winks a sphincter for booty bumps.

Meanwhile, blond mouseketeer – long
Sinuous arms, stuck-out ears, skads of tanned flesh,
Loinclothed groin – hires himself out to hump
Some turgid mother's dank hill of desire.
How limp to find the pup piddles a knob
   instead of a prick!

Dinky at an inch or so, it finks. Wags.
As if all those lovely summer hooks tendrilling
Outward on the intake, slacken, flatten and dull,
A-wilt in *Saran Wrap*. The death, not by intricate
gyration, *but sold-short, trick-shafted*
   Cougar after bicep mustered luster.

MJM '84 Manhattan Beach

In Praise of Joni Mitchell's Agitation

Agitation comes and goes in throes
Unlike passion climbs to climax
 bitch got me up
Axes me out on
Bunioned, yellowing toes

In this *nervous* cycle
In before or after a pickle
 insane evil men do frivolous
Fickle as kids smashing bugs
Post Office clerk with a sickle

Wantonly
I too do fray like Blanche
Dubois, loathe of all beneath me
 Still sweating
Bullies on the ranch

 But an in-school
 lad
The world teemed text clear;
excitement all ways
 Coming Next Year

Humanities "Dear,

 Feminine fear college
 All that knowledge 'n riches
Boston girls, product pitches

A *Clearasil* wife/two sons
 trekking
Odd art ole friend
Would smear off my mind's
Eye's terrorist mascara.

 I'd belittle town
 blues "New York, New York"
 Is sung to melt away.
What went wormy Big Apple,
 framework of the fray?

Your stage, my cage, the
Other guy's shit-faced rage?
Stockbrokers' spillage
¿Mañana's bombed & burning
Chinese village?

Patriot's blandage,
That salesman's adage?
  Turbulent indigo
Sagesse, your agitation:
  dawn predation strife

  overpopulated life
Chill shrill Mayflower fife.
In traffic everyone hates everyone
  Doctors' pills
  give you brand new ills

The bills bury you like an avalanche.
Sex cells and *sells*
And lawyers haven't been this popular
Since Robespierre
Slaughtered half of France.

Eskimo bone
Your Indian known
Your rock-and-roll God-sewn
Yvette in English
Your sage agitunetome.

(Most italics taken from Joni Mitchell, Turbulent Indigo, CD)
MJM 2/95 SF

In Spiriting Wealth

He believes Providence will grant him what he needs, not
All that he wants, indulgence, once vaunted now taunted.

He nearly always contorted his gains to shame – down dim-
med alleys, evading, blurred arun in mind-fleeting games.

He's living on little – every day's dollar a whittle of stick
Bobbing above his humbled eyes' downcast, carroting toil –

And grows anxious at God for not sparing a nod he despoil.
Then what is shaking one's fist to the heavens but out-

Rageous assumption of the tree-fruit of the knowledge
Of good and evil? He would use his Adam's apple to

Bray to the Lord for more of reward and less of this dript
Water torture. Thirst slaked not by the glass, he seeks not

To amass, but to pass into innocent, effortless bliss. God
Only knows if things of this world bring joy again, amiss.

Lord, a word on religion: he's a wing-stunted carrier pigeon.
He misses the Mass, towards which his PTSD won't trespass.

MJM 9/15 SF
"What profit hath a man of all his labour
which he taketh under the sun?" – Ecclesiastes 1

Infinity Twisted (88)

How You might have dislodged me from Your light
To displace my lust, left to eyes of scorn:
Yet right-havened, reined me in with Your might;
Proned me tortuous – evil arts forsworn.

My sworded, black warlock, least acquainted
With my heart, You'd ratchet down such gory
Haunts to reveal wherein flesh I tainted.
In ghosting me, ecstasy pled glory.

Satan tricked me in wicked rhymes or two,
So bending all my carnal thoughts love-free,
His injuries I to myself would do.
Yet graced my sinner, double graces me.

He bridled me, to whom I so belonged,
Then righted bowed infinity, lust wronged.

MJM 1/11 SF
After Sonnet 88

Innocence Riven

To wonder, to inquire, perhaps to speak
and speak as tho' you were innocence herself,
the wide eyed beauty of simple questions.
　　　　　　　　　　　　– Hamlet

Full innocence is guiltless of a crime.
In part, she stirs self-pity and its wants,
As fair children are scolded at bedtime,
Or as nausea, just jilted lover, daunts.

From this crass world never do sins depart,
All lacey souls lanced rude by bloody news.
Rich men gain armor, making money art.
To gangsters full of fault, the gunless lose.

If only passing time would virtue gain,
Innocence might look ahead to perfect.
Yet naïve hearts crush, out-braved stain-to-stain,
As hotheads gaming, buy-and-sell us wrecked.

If innocence be pre-pled to heaven,
Why this sad heart, fear-and-envy's maven?

MJM 2/11 SF

Insert Adverts

When it comes to porn,
I still like my magazines.
                – Heard anonymously in San Francisco

Everything's online, including the Feds and fucking.
How strange to notice the odd *exception:* cheap food
Adverts tipped into *actual* newspapers. Plucking
One up, he sees how feeders get sped into food mode.

Brilliant – as if sprayed by a tri-color cartridge –
Each grocery, as intense as a garish print.
Triptychs of goods, three per deck, and scarcely a midge
Of space: hues sharply outlined, as if by some Mint!

How scrumptious they are to lead with meat, priced
So little per pound, it reminds me we carnivores
Came from chimps to the plate – as sliced   *
Peaches, apples, oranges, fake 'omnivorous!'

The flyers skip any hale, green vegetable,
Not *one* depicted here under the logo's *sunburst!*
Huckstering, corny copy crows to re-call
The obese with coupons, advert-amazed! First

Shellfish luxuriates on an ice-tray, plump, hard
By corporate trash-snacks: *Cheetos* & six-packs
Of *Pepsi* so cheap, *"Dude,* drink your soda with lard!"
From here, it's a sheer crash into hella tacky junk racks:

Chips, cakes, cupcakes, cookies, candies, wine –
  As if all, set up to get us back into line.

**

Last, the hardware ads get tiny, like back o'magazine porn.

[Starved nuts, he'll eat both boys and girls, junk-to-melons torn!]

MJM 2/11 SF
* Chimpanzees, especially males, are known for their habit of killing monkeys
   and other small prey to savor meat (high-caloric) and gain status in their troops.

Insider Mating

"*Entremalheur:* one of those rat-pack
      Entrepreneurs on top, who fucks everyone
      On bottom with his greed: plural, a crass
      Pack in need of a six-pack's fist-pack."
Over dinner, she quizzically traces
His bizarre etymology back to its root,
Peeved, rolls her eyes, and leaves for TV.

MJM 7/14 SF

Instant Gratification

Thing about A.A. cigarettes – Is that they
make up for burned-out, black'd-out fêtes.

They come in handy when we're feeling
All squirrely – gratification, instant and

surely. I smoke when I get up early,
the buzz of tabac, instead of drinks

that I lack. Then during the day
to keep my working in play;

And then at night to keep
up the good fight. Now

Clean, I need some-
thing bad and mean.

Crush it out,
still all lout.

o'punk
Dun'd

kill'r
fun ~

MJM 9/15 SF
And mocha java
instead of Cava!

Intersection

At a busy, happy holiday intersection
Criss-cross, spot thoughts of people,
Places, things – not to mention urban
Situations, pile up behind him like an
Avalanche of Christmas gifts
He's loathe and broke to buy.

The house sold, but profligate,
He netted no money. His art market
Freezes up for department store
Bluff week. A new car is a blessing,
But all his good stuff is still in storage.
How he misses his green patent-

Leather alligator loafers. His son's
Found religion, no longer sleeping
All day and evening until seven.
Godspeed to teenagers popping
Rx's, injecting, smoking, and snorting.
The ex wants an *Hermès* scarf,

Always *Town & Country* classic.
The young ones only want money.
Dad's got a gig in this annihilated
Economy, making less, and now
This heaven-sent, part-time job
With classy Russians, grad-school

Brainy but shaky – when right in
Front of him, he notes a pudgy
Black lady in green velour and
Red Santa hat, as she passes his
Windshield with her cautious cane.
She harrumphs, each step nego-

Tiated on her merry way. She's
Smiling, almost laughing warmly
To herself about her "red velvet and
Ermine" doffed. As if all the universe
Were inside only her, content with her
Contents. In this quadratic equation

Here at the stop, she so seems ten-
To-the billionth-power with just her
   One-plus-one double-AA to light up.

MJM 12/10 SF

Island Singer

The luscious, wealthy singer downloaded
To our PC sings with the coffee-brown voice
Of elixir islands: palms sway in her vibrato,
Asia in her tone, as New York, London, Paris
Spark her diction. Plaintiff, she mesmerizes

Listeners with a sad chant: a lamentation of black
Ghettos in America. She grieves how the young
She resembles scare up no jobs, while their fathers
Deal dope, so Mamma may use and papa may bruise,
Themselves lost in this re-production of violent souls.

Ignorant of their place, their voice, their benefactors,
They latch on to the errant gangsta' rapper and sports'
Star, gifted swell beyond them. So they own the streets,
While their betters rush from cubicles to sandwiches
To meetings, seminars, and raises at polished desks.

Surrounded by fearless punks, the Grandmas hover,
Right-good church ladies. Sunday hats await: wisdom
And faith detectable to connoisseur kin, gleaning.
Aggrieved, not God, they lack the power to wave a plume
To stop the doom of children in gloomy, slum's rut.

To crime's excitement, manning up to risk, annexing
Turf, all testy bucks attract, harrowing with their homies –
As skinny beauties – 'the weaker sex, the speaker sex' –
Exchange hysteria, hair-do's, nail stickers, exaggerations.
Eye whites on the guys, they wait. Wasted, the drug-

fizzled homeless scan it: warrior black boys to thugs,
As old drunks bleat they barely bleared at these kids' age.
How seldom youth digs into its future, once twenties' strong,
Now crap-assed men dimmed by base things: what pumped
Them up as lads were merely hormones, parched to a trickle

In latter days. What happened to forever they'd be heroes?
Ever heady for a fight? Yes, it's better kids read computers
And TVs to see themselves in great stations of the globe:
Behold, the Oval Office! Like 'the experts,' he haggles
The links missing, though: that *program* – that do-or-fie

Discipline, that schedule enforced in adolescent homes.
He thinks back to the two will-do sergeants, who ruled,
And drilled, and ran his chary self to the Ivy League.
Given choice, lax kids won't elect to wake up. Out late,
They'll smoke and drink their '40's and their sodas

To avoid money fears at home, and tweak-lean will starve
On corporate food: chips, gum, candy, beef jerky designed
By the guys who enjoy a farmer's diet. Drug flooded,
Mexico falls uninhabitable for the gruesome violence
Of her de Sade wars. Nor even a gangster is guaranteed home,

Beheaded or blasted by the rival cartel. We hear it over
And over – how to break the circle of chemicals, job-
Lessness, audacity to favor education? Not easy to incite
The strongest, youngest, and most handsome to do what
Elders cray is right. Not on streets, they'd be in forest

And field to fight. They'd hunt meat and collect fruits
For their families. Pride would gleam on honor, babies,
Saves, and deeds, and affluent, artificial us would do
The same, same needs. Had they our houses and our 'hoods,
They'd find their kids popping pills like ours do, but instead

Of jail, they'd get therapy, checked into poignant 'programs.'
The singer repeats her theme . . . she now in a limo-jam.

MJM 2/11 SF

It Takes All Kinds

Mavericks get-rich-quick in McMansion Hills
To live lordly like margraves in old Germany:
Counts' countrymen short-shriving their souls
Of a Sunday, demonstrating faith to community,

Duty rote –

As lost souls on craven, crack-corners lock in focus
On craves, high-spiriting their bodies with pipe puffs-
n-torrents of unfined spirits. Bar none, self-centered
Fear, the cyclone, booze-n-drug-medded cold-comfort

Control, lies spun.

Now his turn has come to lose worldly fruition,
Wealth and walls taken, though mentors say more
Of calm and grace will be given. Will it be a
Pious path – Sisters-of-Perpetual-Silence –

Cloister quiet?

Or will *The Force* stage a comeback in this world
To ferry him to affluence again – this time thrifty?
Or will he in old age cower, fallow of his passions,
Save the symphony? Or will the comfort of cars

And *opere*

Be doled out, the cosmos beaming him a narrow path?
Is equating his soul's size with 'our' universe narcissism
At its most absurd? How deep and engrossing our lives
Are to ourselves, and how *we* proffer Civilization back

To God

As *his* main work. It's easy to backslide into *nyet* –
Galaxies and his jettisoned courage spiraling.
There is melancholy and a dead sensation, catapulted
From goods and glamour. Yet, somehow starlight

Beams joy to live in this moment, pleading
  Neutral charge, 'Not hero nor zero.'

MJM 3/11 SF

It We Can't Understand, See, or Say

God inscrutable, ancient Hebrews mute
A strophe that meant "Don't dare say,"

As Christians and Muslims honor sacred,
Immortal prophets heaven-blest and pray

To holy names that personify for men the
It that one can't understand, see, or say . . .

Outside their illuminations of Sons of Man
And God. In Asia wise spirits of the way

Em-path integrity-discovery, gentlemanly
Grace vertically aligned | no loss of face,

As tribesman, native, occultist, 'original' feel
Nature's and stars' indicated ways to be.

Then in zips Hollywood with its *The Force*
And matrix webs and nets and chain-link

Fence that seem to criss-cross physicists'
String theory and math, cosmic conjectures

To test, and experimenters star-a-spar how
It all came to be and why this aftermath?

Maybe due to Santa Claus we desire
Our white-bearded Sire, and from historic

Kings that Throne. Then existentialism de-
Flocks hell and heaven, as some bemoan

And groan with a'lone wretched atheism,
And others feel awfully right at home. He'll

Attempt to abide their foreboding stricture
Not to say *It,* nor adjust its face or person

To a peopled, sky-high nation. He feels the
Electric web of karma-charmèd math, yet

His younger inner eye retains omniscient
Bearded father with golden scepter, Son,

& Holy Ghost on High. Daily wash over him
Catholic surges to pray to Christ, archangels,

And saints; and daily, he hail hale inhales Our
Blessèd Mother. Yet he owns it's so unknown,

His mind cannot fathom *Its* totality beyond
Vacancy to love to physics to astronomy –

how even heavenly

It
may
be,
not
be,
or
else
be
that
strophe
we
shan't
read,
say,
or
see.

Yet these r vrbs, & *It*$_{\infty}^{o}$

MJM 12/31/10

Ivy League Fatigues

Je suis fatty gáy – Fatty Unbuckle

Harvard Ivy grows on walls: you can see it from the study halls.
Poison Ivy grows in bushes where valedict'ry boys implant others' tushes!

Ivy is a metaphor: it flourishes on bricks, like pubic hair 'round freshmen pricks.
Or walk up to a sophomore trick, to nip the Ivy, clear his dick!

And if that isn't all, trim a tendril off junior's ball . . .
Nightfall, who'd want a virginity, fig-leaf over-all?

If the Ivy *is* poison, switch to snatch,
Otherwise be prepared to scratch ~~~

(Now mons senior high, give up *upright* Divinity for Infinity School ∞
 and see your member effloresce and ambush overnight, a-drool!)

On Soldiers' Field, imagine Ivy League fatigues
We'd doff, gnarled vines cascading up and off*!*

Of tighty whities, we'll have none.
We prefer to grow our Harvard sons

Naked and bedecked by leaves,
As serpents-in-the-bush wriggle up appled Lady Eves.

And if ever Ivy in the Yard should die,
Substitoot bulrush and cattails hard-by.

MJM 9/15 SF
With apologies to Alma Mater ~
Entwined in my bloomin' Frater/Frau'ers!

Jackhammers

The grinding, growling, motorized whining,
whinnying, wailing, humming-n-heaving
Next door is only *outsized* by the clangs,
Bangs, thrusts, and hammer-pounds hitting
The wall behind my head, workplace a-dread.

How all this garrulous, sonic booming rape
and carnage, pile-driving, and pulverizing
Torts and invades our village of galleries
is one horrible thing, but that that thunder's
Din harrumphs my head through my drums

To a migraine is another, insidious pling!
As in blasts & napalm's screech in Viet Nam
rived soldiers' PTSD, I scream to flee to some-
place cool, Arcadian, and leafy with bab-
bling brooks, quiet books, and his-n-her

nooks to nail. How pounding in bed or on
a blanket be so soothing. But on the wall
Behind my head and earthquaking through
Glass gallery doors, now a-sliding closed, is
not the same, gamine repoussé nor *repose*.

MJM 7/14 SF
DRFA

Jacqueline Elodia

The week that Jackie
Kennedy died
felt like when
my grandmother did.

As if a richly mineralized
topsoil had blown to sea
exposing our poor
bedrock beneath.

They soothed with the aura
Of velvet evening purse,
handmaidens of Hera
not quite holy

sisters of Mary
but misses Mother Courage:
finesse, largesse,
    equitesse.

Family, opera gloves, symphony
Dior, home cooking, Lanvin, horses
Ne'er a mention of any label,
any store. I love their looks.

I *riff* your books, your nautical
Navy & white, *Givenchy*
Spirits of spray *parfum*
Flying over the main.

MJM 5/94 Dallas

Jilted Heart

I

The greater part of what I want
decided *t'was all for me,* long before
I became this SF person secretly

Believing that to say, "I want,"
Is to mark yourself a shallow
frivolous man with enough

Already! Do the four billion
Poor beneath my tower door
Know guys have it so swell?

Or do they bypass little me
And dwell on movie stars &
Waxed pussy? I'm as unhappy

As they are mute. And why not
Dismiss this boring male poetic
Interlude? Rambo to rice paddy,

"Who da hell r u, gay crybaby?"

II

I've attained this erudition
Where everything the world holds
Dear I adore except the people.

I'm an engine swamping the moor,
My geyser and suds to find
A marble tub with room service

In which to wrinkle
My duty to make a living,
Or finally *do it honestly*, as in

A calling, contribution, *their*
Roof and regular meal. I'd squeal
To be wrapped in Aubusson,

& yen to trek Tanzania – again!
I want up up up. Or I want out.
Corroding from supreme to lout,

Embarrassing presbyter,
Boyscout. How did everything
I gave myself turn out

To be from off the shelf?
And clichéd hearts, though
Bitten through, the only

Proof of true remains?

MJM 2/96 SF

John B's Last Martinis

The last time John Barrymore died,
His passing halted to a balk, friend-
Imperiled. To deter his drinking,

Loved ones sailed him out to sea
To oversee he dry up, no booze
onboard the boat. But John began

To pass rather toxic gas, stumbling
Blind as a sailor, storm-raving aft.
They tracked the alky-actor all night,

These few dry, intervening, spy him
Toddling fuel from the yacht's tank,
Albeit stomach-buffered with milk!

Nose for pickle juice, he fords their plan,
And flows forth – as drunk a great man
As Barleycorn ever bilked of bile and blood.

Star now aboard dry land, he downs shots like
Shooting stars onto wetlands. Until liver-hard,
J. B.'s organs puffed; this balloon, succumbs.

His mates, Errol-the-handsome and sly W.C.,
Flounder in their *own* alcoholic paroxysms,
Their gamely, lordly friend, *par excellence* –

Gravely missing tonight's trio-on-town itineraries.
Kidnapped by a mortuary? Arrows pierce their parts!
Is fabled J.B. – drink-starved – plum-plucked legal

From their quivers? With toxic dedication,
They'll rue the family funeral and public burial
To follow. How dare relations take *their* man,

Snatched away to be boo-hooed by mere family
And fans; when *here* their deuce is suffering
Such a mighty loss – valorous, drinking bud, dead

Ginless, jailed. "Eegads, Mr. Flynn, what horror!"
"Yes, most dire I should think." The better to brood,
They drown several bottles, toasting

With booze-spiked tears, the tragedy of their
Three-leaf clover plucked-shy o'trine <
Common as carrion-fly's scissored-wing buzz!

When, in a flash, flies an inspiration of ice
And mash: bingo! They've sourced their passion's play . . .

Announced royally into the chamber

Of the mortician, they use all their patrician
Guile, fame, myth, plus a few thousand to bribe
The mift, old-man fan to give up the corpse!

As he stalls, the gruesome-twosome oil
His crank with a small flask's lubrication,
When, "What a lark!" he connives at their intrusion.

Back in Errol's great room, beau bar to-the-ceiling,
They prop old John B. up, in his easy chair, of course.
Gents, all dressed in white tie and tails –

Noblesse above impending tomb's prohibition.
They arrange Lord B. in raffish fashion:
His body, back-a-bit-stiff, as often, and his

Legs crossed with hand held up to clink.
The others chug a'hale, yet J.B. doesn't drink!
"Squire B., may I refresh you with a jigger,

Quothes Mr. Fields. "Or wouldst thou prefer
Another from the shaker?" Errol frowns,
"John, my man, whatever is the matter?"

"Your stem is still full, alas. Surely,
You thirst – slabbed-and-slaked, days dry –
Most especially here! To our wedicated triad!

"Here then, allow me re-make this old gin.
Take it off your hands." Whereupon, he gulps B's
Olive-grimed-one down, exchanging it with a *fresh* martini!

Heroic, they drink the night away, parlaying old times'
Bravado, surly staged and quaint, their few times' police-caged!
They even swill to tears, recalling fond ladies

First embraced by John B., then later divided
By three. Foil-laid, in utter gush, Errol kneels –
Rheumatic W.C., disabled, in so he leans.

Cautious, expecting the worse, Errol queries
His hell-bent brother, "J. B., my Knight,
Are there martinis in heaven?" Just then,

Rigor-mortis meddling, John's fingers
Tighten, splashing a lick of gin
Onto his fine pants. It lands right near

His privates, stained. "God be graced," exclaims Fields,
"He's chirping! 'Not only is there a bar in heaven,
But behold: women galore to mink and clink.'"

"My earls," Errol intones, "This auspicious secret
We shall toast in paradise someday – when we
Three finally die." On point, they regale J.B.,

As the cad, corpse-a'cold, keeps twitching gin for re-fills.
"Funeral be damned! Whosoever loved J.B. as we,
Is but a dame on the make in his hay, anyway.

  "Let 'em all wait," they caroled. Smug,

They both own and owe him most. *J.B.,*
To parlor pallor, toast! . . . *W.C.'d* and *Érrolled.*

MJM 4/11 SF
To Marianne G.

Junk Food Triolet

"Candy-coated popcorn, peanuts and prize –
That's what you get in Cracker Jacks!"

Lady Luck once suited him *three* threes and two sevens.
Now he begs small change – cash-and-prizes prized.
He's humiliated trading *Morton's* for crap at *Seven-Elevens!*
Lady Luck once suited him *three* threes and two sevens.
He twists & rocks & stirs for dollars' dough, green leavens.
Tho' Thrift pay peace and calm, pocket ego just right-sized –
Lady Luck once suited him *three* threes and two sevens.
Now he begs small change – cash-and-prizes prized.
He's humiliated trading *Morton's* for crap at *Seven-Elevens!*

MJM 1/11 SF

Just a Joe

Scalawag in the kitchen, he barks at himself
Sliding lice off his hair and *swearing to fuck
Qwell* also kill fruit flies vectoring to-and-fro!

His face's burned by booze. Via central casting,
His goatee and 'stache match him to zombies
Hare-eyed – no, *headless:* the amped meth-dead

Trudging lanes in Lake County, pieces of mind
Smelted by compounds,"Could yank yer *skin off
In the vapors!"* Housemates, next you find him

Couch blank, hands in his sweats – *ew* – focused
On a silent TV 'on.' *"Yo!* Cantonese channel!"
Tú piensas,"¡Ay, yai, yai!" & nerve up to ask

"Why?" Fast full-alert, Joe leans in to matter-
Of-fact him, Chinese characters subtitling the
Newscaster mute. "I come from a Mandarin

Family," he scruffily gruffs, half-Anglo as John
Wayne's boot man, polishing off everything
In the Saloon except his boss's *Houstons!* You

Get the TV's broadcasting for two languages,
Volume 'off' for Sino-elites, you reading Joe's other,
Other tongue, "Or, why call them Mandarins?"

You jingo,*"Strange:* addict-drunk drying out
Here from an arts-and-lettered lineage." Cued,
You rehear that high-class*'sthesh-tche'* that

Delights the ear far more than Cantonese's ass-
Sonance and hacking at "k's" like crack Anglo-
Saxon, much less *Qho Gon Khow!* grunt-growl.

Next day at the fridge, you find Joe standing
Statued before the microwave. "So, you have
Mandarin family and read it too, that's cool!"

Joe direct gazes. Perked, you spy the polished
Almond zenith of baby blues shaped by Asia.
Joe takes up scolding the timer *a-rail* in jacked-

Up English, wholly emphatic like in movies.
"Icky to think his nits could boll my head hair
And his crabs go you know where!" *You pray*

For Joe later, but not until you check the
Floor and garbage pail for his swarm. You ask,
It's being Christmas, "Would I do the Christian

Thing and go buy him some more *Qwell* shampoo?"
Joe pops in again, "Did ya see the UFO last night?
"Real purdy, kind-u, ah *cross* with colored light."

MJM 12/10 SF

Kidney Cancer

Why would two people who didn't fit
Only fight stay married for so long?
Am I right that this is wrong?

His cigarette cinders flicker like
A lantern at three a.m. – your favorite
Obnoxious hour to bam, bam, bam, bam, bam him.

I've avoided your lichens like a pox,
As snow from sea clouds quickly melts on rocks.
I feel I've swerved around some *Oresteia*,

And moved from the wretched desert
  To this most fashionable La Playa.
That a family's supposedly a wise

Mom and dad taint necessarily.
  To add to cage rattling,
He saw, "Fought till the light

Wouldn't go out right,
Never not some co-dependent fight."
Pops, to be sure, snuffed

Himself untimely, his arrogant, careless
Mug all smiley, smiley, smiley.
Instead of eating well, getting exercise

With his boys, fun in SoCal sun
He only burned the calories it took
To smoke and invariably die young.

Today, mom's charms come back,
I so see, and I forgive them. They
Could not *be another way for me*.

MJM '06 SF

317

La Minnie

It's hella raining outside
And cold as fuck. Mean-
while, Minnie *la callejera*
Cat is somewhere hidden
In the 'hood. She's a hit-
And-run driver, diving in
For food, then dashing
Out our door in a feline
Flash. Redheaded, she's a
Sucker for shadowy cats.
Why it wouldn't surprise
Me if she were the moll
Of some dog! How could
A family like ours board
Such a tramp? That scamp,
That whore! I'd warn her,
"You'll freeze your *tail*
Off ," but she's a Manx.

MJM 1/13 S.B.
con Don A.

Late Love   (28)

Will I re-love, debased by best boy's flight:
Prisoned, my heart, will-barred, drug-numb, obsessed?
Melancholy fate, plangent nightmares' blight,
I brewed his stud-hood, female-dread, possessed.

No one pities me: heterosexuals reign –
Content, share sexy cribs, con-blearing me.
I roiled, then enveloped this hate, my bane –
How forlorn, my toil – mind-eye rant: *past be!*

He thrilled all day, love-laughing me/us bright.
I graced his room, rook to heaven's checkmate:
Stupendous beauty, flattering the night
Till twin-sparked stars, we'd rhapsodize, cub fate.

Then he dodged this blown-out fag of borrow.
Day, tread night. Whom do I have – to arrow?

MJM 4/11 SF
After Sonnet 28

Libertine

On his table is a *Bible;*
Slipped in a garment
Bag, porno magazines.

From the toiler
Night to night
Victory slithers

To the spoiler.
There are good reasons
To drink. It's so

Ugly out there.
Yet over the long
Haul, messy carpet

Come smelly, you revulse.
Toweling oil,
Disregard the hot pics,

Though leave
The Word lain.
Hobgoblins imprison

Red devils – tubercular
Rattlebags jostling
Gleam-white in the dark.

Inward, flesh
Falls randomly.
Inside selves

Inside-out shuffle
And, sandpapered,
Cry, "Air!

"New dominion!
Bright future.
Vigor! Manner.

"What do we care for
Your migrant wino
Bugling the pigeon past?"

Death conjures thus:
Outside reality thugly,
You lick up ashes

On the insanity pile
Made by inner fire
Down to the marble.

MJM '84 Manhattan Beach

Life Lake

The aftermath of rant and rave
Is a pile of charred stubble.
No retribution. No visionary chair,
Nor messy masses awash in precision.

Harridan hagglers divest grace
To free up room for pandering
To public ill will, spent/unspent
Figures stacking up just so.

Your thin, bitter broth,
Trickle of nettle soup,
Is no ambrosial lift to Olympus
Nor necessary serum.

In *your* deck under
Clear water
Stagnates to bilge –
Wormwood slats

Of hull for bones –
As thirsty mad dogs,
Each a bald eye out,
Lap it up at Peace Harbor.

MJM '87 SF

Lion Bird

An adolescent lion prowled across the street.
He stood staring him down from his grandma's
Yard a second too long, when the scoped cat
Pounced across the street to maul him to meat.
Just in time, the careless lad slid behind
The screen door, the beast about to claw
That lattice to litter and to bound in the house
To havoc him.

Half a second late, he slams the forest-green
Front door tight. But instead of latching it,
He lets test the force of his own body against
The pummeling – leaning his slanted weight
To stay that slayer. Each time it leapt
And banged against that timbered shield,
His loafered heels wedged farther under
Granny's sofa. His palms annealed and fingers
Splayed open against the door, he withstood
The pounding that, were it overwhelming,
Could crush him – hot-blood lunch, fat cat's.

Sweating fear's sense, he bang-bolts the lock.
Panting and proud of his own puissance, he slides
Down, his back on the door, as in movies. Then, up
Again to peer through the portal window to see
If he might tease the conquered cat: he incited
That beaten lion to leap for his face once more.
But this time, afraid and shamed he do idiocy
And die in front of darling 'Grams,' he sprints
Through the Old Vic house, room-to-room,
To make-it-to the backyard safely.

There in a cage, his brother's overpopulated
Atrium *cum* county prison eked by threat: half glass,
Top, staved. While the snakes, lizards, beetles,
And scorpions lay rapt, the one big bird
Hops, worried from perch to rail, looking
Up and longing at the open sky it craves.
The pit of his stomach, retched with pity,
He firms, determined to liberate that slave.
Given what's passed, he thinks, he might have
Thought himself 'brave.' Then, he comes
To comprehend this hero trembling to be saved.
"I had choice," he thought. "And the lion, teeth.
"But the poor bird only has that chirp –

Voiceless, unsung-an'-terrified to dread.
It's one thing to fool your own life away
Daring fate for a thrill. Another, to leave
An innocent displayed 'on-stage' for a kill –
Terror-chilled, by your own grievous will."

Freeing that flier, he gave wild right to wild,
And proved himself empath, no petty jailer.
"What would make blood kin so calloused
And so cruel, as to let a pet's mind be mangled?
To torture someone in a cell equals hell."

He thinks about returning to trick the lion
More, but recognizing wrong, he goes inside –
Foe of evil men of woe, and latches the door.

MJM 3/11 SF

"Listen to Me, Love & Mercy!"

"Stella! Stella!"
> – Stanley Kowalski

But now my branches suffer
And my leaves don't bear the glow
They did so long ago.
> – Beach Boys

Devastating docu-dramas: stars hid
Or addicted in pyjamas, lore abashed,
House-alarmed, be-trauma'd.

Sensitive poets to a man,
They come to art by chance and part-
Kissed youth, fletching as meteors pan.

The early days be climbers' thrill,
Eating what they kill, of slight re-
Nown, but ample fill, agrin.

Then come the lustred heights,
Red carpets but obnoxious lights,
Binding doom to the undarked.

To see the genius-agile, tackled
Hearts torn by plunder – gnashed apart,
Celebrity's vain inhuman torts.

We give release to neighbor and to poet,
But to the stars who didn't see it
Coming, rape them of their peace, chagrined.

Now no way to go about the streets –
Normal, easy, rallying successes
Might as well have been defeats.

To be sucked dry of your blue blood,
And the fans a tornado, fire, flood.
Over and over superfame, ungood.

You have to fall, you have to thrash,
You must be crushed, a waste, a'mash.
The hideous bulbs e'er flash and flash and flash.

Red carpets and obnoxious lights
Brash a doom of the undarked.
And stars by suits and doctors sharked ~

Gilled bits of fallen angels like chum
Be of the sea. Stars sparked, then barked.
Floodtide of fame, swallowed by the dark.

Only *zeros/ones* to conserve them.
Felling stars in schadenfreude might be just as
Grave a sin as wishing the poor to ruin.

But *then,* to have had a Dad, who beat you,
Beat you, beat you bad. And Mom, to drink –
Riddance in the dark . . . . a'slink.

MJM 8/15 SF

On the occasion of "Listen to Me, Marlon" and "Love & Mercy"

Living Afterlife

> *First, a man takes a drink.*
> *Then the drink takes a drink.*
> *Then the drink takes the man.*
>
> — Ernest Hemingway < Japanese proverb

He gave you life with one foot in this world,
The other, most o'er-fenced to heaven's prayer,
That as you drank your brain and body churled
Until your boozy realm became half's slayer.

Most men are put on earth to live and pass,
Their spirits, one aligned with head and heart.
But called to afterlife at birth, alas
Your soul be born with mind plus limb apart.

Some saints like John, Saul/Paul, and Joan of Arc
Could not contain their countenance on this rest,
Perchance, born eye on sparrow and the lark,
And when time came to live, they lived abreast.

Poor Teresa, cursed by levitation,
Half-here like drunks' agitant salvation.

MJM 7/15 SF
St. Teresa of Avila is recorded to have been plagued
by spontaneous, bodily levitation, especially during Mass.

Loathe to Falter

In Spanish prayer, anguished men
To edges of deep ravines are drawn.
Palavers, wails and wavers, eye-whites
Loll above lips that feed
On the dark calm of dispirited cadavers.

Praying further, strung taut for the leap,
They slip on a
        transport of mind,
Where, bathed in new hope – as stained
Glass in a pane, granite-white – they rest,
Dry, relieved, late to make conciliatory
equipage of pageantry.

I am a healthy Zurburán man with sores,
My vision, buried in the shadow
Of a horsehair shroud. My knack
For cures for others, immense. All terror
Is as water brought by pails
        on a waterwheel
To the uppermost limbs, the treehouse.

My horror is not knowing the river,
And if these cups stop, do I slide
The trunk barefoot, ripping my soles on bark,
Or free fall and give it to God
Who knows the sparrow and the lark?

MJM '92 SF

Lordy, Lo! What Have I Done to Yous?

I've lost all taste for life, I'm all complaints
Tell me why do you starve the faithful? Why do you crucify the saints?
And you let the wicked prosper, You let their children frisk like deer,
And my loves are dead or dying, or they don't come near.

– J. Mitchell

Bifurcated, fork-tongued, dual-lobed –
Mouth to bung, auricles/ventricles, left
And right, good & evil, divided night,
Dreamy, fright from *It* on high – we below,
This and that, Boy Scout, Webelo,
So and so, yes and no, etc., et alia.

Hetero, homo, bi. Semi, demi, di.
Schizophrenia, bi-polarity, hilarity/
anemia. Sober, drunk, glamour, punk.
Master race, black as ace, cody passive,
In your face. Online, off, smartphone,
Dumb, Democrat/Republican. Boys

and Girls, birds and bees, can't see
The forest for the trees, elbows, knees,
Steal or "Please." War, peace, Christ,
Mohammed, Buddha/Zen, *Bible, Talmud.*
Field and stream, oasis/desert, ocean,
Sand, Yin and yang, foot and hand.

Sex-addled, celibate, orgiastic, masturbate.
Cougar/boy, lecher toy, happiness or joy?
Moody, not, hate your family, forget-me-hot.
Rose & thistle, Pax Romana. Each man, his
Own arcana. Evolution, devo too, you're a liar isn't
True. Blank and wit. Perfect void. Full of shit.

Innocence to the bone. Guilt and shame
For bad undone. Pride and grandiosity.
Low self-esteem, ergo *Español* grandee.

One with all the universe:
not fighting good/bad fight between
Extremely clean perverse.

MJM 8/14 SF

329

Lost Indian River

We're barely afoot.
The odd, critical
Note a cool friend
Drops. The sea of
cars as whispers.

It's no crime, being this shy.
But to be about hiding,
Railing to keep the real
On the sly. Procrastinate.
Dream. Paper.

There is no emergency to get done.
There is no ladder not
Droppings slung every rung.
There is so little distance
 We would have had to go,

Start to finish one. We all merge
        in the middle someday
like former Presidents.
        Our star metaphors paddling
 this refuge of canoes.

MJM '75 S.B.

Lotharios' Lady Eve

Transcendent as the dusk on searing days,
She radiates red-hot light in her disguise.
Young men gaze her sun's sexy, fizzling phase,
Apollo/Venus' rays on town arise.

Yet not supine to middling orange and red,
Her hazel eyes and walnut locks a'curl
Give cool to nightfall's handsome, splendid bed,
That young men alt their plays, Romeo from churl.

Yet churlish bred is rowdy for one night,
Your Grecian Aphrodite licked in lace,
Or feminine temper set the rules aright,
And lads not disrepair at loss of face.

For wherein Sodom and Gomorrha rest,
Tis she re-masks Lotharios a'fest.

MJM 8/15 SF
– to Her Seductive Highness Lexy Alex, HSH

Love Potion

Melting him ignited forsworn passion,
Dream become fantasy, each random touch,
Embraceable twins joined at tipped lips,
Two slips tumble~drying in warmth and

The wind of his breath, and the socks
And the underwear roving each other till
Electric sparks bolt from night's fingers.
His smell, the scrim, the power, laughter

Gushing from him into the shower all
Alone, no cares for the phone or the
World or whatever. His silk hair brushed
His face as he swayed in like longing

Tongue on tongue in ear or on neck
That shivers meandered their muscles.
His heavy sac hung over, most potent
Pony and beau or the belle of the ball.

He thought it was heaven, a third Arch-
Angel annunciating his starred Other,
This prize to watch over him never alone
Lamb in the valley of . . .
                          Then gash! Scalped

*And hollowed out by the devil-driven
Woman,* he mostly sits to hear a still tear
In his red conjunctiva drip – with only
Dreams of you, that won't come true.

Bile bitter he degrades, *"It was the drug,
The drug, the drug, the drug, the drug!"*
He means love, he means love, he means
Love, and *only* love is all he means.

MJM 12/10 SF

332

Love Song on Rain' Day

I

When the behemoth's circuits blew
For a day's wage the bozos
Worked by candlelight & falling dew.

Some toiling per usual some struck
Busy poses while the CEO
Mauled the mail

And a bum who would sometimes
Sleep downstairs scratched his lid
With a blue-'mashed fingernail.

II

Lingering in September light
Two lovers tucked out of sight
Arouse between stacks of boxes

All around the shipping dock.
   He keeps her even keeled;
From their showered-on river,

Sylphen limbs love-clutching
Ankles locked about his locks
Shaking off shiver, he pushes

Through gardens of half-frozen algae
To a mill upstream where they hear
On the other bank

An idling ruck await
Fair weather's toll of work
Upon coal miner

Chewing sandwiches and tobacco.
As doves dream, "Fine-flickering pinwheel
O' rain spinning ferries us long

To the land of moss meadow,"
Where they listen on redwood tables
To the play on tin rain pelts on shack roofs.

MJM 9/84 S. Monica

Love's Pith

He longs for excesses of love ~
Touching thighs ensembled to tornadoed
Release in bed to peace. Wherefore outside?

Hero, he'd glide to the kitchen to fetch
Tart raspberries to his lover's lips; then mouth
The scarlet juice with gallant's kiss.

Anew with neck and ear he'd beguile
Skin to cosmic ritual that roils his loins
To breathlessness overtaking heart.

Mind and soul and spirit would body
Transcendent rest to myths – their lives,
Love's vestigial piths.

MJM 12/10 SF

Loves' Nether Double Hex   (1)

How in youth, we inspired to bear a child
By sudden instinct, more than parent plan
To truly glimpse this universe as wild –
Civilization, just a work of man.

A son, he grew inside his own bright eyes
To burn his flame with self-substantial fuel,
And discharged family bond for friends, Zeus-wise;
Mars at school, forces unkind forked to rule.

Thanks now – he's 'back,' young man, our dining fun.
He heralds jokes to bawdy laughs with kin,
Now adult, it's my wife of me wants none:
Belle of my past – our present now in ruin.

When son was prig, she propped up plenty sex.
Son fair, she's pissed – my nether, double hex.

MJM 3/11 SF
After Sonnet 1

SONNET 1

From fairest creatures we desire increase,
That thereby beauty's rose might never die,
But as the riper should by time decease,
His tender heir might bear his memory:
But thou, contracted to thine own bright eyes,
Feed'st thy light's flame with self-substantial fuel,
Making a famine where abundance lies,
Thyself thy foe, to thy sweet self too cruel.
Thou that art now the world's fresh ornament
And only herald to the gaudy spring,
Within thine own bud buriest thy content
And, tender churl, makest waste in niggarding.
Pity the world, or else this glutton be,
To eat the world's due, by the grave and thee.

Note: My 'Sonnet 1: That Love Nether Double Hex' is an example of what I will call an MJM 'overwrite' of an SS. As one can see, I simply use the SS as a template for subject, rhythm, imagery, rhyme, verbiage, etc. – to greater or lesser extents – in order to write *over* it, an original poetic composition of my own. The degrees of mimesis I deployed from the SS in all their various dimensions – and, thereafter, carried into my poetic imitations – were randomly and variously graded and skewed, faithful to faithless.

It is interesting to note that my own theme of child-bearing inciting frigidity and alienation between a parenting couple is one that SH will himself attest to in his own marriage with Ann Hathaway. In the course of the PS, he will say that his wife went sexually cold on him after the birth of their three children. He will also claim that her sexual indifference infuriated him – made worse by her simultaneously acquired Protestant fervor: what we call today, 'evangelical fundamentalism.' He even declares the infuriating number of times she allows pastors to hold prayer meetings at their house!

The actual SS 1 can be read as a foreboding of the larger PS, to which the brief SS will give *'increase'* – from a mere 154 pages to the over 1,000 in the PS three volumes. SS 1 plays on *'waste'* and blackness (*'niggarding'*) to refer to the evil nature of the forthcoming, but now nascent, PS to be revealed by the DC. The DC is also ambiguously charged for using his own *'self-substantial fuel'* to influence the PS-DC. Is SH complimenting the DC, as in *"His tender heir might bear his memory?"* Or does he accuse the DC of being too *'contracted'* to his *'own bright eyes?'* – that is, *self*-composing the PS, rather than following SH hints and commands, letter by letter?

I surmise that SH is hinting that he approves of the DC-PS, as declared in, *"That thereby beauty's rose might never die."* Foreshadowing all the way to the last PS 154, SH says in SS 1 that the DC 'makes waste' (a double meaning) in 'blackening' the SS into their corresponding PS – not because the PS are not SH-indicated, but because <u>within</u> <u>them</u> (= *'thine own bud'* = 'buddy, baddy, beddy, body, bawdy, booty,' etc.) will be *buried,* in turn, the *female* PS – commanded into being by SH, but not *until* PS 154! How could a DC have made up the 'male' PS-DC and then fabricate a call for a new female cycle?

Because PS 150 is the only DC that I did out of sequence – *after* PS 154 and its SH call to bigender all my DC-PS into a new, 'female' cycle – PS 150 is my only realization of an actualized 'female PS-DC.' Did I find 'her' because 'she' was lexicographically inherent in SS 150? Or, did I find her only because I was told to look for female content *in the wake of PS* 154? Either way, if the PS are 'a waste [of time],' not just 'waste' = *'merde, alors,'* then it is SH, himself, who has wasted *our* time, yours *and* mine, by his having lead the DC into *niggarding*/blackening his SS, in the first place – as stated in:

> *Thou that art now the world's fresh ornament*
> *And only herald to the gaudy spring,*
> *Within thine own bud buriest thy content*
> *And, tender churl, makest waste in niggarding.*

Note: front verts in the *ibid* stanza = 'a twat!' *and* 'what a [double] AA twat, at <u>that</u>' ← both "<u>H</u>" insinuate themselves into the given "TAWA," *silently*. Since "H" will come to be SH code for a heroic couplet and/ or heroic "couple" throughout the entire DC process, SH is already jesting that he has silently implanted both PS-male and PS-female cycles of 154 DC each, into his 154 SS. This book only deals with the PS-male cycle, except for PS 154, in which the call for a female cycle is finally elucidated via SH hints and commands, and except for PS 150, which as stated, I did out of chronological order – as the last of all my DC – therein following SH orders in PS 154 to DC now for female content, and thereby to start another entire female cycle of 154 second-generation DC! I'll leave that to another slave DC or to another slavish day.

Luxe, calme, et volupté

The first hotels, all on the companies, were luxe and voluptuous.
Calm, he didn't need, since he ran the business on verve and talent.
Now the hotels, all on you through our divorce, are mean and corroded,
And I need Calm just to not jump out of my own skin, no job to rise to.

You were only beauty, brashness and ease. No, I take that back.
You were also the better banker, businessman and class climber,
And I was attracted to that way I could see you'd take care of me
Like my own mother did my crazy, ballsy father who Gambled.

   If my favorite childhood movie was *Gone with the Wind*,
Then you looked like Scarlett, exactly really, but operated like Belle
 – all the Graces to loved ones and the Furies to god-help-the-others.
No to mention, she'd only talk inside carriages soundproofed by plush.

In the end, we all come out like Rhett and Scarlett, knowing
We've had a part in each other's resentments and our own in ours.
Who gets to check into The Hotel California lovely place when
The money comes back, and who repairs perforce to Nokandú?

MJM 7/10 SF

M-Damned

He pined to near him outside his house, wherein he might smell
M's fragrance in his chamber or drifting through cozy rooms.
As he skirted his driveway, he stopped to nose-nuzzle M's
Carnation beds. White, their spice shocked a feral delight,

And he vivified that wild, cinnamon-inflected bloom to be
M's own pepper-and-clove nape scent dript on ticklish
Flesh at M's angelic ears. Warmth inside, he wiggled as close
As he dare to M's lithe, slouched, athletic body on the sofa.

He stared in awe at M's shy mien, hero caged indoors to jit-
Ters, yet cool and brave serene with porcelain-fragile poise.
He beheld M's casual slant of head, silk fall of radiant hair,
Eyelashes thick and long, café-brown, his nose Scarlett-fined.

"Oh my god. You look like Garbo!" he camped, and M took
The jab ardently in the know, inwardly bashful, now broken
Open to grin at last at this feisty, voluble friend who knew so
Much about Hollywood and so nervy, never met a stranger.

As M gyroscoped around the zest and audacity of this new
Crush, the other delved, toe-tipping and lapping M's broody
Piscean waters, so that Narcissus' reflection in that mirror-
Sheen transformed into his lover's. He made Martian jokes

In those onomatopoeic tongues of jest that only descend up-
On adolescents – *ad hoc* lingtastic twisters M peeled over and
More over. Suddenly, he dazed on M's Paul-Newman teeth.
Again in a bulb's flash he conjures *Ninotchka!* "Garbo laughs!"

This sphinx, his M animated by this reflex peer and mate who
Wisteria-in-mist nostalgic explodes recollecting M at granny's
House when they were little boys! M's mother, his secret lover,
del Sarto *flamenca* in high study with his castanetted uncle.

The click, his gasp, the current this sorcered up and down
His spine-tongued neck, his own ears flushed, and he re-
Membered eight-year-old M in his lad-plaid shirt buttoned
Up to the neck, even at the beach that summer they swam –

Then parted ways, wicked bifurcation to rival middle schools.
Re-braided, in his Camelot-virgin heart he dubs M, Knight,
His Lancelot – love at grasp! or sundered, lest M incline
To the manhood of his father's gutsy, beer-imbibing rake.

The duets and days zigzagged in an utterly rich, consuming
Adulation of this pet, his beauteous boy, "My Best Friend
M," romantic, a scholar, dim dreamy, and boon a split-end
Star at high-school football matches, where he sat President

Shouting rallies to bleats, throat-hoarse on shifty bleachers.
Grandstanding, fans sensed his haunts of adoration, and man-
Y girls abounded jealous of their pairing. Game after game,
They lavished M with their faux-frail chirps and charms.

Lusting, they scrutinized and mimicked how his hexy other
Half would tease that gallant, withdrawn beau out of his mystic
Lamp. Harridan harlots, they turned up their skirts behind
M's shed. And he led them by instinct and Braille to his bed.

Tossed-off Palinurus, he espied M's dark lady with that
Demure the recently fucked tuck in their dimples, as
Mad, he stayed to staunch her. Bullet to heart, raked in
Stomach, brained to fever, he shot onto the scene like

A startled, vile, headstrong dragonfly that swoops right
To eye level, staring one down, fearless and pissed,
Black marbles en-orbing the pug-nosed buzzard, nostrils
Aflare. Then he fled the size of that bear he'd attacked

And darted away, fast winging it to fizzle on a solo lily.
Now agonized and bulimic with M, he heaved up every
Day's lunch in the stalls of their fast-food joints, lady
Lazarus dead divorced revives on M's Tahitian island

Where the two of them would live again co-fetal as before.
   Lance and Guinevere, Gable and Lombard, Spence
And Kate, Garbo to her adoring public, "I vant to live
Alone (with him)," alabaster M would say, turning his

Back on cheaper times to an age of boyish love for his only
Bosom bud. Alas, M. Garbo fled with girl, not answering
Rotary phone in the days before message recorders. He stewed
Tar-bound in angst gut under, flying mind over sea-volcanic

Flares' vomits of lava. He would never again hear from M.
"You made a pass at me." He convulsed, he stabbed dead
Dreams on steeds to a pity of being alive. Faint, he went to M's
Funeral, where his magnificent loss eclipsed all the others' . . .

He gasped, he choked, he lied, he spied, he ached, he died.
The noose crammed down his esophagus each time he
Passed undedicated, distant M by his locker – with a new
Belle or two – still stickered with labels of his passion – he'd

Replace with hot inhales of oil of THC, smoking amnesia
Anesthesia by a lower companion who looked like a hound,
Skinny head, thin body, and a big mole on his face like
An in-bred spot on Fido. He drugged and jaundiced,

Love's flush and thrill gone sallow, and for the next
Thirty forty years the porn to pain to panic to self-pity
Annihilated, like Orpheus in hell, wretched Apollo, his
Adonis M. traded by gainful youth to dread husband.

MJM 8/76 S.B. – 12/10 SF

> *"To burn with desire and keep quiet about it*
> *is the greatest punishment we can bring on ourselves."*
> > —Federico García Lorca

M'Canned Beer Blues

Ain't nobody wanna know ya
  When you headed to AA
Ain't nobody wanna know ya
  When you headed to AA

All them friends you fed and partied –
  They *so* OK you out the way.

Now, nobody wanna see you, baby
  If ya ain't the one to pay
Now, nobody wanna see you, baby
  If ya ain't the one to pay

All them times you picked the tab up
Ain't coming 'round again repaid.

I gotta sit here
With my canned beer

Gotta live 'lone
With dat blank phone

Gotta tune in
To the TV

And forget you
Can forslake me

Cause . . . .

Ain't nobody wanna know ya
  When you headed to AA

Naw, ain't nobody wanna know ya
  When you headed to AA

All those friends you fed and partied
Now they pray, "We gotta get away."

Gonna sit here
With my canned beer

Gonna live 'lone
With dat blank phone
Gonna tune in
To the TV

And forget you
Could forslake me

Cause . . . .

Ain't nobody wanna know ya
  When you headed to AA

All those friends you fed and partied
  They sez, "Man, find another way to play."

MJM 7/10 SF

M's Crush on Sober

Clear 'n bright, down to fighting weight
Bodies ring bells, and meds you sought to sate
Pugnose the face, allergic from throat
To butt. Neurotransmitters jitter and float

Good vibes morning noon and night
Not just in too-rare collisions with outta-sight
Sex. But that puberty ache: naked him in the gym
Cuts to 30-inch high-school waist and him

You lusted for in a phys-ed shower –
Hard right in this bed of equipoise and power.
Five hours' sober sleep tunes the mind
And intuition, not the wind-unwind

Confusion committee vs. remind what selves?
You-yourself? – shackled remora-wise to else's
Diseased fascist? Scalding, it chaffs obsessed
Morning dressing till blacking-out undressed

Unsleep, as grogginess after anesthesia.
How near divine to be 19 again and every cloud
And glass and bath and customer to please you.
Your love, out loud – and *no me jodas* proud!

MJM 2/03/07 SF

343

Mahler 1st

I

Predawn tremulations; night's gnats weaving to 'n' fro 'mong
buds in the brambles. Bees awak'ning in the chill air, their
knees kinking awake, pollen-less. Blackberry boughs unsheath
their stickers, droplets of dew sliding off leaf serrations on-
to selfsame below, vibrant, their taut shoots releasing flex, ten-

sions warming off in the breaking aurorean rays, aglint
'like slim lasers.' Queen Anne's lace and clover flowers
tremble in the cooler dry winds of dawn, birds warbling
sleep from their ruffs and the gentle swish and rush
and switch of air layers cold and heating, exchanging

layers like figure eights laid on their sides, so many
infinities of discretion, smallness, and Libra's balancing
measures in wafts, tiny vibrations of brass and chain
mineralizing the morning, and the cuckoo beckoning
the horns and trumpets of triumphant dawn, yellow,

blinding, ablaze, real rays like splayed hands taking
charge of the skies, like panthers ripping the grey
t'Hot orange, azure, Red, all to all Coral white.

II

Suddenly, with violent charge, harrumphs of animus
bellowing, binding manses, barking palace to palace –
the burghers stomp through their beery breakfasts,
vests bulging, canes corralled, hats tipped, floorboards
flounced and pounding power of Hungarian empire. Slams

of front doors, the granite and marble ovations
to stallions and footmen, henchmen, each a terrifying
lord of his courtroom, beats of lawyers kowtowing to
judges, slammed doors of boardrooms to cognac
'nd cigars of 'second breakfast.' Each King in his Castle, fat.

When, vanquishing the mighty, conquering legions –
none massive enough to staunch him, the Kaiser collides,
vast pavements O'the *Ringstrasse* laid down like
slaves kicked by his Lipizzaners, no end to his lands,
His music explodes in the morning dome, an A-bomb!

Punying ear upon ear, face over face, terrifying lips, Caesar
& His Romans, the monuments crow, whose estates
Colossi root to rent under their cupolaed peristyles,
even the mountains bow:

The huge roar to rally an army to cut down his cousins
across the palm of Europe!

III

When, in the ghetto dark-odd and embarrassable a dead
Jew's funeral slinks tunneled down Aryan airs. The old God
still with exotic standing allures his people to blind of Church
and State. The inexorably muffled crimp and crank of folkish
tunes giving the lie to assimilation, no Mary here on a donkey.

The schlep and pull of a race forced stubborn, adherent
wavering to Original Cause, shimmies off the forces of
blondness, quivering
to walk in the wake of the chosen chastised by death
to the black of the blankets and the ringlets of hair at
men's temples. Oompah gives way to half-Slavic dirge

And the strum of Jerusalem chorusing in a time before song.
Incantations, chants, and Kabbalah in the black top hats
and brimmed bowlers, Romanian, black-scarfed, swathed,
and reverent holy in the polkas of people klezmer, läutari,
taraf. They move solemn single like weave in prayer shawls

overcoming the woof. Slouching toward the dirt, slaking
their thought of thirst in a second coming, somnabulent
Gift a'drift . . . beyond and beyond the ledgers of town.

IV

When lo! what inner window, shaded mirth, rebirth
of quiet, cloistered calm ~

Invading locks of hair, cascading gowns of the *boudoirs*
The feminine first cause defuses the law of noise ~ as water
spouts on smooth stones in the mansions, the felt-soft faces
of her children, too precious for school, and she their diurnal
Madonna. Crescendi of sweet strong sound, her maternal touch

rises like the swirl of St. Peter's Solomonic columns, she a
baldachin cataract of holy chrism poured down the forehead
of commerce to sog it ~ rained-upon lark in a swamp! Her
love towers above and through the ceilings and floors of rooms,
dry and aery. No emperor holds his globe and sceptre, arms

raised to embrace the Hera of his loft, the Venus of his heart. Her
appurtenances now resounding: veils, gloves, hats, melodious
parasols, stopping the chiefs, out-ringing the champions of order.
Her secreted extravagance of soul, the boll of her universal cup
births twins of Stadtrat and Sanhedrin.

                    V

And right Beside her, The Composer, the stringer of lights
blends a Christmas tree in the Holy Land. Grand synthesizer,
words would describe how the genius scribe makes swift work
of difference and prejudice. He is the seraphim of Almighty,
hybridizer of covenants. In him is the end of gore and the

Righteous glory of the eye of the hurricane. He is today,
he is now, not arcane. In him, all bluster and muster is tuned
to the tympanum of Olympus, the throne of the pontiff,
the coat of many colors, he preludes, o'erpowers, and bom-
bastic, outsings and Outshouts even the trumpets! His golden

Horns stand up and seize the Empire, every citizen in his sway,
Every soldier and lover and jailer swept up in his rays of sound.
Behooving the very ground to rush to music's altar, all trident
and psalter, all egos and alter distaffed and enstaved, from Kaiser
to slave, they lay about on couches of glorious, storied glamour

The clamor of coaches arriving to theater. The here and the now
of God's single creator. In a din, the celestial orb's Alladin.

MTT ~
MJM 8/15 SF

Wittgenstein said to his friend Drury:
"It is impossible to say in my book one word
about all that music has meant in my life,"
adding, "How then can I hope to be understood?"

Man in the Mirror   (3)

Stare in mirror, and tell yourself you see
A loner never paired to love's shared fest –
From soul to face, ne'er loving husbandly,
Your lacking courage to wait, all sex unrest.

You've always tricked to bed in surge of lust,
And never waited for your bonds to bloom.
You've touched both man and girl in your distrust
Then closeted away: half life, no room.

Be lover's gift to every boy or lass
With abandon and ravishment, none won,
And Cupid's prize will show not only ass,
But fletching heavens' graces, all for none.

Remember love is knighthood blest by kings,
Exchanging hearts' courageous offerings.

MJM 3/11 SF
After Sonnet 3

SONNET 3

Look in thy glass, and tell the face thou viewest
Now is the time that face should form another;
Whose fresh repair if now thou not renewest,
Thou dost beguile the world, unbless some mother,
For where is she so fair whose unear'd womb
Disdains the tillage of thy husbandry?
Or who is he so fond will be the tomb
Of his self-love, to stop posterity?
Thou art thy mother's glass, and she in thee
Calls back the lovely April of her prime:
So thou through windows of thine age shall see
Despite of wrinkles this thy golden time.
But if thou live, remember'd not to be,
Die single, and thine image dies with thee.

Note: a close reading of each of the foregoing SS 1 – 3 yields a SH warning that his DC not just stop after the male-homosexual DC of the 154 PS (*'the tillage of thy husbandry'*), but to, then, RE-DO all 154 in a DC series focusing on females (*'die single, and thine image dies with thee.'*) SH *mirror* is a symbol of homosexuality.

Mansion for Men

> *– Jack and Jill went up the hill*
> *To fetch a pail of water . . .*

The Victorian Mansion atop the hill
Once stood unsurrounded, grounded
On granite gripping its foundations,
Grazing goats on grassy knolls its only

Neighbors – no doubt the domain
Of some curmudgeon, allergic to other
Fancy folk of his ilk, kin, and class. Alas,
No lass, no laughs; but the shuffle of butler

and maid, and the tinkle of ice in his glass.
Where along the line of his decline into
drink, drudgery, dementia, Noblesse dolor
Did DTs shake his hands, *Agita prodigita* –

His rocky hillock sinned to sand? God
Pities the solitary. Their tendency in crisis
To gut their hollow: "Help me! help me!
Save me," they yelp, so angels of the Lord

Rump them up slumped to some doctor
Or hospital for help.

Today, the manse on the hilltop gives
For good to the ill: house of recovering
Drunks. The grandee still boasts its
Formidable façades – all stained glass

And brick-upon-brick, and cornerstones
And polished brass. But inside it's gone
Dingy. Stately rooms, carved into shower
Stalls and dorms. Bunk beds, where once

Mirrored dressing tables looked back
On no one, except the foggy, annoying,
Occasional cousin or Brahmin. The carved
Oak étagères' grains grate like strangers.

Rococo stuccos, faux over 1970s' chan-
deliers. And the mantel's porcelain-tile Hera,
reclining with doves, too British – stiff
And tensed, no Greco-Roman smoldering

Eyes, nor *contrapposto*. Paint's faded
to anemic. Couches for slouches, brash

And monochrome in Naugahyde – yester-
Year's bounty, today's imbalanced budget.
Pipes break through ceilings. Slams dent
The doors. Knuckles bust walls. Shards

Fall on floors. Or into mouths of those
Snoring. Cell phones, hornies whoring.
The old loner stuck in a well; now here
We are, 45 ne'er-do-wells, once upon

A rhyme swells, scorched and pickled
In alcohol hells. I wish I were still that
Façade, glistening glass with indoor
lights. But how the wrought-iron fence,

Now painted green, gives way to ram-
Shackle redwood planks that crudely
Bend from the weight of these hunks
Of humanity, asses slung upon with

Smoking agitations. Thanks to an odd
Fellow's philanthropic rehabilitations,

God, House, and bros give us back ourselves.
Just now tis only I, bitching at ersatz shelves.

MJM 6/14 SF

Manson and His Gang

A sudden crash: the great doors rumbling ill
Behind the staggering star, her throat redressed
By the dark cult. Unborn shocked in his still,
Thugs hold her helpless, beards upon her chest.

How can that terrified dazed mother push
The leathered hoodlums from her slackening thighs?
And how can body, knifed in that red rush
But feel her son's heart beating where it cries?

They jab her in her groin, spun tresses fair:
The broken sac, the burning hate and power,
And baby, mother dead.

Being so caught up,
So mastered by the brute news on the air,
Did I stare through my homework: at this terror!
TV scenes engraved – to map me for fear?

MJM 1/11 SF
    After Yeats

Mario (126)

– Now, and at the hour of our death . . .
At only 23, he died of purpura, bleeding from every orifice.
May he and his mother, my granny, be joined in heaven.

O uncle, lovely boy, who in your flower
Bled in Time's fickle glass, your sickle hour;

You have by passing star to heaven's gain
Exuberant mother, now not kidnap's twain.

Your youth, our sovereign mistress under-lent:
She spent you onwards, kin to keen lament

Yet, sped you to her betters. That she sand
Lads, let shatter her skinny minute hand.

Fear her jots? Dominion of our measure
She obtain, will ne'er tears nor wiles forger:

  Her short shrift audit, we will granule free
  See aloft mother pair him timelessly.

MJM 2/11 SF
After Sonnet 126
In memory of E. & M.

Market Crash

What good's the U.S. if failing money, economy, banking?
Country gets an "F" in Anglo-German, its metronome, and like
A parent whose kid untopples the china in Aisle One has to buy all
Them broke plates. It leaves me twenty-five again, earning more

Than a college pup but less than at twenty-six: I never looked back
Or down at a budget: *spend, spend, spend* until the bank rang
Screech! through the iron-clad retorts of addled ATM machines.
So I re-start at fifty, farther behind in my field: entrepreneur!

Lifting and schlepping art instead of that fancy boy who once
Sat behind his desk to hold aesthetic court, or who drama-
Turged in sacred viewing rooms, romancing and vaudevilling
For those with the confidence to be seen to hand over "plastic."

The Great Generation won the big war and saved the world
From Hitler. Now their kids *still,* like melted fat in the afterglow
Of the A-bomb that was *the new wealth* of our country, blown-
Up lines of credit, burnt bonds, dump of flaking cell phones.

MJM 2/10 SF

Matt Goes Methadone

Come here, baby blue eyes: shed the syringes
To street toughs, trannies, shonuf crooks, hookers
Phantasmagoric, lolling like x-rays with twinges
Of glitter, eye-white bling, meth butt-fuckers.

Poor prep, they'd fleece your department store
Jeans 'n topsiders, slaying you but for blondness.
By day you lift from fine establishments galore
Better than you cop. They detect your fondness

For good manners, earnest felons, sport designers
Then jip you half a street whore bindle for fancy
Origins, all like where-the-white-folks-live one-liners.
They start jokes and end throaty warnings for pansy

Suburbanites, college drifters gone droopy dope.
I chauffeur and stage direct you for God; I hope
To pull us straight back from that last scumbag curb
Begin ascent to selfless surrender, and disturb

All the dud old ways glamorized by dead rock.
Be a black sheep but *Jesus* among your flock.

MJM 07/08 SF

Me and Druncle 'Mando
(Hendecasyllables of Co-Dependence)

We're a churlish pair, me and druncle 'Mando,
High-jinxed, drama-rama, classic-neurotic
Folie à deux, two co-dependent screamers.

All my wanton life I've glamorized this sot
Flamenco gypsy, poised on a pedestal:
Este hot-house, harrowed dancer on his dais!

In sobering heights at Fox, didn't he arc
For Princess Grace? Boy-oh-boy ballerino,
Light up the spot far above other kin? Now

Stunk, he flares, pleads, like commonly wasted men!
A prude in danger, at sixty – a pickle,
A haggard hawk.
           That I was he, and he, me

Was some kind of little lie. He'd like to die.
Did I? Aye! Yai! Ai! But I've tried! I've tried! I
Pay to get better! While he to the letter

Of some Tennessee Williams' play, sunk, waltzes
Real, real drunk to hold his cups. I'll corral him
With the rest upstairs! Next time, draw boundary lines!

"I don't have the time!" And by and by, should there
Be a next time, I won't want Mom gossip shot,
Talk on dot of grim, dim legacy with him.

The wife, the baby and I – we got rhythm!
Uncle, my Mother! you've thrown *down* castanets.

[It was after a fight. The author, uppermost, owes A.]
MJM 3/92 SF

Men as Such Dogs

"Rugby is a good occasion for keeping
thirty bullies far from the center of the city."
– Oscar Wilde

He started youth gorged on grandiosity,
Ace apace in class, but hungry in the ass.
So, a sissy, he shopped the grandeur of family:
Their Spanish style, class, and taste

A waste on provincial Protestants
With repressions and good-works'
Obsessions – their heathen boys, redneck
To rowdy, endowed, but not with *his* gifts.

The violence and brutishness of the hard-
Hat mob jacked him up and off with fear,
Hiding hands in his pockets, but in bed
With *'manuela,'* the worse for wear and tear.

How jocks and bullies wreck-'n'-check child-
Hoods 'round the nation! Some evolutionary
Imperative that farmers, soldiers, hunters, hunks
Muck up errant fairies: 's a damnation!

Bashed-in by bats in Moscow today –
'N-not far from pre-historics castrating a gay.
Old enough *not* for sex, these nights, he
Doesn't fluoresce superiority, but right-

Sizes himself, man among many.
Style's not important enough to convert
This infidel – Country ratcheting Up to punish-
'n'-edumacate badass goonies, anyway.

Dr. Freud says his using 'boys' as his bottom-
Toys – thrashing their asses with his grower-
Not-a-shower, is a symptom of repressed hate:
Honey's ached, butt-cup, Daddy's sate-fate.

But it doesn't really hurt, and they're of age.
Guess he's still pretentious – if *only* sage.

MJM 7/14 SF

Mexiam (& Bi-a'bête'ick Too!)

Me gustan garlick'd and jitomate rice,
Lard-ass pin'toed beans, fried twice.
'Enchilalas' in m'olé sauce,
Piñatas and a horseshoe toss.

Mariachis in a cantina dive,
Salsa dancers, cha-cha feet alive.
Serapes around sun-browned skin.
Matadores, pinned in the ring their in.

Cervezas in a cock'd hen-yard
With meaty flautas, extra-hard!
Dulce de leche with insulin, and
mijos quien my prick'd skins in!

Cactus and chorizo scramble,
A mother country Las Ramblas ramble.
Moto and low-rider races,
El barrio and policía chases.

Pyramids and indios,
Crisped carnitas in verde *sauce*.
Chimichangas and churros, too –
But not the ones made out of pøo!

Cinco de Mayo sin ze French,
Borrachos passed out on the bench!
The victory over Father Spain.
Barbacoa in the acid rain.

Volcanic fields, rough and bleak.
The high-class way rich people speak.
Aztec history of human sacrifice,
Drug lords in Tijuana jails for life with
lice.

Fiestas with your hundred tíos.
Grandmama's, "Ay, Dios mios."
Tequila and every sea-side sin.
¡Every chingadera Mexican!

MJM 9/15 SF

Mexican Ivy

¡Veritas, viva la raz!

When I yelled, "Anglophile!" at the Ralph Lauren store-opening
In NYC, I was fleering my own style. '70s disco prince, redressed
To Preppy by the manners of Mahsahchusetts, I – crank, suppose
The prank was less protest than envy of rank. Then again, Ralph's

Fashion statements – English countryside & Ivy League a'Wasp –
Seemed contrary to his Yiddisha roots – Ralph Lifshitz, so to speak:
So far away from His Bermuda Shorts and Lauren Hutton Safari
Boots. Not a bad business call, to be sure. And after all, if All-

American, are we not that *smidge* closer to Britain? But the
Designer's insistence on willow-blonde looks and Anglo-
Saxon customer hooks *does* allude to that antique, Brahmin
angle some secret away: the more Plymouth Rock, the more

triple-"A?"

It reminds me of my own mother's auto-racism. A Mexican,
She frowned on the old neighborhood and brought us up as
Lily-light as any White mother could. She made sure to catch
A Lancelot from Old Philadelphia and strove to dress us

Yankee and wealthiah! She'd scold me in summers for sun-tanning
Dark brown to nearly black. Told us to never to marry a Negress!
Said boys don't inherit DNA from their mothers – making bro
And I completely bleached, any witch way! It cut me to the quick,

Hearing this sick science thrust on me like bigotry. And only
Made the jeers of my racist peers on the playground sound
Like the truth about little, coffee-stained me! That's when Uncle A.
Came to the rescue. Shocked by his sister's self-defeat and snoozed

By her Gringo-power milieu, he took us boys aside to teach us
All about Mexico's ancient history to Hispanic pride. Stories
of Teotihuacán, Tenochtitlán, Inca, Maya – even the raucous
Fun of the Baja California la playa! We heard of Olmecs, Toltecs,

Mixtecs and Maya. Inca and conquistadores from Castille –
Flamencos, toreadors, and even gitanos, Andalucían. I swelled
with dignity I knew was ours, all along, and cemented my
Strong conviction that Mom was wrong – so very shallow

And self-loathing in deep-down, buried ethnic funk. When
I made it into Harvard, discovering the world wonders of
The Yard, I carried my Indi-Latinity into that august vicinity
With the same naturalness and national pride of any 'purebred'

European. As I saw the Ivy growing thick upon the Bricks,
I thought of my *other* grandpa, who laid bricks in Philly
For old man Kelly – Princess Grace's dad. Her own niece
Was now a classmate of mine at the College, and I basked

In the art-felt knowledge that Uncle A. was dancing flamenco
For Her Serene Highness that very day at a party thrown at Fox.
Thence back in L.A, we all choked with laughter one playful day
When our *Carol* tagged me and José the Harvard Mexicans!

MJM 9/15 SF
Dress British, think Yiddish!

Mi Manzanita

You are a very special tree for me – Red-violet.
Your bell-flowers, tinged rosy, your bark ripped
As if by cats, j-curled, a'shed. I would wed

Scarlett O'Hara under your boughs – with beau's vow's
beau·tan·o'Cal bow. Your small fruit, an imitation
Of apples – *manzana* in Spanish and therefore,

Here, 'ita' – "manzanita." No one sees your
Bluish-Red beauty, except Matisse and me:
There is no brown bark. *Señores,* see?

MJM 2/15 SF

Mi Miró

Sex in the sky and stars in the guy
Whose chick in a nest looks fish-eye
But then turtles and sharks its way
Back and forth, in-and-out interplay

Of penetrations of our heroine.
And in space pictorial, _Rubik's Cube,_
I mean those same colors even,
Wherein a stake, a block turns tube

And concave/convex revolves planet-
Wise, solar system pulsing pastel.
Could be a kid on a swing or a halo
Angel angling for a soul in Inferno

Red, suppressed like lava – carborundum
Minerals cooling their shine to black and blue.
Now, whilst Picasso kneed you, Miró seldom
Perpendickled, and as suave Catalans do

Took it degree by skeptical degree
Or, schizoid, polyphoned wild and free
As kids choking and running the stairs
Of _Sagrada Familia._ Everyone stares

In the gallery, vaguely connoisseuring
This tourist, painter-laureate of Spain!
One minute grave, the next cartooning,
Whispers in abstractionist ears, _"Not insane."_

"When all is laid and done you're the one!"
No matter how many time-dependent differential
Equations in non-Euclidean space the lace,
Howsoever big _Joan's_ initial dream, cause or dial

Only you and that brainiac parolee,
That deferential dreamer-committee
Of your paradise/hell make it done.
Not self-centered fierce or free one, you won.

MJM 3/30/08 SF

Moody, Man Monkey

Irritable on the freeway's ground
I look up at the sky: light glare
and Caribbean islands everywhere.

It does my heart good, now pump-
Ing blood, endorphins at last. Man
is a moody monkey, eyes down-

Cast or daydreaming depressed;
or his nose up in the air, arrogant,
Putting on airs, perplexed to be

the top heir. God's not fair. We
Want his throne. The dog has it
Off so well – food, water, love,

Bed, and bone, all givens. Save
in Thailand, China. et al. "I want
to come back as my girlfriend's

Dog or God," and all such manner
Of spoiled, fantastical clap-trap.
Turns out it takes a lot, a *lot,* a

Lot to make a man comfy: pro-
Tected against the elements
and the slings and arrows

Of outrageous nature. I mean –
Discomfort at every turn, starvation
Round every bend, waterless

Desiccation. Then, once deluxed,
He has heathen mood problems,
Big brain kicking up fear, anxiety

And tendency to seven deadly sins.
Unselfconscious creatures need
No word or work for 'enlightenment.'

They seem to know sun's up or out.
But as they disport, I report. Alter-
Eagles and another thing to fret about.

MJM 8/14 SF

Moon and Mars   (20)

Your harlot's piggly face, lust transparent
Through all too-blushing cheeks, she beds to deed.
Years-fleet, you discharge me, now repellent:
Brace-toothed, her dent-prickt mouth to feed and seed.

Her eyes glint guile; call it call-girls' glitter,
Disingenuous whore faking tweener, sauced.
Depth's boy nearly picked me: how now litter?
Your spiced warmth, shifted by her vents – rake's frost.

I dreamt us ancients, tenting love through war –
Translating lips, sword-bold we'd each awake.
I moon'd and Mars'd you'd never orbit far;
Now nature's many, common ways I fake.

Did you kicks-trick me, feminine resolved,
Or orth'dox nix me loveless, un-evolved?

MJM 3/11 SF
After Sonnet 20

More Shall Be Revealed

He's a knave toeing this new network,
Unsure how it will trick him, tuned
Into the matrix. Footwise, he sees a
Chain-link fence: the goal, to walk its
Wires, or tune-in at its intersections.

Often the cosmos caresses: one charmed
Save after another – blesses with luck
In nixes of time, and coincidences
Against odds in ten trillions. Then to
Test him, punish, joke or jolt, some

Alarming force shakes that nexus,
And he free-falls through the inter-
Stices, grabbing about as if to grasp
Tarzan vines, while mid-air praying
Archangels in heaven re-leaven him.

Is it tit-for-tat? It seems arrogant to play-
Bargain the universe like that. Karma? Yin
& yang? Good with the bad? Demons/saints
In tug-of-war over his hassled hide? Or just
Life showing up? *Natural as the weather.*

He'll be *all* connected to that grid, full heart
With fate going his way. When suddenly,
His brain trips astray, and rat-a-tat-tat, his
Prospects and past shoot down morbid chutes.
Big It each day shows him signs to align by.

But he hasn't mastered much vocabulary,
Nor understood the syntax of this endless helix –
Its orders of merit & which wire cutters will drop
Him to relic – nor which tools, and whose, will
Be flexed by whom to fix the next, fence hex.

MJM 2/11 SF
Dedicated to Dock

Mosaics

I lament the earth was meant for men
Who'd rape and cannibalize their own humanity:
The ornery-evil ape insides' proclivity
To murder after civility . . . on to cyborg.

I lament old S.F, rived, the broke afraid of tech brats.
Lament the byzantine
                              mosaics at Trastevere apse,
Glimmering down on the brightly colored
Squares of apps on smartphones in pews.

      The people don't look up.
      Everything's a screen
      Fast & Slick money's means.

Funds are slow to fix the monument,
for decades, half-scaffolded.
  But lines round the block for some
      puny astonishment.

MJM 3/15 SF

Mucky Mucks

Everywhere you touch the Earth she's sore.
– J. Mitchell

Head down, focused on the ground
On this gusty, downpouring day
I walk amongst a sidewalk display

Of tree detritus: pods, seeds, twigs,
leaves, misarranged in an aesthetic
Way. The leaf litter scatters like

Found art, but unlike art's effort
Apparent in, say, a Rauschenberg
Combine, this is stressless nature

Giving her produce a toss, a theory
Of organized chaos – lace-like,
Delicate, ginger, pelt down by wind

And rain, elements and Her materials
Lovely as an AbEx Persian silk, yet
Handiwork, unlike any human ilk.

On this garden planet, we loot,
Shoot, and pollute, caring only
For our comfort. We may talk

And teach one thing, then make
The Earth screech. Why are
We, the species being, the only

Ones with power to alter the face
Of our sacred space? E.T. infusion?
Evolution? Creation theory? Rein-

Carnation? Acquisitive like us all,
I think: "Shall I take a photo, do
A drawing, paint this ground-scape

En plein air? Or is just stepping
Among it my where → my there?
Suddenly, a few feet down the street,

Trash-n-garbage *have* to appear.
Sopped brown paper for vodka
Half-pints, slushy plastic shopping

Bags, omnipresent ciggie butts,
Styrofoam cups, children's toys
From pre-Christmas 'clean-ups!'

The frisson of man-made crap
Is a slap on this dream of my
Leaf-like map. How inferior our

Products seem: wet, misplaced,
And dour. They corrupt nature's art –
As *we* do the planet bandits inhabit.

MJM 12/14 SF

Mustache Rides, Five Cents

> *"All actors are cattle."*
> – Alfred Hitchcock

They come on strong on dizzying days like these,
Peeps, shrinks, confidantes saying what they please
To wring me out aright – save me from "my disease."

Relieved, semi-fortuned, I smell 'em read my tealeaves,
Hear X-rays buzz, scanning my unmaking. Ego grieves
Pestled to pint-size. Friends panegyrize, but art believes

Me! The symphony, theater, opera and ballet where I
Wax transcendent, deliriolusional: *tra angeli sereni-*
Ssimi, my notes staff – rabblers booing off high-

Octavian for sports' noise. Midway *Mustache Rides*
5¢ and titty-toy cinema blather where Malibu hides,
BGBC digitizing "*wow* celebrity," low blood tides

Portending devolution of my kind. The end is near.
Do I entertain this allergy-obsession until "I fear"
Collapses me? Or do I stick close to the voice I hear

Say, *No doubt there are better things to do in life*
Than live, but just tough it out for the duration, rife
With impatience, phobias, insanity – or conquer strife

By giving up my host? There is nothing more absurd
Than boyhood instructions to dramatize your nerd
Then find out the audience prefers a *smorgasbord* of turd.

Better animate brain in formaldehyde set live in the aisle
Than chump cheek to butt with these abortions of style.
Bless music; it keeps me in this time game I would undial.

– to the W-Gallery gang on the occasion
   of our hideous and boring movie debut
MJM 10/08 SF

My Friend at the Pentagon

My passing friend at the Pentagon's I.T. Security Division did confirm,
'They're always gathering off-limits information: – illegally absconded
Cell-phone lines, PC peeks – even hijacking TV screens to see yr wanking!'

Viz widgets under car hoods, as in that Asian boy's, who's suing to *correctum!*
If we make certain friends or enemies, alas, we're on their list. Perhaps not
Whom they're looking for: yet getting little guys out-of-the-way clarifies

Which mice, then mobs, then moguls to thunder in those knock-down-door
Raids. Intel must be inured to human depravity. Still, one wonders if they
Insult us, laugh . . . go incredulous, as they peer at us with their techniques.

Or, it's no one we meet, just the strings of words we type, now scanned
For evil patterns of interest. Certain sequences, he said, give cause for alarm.
'There's a set for terror, one for thugs, and one for sex-crimes on drugs.'

That much, we established. I wonder if the day will come when deluges
Of widgetal-digital Info on the spied on – banks of chips, keywords, IDs –
Will cloudy to ennui, even at the Pentagon, as medical histories do in hospitals?

The whole country will run on two sets of laws. Of criminality's
Spies, so as to give judge and Congress, pause.
And too much data to care what, whose, where, or why it even was . . .

MJM 3/07 SF

368

My Neighborhood

I live in a Chinese neighborhood –
Serene, modest, mild, at peace.
Families make no show of their
Money, as do the Stanford grads

Uptown with their sharp, upper-
Middle class agglomerations that
Ensure those who score the more
Peeve an audience of 'also rans.'

Why would graceful, smart people
Social climb when they're already
There? Down here, the toddlers
Tricycle in driveways, and every

Clan sits down to a table-clothed
  Meal each eve. Yes, teens
Go their own way on Friday and
Saturday nights; but they mustn't

Stay out. Their grandmothers wait Up,
Hearing each sound. She'll wake up
Their parents if by twelve midnight they
Don't come around. By Sunday night

Re-arrested students get herded
Back to their homework, Asian
Travail toward all A's, the only
Acceptable report card to ensure

These young ones some day fill
Elite slots all over town, never
More to be degraded to 'railroad,'
But firm of mind and in *Benzes*.

On the hill, parents fly out of town –
Teens fed by nannies, not grannies.
Our rich kids are, to practical purposes,
  For-profit, illegal pharmacists!

If looks aren't deceiving, the Asian
Kids run the *actual* pharmacies – kind,
Clean, and efficient in their whites.
The dads uphill donate so that their

Wealth known may attract other
Deals. In my neighborhood, dads
Drive the family here and there in
The spare SUV. They'll splurge

Tonight to eat out together around
A big round table with lazy-Susan.
So disposed, their money grows
As the wealth they own gets vaster.

At the same time China booms, our
Own Asian kids master discipline,
Obedience, health, and career. We'll
See if decadent us can outlast Her,

Inventor and founder of civilization,
Empire, and now transubstantiation.

MJM 2/11 SF
(Huge stock-market crash in China 8/'15.
Welcome to the Western World Bubbles!)

Natasha, Patricia, Sean

To see all of you again in a rival gallery,
but all concern for business shoo'd away
in your smiles, our hugs – two Venae
twinned like Gemini in your black silks
and gold dangles. Salt and pepper svelte,
you two leave male bodies in your wake
on the floor of that fancy bar. Then S.
comes up to say, "I do love a good thespian,
but it was only that one time in girl's
school." All our time in art has made
you intercool. Light velvety. Soigné/e.

MJM 9/15 SF

Natural Fibers

His grandmother opposed plastic clothes.
Serene, refined, and graced, she was blest
To silk and linen, moiré, crêpe
de Chine, *peau de soie,* chiffon, velvet,
Woolens, and satin. No way, she'd let *Leisure*

Suits, "Made of petroleum," into our closets!
"An insult to oil men and designers alike."
Polyester and cellulose, *Lycra* and urethane,
Viscose or rayon just didn't cross her threshold.
Even her hose were silk – no nylon did she entertain!

It took her two hours to make-up to go out.
Woe to him audacious in her driveway,
Who'd honk. "I'll *be right there*, coming,
Coming!" She'd get in and stare at the wind-
Shield blithe, no affair to fuss over,

Finishing her lipstick with lipstick liner.
The mere sight of her at functions was marvelous,
Black hair piled high in the perfect Givenchy
Or Christian Dior – off the rack, of course:
"No one can buy couture, except

Those *way* up there." Her glowing rosin
Skin, red lips, and mascaraed eyes nearly
Large as Garbo's, stopped a room
To quiet. She always deigned humble, not vain,
Taking compliments as if a snowflake too frail

To touch, yet haled to crystal by gracious wiles,
And modesty, half-blushed. As he grew up
Beside her, she'd coax him to outfit in finery
In kind, like times they dressed for the symphony.
If he entreated for *Levi's* or corduroys, she'd coo:

"The musicians perform in white tie. It's the
Least *you* can do to honor their talent. They
Sure can see us from the stage, all right.
Pay them respect in your jacket and loafers."
Now he's in hip San Francisco, where nearly

no one dresses up spiffy – except society
Gals and business wonks in boring suits,
Who'll sport down, or shabby chic later.

Brown, grey, black, denim, beige are
All they don – a bunch of dirt-clods.

He broods, what murk these city schleppers
Convey to all around. Whatever happened
To glamorous hippies, city slickers, Goths,
Cary Grant, and dreamy couples clad in
Romantic clothes? The cool class isn't broke!

& the thrifts are chock full of color and cut,
All there for the rhyming. What a town
It would be if they dressed like she – a banquet
For the eyes: New York in Los Angeles.
Though she spot-checked in quiet before the mirror,

She gave the rest of us 'wows,' her glow a gift
Of Hispanic art. Did she donate her style
And public allure just to grace the other
Guy? Here in these grungy times, he misses
Her most of movie stars, old Cal and its patricians.

Today he dresses for grandsons of musicians
On his own in orchestras that outlived her.
From heaven, she shrugs off those ill-doffed,
Favoring pearls, and those in black-tie to honor
Achievement. She is fond of the Nobel Prize,

The waltz in Vienna, and the White House
In State. Of him, she yet beams on his dapper
Attire, mid seraphim and saints not pleading
For casual Fridays. She prays we deck-out
In better apparel, if only to dress up: art.

MJM 2/11 SF
To E. *à la mode.*

Neither Bang nor Desperate End

There's a wall
Around paradise
Talking about

Won't climb.
We never have,
Yet you fall for it.

"You all climb
Wrong. You wait
Wrong." You query,
   "When

Will our eyesight
Bubble, bubble
With a million

Red eruptions?"
I butcher me,
You complain

To the grave,
"The world's a tallow
Pit." *Die young*

Your parents' blood-
Tears stain it.
Batty sad crier

Set on careen
Or crammed in a slug
Carpool, you jump.

Sorry, Mom.
Sorry to do
So little time.

You leave grime
And their teeth
Grinding graveside

Behind.
The razor's
On the commode

Next to the guest-
Soap roses.
The committee

Does suspect
He can barely
Rhyme a clock

To contrive
A handle
On bald fury.

I hear your
Red embers
Hiss, *slidden,*

*Swallow
In the doldrums.*
Mid spume

And spunk
Up fumes your last
Gaming steam.

MJM '84 M.B.

Nemo me impune lacessit

*The longest distance between
two points of view is opinion.*

No one provokes me with impunity.
Logical in arguments, my almighty
Point of view is your ego's surety.
Seeing all you say and do,
As gods know the sparrow and the lark,
I know with my omniscience
What it is you ought to do,
And with you, what is false and true.
I see your every move's mismark –
Like Prussia's did Bismarck –
And what the rules oblige you to.

So choose an argument with me,
Your torment is to exhort my retort's
Faultless continuity.
But if you passive rest your case,
Then we shall not disagree –
On which either, is whose place!

MJM 3/11 SF

Never Soothed by Care

Never soothed by love's tandem touch, his life
A road of errands, isolation, work –
He fumbled thanks to friends whose jokes mend strife:
When winsome, generous pals gave him the shirk.

Tears churned, he sits in sorrow in the car.
More than friends' the less their loss, he's known no
Dark impassioned, resistant, hexed by star –
To've lived, not loved, so sadly sped, all show.

Fie! Unrequited love's obsession takes
Blood, breath, hiving drugs and drinks, death's bequeath.
Oh beauteous boy, how he saw you through quakes,
While she, serenaded, won your laurel wreath.

  She came, she strove, she conquered you – you turned,
  Lain upon her, jilt I laid out, start-burned.

MJM 7/14 SF

Nightrun

Run upon a Doppler shifting train
Who woos the slurry moon's cold
Blue ring Pulse of the wind
A swimming eardrum *pain*.

MJM '77 Cambridge MA

Ninety Days

90 days that mind rent
rant pancreas explode in
furniture fight, cops, cops
ambulance blood and shyte
hospital, locked suicide-
possessed, hex-posed.
Can't get a gun for five
years, law-bleared, pure-
panic fear and slit-wrist
tears, quelled kneeling
again, unswilled to pill-
well. No one who isn't
an alcoholic really knows
the trash-burnt body and
brain of the ill-liquidly in-
sane. How he can't get
drunk to relief, and how
he can't stop drinking
to stop this Chief. One sip
robs him of all the will
that medicine and science
to a wo/man cannot instill.
When you woke up today
you probably didn't say,
God, I need that first drink.
That is all I think. And then,
on the brink of death and
gutterness of crab and lice
wet-brain vise, I come home
to abstinence in this anon-
ymous Us. 'God' and our
kind in a *deadly* friendly
room we find peace for
disease, disrupt. Some
bodies and minds are
wired for this pitiless
fate, you can't drink your
way out of: tissues incinerate.
Of all the things we take
in, alcohol's poison – not
inherent to the body like
cannabis, opiate, speed.
And one drink is all the
deadly drunk need to steal

that gun, steel upon
temple, triggered, pull
relief to shoot a Thief.

MJM 8/15 SF

No Cure but to Recover

I

Most of us do not arrive here rid-
ing in on the wingtips of victory.
Rather, more submerged in fatal
   tipples of misery. Behold

That scabbed scrape on Fannie's
Face, that scar on Dan's nape
That wraps around and up on
His cheek, one ear wiped out,

The crab lice crawling on the
Brutha's *Salvation Army* sweater,
   and you no better sucking pipe
In this trashy, perverted motel.

II

What hell,
Suicide pell-mell
Fending off homelessness
   and a death knell

As bile and blood expel
   from both ends,
Families felled.
   But then we surrender,

Brain in a blender,
Spirit asunder,
Judge to jailer aghast
   and a-wonder.

Surrender to yelps of ardor
   To the Lord. Guttural.
Pitiful. Blinded and feral.
Until the pink room's

Warmth and serenity
Vibrate "community."

MJM 11/10 SF

No More Noons   (7)

Lo! in your Orient when fevered might
Lifts up my burning head, sigh over sea,
I scrimmage from the new-transcending light,
To haze obscure – the dawn, sun's travesty.

We have plumbed the gorgeous canyons downhill
That one sees inked by Mandarins on a scroll,
Then rest indoors for love, your passion still:
Profane, rare orbit-entourage, o'loll.

Then next we see – there in the setting sun –
His days go by without our noting age,
Still in a trillion years, his star-book done,
My duty, pain to stretch: pen-out my page.

My advance be phased someday, now a noon –
Guard dour days, till love deeps his gage, fazed moon.

MJM 3/11 SF
After Sonnet 7

SONNET 7

Lo! in the orient when the gracious light
Lifts up his burning head, each under eye
Doth homage to his new-appearing sight,
Serving with looks his sacred majesty;
And having climb'd the steep-up heavenly hill,
Resembling strong youth in his middle age,
yet mortal looks adore his beauty still,
Attending on his golden pilgrimage;
But when from highmost pitch, with weary car,
Like feeble age, he reeleth from the day,
The eyes, 'fore duteous, now converted are
From his low tract and look another way:
So thou, thyself out-going in thy noon,
Unlook'd on diest, unless thou get a son.

Note: From SS 7, it is commonplace to draw the theme and plot as this: even though the speaker, SH, admires the beauty of the 'golden youth' for his own romantic pleasure – the latter, typically characterized as the hero-spoiler of the early SS, as SH object of obsessive homosexual affection and vexation for his infidelities and changeling nature – SH is said to, nonetheless, warn the youth not to die without a son, lest he, the father –

once a golden youth, now in middle age – die without an heir, thereby dying without passing on his fatherly beauty to his next generation.

As you read on, into the PS, you will find SH skewering both the ideas of the 'golden youth, Sean' and, later, that of 'the dark lady' as completely false constructs of his self-proclaimedly wretched and doltish SS. SH will deny he ever conjured the two figures to be taken seriously. In fact, SH will insist on the primacy of his own promiscuity, and deny that any one object of love could ever have made an unrequited fool of him in romance, since the satisfying of his animal appetite *qua* sex addiction was always and foremost his quest. At dumb love he will scoff, even to the point of insulting academic analysts, who, even in SH own day, to hear the bard tell of it, were already monumentalizing the 'golden boy' and mystifying the 'dark lady' – both of whom SH will declaim in these pages of the PS as nonsensical precipitates.

My own account, as DC of these 154 SS-PS, is that the SH of the early PS *is* jealous of and tormented by the philanderings of a young, homo beauty. Only as SH finds reckless solace in orgies and promiscuity will he, in fact, gain the narrative believability that he is done with the youth as an object of his affection. The opposite is true of the 'dark lady,' as you will encounter her in the later/latest PS: SH will give no account of her in the plots of his DC. She will 'not exist' in the PS, except to be held up by SH as an insult to the 'no-nothing' hermeneuticists of his SS. At most, in my opinion, the 'dark lady' – since she has no dramatic presence in the PS, while the 'golden youth' *will* have, despite SH denials to the reader of him – is perhaps a mere foreshadowing of his call at the end of the homo-PS cycle for a hetero-PS cycle to be re-conceived in a second series of DC-PS. Therein, 'dark lady' would = 'shadow text.'

What is most important for my case here, however, is that unlike SS 1 – 6, SS 7 does not call for a doubling of the SS into both a homo-PS series and a hetero-PS series. Taken in the context of my thesis, SS 7 actually relieves SH-DC of the responsibility to conjure the two PS sequences, for it is here, in SS 7, that SH *only calls for* the lovely father ('golden boy') to give birth to a lovely *son*. Furthermore, since "7" is such a powerful climacteric integer – most often signifying luck and encouragement – we may conclude that SH is unilaterally calling here for the homo-PS cycle to be realized, first and foremost:

> So thou, thyself out-going in thy noon,
> Unlook'd on diest, unless thou get a son.

. . . in which the vertical front verts of the foregoing couplet = 'son, sun' + in which the double "OO"s and single "O"s are cleverly juxtaposed at front and back verts. Since "O" will become SH concrete semiote for 'sex orifice' everywhere in the upcoming PS, the bard is again up to his old trick of asking: 'two holes or one?' – a riddle that can, then again, as easily be ascribed to two homo, male lovers, as to a man facing off with a woman!

The reader must also remember that I could not have detected the call for an additional hetero-PS cycle in SS 1 – 6, as my Notes heretofore indicate, until I had gotten *to the end of* the homo-PS cycle – for it was only at PS 150 that I, in my original quest, was called to 'female' action. To clarify: all my Notes under SS 1 – 7, thus far, have been done anachronistically – that is, after I had already completed all 154, homo-PS. To wit: SS 7 gives the SH-DC the command to create 'male after male' – the homo-PS cycle, which *actually* begins in SS 8, as you will now see.

Not *It*

Those in my family whom I despise are low-class,
Ignorant, and gossipy. Whereas, I am just decrepit –
And frosty with cold indifference. There's a big
Difference – look how much bad karma lowlifes churn.
Might as well burn comic books in the desert!
My "corrosion" obtains from high-altitude attitude.
Frost-bit, I disdain their dearth valley from my summit.

MJM 12/12 S.B.

Not One of the Guys

On this freeway of strangers, classic music
So sweet and high – I'm all sky. Death metal
Around me, and straight studs galore I'd
Like to be or adore – giant rods a'pounding

Girls who can't decide whether to avoid it
Or want it – then prone to be sore. The good
Citizens in modest new cars – all business
In their trifocal lenses, they waver not

Saving, some day to retire, relax, and travel.
See all the places disorganized bohos saw
When we were all twenty-four. The leagues
Of jocks, the college girls, those who buy

NFL tickets, and those who don pearls.
The legions of lawyers, and bankers, and
Health-care whatevers, techies – us, wankers.
To be a dissipated genius, to bear a poet's

Soul, to have travelled the world to conquer
Museums, symphonic houses, and opera
And then take a nosedive with the economy,
Unprotected by stocks, bonds, investments,

Property, savings accounts, 401Ks. It's a haze:
I remember all that I've read, and nothing
That happened. Like Joni M. enchants, *"What
Have I done to You, that You make everything*

I dread and everything I fear, come true?"
She and I: this world is two black eyes of
Video gaming and TV horror domestic violence.
Whatnot amplification of tech-savvy destruction,

Evolving those ready, willing, and able to slip
In as 'Knights of the Future,' warring with galactic
Sang-froid. *La* M. gives reading a "D" (dread)
And music an "F" (fear). *Everything I d'read*

And everything I f'ear, come t'rue. The world
Is a commoners' hash and what's in your
Pants is your stash. Cock and cash; race
And trash. Short on Pop, I doubt I'll long last.

MJM 10/14 SF

O Caqui with Orb Irises

> – *"Caqui, why are you so pretty?"*
> Uncle A.

Now, you're my charge, poor old girl – so used to your "Daddy A," new passed –
I don't sit in his old chair with you on my lap. Yet, I strive to stroke and speak
To you, just as he did, in order to bless the air of your awareness with symmetry,
Not mystery or dislocation. We stare each other down, but I know not cat thought.

Other night on TV, a zoologist on one of those amazing nature shows said that
"the smaller cats" – from pets, right up to cheetahs, all have marquise irises that
Open and shut their slits, depending on the light or dark, like a Caravaggio art.
Authority, he pointed out that big cats – from leopard to lion and tiger, puma,

Jaguar, and panther – all sport round irises – a fact unknown to many, since too
Close is close et. Even elephants and rhinos would rather steer clear, capacity
To stomp them out, not a good alt – tenacious teeth, curled claws, withstanding.
But A. quoted Collette, the month before he died, "There is no ordinary

Cat." Staring and caring, you and I face off, when suddenly I see your eyes
Open: un-slit! Your irises aren't ovoid, you mutant beauty – you touch of class
Uncle A. always attained: you are round-eyed: come rain or sunshine a'flood –
A house-cat with 'tiggerish' orbs. Big blues, they neither contract nor expand

On their axes, open day and night to rival Garbo, Paul Newman, Liz Taylor.
Are you trying to freak me out? Making a mockery of *National Geographic?*
Zoologists, lacking observable fact, let alone insight? No wonder uncle always
Asked, "Caqui, why are you so pretty?" – he, no scientist – art visionary Neri.

MJM 5/13 S.B.
"after" A. N. (2/1932 – 4/2013)

As a kitten, she shat to and fro, thus earning her moniker – and, having been rescued by A. from a woodpile, she would treat chez lui like a wooden outhouse – but then get potty trained: yet, her nickname stuck, like shit on a shingle or shoe.

O Limp We Had

The quaking head, craving relief from reality,
   shunts treacly resentments – fear, self-pity
fantasy at any cost to body, brain, the family:
Son of a Bitch, *Everything's Real!* – to hapless heart

beating booze
bruised
by coca's
pounding pericarditis.

The bloody end: *beau geste* in a jester: *666*.
Four acquaintances dead in 24 hours.
One, a local movie-star/
comic hung o'er his Oscar, the others friends.

This is serious shit.
Thank God, you have
Sisters and Bros,
understanding it.

A cyclist's psycho aptitude
for X Y Z co-ordinates:
Manic – funny – fine.
Drugs & drinks, no *9.99* . . .

MJM 8/14 SF
– In memory of R. W, d. 8/14,
   entertainer and cyclist, et alia

Obra Maestra

As much as he ranks Rembrandt first,
He often can't hide inside the red meat
Nose and dim-squint pink irritated eyes.

There's more flourish in the Spanish,
His elegant brush rushing arabesques
Upon *Felipe Segundo* or *Las Infantas.*

Whereas Rembrandt gilds with pin-
Lights this glorious damask and gems
Sparked upon nubile mortals, so he

Marches time's etchings on grace,
As sitters beam the world to unwind
In their silks, rosin flesh withering

Until museums' costumed husks.
Ecco! Velázquez, embed lute bows'
Curves in paints' pushes, and the

Flamencas' faldas ignition roil
Idealist sweeps of moustache,
Saber, file-ribboned hair, even

Pages of paper swept with ochre
Veined black, each ailed leaf a rift
In that splay. Were he ennobled

Caesar, so Rembrandt he'd elect to
Foretell laurel labor in untold lives
Unswept in space-time by pontiff

Gravity, till last marble bust dissolve
In Rome's *fora.* Wedding night,
Coronation, *el Rey* on riled stallion,

That Velázquez' *maquillage*
His Sire's mirage, King of State.
Yet let Rembrandt scumble lost fate.

MJM 1/11 SF

Ode on a Sexagenarian

Harsh fact is, we're the spoiled generation:
Grandparents' Great Depression soup lines
Parents' World War II sacrifice and trauma –
Accounts we in sin din yawned, "Maudlin!"

Sex, drugs, rock 'n' roll, Summer of Love,
Me generation, then *MTV*-cohorts X,Y, Z;
No one had it finer than we. I'll take
Some coke with a hashish back, please.

(Perhaps, why we don't recall
Viet Nam forest for the trees?)

Now, I foresee assisted suicides at our behest
Of doctors public health care won't pay for
And forecast gloom and doom and our drool +
Kids not caring, neither tools nor fools' fuss.

We've spent the country into bust on credit,
As younglings barely make their rent, pathetic
Hordes of us back at zero where we started,
Wont to leave this harsh world, jump-hearted.

MJM 8/10 SF

Ode on American Ruins

We've ruined each other's hands.
Fist-in-a-glove you and my half of
That pair I bought you in dolla
Pride scrunched in the back of a
Drawer I have to bat at to eject.

Fire brand, I kicked the periwinkles
in your tide pools to death, the Ram
In heat, and so they clouded my
Sparkling tap, milkened by crab juice,
a pasty steam. I still stress to get in,

And again you slip in to be out.
My rack scumbling you on the
Counters and floors of our loft
Were as a kamikaze bombing a nit.
What I whipped up in sound and fury

You countered with tiny resilience.
My head would honk, and you'd have
Your chance again to side-step up,
Call the cops on me for arguing, then
Go out and multiply in the marketplace.

What is a ruin? A tumbling castle
With one *quartier* decorated and heated?
Or a vast complex in which he leads
Her at 20 to lichened grottoes and moss-
Covered chambers, cobwebbed but

Fixed up like a boyhood fort just in
Case Indians or a maiden on horse arise
Around the bluff? Or has a ruin two
Quartiers glassed off from lice so Mr.
and Mrs. Parvenu can come and go unno-

ticed by the crumbling bits, visiting not
The off limits? He still smells the
Moldy caverns utmost in his heart
While you sell the old place, submissive
To the stager who said, "We have

To remove your beautiful stuff
And make it look bigger."

MJM 7/10 SF

Of All He Loves Most

Of all he loves most, a son, so much fun –
No hassle, heartbreak, the blues. *Not* he's been
Easy – even by heroin's grip inun-
Dated, dear old dad *under*whelmed, akin.

Maverick mom with no conditions cares for
Him, his divorced 'rents suffering no hatred:
Joined alike in support of their scion, poor
In genes and good sense, now saved by dreaded

Consequence – withdrawals, car wrecks, and his God's
Blind eyes for him, unsober. O'er-'n'-o'er
They did second best, spoiling the child, rods
N'er used, relinquishing teenagers power.

He warned indulgence would come home to rue,
Having snift-drunk himself similar undo.

Now baby boy and Pops in sobriety,
Back to humor an' stand-ups' not'riety.

MJM 7/14 SF

Oh, Say Does That Star Mangled

"The other day, when I went off the reservation . . ."
– *Meg Whitman, eBay CEO, in a meeting*
with Buttterfields' auctioneers

Rockets' red glare, bombs
Bursting in air – and that was
Just the meeting with his bosses
And colleagues yesterday –
A bloody, screaming scare,
Temper tantrum on a tear!

Ask him, and he'd say he's
An odd poetic mix of over-
Sensitivity and sky-high ethics
Plus, nasty, brutish, and short.
Latino blood on fire with snot-
Wired, hot-rodded head

Steeped in Granny's genteel
Manners, *d'un amour raffiné.*
Raffish, rakish, wrong-steaded
Angel dancing on the head
Of a din, *"No me pica! Puto!"*
Must be DNA or the chemistry

Of noxious flare-ups. The latent
Toxins of upbringing and his down-
Fall, so well-authored in this hella
Church, his privileged berth –
Not worth a shit, and yet worth
And worth. Bro and he,

scions o'crazy ions.

MJM 11/14 SF

Old Man

The flames and pangs of pain
torch and dart an old body . . .
How far from the devil-may-care

laissez-faire of youth's profligacy:
  High as a kite all night, then ready
for the daily grind, fight to the light!

The brain is a fascist, ego organ
of appetite, seething cobra
as the eels on the Gorgon's head.

The rest of the body, dragged
over glittering glass, bloody,
gackled, hit and run, near dead.

It isn't his death he fears, but all deese
unwise years, riven, fatality-lead.
  Wherein not unity

          . . . peace breaking bread?

MJM 11/14 SF
To M. W.

<u>One Won, Too – One, One-Twoed</u>   (112)

"In so profound abysm I throw all care."

W.S. Sonnet 112

'Son-sewn pro finds abysmal babyism; I wreath carrel.'

MJM after/under Sonnet 112

Your love and pity doth the impression fill
Which vulgar scandal stamp'd upon my brow;
For what care I who calls me well or ill,
So you o'er-green my bad, my good allow?

Royal rowels youth: rove, dot-unraveled empress.
Candles scan dell – scarecrow damp – paste-templed.
Frau-frat thwarts skullèd lass, dick's *Salle Duchesse.*
Ogre's prole log, prog, rams imp-pimp, limp-stimpled.

You are my all the world, and I must strive
To know my shames and praises from your tongue:
None else to me, nor I to none alive,
That my steel'd sense or changes right or wrong.

Lord lurid lured, prowl-rowelled, dined land my Eve,
Tokened monk's name shows mission: tongue Shakespeare!
Nestled essence, lone tome lorn: not naïve,
Testy mystery peeled, writ sense insincere.

In so profound abysm I throw all care
Of others' voices, that my adder's sense
To critic and to flatterer stopped are.
Mark how with my neglect I do dispense:

Pro's proof finds baby-abysmal pabulum.
Timed mate masters matter, readers' essence.
Tossed rhetoric, Pan's point re-rattles problem.
How myth my time neglects – dialect peasants.

You are so strongly in my purpose bred
That all the world besides methinks are dead.   (sic?)

They are so strongly in my purpose bred,
That all the world, besides you, thinks me read. *

MJM 6/11 SF
After Sonnet 112   * 'you' = The Porn Sonnets' decoder

Only in S.F.

– *gymnós* (ancient Gr. γυμνάς) → 'naked'

Amiable Winter starts cold and ends up frozen,
is ruled by Water and phlegm, so cool-phlegmatic –
relaxed and peaceful, like a fireplace on New Year's Day.

Expressive Spring starts wet and ends up hot,
is ruled by Air and blood, so sanguine –
pleasure-seeking and sociable, like dancing in a disco.

Driving Summer starts hot and ends up dry,
is ruled by Fire and yellow bile, so choleric –
ambitious and leader-like, like climbing in the Rockies.

Analytic Autumn starts dry and ends up cold,
is ruled by Earth and black bile, so melancholic –
pensive and quiet, like motoring amongst the leaves.

***

Crazy San Francisco, unorthodox in all respects,
including sex, makes Winter of its Summers
and Summer of its Falls like changing one's gender.

Ambitious and leader-like in the driving heat
of Autumn by the Bay, we hightail it to the beach
in October and November to sunbathe in the nude.

Husbands turn-on gay boys, and wives alert boy
toys with pert nipples and low-hanging 'fruit,'
irrespectively, one season not following the order

Of proper calendars, nor the rhyme of time. Maybe
People flying round-trips, Buenos Aires to New York,
Feel the same oddities ~ atmospherics ¡upside-down!

***

We just can't get our seasons right,
And so capricious be sunlight,
What we *most* like to do, we do naked or at night

During The Fall with him or her, or her's a him –
In our 49-square-mile weather, genderqueer,
Mum's-the-world Gymnasium!

MJM 8/14 SF

Open Your Golden Rakes

The days are always
Chased away at night
In San Francisco

By his Pacific air-
conditioner sweeping
Away all sin, misstep

And doubt, rendering
The locals impervious
To conscience for very

Long. Tonight is another
Day . . .

    Daddy's way.

MJM 6/10 SF

F   F
a   a
n   n
g   g

Orb *et* Octet

(H   H
 e   o
  r   m
   e,   o

pedipalps   ≠   heartbeats.)

Poets knit wit as   Granma a'Go-Go

Crochets no pret-   À-   Porter clichés ------

Her yarns – a dif-   Ferent ilk: a kind of

    y-Finger'd   Tarantula
   l   S
  st   i
  i   l
 r   k
B   ~~~.

MJM 9/15 SF

Orbit   (38)

Why does my love stalk lovers to relent?
Your boat nearby, you swell my brackish tears,
Rushed from river rapids' run, I re-tent –
Old – no fresh froth to spume my sea-salt blears.

Laughs you craved, flamed your beauty into me,
Revived warm campfires, each eve I'd relight –
Yea, so torched, picked you – beau off husband tree –
To writhe and burn in youth's invented night.

Your stellar face flashed mine to orbit bind.
Three years of summer you and I would mate.
Thrilled to beam as suns, our two moons aligned,
    Your gravity, I'd satellite to sate.

But love, no King, in shad'wy nature's ways,
Eclipsed planets trined – I tailed runaways.

MJM 4/11 SF
After Sonnet 38

Orgy   (77)

This mirror re-finds why you fear that foul scar:
Doctor bills, you nearly lost eye and life –
Kink and bars and vile lust that you piped far
Too hard to hospitals, a-swell, death rife.

Man ravaged, the hours it held you blaze-borne
In smoky cribs, *hole*-dazing demon whores.
No love, you'd page-control butt-orgy porn,
Tweakt powder freak, long-stiffed to slivered pores.

What de'vil'ry you stroked to torch eye's bane,
In which man fucks himself to fame to squirt
Victims curse-conjured in to stretch, insane,
And rise, cock-cruel chieftain of pain and dirt.

These pastimes, sped as often as you've drained,
Will coo brain dark, thimbles of evil stained.

MJM 2/11 SF
After Sonnet 77

Out for High Holy Days

I

I went to the San Francisco Opera between
Yom Kippur and Rosh Hashanah. Half the seats
were open and it had the air of San Diego.

A cracker is a cracker
  but a WASP
is a *Ritz* cracker.

Do the *goyim* realize that the Jews
are the *salsa picante* of High Society?
  Life is just not worth living without
Israelite neurotics and heartburn.

II

There were no Jews at the opera
tonight. It was like watching Doris Day
pine for her Golden Retriever.

So, I glanced around the dining room. It felt
like *Cancer Treatment Centers of America.*

Between the Semites and the Sodomites,
Now you're talking New York!

III

With only WASPs at the opera tonight,
They decided to start at 6 instead of 8.
That way, the boys get in a game of tennis
In the morning before the market opens.

At least with the Jews you get extremes –
Everything from seven-foot and thespian
Senators like Feinstein and Boxer
To full-wit, half-pints like Cousin "It."

With WASPs you get The Links.
With Catholics you have to drink.
At least with Jews you get a <u>Variety show</u>.

MJM 9/10 SF

Oy – for Shy Kidneys!

I have to piss so hard
and these finger-freakin'
button-downs,
all to save a zipper!

If I can't unfurl my
weenie out,
i'll wet my pants,
a dripper . . .

Split seconds that
my kidneys clench,
farklempt! I squeeze
to hold the salton seas:

So as not to gush
slacks, front
and back,
to tush!

Here it's at last!
one-eyed piglet
jets,
hahhh!
whoosh¡
'

  '

  '

  '

  '

   '

   '

  .

  .

flush . . . ~

.

.

MJM 9/15 SF

Paint in Cement Sestina

That 'Pepe le Pew' be bathed but not baptized! – Henri & D.

Imagination shrinks from your art history lecture that such as fine
Painter or sculptor will always be confined by thirteen criteria, a recipe
For quality – universal, obvious fact decipherable by those in the know.
Hue, value, line, rhythm, composition, technique, ground play, scale, detail,
Facture, texture, finish, and supreme attainment of a new language in art.
It's not that you are *just not right,* but given this approach, why not be

A dentist reciting a man's teeth types? Or an accountant who'll be
Sure each entry adds up to bluff an IRS sentry, 'B.S.' *Excels* summed fine
By *which* craft of math? How could a Frenchman cook up a *policy* for art?
One can smell you're a philistine by hearing the feeling your recipe
Lacks even a speck of emotion, synesthesia, atmosphere, aura: all detail,
No sex! Even the straightest Albers or Mondrian aches that we know

Flawless measures can re-vision man in the image of gods who know
How to set every star in the universe so – that big and small dippers be
Our soul's guide to North Star in this blender of lights; that every detail
We gather will nest us the day after death; that we may kiss within fine
Music-tuned spheres resounding "Broadway Boogie Woogie's" anti-recipe:
This griddle of hexy horizontal and verticals saxophoning color. As art

Whose formal order you re-border – we, jazzed, taste *color* to an art!
Instructing us into hive cells, all you row is you know what you know.
Then a bold one raises his hand, adding foreign spice to your recipe,
But you grouse to sink his soufflé, knock down his *grand jeté* to be
Back on point, the only goal *tout à fait* hustling up the public to your fine
Price indeed: six times what your waiter-artists get, every sell-high detail

Aligned to rapacity's retail plot, art-professed to scalp newbies, a *detail!*
Let's say a bright lass with a future in music were drilled in your art
Course, novice violinist start-to-finish, *only* right/*only* wrong. With fine
Poetry of trembling, bold, ecstatic, or subtly impassioned lyric, we *know*
She won't *vibrate* hundred dollar seats: her rotary play you've bowed to be
Just a band breeder. Sure, any high-school need force-feed song's recipe

On freshmen unthroated in basics of music. Yet, interior-decorator recipe,
You match up jeweled tones of the moment to chairs that in fabric detail
Contrast boldly, but so fakely forced symmetrically, derring-do *looks* to be
Formula! What every domicile magazine is *not* touting, your tandem art
Would parlay to trick clients about your *idealability!* We & nymphs know
The way to coursing imagination to peal & appeal to slips is to crest a fine

Rapids, Grand Canyon. False or true, she *may be* mundane for libraries' art
History to rift-raft her magic. But detail dull, how birth/death dates you know
On recipe tests paint cement – *rapturous courses under us bursting froth-fine!*

MJM 1/11 SF For Sean & Steve

Pantheon

A great city, whose image dwells in the memory of man,
is the type of some great idea. Rome represents conquest;
faith hovers over the towers of Jerusalem; and Athens
embodies the pre-eminent quality of the antique world, Art.
                                – Disraeli

Lord Byron, to get this aller-retour off to a somatic start,
with a few drinks, smokes, poems, and lovers, purloined.

Oscar Wilde, to turn the lusty party to wit, disestab-
lishmentarianism, curmudgeonry, louche laughs. Cary Grahnt for his accent!

Alexander the Great, to take in the arts of conquest, empire,
stallionry, and to study the face of homo beauty, hetero-charged!

Michelangelo. Watch him chip away at marble, smoking a cigarette.
Caravaggio. We'd get drunk and visit his Matthew in moonlight.
Bernini. We'd crash the Villa Borghese, winding in the midst of his marbles.

St. Peter, to tour me around the Old Basilica, high of holy ghosts,
        confessing I took his name at Confirmation to be the big shot that day.

Maria Callas ~~ she'd sing to me alone at La Fenice, and we'd both go
depressed, shedding tears together in the *Rio del Santissimo di Santo Stefano.*

Mahler: I'd be speechless and listen, could only listen.
Ella Fitzgerald and Frank Sinatra, singing at Carnegie Hall – all of us New York
loudmouths, stricken amazed and dumb. Whence, *encores* to howls!

St. Michael Archangel to foist me on high mid his furls. "I must see the devil,"
I'd say, and he'd show me and save me in his lance-hurling way.

Walt Whitman would read "Leaves of Grass" and I would tumble
in the to and fro of his green. Joni Mitchell to study the science of love with.

Greta Garbo to inflect the tragedy of beauty and glamor, of audience
and adored. Vivien Leigh to marry me. Montgomery Clift, to whom I'd

open up true love to sooth his fright in the light. Elizabeth Taylor, to give back
to him, and to dazzle us with magnificent gems.

Achilles and Patroclus, to *become* them with M. and suffer a broken heart, anyway –
even unto war with self, that unrequited love would see him to the tomb,
instead of the arms of another, that the rest of my life be for ghosts, anyway.

MJM 9/15 SF

404

Parents Parent Anger of Angers

– Got Mark(s)?

Almost nothing you did Dad raising us hit the mark.
The only thing you felt were our school marks,

And of Mom's bouts with family appearance
You were about ripping down our sails for appearances.

The elder, I seized her bait, racer in a faint pant,
While suicide bro' *Flexi-racers* down mountains to tear his pants.

You were ambition without work – aspiration a phase.
Now, near forty, my disrespect works deadly and faces

The fact we boys were aliens in a strange land
Where good-ole boy orphans & disabused poor lands

Us smack in the middle of no relative love for you,
Nor insulted Philadelphia relatives saying "yous"

To mean "you alls," or in Spanish, *Usted es*
Una madre-fucker: All in the family? *Ustedes,*

You are not my parents. I have, sire, this lone
Alien orphan forgotten proud-eyes dead loneliness,

And my gorgeous *le cirque* life, wife, & son Lex
Whom in my manner I Father Circus Maximus.

You gave so poorly, selfish lazy little
That the memory of your thus and so's belittles

Family love, lives, action, visions
For more than life, you stared at television.

I'm not heartless:
I know all the knots in your heart

. . . of its pain
But it pains

Me not: your once-I-was-a-hurt-kid excuse:
Kids conscience no excuses.

Whosoever would mess with these,
"Least of mine," messes with Thee.   *MJM 3/96 SF*

Pendeja dolor

Allá, donde no hay valor
San Bernardino hace calor
Anti-vida, sin buen sabor
Las cosas no tienen valor
Pendejas prietas ataquen honor
CoÑos, ¡vos jodé, pues, por favor!
Y dejen esto ángel y su
Mayor Gran Señor.
Perdón, pero tus putas
Me duelen, ai, ai, ai, ¡que olor!
No sirven nadie, pero cambian color.
Son el sujeto de más reciente rumor
Pero vivo al norte, con total humor.
Mis pendejas parientes penderán 'no more.'
"There's the dumb one, the snob,
And *listo* me, here, to adore.
Open your mouths: watch the Judge snore."

MJM 7/13 SF
You can lead a cunt to water, but you can't make it pink.
Salud, amor y pesetas . . . y el tiempo para joderlas.

Perfect Lover

Shorter than he by a long shot.
Alabaster skin, tissue thin.
Spongy butt cuppable in two palms.
Blonde with green eyes. Lashed to the bed.
Ankles by his ears, and afterwards, hand-fed.

MJM 12/10 SF

Persian Boy

'Scopophobia:' the fear of being stared at.

A young man: his tide-pool eyes took
In the gazing longer from the older man
Than most, averting his focused look
Only after minutes passed – more than

Most people shy from. Where does
One gawp in conversation when one
Fears too much exchange? Our glances
Away are many and fast to set a tone:

*Not too intimate, no sex, no sharing
Of my soul.* "I can't even stare at my
Wife that long!" Set widely, pairing
Beyond the other's eye periphery,

The elder loved his vast stare. Because
His own, narrower gaze fell flickered
Between those orbs, self-conscious buzz
Shushed. He shared a saga the elder heard.

Stilled, they shone, beaming care easy,
Not odd. The older attracted to his solid
Brow and handsome face, coarse goatee
Echoing cunnilingus. He sensed his id.

Gazing straight and long, do we lose
Confidence in our own separate being,
As if free falling in fear into another's
Essence? See no ego, therein seeing?

By the end of this swim in each other's
Fast-brooked looks, they traded cards, new
Friends. Why turn askance, our brothers
Shy and wary: if eyes shade insight, too?

MJM 3/11 SF

Persian Silk

Imagine me – washing wool:
A Persian "silk," heaved, buckling,
Fortune-cookie torus of tons
I grunt to lift like a carcass.
Since the house-fund ran dry

I have no luxe van-man for pick-ups.
Toil on the heels of a hangover,
My breath vaporizes, as muscles
Burst sweat in our dank Japanese bath.
The beast apexes twice, Giza-like

On sand-ceramic tiles, its paprika fur
Restraining me back like a bear.
Now the place smells of wet dust,
Grey water spilling down wove banks
'n' slopes ~~ dirt of a hundred parties.

In the high window November notes,
And the nearby porcelain tub shines
Like a runway – I take off to the banks
Of the Tigris, where a stick-brown lad
Drowns a rug in the swollen currents.

He beats its back on stones. Round
About cranes fly, fish freak, reeds
Bow onerously, as bracing breezes
Yellow yonder blue with butter pats
And cotton balls big as Montana.

I wonder if he imagines humbled me,
Searching the same sky for daydreams.

for G. Underhill
MJM 11/09 SF

Rather than words comes the thought of high windows:
The sun-comprehending glass,
And beyond it, the deep blue air, that shows
Nothing, and is nowhere, and is endless.
"High Windows," Philip Larkin

Pied à merde

> – *"From three feet away, I can get you pregnant.*
> *Not that my dick's that long – but mind over matter!"*

Dancing comes so naturally,
Everyone wants to fuck me!
Gyrations, hip dysplasia,
Prancing on point that all
Recommend this stag to
Nubile boys seeking stamina
At rock-the-cock for later!

I told Cameron how I lust
After his skinny trunk, lithe
And writhing under the impress
Of the heels of my palms,
Tufts of torsion that punch
Him up against the disco
Tin of plastic colored lights.

He's pinned, then I slither
Off him, letting him know he's
junior-free to away ~~ but all
The more likely to flay 'n stay
"Daddy-play," since he feels
In charge of my re-advances.
"I'll eat your ass raw," I say,

"And take out all today's
Aggressions on your butt-
hole." *Hey, how gay boys do
Talk!* But he doesn't walk.
"Not tonight," he'll purr, "but
"Sure wanna dance with you
Again right here on this floor!"

I limp out the car, up the
Elevator. God forbid the lad
See me on these arthritic
Feet! What the fuck, these
Uric acid crystals flare my
Gout like some Middle-Ages
Lout with *rich-man's diseases.*

I told him it would be his ass
In my face tonight as I whack.
And yes, I told him I'd be back.

What he doesn't know is
My hammer toes and corn
Confer Baryshnikov's r the norm,
As I grasp for my 800 *Ibuprofen*.

MJM 7/10 SF

Pigeon *du jour*

A male pigeon ruffs his neck-and-body
Feathers, goose-stepping puft to get laid.

Faux-big as a game hen, tensed, he ought
Hackle back to thinner ~~ else die,

My dinner!

MJM 9/15 SF

412

Pillow

With no one to touch his body, no mate,
This second pillow is his surrogate.
He fluffs and punches it up to his chest,
Under his chinny chin's shameful rest.

If inserting erections was his merely best, blest –
Now, with no one or nothing, this horrendous test.
Sleeping all day with his pillow of foam
In this psyche ward where peers aimlessly roam.

He's got no resort but freeze, fight or flight –
Terrified lonely in this strange pillful plight:
Crashing outside overnight after night
Slit-throat gangs and gunned thugs in

No-light might is right.
First-pillow-gone so and so,
He'd be the first one to go.
Second pillow, gone, say *adieu* to John Doe.

MJM 5/15 Los Gatos

413

Pit

For giving up drink he gets manic-depression
And bankruptcy from blackout vanity to shop.
With no *Rx* of booze strange ways crop up
To make a dismal citizen a sober succession

Of head shrinking and talk at group level won't fix
As fast as a double once did. Now drink fails to
Numb his brain down. Repeat boomerang, staccato
Thought, obsessional fear, hexed sex, double-helix

Mood insanity dodge his third eye in guilt and blame
While the cells of poor animate organs crush under
Fascist ganglia and his suicides a-plunder sunder
Any hope of wellness – joy, love, status, name

Long gone like a flip through a high-school
Yearbook – his keen superiority in youth now
The faded charms of puppy rambunction; how
Absurd extended into manhood, more fool

Than eccentric, more tossed than maverick, he
Ages without maturing. In his path the ward,
cell-block, cardboard-box death fast-forward
Heaven where the Blessèd Virgin and Trinity

Love whom sure as hell he could not. He's told,
Surrender to the Tao path Providence reveals
To those who in faith seek guidance. Appeals
To a higher power will relieve you. Self-will bold,

Your kidnapping brain's on a high-jack flight.
Your mind's a bad neighborhood, not the sum
Of you – which art radiant spirit, awesome
Consciousness. You are not ego; your parasite

Masquerades as you when your cephala selve –
Untuned to immaterial non-Euclidean cosmic life,
The soulful way one dimensions or loves his wife
Not yours for the simple taking off the shelf

Of news, of non-fiction. They instilled your damaged
Wiring to form flawed in trauma, a baroque shape
Disastrous to any electrician, extra amps in the nape
Of the neck where instinct and appetite ravaged

You into the influence without enough juice
Where higher *self* comforts in one's own skin,
Feeling all right with anyone in anyplace he's in
Aligned with the next right step, not some loose

Conjecture of a divided mind, convent of nuns,
Of chemicalizing moods that evade and fake
Whatever course civil reality is about to take.
The world wants to nay and play him, or stuns

His kind. When grandiosity and low esteem
Collide, he kens no brother, lover, leader with
Whom to gently root. He's hard like the pit
Buries the little life-germ inside *in extremis.*

His potential can't crack its shell, or his yolk
Was always rotten. Some take lunacy like a joke
And make mostly nonsense of what others think,
While he was born with its propensity to drink,

Anaesthetize his fears from these hellish sinks.
To life and what others have! Clink drinks jinx
Till his own dry heaves and hemorrhages peal,
He'll out of this cesspool of self to heal, to heel!

He'll out of this cesspool of self to heal, to heel!

He'll out of this cesspool of self to heal, to heel!

MJM 10/08 SF

Pity Plato

– for W. Bailey's pagan Chinese pig

Alone on the roof, one man's cold, pure thought
Is more than the entire party of revelers
Babbling inside.

It's not *him*: would he change places with any
One of them, then his cold, pure thought would
Supersede.

As the philosopher said: One man's contemplation
Is more to the finish than all the republic's
Arguments and archives.

That night, their Bay Area stylo-chat sounded
Like trash trucks that wake you in Soho 5 a.m.
Or the TVs

Interfering all at once in a *Circuit City* – prosing,
Yelping, preening, prying, really trying to be nice
And cool and sexy.

Drowned out/tuned in, they connect as plugs in sockets
Do Christmas bulbs in July in a popular
Mexican restaurant.

Salt on the rim of your honcho "Margarita"
Has more truck with golf than delicacy of an *abuela's*
Mexican table's *margueritas*.

His one blue light, his burnt-edged acid trip,
The sole bare bulb each one has in order to see
In the dark

As New Yorkers care what others think,
No one stays in his glass cell. Withstanding,
You are the museum.

It's not that we've contempt for parties, hell no.
But Plato was right: give me solitude, I'll show
You the man.

Show me politics, I'll give you mouth-organ mythics,
Satellite-dish party of chatterbox specimens, each
His own woof 'n' tweeter.

MJM 2/96 SF

Planned Intuition

When I joked, "The road-apple doesn't fall very far from the asshole,"
I said it with that type of indigestion that folds heart and stomach,
Grinning like a soft taco, stapled. All my life, these intuitions

Girding the mind's eye in my torso, seething seerage yet to unfold
Around *Mons puny* fright – will it *be?* Dogged by vague nausea
I saw my father's end, my brother's estrangeanoia, and now your

Recovering from heroin – as if my subconscious had fielded these
Out, per se. This is narcissism, I know – but why the forecasts,
So long back, now made manifest? I have old, Mexican hands –

A shaman's digits, o'er-wrinkled. Ten knuckles peer out at me: Aztec
Eyes. What anachronism lets in-vision true? Einstein time-space,
Méjico mágico, illusion, genomic fruition? I'm the kangaroo mouse

That senses the snake 'round the rock in the desert. He freezes –
And can't let go terror – the granite, hot enough to burst.
But the fangs strike first – though our rodent, already knew it.

MJM 1/12 SF

417

Plateau

Young and dumb was always side-stepped
On *his* plateau – where to go, what to do
Bigger, better, richer, leaner?

Now aches and pains and petty crimes
Ping-pong for the orthopod and shrink,
Family insanity billabonging

In whose head? What heart! Lordly
Art World yodeling, "Fame
is a wig. Family, a frock. Power,

a jig. Love, a jock. Money, the car,
and its spare their own motive!" Scion
of sailors tattooed with no coat-of-arms

In uniform or apron, he goes higher
than kitchen rinsers in stride! Spit-shined
Lunatic, backyard bubba trades

himself to secure enclave's financial
capitalette, wherein socialites zany
& Restaurant-crazed tourist

couples don't fuck as swell as Bohemians
do: *his and his* place down in the Mission
ain't the missionary position!

He wanks, whether-ing heights via facets
of books, "None mine! Dostoevsky to Fitzgerald,
Either Ella or F. Scott, I'm not."

Hot potential with a chilly spirit,
Brittle spine, swervy nerve
He thinks incessantly of Truly Greats.

Does poet saying so become slightly
great? Though critics plucking lately
Pronounce him outplumed by Smoother?

"It trickles down to little me
in the wee, wee hours of the night:
Paris, Shanghai, Buenos Aires, Milan.

The élan of good looks in old books."
See how swell he'd fit in, foul-
mouthed with elastic crooks: Warhol,

Napoleon, Nixon, Augustus, Scot Mary,
John Mellon, where has he been?
"Is the *real me* the one I like being in on?"

   His granddaddy druids peering
Down from on top? "Or is dorky, chubby
cross-bred homey from San Berdoo

with the Cabernet legs for eyes
   chasing a carrot that's turnip?"
Luckier than unplumbed continents

Yet lack-lustre, outshone by twinkle
Wishing to be blinded by flashbulbs.
Yet comfort,   death's slipcover.

MJM 11/96 SF

Plato Pyramid

A Plato pyramid, Gauguin refrain, *"Why am I here? Where am I going?"*
Point to hope in a universal hereafter, my fearing the Lord by upbringing
Or discovering in adulthood synchronicities too perfect to be random:
Karma kicking ass or discreetly rewarding as intuition tips brainstorm.

We find unlikely wise men and true prophets from every time and corner
Evangelizing Love, the greatest human gift. From Yahweh to Dr. Phil:
Love, love, love, which perforce brings up Sex, the two quarreling or
Harmonizing if we're lucky – though many a dog in love's gone rangy.

After God, the universe, and *l'amour,* it's a dead heat between health
And work; although in this fat country, the job's the thing to snatch
The blessings of the bling. We jog, fuss, climb, fear-n-peer, squeeze
And rend – or lavishly paid – investment quest to power part the rest.

For the poor and lower-middle, family remains vital as food stamps.
Can for richer man, although on slopes, boats, and boards, he seems
Invincibly his own, paying everyone else's way and fleering relations
Who try to sway and interfere with his wife, the kids, or his alpha bet.

Per se the good contain their envy, reaching within and up for Lord
And Hope, counseled to pray for the enemy, "Untaint thine heart!
Don't drink poison to kill the other guy; *don't compare his outsides
To your insides."* Scolded, we hold, cozied by Godly emendations.

The renegades run to Zen or drink and drugs, reformers exhausted
By games of buy and sell, and us abusers said to be half-alive in a
Kind of mental hell, not born with the right neuro-transmitters
To live a decent day comfortable in our own skins, not craving.

Do scientists, scholars, engineers, politicians, philanthropists side-
Step crasser tumults, given to *veritas*, progress, polis, and the poor?
And do scholars get the best of it, paid to teach and read and write?
Or philanthropists buying art and relaying the Mediterranean life?

God, love, sex, health, family, money, rebellion, contribution –
Are friendship and warfare all that's left to discretion? Or stark
Existentialism, doing what's good for its own sake or Evil, no
Retribution from on high, no afterlife or aftermath to figure?

Plato told peoples, "You are bronze, and so you shall be a bronze-
Man; you are silver, be a silversmith; you of gold, go be golden."
How his noble lie carries to this day from prince to poet to groom.
Real Thing: a shadow cast on cave-wall earth. Light so far awAy.

Poetry

Down in the trenches
with ideas, sounds, images,
and signs, he's stretched –
head-ached and half-
blind. They change
electric charge, mass,
color charge, and spin
like quarks. Does my
lack of control make
them quirky turkeys?
And does controlling
them, therefore, vie
'em immortal works?
Syntax is so taxing.
At least in poetry
it rushes around
smooth stones in a
cliff river-stream like
seen at Yosemite ~
no up or down, just
randomly over, under
around mid-spume
and roil.

Last year, a tragic youth
ignored the rangers'
sign, and stepped into
that boiling rush; slip
slipt on a rock and below
was crushed – *loss to
his parents a pity beyond
fathom.* I want to stay
on the bank and observe
the signs, but how can I
when art and fate are
most oft off-rhymes?
My poems, I'd like to
see them known *now
and then* when I'm aloft.
But to bring back the lad;
that's a masterwork of
which I am incapable,
only being a Dad. Re-
surrection is beyond me.

And I don't have to be
a wordsmith to rhyme
myself there sad.

MJM 8/15 SF

Ponderous Sky

No more moored in the heat of the night,
Room and mood in my room, June-gloom's
Alabaster, dove-grey vaporous dome
Soothes the inferno . . . lofty slathering fog
a soft powder . . . as when higher-class
Weather plumes through Bay windows,
June blooms wet October witch's broom,
Skittering the sky on grainy upside-down
Carrara floors glowing moon in a Pacific
Heights palace. I can marry this day –
Cool as a bride groom with grey eyes,
Creamy crêpe de Chine coat, and bow tie.

MJM 6/13 S.B.

Porch Light

Amusement, not your forte, *per se*, yet you were a party boy –
Spawn of the Muses: painter, dancer, architect, writer, handy-man
Sculptor, like your famous great-cousin Manuel Neri. One wants
To say Renaissance man – and yet, you were *so* against clichés,
I cannot memorialize you that way, ancient Greeks be hanged.

Tonight, out on your patio in the porch light, I suddenly saw
A shaft of light, beaming from the spiral bulb, now commended
By law – not those incandescent ones we were born under, nor
The candles that lighted every room, our every meal, as if we were
Ever lodging in Segovia in a tavern in the golden age of Spain.

The beam, naturally, nothing more than a reflection off of my
Smudgy eyeglasses – at least to scientists – then vectored
Into two, the one on the left, wider than the right one, whose
finesse, I took to be a metaphor for 'little me' – and your thicker
One, a ray more robust with wisdom, yet blunted by death's blur.

Is this "V" – of which, when I blinked, the thin side disappearing,
Only to reappear, as I concentrated on you: all visuality – also
Only a stupid cliché? – "V" for victory, alas, even Queen Victoria,
After whom you had old, grand manners and never swore?
Or am I just an illusionist, full of eyesore at your death:

Just now, manic moron, melancholy baby, even a bore
To someone who always lived under the radar
But above the stars, onstage in your strange calling
To Flamenco. No one knows where that word comes from
But I came from you, and now your spirit goggles my glasses.

MJM 4/13 S.B.
Nursed by a nephew for four months, he died 4/12/13

1932   **A. N.**   2013

Artistic scion of San Bernardino, Hollywood hidalgo and flamenco maestro – Sevilla to Santa
Barbara – ballroom ballerino *primo assoluto,* he thundered the floorboards of world stages,
mastering manifold arts with versatility and aplomb – even as he shone with wit and acid
amid a constellation of ardent students and comrades in brilliance.

Here rests A. X. N.. While he danced, fluid Terpsichore feared he might outmove her.
Now – him stilled – she fears she, too, might falter.

Potted Palm

Settling in at forty is like throwing in the towel
No more three-day, snort-induced erections
No more boho cronies resurrecting "Howl."

He knows he ought for joy to jog, re-encapsulate
His youth with *Metamucil,* but he's an addict
Dining in a red wine fog. Here's what he ate:

Ten years of misery under his parents' rule.
Ten years of sycophancy, teachers' tool.
Ten years of puberty tortured he was gay.

Ten years' pseudo-notoriety in smoggy East L.A.
Four years, Harvard's pet lower-upper loser.
Four years on minimum wage – a snoozer.

Waiter, busboy, writer, European gigolo who
Por fin gave himself the gift of San Francisco.
First time in a go-go economy, Alfa Romeo

With money's buzz, albeit lower-middle ego
Eating crow, fell in love, fucked hard,
Did/do credit card and rent and mortgage

Now he has his own backyard.
Then this mid-life crisis: fat and neutered
By a gorgeous wife who loves the bourgeois life,

Or by booze, or fear of *San Bernardino* strife.
Yet Cabots and Lodges take their doses – see,
Some even have red, spider-veins on their noses!

Of course, those larger than life are blue.
"Me too! Me too!" Oh, the unexamined path,
The dumb poet's and poor rebel's wrath.

Oh, the humiliation of not being rich and thin
And famous in the media, wannabe, wannabe.
The boring way a one-star life gets short shrift

In encyclopedia Who's Not Who, but *brief!*
So he settles for a recorded message
That his son at eight is wonderful

To have over for the night. Is just being
A good father his good fight? Or will he find the might
To get "A's" and win again, right?

Or Zen anonymity to see ahead into the light?
Poor soul, is he to philanthropize some plight?
Or plot against the buck's and body's blight?

Or is he already blessed and done
And re-loading for a second sight? The way
Nature works, one feels like an old hag.

Not a fag, college gag, youthful drag, island jag:
Just an old bag of wind and water praying to God the Pater
As the nuns said he should, since this life on earth

Doesn't matter. "Hail, Mary, full of grace,
I don't comprehend my face and certainly
Don't understand the human race.

"Where's my Oscar? Where's the pace?
Yo, forty Shorty, I do not like this ordinary place."
Then an earthquake hits Istanbul today, killing

Ten thousand. He's a spoiled fuck choking on good luck.
Butta bing, butta bang, but a million-dollar-bucked pup
Discreet charm of the bourgeoisie, so suck it up.

At forty you wanna run amok? Duck, cluck, truck
You potted palm. You might even try your luck.
No and please! It may be, there's a forest fr yr tree.

MJM 8/99 SF

Psalm to Cure the Jitters

Called to the priesthood as a lad, he flipped out when he found out
Sex was barred – even masturbation, a deal-breaker – he, a chronic
Wanker yet hellishly allied to Christ and Mother Mary, nun-torqued.

The dark side, the light side – like the earth at any given hour, the brain
With its starved, reptile stem, our id, our demons, our cravings and sins
And the frontal lobe, full of humanity and its charge to aid others.

Lust, his retort to rule, and pride, his wont, given brains, books, looks,
He scaled the heights of this material world, driven by fear in L.A.
To comfort and glamour. People envied his place. Friends loved

His crumbs. Fancy pants historian, he might have guessed how
The platinum 30s' crash would bubble-re-bust at the top of his bucks.
Mea culpa, mea culpa, mea maxima culpa: so the mighty have fallen.

Lost in the coked-up valley of the shadow of Wall Street kills, he
Digests humility to shit – lets slack that upper-middle class terror
Of egoistic shame: career, money, position, wealth, flushed out.

And without a blush, he turns his back on this world, challenging
The banks to fuck with him, even as they fucked their inferiors,
Stylish cheat, back-to-bohemian, sick, insane – mid-'40s *crisis*.

Now a market of nice people are palming out decent bait, he alluring
Back like a deer hungering after urban garden roses. Then a voice
Says, "Rejoice in the Lord, and He will make thy heart glad."

He's learning he mis-processed. He's grasping, "It's _His_ process!"
He's dope-sick of success. He says, "May I come to fear excess."
Alert and glad in the Sacred Heart of Christ, he wary to chess.

MJM 5/13 S.B.
For Marilyn and Glen: May they take the swear words as art –
Words their own hearts don't need to transcend any art world.

Quivering to Acquire

What a country of consumers bred to acquire!
Not in the sense we're the only acquisitives –
God save him who would stave off squirrels
From nut-hoarding for harsh winter's larder –

But as if *to buy* were *to be:* the national pastime
To *accrue,* as in Americans, who first dissemble to
Stock their world, stuffed, now pile up the most
Part II to prove merit. That old, "We envy guys

With more toys than I when *I* die." As if Ramses,
Napoleon, Genghis Khan, or Alexander only came
To claim, not leave behind, their kingly riches, rites,
Might, and power, gloriously intact – here, undead,

Wondering would their stakes stack up against
The counter-culture's? Not everyone's ignition flares
For fabled days. We're simply born in similar fashion
And die of all the known ways, just like despots, not.

What is it that drives our cult mad men, cut-throats
To bash friends to rise to boast of yachts, a copter,
And many mansions prepared for them? Spoilers
Like he, what causes him to envy?

MJM 12/10 SF

R.I.&D.

Restless, irritable, and discontent.
He had money, property, prestige,
Family: his lovely wife and child,
All cruelly spent, or went, or rent.

Members of his particularly afflicted
class make much of their differences
from you, the rest. Yet don't normies
Get it too? Self-pity and resentments

   Take us out to bars and ghettos.
Don't they you? – Boo-hoo blues,
Drunk to drinks and druggie nixes?
Or do you endure until time fixes?

MJM 7/14 SF

Radio Cascade

"Samba to oblivion," he said.
"Vamp a tango, or rumba
The dead dears from their
        sleeping chambers."

Prismatic earrings dangling,
She arced the wood floor,
Limbo in firelight, shade
Flit over red embers.

MJM '83 Lake Arrowhead
– In memory of M. Miklaucic, king of trim

Ramparts

"I go, and it is done: the bell invites me"

Macbeth

How does a heart bruised and scrambled in its youth
Regret not having loved, save that first, unrequited time –
Strafed by parents as a lad, his false lover turning on a dime.
Scabbed and callous, he retired from cupid-ties' untruth.
At first he stalked lust – orgiastic, criminal, uncouth –
Then drug-infused, dreamed pornography as real to rhyme.
How in winter of his sewn years, he tears, only once sublime:
Unpracticed, romance as dim a deed as pulling out one's tooth.

He rejoins humanity yet cowers as a lone fox. They say,
"Why so unapproachable and defensive never letting go?
Your cure is neither satisfying sex nor daring love your way,
But tearing down the battlements and breaking their embargo."
He imagines high-flown romance in Paris, Barcelona, Rio,
Where movies make love for him. He'd elude, away.

MJM 2/11 SF
(Petrarchan)

Ravenous Villanelle

Yea! the City's green parrots bleat so stern, they even shriek
      At ravens plying boughs and leaves like rats.
Still, in hunger the peevish crows hunt parrot meat all week.

The crows lose often, stalking tiny finches; might as well be gnats.
These exotic parrots from another land, one can spot by beak.
Yea! the City's green parrots bleat so stern, they even shriek.

They dissertate so gaudily so quick, the ravens have to sneak
Them down, even City-law protected by a vote of bureaucrats!
Still, in hunger the peevish crows hunt parrot meat all week.

Our green parrots thrive up high, where no troop of pigeons splats.
Bigger than budgies, smaller than macaws, they hide and peek.
Yea! the City's green parrots bleat so stern, they even shriek.

Exotic flowers, bohemians plant as sweets to fuel their parrot chats –
Such a lark, so queerly lavished in this town of fogs to freak.
Still, in hunger the peevish crows hunt parrot meat all week.

On and on, the crows in their murder crave these vocal brats.
Fruits, they eat more readily than ravens, each in flying frats.
Lo! the City's green parrots bleat so stern, they even shriek.
Still, in hunger the peevish crows hunt parrot meat all week.

MJM 3/11 SF
To Robert Fitzgerald's *obsessive forms!*

Re-Tooled   (17)

Who will relieve his arse in time to come,
Ass route, lulled moist by their wormy inserts?
Will they heave, swoon for his butt's bottom womb,
Or ride his rifle and swallow his spurts?

Foul, old bride, oft his beau'd booty soiled kings,
Kneeled for fresh bum to numb their dumbed faces;
Eager to come, young tops diddled his rings,
Now heathen slouches, douched not by graces.

By stretch, if decoding the bard's sonnets –
Old nascent tittle-taled tops, bottoms, tongues –
Offend scholars, youth cramming Internets,
They flatter this author's deciphered songs.

If my retooling love's bi-sexual blight
Be insane, how that I, bard's voice rewrite?

MJM 3/11 SF
After Sonnet 17

433

Relatives

The trouble with this curse of a blessing
Is he indulges them more than Others –
Automatic Cody, as shrinks would have it.
More trial than visit,

The day after the fun has faded
Retrospection *chez nous* split-
Screens with their gossip on another line.
"What's his trouble, up there in Busy Town!"

He objects, abject,
"Was it me? Are these mine?"

MJM 12/12 San Bernardino

Repairs

Smoked out or drunk, he gazes
Upon your square face, borders
Tremulous, as ships trawling
The lines on your forehead
Fall clean off. Heavily lidded

Catalan explorers, Picasso horsemen
Dribble down the sheer frescoes
At your sideburns, your flung
Limbs wavering in a black sea
Of *vino rosso* mixed with coffee.

In tear-hung triangles
At the corners of your eyes,
Those private rooms where
Love accumulates, mangled dreams
Rail his torn sinuses.

Now skin sheds off your zygomatics.
Molten encounters,
A moment ago ticked by,
Ripple a liquid looking glass
Swirled on the jellyroll mattress.

He will explore your congealed
Pieces, what few he can find;
The rest bend-bang back into form –
What he recalls you were
Before the occupation.

He will render himself guilt-
Less one day. In the meantime,
These repairs he barely manages.

MJM '84 Santa Monica

Restroom for Customers Only

In my borne days of late have I seen
Proliferate nannies and dog walkers!

I should think the next mean profession
Emerged from this procession of "alphas"

Shall be that of kid walker – say, ten toddlers,
One per leash, so ten leashes, promenaded

Down the street by some blonde WASP
Or Mexican will-do-well for good pay.

Each day, when the kids need a quick
Shit, imagine it: them all skittering into

A hotel lobby or restaurant to do doo,
Their handler, hand-baggied in case of a floor poo!

MJM 8/10 Santa Barbara-SF

Revving Cars

I get that some would tag you proles or plebs,
And today, what's more, transgressing rebs.
Instead of a spiritual Sunday,
It's your mob's low-rider run day.

I get that as a kid in shop
You majored in internal combustion
And in your own garage built cars with Pop.
I get that those who love the summer grace

Of some high-bilded cloud in sky, apace
Might look down on your hot-wired troupe –
Even as the police trail your raunchy revving group.
I, too, look down upon you from the art gallery

Adjacent to boats on water blue, a-ply.
I know that this is not liberal; attitude, incorrect.
But I have no truck with using cars to insurrect.
I love and vile in word, and you in souped-up wheels, absurd.

It's a class war, I suppose. On TV, your low-brow audience grows and grows.
While mine for poetry is channel-less
And must repair to library, slam, or press.
You like poker, and I play chess.

One argument I would make,
Is that your sport stunts the rake.
You made the same noises as a youth,
And cars don't grow you up, uncouth.

While rhyming ages lads,
And turns them into
Keen old Dads.

MJM 8/15 SF

Rich to Ransomed   (34)

How endowed, he bejeweled the gift of youth.
There – left to travel forth of his own yoke;
Here – to puff base clouds, his broiled trysts uncouth:
His waffled genius, lusty, rot by smoke.

When he fell, did You seek to sane the weak?
To dry the grease off his drug-lacquered face?
For no man well of such a paste can speak,
That seals the mind, but bodies forth disgrace.

Nor can shame loan innocence back to peace;
Though he repent – froze, he profaned to leak.
His plumbs, but mad in mind, he gulps gut ease:
He broke no civil fences, slathered freak.

His tears, Your pearls hailing joy, wonder-sourced,
Shine rich to ransomed faith as intercoursed.

MJM 3/11 SF
After Sonnet 34

Rift Raft

Wasted wishes
Unwind on the wind:
"Waa! Waa! How
   you do blow
To unfeel
   the airborne song!"

Sucker for woe
Reckoning on wrong,
Scum-bottom fishing
Other suckers,
   Would he drain
   His slavering brain,

No more blind bitching,
Dry to a coiled rind
Stiffening in darkness,
   or blow in a row
Sick-sick, life-long?

Limp-spastic throw
Abandoning boomerang
To the well's muck fission.
"How do sick ones rescind

Their babble? Drivel?
   Habit hacking one's own wing?"
He warns the wind:
"Unpeeler, we don't forgo
The cliff wreck later.
   "Now rift us along!"

   Riff-raff

   aloft.

MJM '81 Cambridge MA

Room Ruminate Ruin

Mustering, the 'kids' brave an after-dinner
walk. Flustering, I languish in untired bed,
Only to talk to you, page.

Even among the sick, I am weak and weary.
They try to stay awake, do chores, avoid
naps – as I turn into my mother, bro,
and paps: depressives capable of round-
the-clock sleep. Insomnia. Undeeps.

The hole I've dug myself is steep.
B of A, IRS, DUI, L.O.A., G.A., *A.A.,*
D.A., AWOL, SOS, P.D., State of CA,
12 Steps, *Debts & Debts, Inc.* – a *Scrabble*
 board of bad letters, H&R Blocked,
"Q"s with no "U"s – nor "X"s or "O"s.

It's hard to know what "I've ruined my
Life means." You accuse your addict
with the phrase, then nod in accord
When re-assuring others your suicide
 is only ideation.

What is a ruined life? Pac Heights
 to homelessness? Or the impenetrable
Layers of numb you've mummified PTSD in –
Dysfunctional-abusive family, seven
Deadly sins: lust, gluttony, envy

In a martini shaker, smoking with
meth crystallizing aloft? Jack off
                              love lost
                    in a flash, flash, flash.

In the time it takes to fix it all, you're
done for. Such is the nature of cash flow.
The price on your head.
The cost of living
DOA, S.F.

MJM 4/14 SF

Rosh Hashanah

A furtive rat pokes his fat self out from under the couch,
whence TV slouch Spencer moves out the sofa to espy
the little guy, who freezes 'gainst the floorboard. It's a

rat alright, so Spence goes upstairs for his baseball bat.
Poised like a decisive cat, he smashes that slugger right
on rodent's hind, half-crushing his hips with a squishy

smack. But rat does a disappearing act. No one can
find the varmint paraplegic. It rather makes the girls sick.
I know these surreptitious brats can flatten their skulls

and thighs to slip over a doorsill, as if having no
size. Later, I see a neighborhood cat, eyeing some
prize in our bushes. Stealth itself, that feline indicates

a beeline for something unseen. I just know it's our rat!
The cat flicks his tail in anticipation, not making a sound:
not even air swishing. As I inhale my cigarette, cat fret

bolts to pounce. Hard to imagine *Friskies'* kitty devour-
ing that ounce of wild snack. Spence said he had a
really long tail. To the cat, perhaps a second course to his

meal – now lost to the dark – as I, distracted by the mail
would prefer to see Peace on Earth, goodwill to rats.
Good luck inspiring that lofty sentiment in cats. Might

  as well ask Ishmael to sup and dance with Israel.

MJM 9/15 SF

Rot Title

History repeats, but not often under this macabre a
Dis'aster: those flinting hellfire to form a caliphate,
As when Ottomans stormed the gates of Vienna,
Constantinople, turned Istanbul, Byzántium spurned.

The terror these barbarian beheaders reign upon
All heterodox in their path on plains is Beelzebub's
Wrath – extermination of love and life, dark pirates
Avenged to skull-and-crossbone hype. The missile,

The tank, the sabre, now alluring Christian girls
To join, Jane Jihadi wife! Collapsing apart, World
War I fomented demise of the Sultanate. Yet for I-
Dentity politics that that Armistice has renewed of late,

We staunch bloody gyres that never blanche across
Mother lands and corridors of ancient, now synthetic
Empires. The audacious proposition this army
Of horror-smitten demons will one day rule the

Middle East from Mediterranean to Arabian Seas
Will not be squelched, metastasized ideality of
Antique fealty of fez, now re-ingrained. Dormant
Theocracy newly re-godded by maelstroms' thugs,

High-jacked sands and black flags re-taunt civil-
Ization's mand. The Talmudic striving to Israel still
Enjoins a keening damned. And now this brutality-
Defamed conquest, pitching warfare with the West.

But to some, ISIL's greatest sin of hand and heart
Is the destruction of host Islam's own sacred art.
Toppling totems and razing epiphanic temples,
Crushing effigies and sledge-hammering exemplars

Of pre-Muslim wonder, one-of-a-kind, the earth now
Blind of a glorious past, these heathens blast and
Havoc their own backyards. May filthy Feet black
Their faces and Dogs revenge their heretical erases.

MJM 10/15 SF

Running through Town

1

Luck brought day a hit of background noise.
Motorbike. The voice of a dominant beast
Arising: red-dog, tusk and brick
Honing colors on the hill,
                              mid a play of chinkle-chankle.

2

As alien altars bevy the sky, the squat
squadrons of children running reach
their low homes, decrepit flats near
                              an airport stumble.
Everywhere, trees evenly brittle and brown.

MJM '79 Boston
To M. Selig

Rx's

Depression's unromantic: *Prozac* ratchets up
Stubborn. Lush life doesn't need a blue lagoon
Passing by, *nor birth-to-death of the blues.* Hip
Hopper, Moody works the room on the Strip.

Joni, Lord Byron down in their bottles with all
The houselights turned up bright, he guzzles
Not the mistress but brain-stem science's little
Pills to jack-off neuro-transies. Buzzes 'n Diddle

High-jacked your right mind all those years
Of not knowing the extra wiring got in-tracked
From the fighting and Dad's gambling: fear
Of family shambles, house shacked, a career

Of false pride, elevation disease, grandiosity
Be-knighting this gowned lad receiving the Nobel
Eyes' ayes afore a billion fans. New York City
Pied-à-terre, Venetian *Orient-Express* car, ditty

Onstage thanks God, Mom, celebs, L.A. award.
Now . . . no longer crazy, or inane – just prophylactic;
No longer fey, or tortured A+ list, nor coward.

MJM 7/13/07 SF

Sails on Blue and White Bay

As today, all the sails on the Bay look like stately
Slices of Boston cream pie, up on wide white smiles
Of hulls. Yonder blue: ocean's lacquered table.

They seem still; all motion does from far away.
As stars steer a-still, here boats pearl-pin aglow.
He imagines Anglo suntans, ultra-coolest shades,

And yellow Nordic hair on the men's brown legs.
Often they doff these cotton colored clothes; even
Ankley sneakers like those sexy slip-on *Keds*.

Sailing, like target rifling, did not course into
The world as sport. Descended from forever ago,
Old ships were the wildest bars, survival cars,

Where scurvy to pox and plague, made 'tross and rat
Good dinner! Boats charted the world, started most
Wars, carved cities upon bays, and traded goods'

Divided labor, year after day. Once a *Caravaggio*
Set sail from Malta to the man himself at Rome,
Whereat, even the pope prepaid! Not one false hand

Lay on that storied painting; it was crated with rules
For execution upon him who would take it. Not to
Mention excommunication, though this ought be

Of less alarm to catch a thief to conscience.
That this harsh, profane, mercantile network
Be secured by an *identity system,* depopulates

His mind's-eye view of that voyage, reliant Malta
To Rome on a folkway, shipmen-driven. From here high
Up, the white peaks are daisies, petals strewn on The Bay,

Or whorled, stiff-peaked meringue, or mirroring kites
In southerly light. They triangle up for our sport,
For love of nature, for peace, for lunch; certainly

Adventure. Any which way, it's the good
Adrenaline rushing the blood that hales
A mariner's looks. Here he sits, the Other,

From a Mexican line of feet, soles adept on clay.
Ask him to build a pyramid, to swim a lagoon,
Or oiled seek a suntan on the warm arena's shore.

'All sail' is *not his thing,* too mechanical and ropy;
And he's testy 'round Northern whites. As "WASPs
Are all that sail," he chimes, jingo-bingo, racist-asp.

MJM 2/11 SF

Say Your Grace

I had a hundred dollars
Yesterday, but am
Broke today.

I refuse to eat
Subway $5 "Foot-longs."
I'd rather pay

For restaurant food
And wine by troy ounce
My budget trounce,

Parsimony denounce
On debt delay
Than eat by the inch,

Like some
anti-gourmand
Grinch!

God bless us with
this creative food
& festive SF mood.

A'men.

MJM 7/10 SF

Schadenfreude

Heather.

                                             Sean.

                    Chilled sprays of lavender bristle-quake
On limestone rocks and grounds like electrocuted hands ~
Far up, far up on Orkneys shiver-shake to sign your lands.

Down south you stood on auto tops insane and daring cops.
Down south you scared the boys away lubricating for a dance.
Far down, far down the Golden Gate survivors in hysterics

  Replay your deaths' advance:
The one you swallowed all those pills if only for a sleep.
The other sloughed off the bridge into a terrifying deep.

The mates who knew you relentlessly report
You're dead to me – pulsing, typing URLs
To demonstrate your *Facebook* faces recently.

            They twitter and flutter around the desk.
            They grapple for pictures on *Xerox* stock;
            From messy-girl purses flash elegiac giclées.

                Now I'm full of curses ~
I no better than they: their *National Enquirer*
Energy tonight has me writing verses!

Dysfunctional siblings, all a-wrought –
They in comparatives, I in rhyme –
That seem to say:

What one private tear and a hug
 from me to you would do;
We can't have condolence in the ordinary way.

Far down from far above The Orkneys
See how we replay,
"Look on. He's gone! She's gone! Look on."

Both gone, we must announce ourselves
The lucky ones, the God-blessed
Ones here on over-stay . . .

I shouldn't jibe your sincere grief;
Your friend is newly gone. How can I know
All you feel and felt in brief?

But nervous energy
Is your excitement, nonetheless.
It isn't wet; it's not at rest. It *is* about us.

I savor tastelessness.
Would I give Sean-Heather one true prayer
Far from this publicity we ensnare.

MJM 7/10 SF

Carlos,
The same day this word came up at lunch between us, I heard of my friends dead that night.
Sending you this extends the irony of *"schadenfreude."* The more one denies it, the more it manifests.
The more one shares it, the less it is confessed.

Scorpions, Self-Stung

Night terrors rip me out of my sleep into a freak deep
Panicked search for mental retort, "Brain, oh brain!"

Anything to alleviate the fright, the pain, intense, insane.
I think aspirin, cocaine, beer, wine, broke, masturbate.

Then it comes to me last and late, as I recite Hail Mary's
In the white noise background, full-loaded daemon trait

That in perverted sex dreams I conjured against
Women and the innocent to make my dick hard

On cock-numbing drugs is the sin I now pay for.
I will not be let loose unless confessed. "Hell, *how?*"

It's a process of removing guilt in dead-skin layers
Like serpents ache and arch on gravel to shed shake.

. . . About seeing the interconnectivity of the universe
And knowing that what I dread is what I sinned filthy

Upon others. Though I never raised a finger to harm
Another, perverted thoughts would steal and fuck

Your own mother, brother, or any *lesser* speedy lust
Could control and own and dominate, gorged by

Vitriol, his great big ego on patrol, money roll
Giving him the right to rape and pillage, life light.

Then comes this karma reckoning my ruinous plight.
Instead of drilling and coring and knifing him or her,

It's my own evil I must surmount and plunge in
Order to be cleansed back to the innocent sponge

Of love I was when I feared even thoughts had wings
And wicked thoughts auto-stings scorpions die by.

MJM 9/11/10 SF

Serpent Swallows Own Tail. Reports of St. George Mistaken.

– Honi soit qui mal y pense.

History eats and repeats itself until Its shit is all over the news again in the short course of one life, Russians taking aim to be Alter -It and Islam against the Israelites, whose force Be nowadays doubled by Yahweh with *arms* – Black folks raging/marching against white police, Beset upon by dogs and racism rife, swarms of refugees bayoneted out of town, nil peace, unlife. Beheadings, Christians routed, hetero animus against the gays, return of San Francisco's Moneyed ways, and movie stars, a plus, Found dead in dorms by powders, booze, *Rx* woes. It's hard t'be proud of *Homo sapiens* today, remembering I thought these things had pass'd away: Berlin Wall down, Obama elected, lesbian and gay Marriage, A.O.K. – ¿ Olé, another charmed Mexican holiday? ¡New-world's old country, damn ruthless as *auto-da-fé!* Planes downed in fields by terror – on purpose and in error. Nam-napalm, Manson, A-bombs, commies aborted child's play. Billions of good works today, and yet I see the worse return ← devolution's turn ← yearns' evolution lost o'spurn.

MJM 8/14 SF

Seven Deadly Sins

1

Envy

Like finger bones riff *Grateful-Dead* skeletal logos,
Tarsals prick his pump. Gashed by stiffs in ten stuffed
Holes, his aghast chest-chakra swamps with blue
Blood. Mortised digits rake his chambers to muck,
Till auricles-ventricles, stabbed to stew, bleed esteem,
Grace, courage, hope in gorges of loathing, money-
and-fame shamed eyes, slingshot livid on gilt others.

2

Greed

Praying for-wife's-downfall *mantis,* she covets her boyfriend's
Legacy dick tweaked in swanky offices full-high in the air. She
Waxed and diddled, he gallops for banks to vaults all executive
Hegemony sodomy. Big-ice inclined, she drips in his ecstatic
Gems in spreads for fashion and her functions. Funds, boats,
Jets, power sunned company jocks to martinis in *which* mansion?
As he ponzies a book *of clients uninsured,* inured by backed billions.

3

Gluttony

Leek soup with parmesan-*Reggiano* croutons and *Sauvignon blanc;*
Cochinillo de Segovia, pinot noir with fries, *haricots verts,* and salad
To finish it, à la vinaigrette with eight cheeses. Champagne & *hors*
d'oeuvre of Sevruga caviar from mother-of-pearl spoons; Norwegian
Wild salmon with white asparagus *à la crème* and white Bordeaux;
Quail in soy-and-berry sauce with Burgundy and carrots with clove;
Filet mignon *bordelaise* with braised chard and Bordeaux; *financiers*
For dessert with nuts and chocolates. Sparkling H2O. "*Chef,* do do
It again tomorrow, but different: and make sure we have Beluga!"

4

Sloth

Tees and three pair underwear soak in his bathroom,
Sink-sunk in bleach, may they dry on a radiator in his lair!
How handy that peanut butter and jam stay unspoiled in plastic
Jars. Mom's kitchen beckons so *hella* far, he'll drink tap water and
Hop back in his flannel bed to nap, nude and bored; his TV needs repair!

Once he took a swim in the pool to bathe; actually, he only waded. Chlorine
Stinks up his hair. He resents his rope-soap lost, and his lined-with-mildew shower.

5

Wrath

Stomach cyclonic and intolerably gassed, his panic to power to
Power to panic beet his scotched nose redder. Devil to pajamas,
He swore to *mother fuck* as before, he would share her no more
Grabbing a fistful of pistol. Stunned, insulted to outrageous, he
Hollered, then throated and demeaned her, mimicking her shrill.
When snapped, he slapped! his eyes shrinking to greed. Waving
Carbine up in air, he said, "Get stripped, get high, your mine."

6

Lust

Juice backed up, his reptile stem swelling full, he never loved
And can only remember his torrid member in conquest at pump-
And-hump a rump to drill tissue to tear to pain to pant to dump whom-
Ever is dressing to leave: he or she. Alone with dragon smoke
He'll elongate his XXX-rated sessions. Enthralled alone,
He'll tease dementia from the devil. Laying love low,
He'll screw himself to prison for life without lube.

7

Pride

She holds her nose up in the air, smug over Dow Jones pricks after her teats:
How her bantering voice uncoils her lover, her rules. Esteemed in career,
She deigns to weekend's cowgirl in bossy bed with Romeo's prestige bottle
And toot. Self-5-starred, she ladders up office escalades: such damn stamina;
Must be her strong brain! She rants to own more, macho market magnet
Exquisite. And thus fired, un-grieves her heart's hole. Deservèd, that her
Grandeur's gravity fell what bankers strive for. Work *or* play *her way.*

***

As for *Seven Deadly Sins,* surely yahoos conceived wo/men's features:
Centaur & mermaid ½-hatched to fair and mucked, god'-n-devil's creatures.

MJM 1/11 SF

Seventy Winters Lex   (2)

When seventy winters have salted my mind
To freeze-dried *gyri*-and-*sulci* flat brain,
My so-called genius, flattered by my kind,
Will fan like crystal grit, blown sparks in rain.

They'll note, "He has a 'touch' of Alzheimer's
That steals artfulness from his show and speak,"
As puzzles sap him, bereft of rhymers –
Son-fluoresced gods and Anglo-Saxon, bleak.

How much more will his comic son create
To wrangle wit and kids to brilliant heights?
Gild his gags; make the Muse re-luminate,
So, quoting Sire's art, "Ante up your sights!"

If son's humor cripples crowds to lather –
I'm alive – he's sharpt his high-jinx father.

MJM 2/11 SF
After Sonnet 2

SONNET 2

When forty winters shall besiege thy brow,
And dig deep trenches in thy beauty's field,
Thy youth's proud livery, so gazed on now,
Will be a tatter'd weed, of small worth held:
Then being ask'd where all thy beauty lies,
Where all the treasure of thy lusty days,
To say, within thine own deep-sunken eyes,
Were an all-eating shame and thriftless praise.
How much more praise deserved thy beauty's use,
If thou couldst answer 'This fair child of mine
Shall sum my count and make my old excuse,'
Proving his beauty by succession thine!
This were to be new made when thou art old,
And see thy blood warm when thou feel'st it cold.

Note: This is another example of an MJM over-write (OR) of a SS. It should be said that I composed most of my very first OR out of sequence. At the time I began to OR some of the SS, I selected SS numbers that randomly appealed to me, like 69, 7, 3, 88, etc. I would later be prompted by SH to uncover the term 'climacteric numbers.' These are numbers like 333 or 77 or 11 or even 13 that, in medieval and Renaissance England, were thought to contain extra numerological power or special properties, innately. It was only after I realized that the SS were, in fact, hinting at pornographic content, that I set about to OR *or* DC the SS in *chronological* order. And PS 150 is the only one of the full-fledged PS thereafter done out of sequence – last, after PS 154. It was during the execution willy-nilly of climacteric numbered OR, that I suddenly realized I was being prompted by SS with encoding, and so I thought it prudent to switch to numerical order for the rest of the DC, rather than my initial, random 'cherry-picking.' Alas, several out-of-sequence OR were already finished by then, so the reader will find them scattered throughout the overall order of the PS-DC. You will forgive the indulgence of my having left these OR intact, as I have tried here to present the entire sequence of how my DC discovery occurred without editing, in order to demonstrate these 154 works of DC as "process art."

Sexy Boys of October

The Big Games are finally here!
Our boys seem to slide in every year:
Posey the Poised, Hunter the Viking,
Panda the Giant baseball pandemic.

A cast of eccentrics and thinkers,
They reflect our City's bizarre panoply
Of treasure seekers and drinkers.
Nose to the grindstone, but hands on

Champagne, they mirror S.F.'s refined
Urban game: do your research, bring
Home accolades. But when the work's
done and won – party up to your name!

MJM 10/14 SF

Shakespeare's Porno Sonnets

Why lov'st thou that which thou receiv'st not gladly, (glad lad lies)
Or else receiv'st with pleasure thine annoy? (sir hind annoy'd ➜ [oy'd backward] ➜ a'boy'd)
   ➜ Glad lad lies, Sir Hind, annoy'd. [Or:]
      Glad lad lies, Sir Hind, a'boy'd. ['Sir Hind' can = Golden Hind = Sir Francis Drake]
                                                             – Sonnet 8 + MJM

Everyone thinks Will wrote the Sonnets for love,
Whereas, I see under their surfaces sons behovel'd.
I see e're ass under heir sir faces, sons hove-b'el'd.

Love backwards is 'evil,' and 154 – the total number
of sonnets = 1 + 5 + 4 = 10, the number of beats (off)
per line in a Willy ditty. What's more, 1 + 5 = 6, and 4 + 5 = 9,

thus 69, a bad-boy number if ever. 14 lines in a Shakespeare's
on it = 1 + 4 x the couplet (2) = 5 x 2, so ten again, the inches the bard
claims for his dick, diction surmised, when of a sudden

we are cocaine surprised. Willy says that London's Portuguese
sailors bring it in to Dock 12 all the way from Peru to London,
and that the king, queen, and nates' nats are all snortin' and smokin'

to lusty depths and illegal heights of sexual perversion.
He makes fun of the obvious version of his Sonnets,
and says the decoder is the only one who can read the ones

he meant, hell-sent. By some magic, the decodes all self-justify
on the right margin! And here's my bargain: you read all
1,000 pages, and I'll show at Sonnet 150-something how

the name of the 9th Earl of Northumberland gets spelled down
the right margin. Northumberland in the tower shares the same
birth year as Shakespeare! Look it up! (As I had to, to 'get' it!)

What they hatch together
is coke-scrambled regs and eggs
round donkey-dick legs.

And what's worse,
Royalty at It,
Purr the privy purse.

Ur, the rivy urse.

Sonnet ➜ Son One [Prince] on it, et.
MJM 9/15 SF

Shame Equations

Exhausted as card shufflers in Vegas on triple shift,
Heirs of debt go groggy – oxygen-stuffed-casinos:
Uncle Sam, Mother Europe. Mr. Red, "It's pay-up time!"

Velocity of money, hah! That title – *Inherit the Wind,*
Fools bellowing *Eureka!* Wise guys know, no slackers here:
What's being traded. Money-sunny-calculus poufs?

They see us spend – how we make due, high on high
Standards, none to savor-save, but, havened – misbehave.
Sheer-shaving profits, stalking – Rise-for-fall, hedge your

Alls' ledgers. From tall ships, Founders daze – remora-
Schools of nations, rent – beta's, squalled – Great Greece,
Great White Shark, a' brink, and dunces mauled from malls.

They amaze at their offspring – Yankees, coast-to-teen-
Age-coast, trounced, finally appalled. "Oh! Ponzi Scheme
Is what we've built, it's called." Our fathers would amend

Us back to debt-prison! They know not what they smell,
But neck-hairs sense the devil combing groom and greed.
They say, "Nothing unmade, does God come near."

Our people, sucking meth pipes gassed-up, leer.
Others, ducking IOUs that hacked-in viruses may smear.
As fat-cat rats, helicopter to château-solo, rear.

MJM 8/11 SF

Sharp

When in New York City, one has to Up one's IQ to High.
New Yorkers won't suffer fools gladly.
Otherwise, they'd never get stuff done –
Not to mention move a block.
They'd rather pile-drive a blockhead!
But if you ask for directions,
They make quick etiquette corrections.

MJM 7/14 SF

Sharty!

I'm a'feelin' rather shart-changed
Because the boy I *loove* said he would
Shart for me, butt then-'ee-*oo*nly farted.

Now, it's *anoother* thing to have *shat*
In front of yer lover – that won't get ya
Very *fahr* – if you're smellin' m'words.

But a bit of a nutt, I think there's *nuth-*
Ing better than a good-long-shart, t'git m'game
A'goin.' Wuss *moar,* being th'good top, eye *am* –

I implaured twink # two tuh *shart in me bed!* –
  E'r a long-loove uv'*fair* mite get start'd:
Butt, again, he only farted. 'Em

S'a *tired* a'flake-*shites* a'promising
Won, 'n' shart-sheetin' mi'nuther. I *sing*
Of sharts. Have *ye* one in *yar* sharts?
        T'a hell with bloody tarts, a'tarryin'!

Ding dong ding! Let's get start'd,
Me-self, high-hearted,
And mule a'darted – ass ewes fur me,

Ass shur 'es this pooh-et-tree *shit's*
maid-en-bum-barded! Their aghast o'me, now:
B'fooked, and sharted.

MJM 9/11 SF
Ta' Sean an' big Sharty

460

She Does Grout, Too!

'Mamma Leone' of the mad,
Hostess to the once hella high,
And manager of those laid
Low by booze, meth, and blow,

What would the Dock do
Without Sandy? Like Julia
Child kneading dough, she
Must pound and fold the flour,

But then in a minute or an hour
  Spin it, making certain the live
Yeast have all risen to the pull
Of her spiritual nutrition, without

Unsolaced breakdowns or trauma's
Freakin' fear, half-baked here. As in
Our old-TV idealized favorites,
Her *Grande dame* warmth and

'Aunt Bee' concerns soothe any-
To-all these *crazy-ion* o'centrics.
Then, at the same time, she makes
Notes on ½-&-½ and rent's metrics!

You just want to pull back her
  Blond hair with your hand and
  Arch her by the waist like Rhett
To Scarlett; plant a "juicy" on her

I Love Lucy marathon of laughs,
Cries, and panics with all these
Hypomanics and the occasional
Schizophrenic to keep it real.

What would we do without you? Not
Get our hugs, warm words, coffee,
We, all a-loss? Whoever runs this joint
Was right on sober to dub Sandy boss.

Because *He* doesn't even have to guile-
Manage Glen, let alone break up cigar-
Ettes and noise by eleven. Then, clear
This Den of Thieves,' dashing to *re-tile*!

MJM 1/11 SF
mwah!

461

Shell

Light smoker, the sight of an abalone shell stuffed with spent butts
makes me sick – nauseating, recyclable dead ends stinking stale.

But as I gaze at these putrid punks, I realize some of them are
yours. Now reviled out of the house for your relapse, are you

Recyclable too? These snuft cigs signal your DNA is actually
here, still with us in our smoking cage between the front door,

Out of which you were unceremoniously escorted, and the wrought-
iron front gate, meant to keep out goners, criminals, and skunks

Spraying in the 'hood: attacked by recalcitrant racoons and coyotes.
Your remains, your ashes, remind me of the time we buried Leo.

When we went back to his house for the wake, red, ruffled roses
withstood there in a crystal vase – flowers he himself had grown

And cut before collapsing. The color and texture of red velvet,
they felt like so much flocking on his Victorian wallpaper. But

No matter, it's they were culled and clipped by him live, now
dead, that made weird work of my standing there all in black.

Jack, you're here now and still, too.
Like and unlike Leo, only near dead, *nature morte,* all ash'n.

MJM 8/15 SF
For his homey J.R.

Shun

It's no fun
This organ of P.C. banter
this shotgun government
this backlash regimen
of sexless, eyeless, faceless
conservative dour
gaining from and giving power
to the reactive mediocre
with their penchant for lauding
media-marauders parading.
Oh red-faced religious
patriarch, is it true
your thumblessness, your ice-
cold persona qualify
you to climb their ladder?

So, non-
controversial, you seem to me
like a blank flashcard
the public will pick
just so it doesn't have to face
the fact it's not good
at deluding smart questions.
We're abiding forces
of brutality, terror, deathwish,
outrageous misfortune, and you think
what we need is school prayer?
What's that thing
Hanging between your legs
you like to snub?
"Was it not you who put gin in the tub,"
  He rub-a-dub-dubs?
  Who are those pissed-off
Tossed off slaves urinating
  in your capitols down-wind?

Of him growing up they said,
"He's a clever, sassy lad –
It'll serve him well in the bigger world."
Lo and behold, he's fallen POW,
loose cannon netted
on your litigious field
  of lightning rods and PTA
potluck dunder, thunder, plunder.
Cast him away. His salsa's too hot

for your marshmallow mouths.
His fingers poke too deeply our tumors.
    You'd rather run down rumors.
His brain sees back too far to caves.
Saintly acumen corrodes to knave's.

Loose cannon.
It's no fun.
This organ.
This shotgun.
This *born again to gain* regimen.

MJM '82 S. Monica

<u>Shut up!</u>

If the world paid for wit,
We'd be choked mute by
Money, and instead of
Fopping would wind up
Shopping.

If the world paid for true
Love, all the whores and
Strippers and marriage
Wreckers would go puss-
Nonplussed.

If the world paid for class,
Nouveaux riches and film
Stars would labor in peace,
Not tonight's plebian news
Release.

And yet the world pays for fine
and media arts, perhaps because
As they peak and pique at our peeks,
Witty and witless need not
Speak.

MJM 1/11 SF

Sick Beds

I

Enrapt in finger acrobatics
The mental ward's lurid
Dance their days away

Knuckles 'n' nails
A collage o'handplay
O'er window, o'er lamplight.

Immobile as you are
Right this minute
They charge: *It's not here*

Real over-the-edgers'
Sick beds beckon ~~
Sneaking, all chronic

Twisters hedging,
"Day in/day out,"
    cacophony blasphemy!

II

When organs ache
Liver kidney spleen
The doc, fey

Don't say
It's blocked-out
Madness.

Then your
dumb dangler
knocks

Why, I've seen you hurry home
Just to wank by your desperate self
Craving to jack one more

Porn part torn.
You erect trusting
Alien selves

Limboing
Scooping ever deeper
To mine in fresh fear

Alone, whimpering exxed
Dumplings of perversion,
impotent.

Fellow wo/man a rear,
You rote gob down
the drain

In the snift mirror
Hide remainder,
Your night habit

Finger-meandering
  Wicked smears
and fading insight.

MJM '83 M.B.

Singing to Birds

When I was young: the birds
Scuba-dove a rainbow,
Carbonated twists of arc
   and color
They would swarm and swallow
Catching as catch can.

But now they're flicks –
Abstract as whistles –
Frequencies of sound
Without music
Or élan.

I hear my own heart
Beat. My breathing
Is the simple code
Of drum and the quaver
Of bow in between.

They float on the message
Of my audience. The simplest,
Stupid creatures – flaps
Without heads – fly in a
   way I never will!

I envy their fearlessness
Of height, mettled wings
And brake-spare bodies.
Tower-locked corkscrew
Keening from a window,

I mean them to collect
The spring fever asleep
On the bed! Get them
To frolic and scream
And flock and fly away!

I hear my own heart
Beat. My breathing
Is the simple code
Of drum and the quaver
Of a bow in between.

MJM '79 Cambridge MA

skin flint

was it vanity
or insanity
compelled her
to the mirror

the reflection
of her corrections'
false face
imperfections

was insecure
frigid sex demure
offending even
venus, let a-

lone narcissus

MJM '01 SF
Basel

Skyscraper Highrise (Not for Trump)

Had he unfurled himself higher,
His 'necktier' looped 'round
One of those antennae atop
A skyscraping highriser, he'd
Have no time for quotidian
Doldrums, thumbs and fingers
  On *songs in the key of life.*
Nor rife with the sadness and
Boredom of city serfs and daily
Slaves, he'd be a'boon with
Contracts, deadlines, headline
Raves, proposals, presentations, law-
Yers' and bankers' amalgamations.
Yet so many meetings as to make
  collectivism of Capitalism!

His decisions would sway
The government one way
And his opponents another,
Guaranteeing a hearing date
To decide the polis' fate, and
Then appeals to cement or
Undo his deals. The stock market
Would wobble for his troubles
To keep his shares blowing bubbles,
Long hours and in-the-office-
Showers, a'reigning o'clocks,
Logistical overseas' Plants to
City's unionized container docks.
  Or intellectual property and
Advocate arguments challenged

'Fore judges, the highest court,
The long, the short of knowledge
  Is power, is content, is asset,
And the inevitable *online* global
Blasts to chute it, to grassroot it!
There'd be shares and corporate
Fairs, human resources and one
  Or two high-profile divorces.
There'd be fundraisers for politicos
And the funds raised, going to God
Only knows. Book signings and
Speaking tours. Fees galore, never
Shrinking from the fore, biz agents,

PR men, image consultants, regimen.
  A leader, a breeder among men!

  And once at home, Golden Labrador,
Gated estate, fine art in the corridor.
Pool in the palace. Scotch and ardor.
Kids, refined, and on their way. Let's
Top mom and pops Phi Beta Kappa day!
It started when you were a kid: you rose
And rose, you did and did. You ended
Up a Harvard 'man,' and went on from
There, postgraduate plan, supportive
Clan, feel-good power, good-looks' élan.
  Yet for this writer, the high life meant
  A dancing, drinking, coked-up gent,
  Hoarding his hours to himself – sheaving
  Market concerns to the dusty shelf.
The pursuit of small art is an assertive

"No" and wild play – eternal child on the go,
To and fro ~ yet stunted old, bored ego,
Qwerty, sometimes jealous, sassy libido!
  He'd walk in your shoes one day to see
If being in demand on overtime felt at all
Like liberty, or being as some higher Be.

MJM 9/15 SF

Sling Afterglow

I want it anonimo! – Henri

All alone on a Sunday eve: a huge *Bear* fest
Going down in the gay leather part of town.

There'll be fairy chaps hangin' up in slings,
And chains on chaps to slaves with Paps.

He can't go this eve. He's cleared the liquor
Off his shelf, fearing he'll fall prey to drink

In the merry stud bars with their booze-beer stink.
How joyous it would be to see, but alcoholism's

Thrashed him low. Better to be a safe no-show
Than risk the *fascism* of that first cocktail that

Only the addicted know. They say someday
He'll walk anywhere sober and not be tempted.

But for now, his chary hairy ass is homeward-
Bound-pre-empted. He wishes he would come

Across some little blond from Scandinavia or cross
The pond. He'd take him home and give him bub-

bling water. Then turn him over, pounding Pater!
Better than pounding drinks, it would lovingly

Elude away this sober sink that feels like
Exclusion from that funky South of Market

Frat, o'nuded. Yet for clean, he's repatriate among
The living, charged with atonement and forgiving.

The sober life is a sacred, narrow path for those
Nearly died in alcoholic countermath. Come to

Me, lad: I want to wander in your space, and
Play for joy, your flesh trespass. Sexy, soothing,

N'er a glass of poison. Your boyish skin o'rosin
and reposed, in an afterglow – I don't know.

MJM 9/15 SF

Smokey Joe

He pops the top off
his half-cigarette
on a brick. Cherry
blows to the ground,
steaming smoke
in the wind
of the bulbette
of tobacco
on the sidewalk
still lit.

MJM 8/15 SF
You can always find me down at Smokey Joe's
That's where all the hip and groovy people go.

– Diana Krall sings Nat King Cole

Snow in the Sahara!

Some of the scientists, I believe,
haven't they been changing their
opinion a little bit on that?
— George doub-yah

Snow fell in the Sahara desert today
For the first time in recorded history!
Immediately, I feared for the animals:
The cold-blooded snakes, lizards, and scorpions

That earn their living on the fly in sunshine,
Or as the great sand basins cool off, still warm,
Insulating them in a radiant bath.
And what of rodents, beetles, and palm trees?

Will man's sky-gassed globe brand them *Frosted Flakes?*
Will oases rot and Nubian ibex
Expire, lost to time, like the unicorn it
Mimicked? When viewed from the side, both horns mirage

To look like one. Will not even one survive?
My second thought was of a recent dumb-ass
President, unbearable on TV: Oil-
Man all Texas, even though his parents talk

Patrician. I guess he slicked up his twangy,
Folk way a slangin,' *to where* the runt tries like
Fuck to be one of them boys. Refusing to
Address the awesome change in temperatures

Worldwide, he declares the melting, down-plunging
Glaciers into icy waters a fluke of
Mother Nature, Father Time. I forgive him
Since, before he was sworn stupid, the damage

Was long done to them by *us*, a human race.
Twice odd, it seems global warming oscillates:
This one to freeze, the other to heat – all in
The worst places. By degree, ill hot gets iced.

Sprinting on oil, we speed up Nature's next kill.

MJM 2/11 SF

So This Always Happens Again

Another blasted god-damned gunning down of kids
in college: 10 gone and 8 a-bed. 13 guns found, six
on the killer, now himself dead, and seven back at
his house. Yet cursed, all the usual stories – mentally
deranged man busily buys a stockpile of weapons
and magazines, easily, legally. Hate crime notes,

illegible quotes. Christians killed, professions of Christ
their last acts of redemption – the apostate taken out
by cops – gunman feeling great, or worse, greatness.
On par, there's mental illness in the assassin's record,
and feckless family allowing his possession of army-
Grade weapons. Magazines stuffed in his flack,

the terrorized huddled on floors at his back, as he
calls out some bogus fealty to some god, shod in
fatigues and craven in league with the damned.
When will the country learn? Is this the price we
pay, that free men hunt game, as wheelchaired
survivors start rolling *out* on the pavements, im-

paired and lamed? And what of the upcoming
funerals, brought to you by TV? We'll see police
at attention, and civic leaders, *well-intentioned,*
an FBI investigation. Solemn notes, press quotes,
and calls from the White House to the stricken
homes of the innocent dead. Someone will say,

". . . so this never happens again," as nicked, smug
I nay in retort, "Go fuck, yourself, you cliché-meister."
Where were you when the vote came up in Con-
gress, yet again, to remove with care and largesse
guns from the hands of mad patients? Where were
you when the call came down to eliminate militia-

style weapons from the hands of Joe Doe and
John Do-Do? Ought-to-extinction, gun-fing'red dicks
and machismo chicks, boisterous for their right
to machine-gun bullet a target at target practice.
Do they think Armageddon is nigh, that their
firepower will keep them alive? When the Lord

is done with us, we'll have wings, instead of
ammunition slings, and may the devil take
the pro-killing pricks who hustle up Capitol Hill.

MJM 10/15 SF

Social Needy Ya – (and the Us Generation)

Now let us see. Is *Facebook* about us, *mais oui!*
Or more about you, her, or *me?* Do we anticipate –
OCD – praise and recognition, especially instantly?
Or do I, and/or you, or big We just flux in the mix?

Avid to exchange and capitulate heart to others'
Posts, one is careful not to focus on oneself
At first face. Lo, when someone offline has died –
He's a slag who mourns *more* for pride of place!

Analog egos aren't *Legos.* They don't perforce *need*
Hook up. Both masturbation and dancing alone
Prove this, covering the spectrump, you might say.
But *then* comes this *Facebook* thang, straight

Outta Harvard, the ole alma mater, where it
Was simply a slim, red-book *Who's Who* –
This fancy, online chatter another matter,
Making self-centered *the* most amiable.

Although, one must confess, Crimson excelled
At recruiting both best! Maybe she's a frustrated
Actor or singer in tired, writerly circumstance.
Instead of *Change-Status*-anxious like 'needy dog'

Or kitty, who hates y'all for not feeding her what
The brat's craving, maybe she should get a late
Start in show business. Yeah, yeah! but that could
Spell mere pretension all over again – *what, art?*

Nonetheless, she'll resolve to forswear as much
Giddy attention to *our* posts, as to her own,
And lick that Aries tick to trickily kick to be
Host of Hosts. Heady Rams don't run to lead.

They just wanna be first! And in the realm of
Social Media, that's a boorish, tricks-of-posting curse.
What's worse, "Sharing" her oddball poems online,
Ms. digital I'm Lime-Light . . . now that's the worst.

MJM 6/13 S.B.
"H" '81 Greenough/Mather

Son of a Father

Sum of a drunk's conundrums' maximums –
vodka and *Gatorade* 24/7 – dims some
to a minimum,
but mea cuppa – yuk, yum – equals
this numb, dumb, amateur brainiac bum
manic liver & pancreas under the thumbs
of everyone making a living – pill-&-skill
pros' aid to the aching, rapid smarty
to vapid tardy. Ho hum, not even a cog,
Vitamin "V" makes limbic lately
just a sleeper and guilt weigh so greatly
there must, paranoid or wise, be a door-
peeper: the one drilled in the house port
brass 'n' glass – the other, this floor
nurse on salary o'drill apace, paid to pass
and re-pass an' report. I could trespass
the bridge on to off, but my beloved young
son says, "Hold on! You and Mom
are all I've got!" How you mayn't scoff.
Ace to spade my lot? Whose plot?
Whose purse? Whose keeper?

MJM 5/15 Los Gatos

Sonnet on Doubly Troubled

Tossed so far from tandem touch, your marble
Athlete in the Hermitage Museum of his mind,
He stumbles, stirred to cry, forbidden to re-find
You wed across the Bay, his desire but a warble
Muted by gender and hexed, covalent garble.
Is he called to *chaste?* Or tri-foiled to rekind
Himself to romance, neutered solo by trined
Boy/girl love's dual dream viable as bar bull?

What sport of nature that he disconnect alone?
Ought he to follow Church – Jesus wed, nun/parson?
Or find upon his path fair daughter or fine son
To un-vise himself from rule to see which prone
AC/DC couple flows, yet tête-à-tête unknown?
Or past lust, revolve the Earth to love no one?

MJM 1/11 SF

Sperm Song

You imported a bean-bag 'chair'
We snuggled in, your cupid
Face limpid, crest silk to stroke.

In brown-eyed love, two deer
Alert for trespasser – love-dumb
One, even for passers-by – we'd

Punch-fluff 'them' beans through
Vinyl, then squint, *'Foggy little
Fellows,'* nor yearling or starling

Ripe to molt or flock, yet a-rush
In our reeling. *Bravi i due!* Your
Oscars in the sky! I'd pen & woo,

*"I remember you. You're the
One who made my dreams
Come true . . . in a* dis-tent

*"Glen, when stars like rain
Started to fall down right out
Of the blue."* How suddenly

You criss-crossed to judge's
Mallet, maid-n-lad. Fire *me?*
Fuck you! I bile ripped-gut's

Punch, bon voyage to *Ivy League
An'* all: I guess he's <u>not</u> <u>for</u> <u>me</u>!
"Then, hey, miss lonely you went

"To the finest school just to get
Juiced in it. How does it feel?
Like a rolling stone" into careen

Unknown and a glam' career, that
Won't allure your dear, *my huckle-
Nickel friend 'Moon River'* toxic

Winding with Sartre's nauseous
Puke:*"What'll I do, alone, and
Wondering who, is kissing you,*

"What'll I do?" scene on Sunset
Set in sun-glassed melancholy
Bars, like yr potted balmy palmy

Chez Chatêau Marmont. I'd
Palm the side of my forehead,
Suicide cigaretted between

Knuckles, lush fingering to turn
And scratch his plush red-wine
Glass stem like I once skimmed down

The downy rims of your Montgomery
Clift ears. You were that tremendous.
Gregory Peck Spectacular: rapturous,

Indelibly funny valentine-phone-o'graphable.
You hand-crush my stem's bowl to slash
        My jobless hands?

My irreplaceable you. Don't be a
Pitiless traitor, *come to papa do.*
Many charms about you, my arms!

Thirty-five years that I may piss on.
Still I, your man's-man past. I still
Sob & die, a 'Daisy' we ever claspt.

"Look out for yourself. That
Should be the rule. Give your
Heart and your love to whom-

"Ever you're 'love,' Boy, don't be
A fool. Why should we cling to
Some old-fashioned thing that used

"To be? So, if you can forget, don't
Worry 'bout me. When the angels
Ask me to recall – the thrill of them

  "All – why kill, *I will tell them"*

    I remember you,

"... And a window that looks out on
Mountain's sea – oh, how lovely!
Now I am lost and lonely, please,

"Please have some pity. I'm all
Alone in this big city. I tell you,
I am so awfully misunderstood . . .

"Won't you suck someone to pipe
Us some speed, follow my lead?
Oh, how I need one, two of you

To watch over my plea to . . . some-
One who fucked over me. Now I
Need a little slam in the 'would,'

Oh, how I could al-ways

  Be good
        to someone
                to fuck
                        under me.

MJM 1/11 SF

Spider Rooter

The one night he can't sleep,
Hijacked, manic-panic, back.
Inert eye scans MRI-brains,
No body: patient, paranoid, held.

Like ignited spiders, hop-to-spot-
Web-works, got insects – silk spewn
On tugs' trembles – arachnids a'tour
Race skullo-pods. High-fiddling

Frequencies, pert alert on skeins
Of antibody, *intense aux xenos*.
He fed his spider a daddy-longlegs,
Insect-famine-fearful. 'Eight-Ball'

Bred, spun mummy-tape his kill.
Without nightly-cocktails – just doc's
Brain smoothies – insomniac's still
Strung-out as *sirènes* disaster hooters.

MJM 6/11 SF

Star to Spark   (15)

When I consider everything you gave,
Held in your perfection for one fleet sec,
I crave your musk of cinnamon, your brave,
And die to kiss and lip it off your neck.

Linked by constancy, twinned to perfect rhyme,
Our love staged Mars to passion in sweet dark.
Now in stars' fabled daze, he burns out time.
I, conflagrated, wane – his smoldered spark.

Then the coldness of my incessant stay
Freezes you, cool in cloak before my sight.
Wasting Time's array on this agéd stray,
Won't change your days of youth to mine at night.

All at war for young man's love unfulfilled,
I'd bargain peace for Time and twice be killed.

MJM 3/11 SF
After Sonnet 15

Storm Ritornello

1

Not wishing wet, I closed the window;
Lost laughter from the windowpane ~
Splitter-splat of tinsel down the
building, when I overheard a few spiders outside
do the talk-of-the-town in the rain.

2

Wash a waxed car in the rain –
What happens? It halos like haystack
needles' *aura* on your back. You dodge
droplets, but your t-shirt's so cold and wet
        you run home to hop in a tub,
Relax, let the warm wash off
your pub-a-drub week, your rusty old
                Cadillac.

3

Outside, dusk and the light litter of rain
bust like eggs on a campfire.
Ransacked, the lane of little boys pelts posters.
The songs they whistle
tugging hedgerow and thistle
at the edge of the road,
they're a casual choir.

4

(Don't jerk off over water, Brother,
  you'll be caviar on the river!

(*As amorphous waves swelled
a pelican pelted a porpoise.*)

5

Outside, sun and the patter of rain
splash the springtime city. Honks a horn;
A bank-cloud leavens the heaven
  above buildings; the wash of cars
Skates by like firelight.

MJM '80 Cambridge MA

Storm-Tossed

Launched from recovery mansion for men,
Paunched by starch and the *ism* in alcohol
To a one-man boat at Emeryville slip,

He's squeamish with fear of isolation.
Will the dock landing cause him to slip
ad hoc – low ceilings, crushing

The tripped-out fraternity
He's come to love under the mother
Of high ceilings – above all, bros

Warranting sobriety in the highest?
The taxi driver says, "Wow, dude!
"You live in a mansion?" His inner

  hipster secretly glad, he snorts
To himself, "Life on a boat, rad?"
To sad's, "no man is an island."

The City's gentrified: no man's land, pushing
Out the needy and artful, the greedy
Cached under mantles of liberal silt –

Balderdash in the Press like, "mixed-
  income housing," as we drool at *Google*
Peeps waiting for their corporate busses

All flush with geekster, now Ivy-League
Cash and 4,000-per-month one-bedrooms –
No bed for even one kid or roomie or mother.

A tithe at $400 per month, he'll live on water,
That cradle of ebb and flow lulling sleep
In brilliant sun and rains' pitter-patter.

Once bohemian-bourgeois, Bobo's all
At sea, nervous about change? a *"little me?"*
Affluence/poverty, frivolity/gravity, wet

Drunk and dry, can he keep his soul sober?
He'd better make himself over or die: *"Ya
Lily-livered land 'lubber'!"* – no more Italian

Loafers for soles of white rubber! Meth diet,
now *all*, group-therapy despair 'round obesity.
Blubber, blather, sea lather, blabber,

"Land and sea, look at me! Living almost
free. Gesù Christo, walk on water . . .
and while You're at it, cure my addict."

He 'don't' do suicide, but come a riptide
What'll flow into his insides, inside
That little float, by flotsam and jetsam,

In the middle of the boat?

MJM 7/14 SF

String Section

Men measure success in strife by their careers
As he once did. Now does he? It's sly to re-dub
Oneself bohemian in the aftermath of profligacy
And madness – dimeless legacy from which

He may never re-materialize to Bank. True, it's
In times like these the soul's tenor takes over:
A violin, as angelic sopranos sing of heroes.
But what of the baritone cello and bass as base

Scrambling after but dollars – pride-slicing fife
Whistling amputees down the toned town lane?
The spirit says he has not accursed his life, while
A daemon says, "You're broker than a jobless wife."

The soul says, "Never mind, heart get aligned with
Heavens." Refrains ego, "All you've done is thrive
On cliffs of excess, waste, and spending climbing.
Don't think only bumpkin knaves, unaccustomed to

"This bigger, keener world, are the only ones to piss
Away what remittance or fortune gave." He knows
English books with rakes, who decastled land mis-
Takes with father's money, lost honor and rot title.

"The fallen world should not be falsely famed
Or fawned. Many a scandal's fortune devolves
Round cruel arms and drug-lord's tweakt, the CIA
On the take, brokers' rapacity, Ivy League snakes."

If there *is* a sacred afterlife, to hell with earthly din!
If there be only human race – then he's all cost, no win.

MJM 2/11 SF

Stript o' Caucus

It starts like tiny termites' or Argentine ants'
Foot jigs on a chad-sized bit, back of the throat.

What tickles, soon sizzles to strafing sickles
   Razing urban athletes like sick kids at camp.

Flagging, fully fled energy saps from the eyes
Soon gummed with dimming coagulant veil,

Until the thought of sun, work, or company
Gives nausea a new name, all points of view

Tunneling on bed, down pillows, hibernation.
Amazing, that ambition squelches at the drop

Of bacteria, survival now sleep instead of
Labor, errands, one's circle, or civilization.

It takes a sore throat to make him envy pigs
In shit and bears, nose-moist, clockt in furs.

MJM 1/11 SF

Stroke

A moment ago,
White bullets
Of spray
Pinned you
In the forehead,

Your bolt
Limbs wavering
All a-dart
Like goldfish
In hot grease.

Then we shrunk,
White to black;
A local death
Boxed us. But
Death was not

An expiration.
It saw land-
Scapes through windows
The room lacked –

Stroke-burned

black-
and-who edges
  red dwarf
Eclipsed?

MJM '83 Cambridge MA

489

Suicide by Prayer

Strange, that he would pray to
Pass on, heart-to-lung soulful,
His car tears and lip tremors,
Our gauge he's engaged God.

On the right-side of our number
Line, he's re-found a refund of
Thanks: his zombie rift path alas
Blessed with lean bed and larder;

Miracles of healing, brain-save,
Of habit, of look up and look in,
But, *haaail*-no, none of outlook.
Profligate, *parvenu* rake laced,

Mere media merchant, he rued
The stockbroker speaking tonight
Intolerably better off. His every
Dark deal, every dog-and-pony

Tricked in gloriously empowered
Light and clouds of sky-scrapered
Offices, paid and repays *him* who
Forecasted high to retire in infirm

Times. Whereas, *he* planned for last
Night's party, top tickets to every
Knock-out gig, he so keen & vervy
Cher chic, it'd unnerve a teacher

To unbook, begging for his classes.
Perspicacity he had not, nor plans,
Nor income tables to zig-zag the
Budget's vectors up and down on

'*Execs*'-and-'*Why?*' axes. Straight
To the money source, that fountain-
Head of us all, they filled buckets
To 'Fuck its!' to the flood of trillions.

As his jittery jazz clinked 'Dionysius,'
Fruitful, he pressed on after Bacchus.
Yet *they* snortled 8-balled bindles and
Mighty vodka to a-right in *their* offices,

Cheered on by their frats and feared by
The brats, alpha ensnarled, as if dual anes-
thesia numb-skilled *Wall St. man* sub-
Conscienceable to drive the deal to dive

For the Dollar – even into gram mama's
Purse; then again, for rife <u>*virtual*</u> fisted
Funds glowing a-pulse on their trader
Screens. As for him, he lashed himself

In bad bed, appetites tweaking erect for
Jane-and-Johnny *X-X cum-n-go nightly,*
  As far away from a desk as Mars,
  Venus, and Cupid from the River

Styx. Lax, not one stifft lover stuck.
  He dours, "I give you them or me."
We hear one sterling-rapacious story
Of the excess we *do* admire, and one

Of pathetic ego-libido in a time when
Love's *so* expensive: *he,* pensive-only-
for-Art-snob; *they,* Bravado in banks.
What a Knox-ious unfair dreampair.

                    ***

That ivory towers shared to fare;
  ¡Ojala! he were well, off dead.

MJM 1/1/11 SF

Sun Wintered

> *. . . didn't go to the moon, I went much further —*
>
> — Tennessee Williams, *The Glass Menagerie*

O dawns, not the blues: this time of year
When sunlight hales cold days along the pier
And every football-game beer leads to
Where I think you are, not kissing me

In the least: girl to intercourse – son, unleashed.
Why did I manipulate you to, 'I, be pleased?'
Blind, that for a girl, romancing friendship'd freeze,
Myself, bulimic round her-Other. Was it that pass

I thought you, *bello,* finally winkled – spiced
To pontiff love? It only dunned you out of groin.

Your allergy to any ass-boy, least of all me, dis-joint.
We held in boys,' fleet-foot, silver time, gold, garish.

Our melt into each other proud, athletic, funny
Smart. A precious, lunar metal to solder youths'
– little, silver slipper of a moon, coupled secrets,
The whole deal was you for mine – me for you.

Don't you remember deliquescing me
With your eye lashes scrimmed down,
Earnest to see me like a sheep dog through Garbo hair?
That was all I had, and that's why I was there.

No decades of riches, no wife, nor son,
Could ever be hell's allure you were. Not
bucks, nor fame, nor venture. Only the
Mystic pheromones of your aura,

Leading me away up close to you – and by the nose
To be cut off by your breed. Now I fare, ex-lariat,
No heart pulleys. My all – ex-transfused-in-you –
to Love's a harm – sex apex, I, elite to kill the near.

MJM 1/12 SF

492

Surrealism

a'dream mind- digging and digging peasants
hand trowel *close up*, dirt coughed up squirrels, -scape,
prairie up to Canada, Millet France museum room, dogs,
I liked gophers, red headscarf, dizzying turn to horizon desert Dalí
Hijos de la tierra, scared boy, frowning mom, bitch indif-potatoes
ferent ant hill, red black, our feet standing, "synecdoche,"
hand trowels, dirt funeral, cranking down casket, she
throws, splash of flower water, museum room, cross white
chasuble gold, coughed up by miners, cherries in the
gallery, ladies, bitch indifferent, blue scarf, horizon, horizon, horizon
casket dirt earth, throwing herself on the casket movie, Brando
mom brother Persian rug, Christmas, feet standing, desert, yucca
cross of flowers, cherries hijos de la tierra eat our white,
squirrels scramble down, museum room. gold and hill, dogs tumbleweeds road
feet, old rabbit foot, chain, meth mom, peasants digging, dirt flies,
they bite blood scarf, aspirant "huhhh," *awake, "Thank God!"*

MJM 9/15 SF
Avída Dollars

Swanky, Kinky, Frigid Ess-Eff

Would that he IM a love a love-song.
Fancy, eclectic town, liberal and wild:
But one nearly never sees a child, only
Scads of girls and cads, date-neutered.

These frigid chicks pay two ways: you
Buy them out, house and home, or drunk-
Drugged on your dime, you may tomboy
Her up the butt some time! Goal, dual control

Of a glitzy life, classified by prep-a-tory
Kids, fine shopping, gowns to gourmand,
And nannies a plenty to save the day:
Ass-chief comes home hard, she'll splay?

Frothy flocks of sisters, wine and dine,
Jack-of-spades, normal Jakes scramble
Just to shave to-make-the-market – alive
In private filth and ever-beckoning wealth.

Lethal-toenails in flip-flops, grime-stubbled,
Monday's troupes man-up the skyscrapers –
He, dreaming one of biggest dicks and how It
Could punish those nonchalant Vics.

They may come together some day,
Suitably extended families in con-tendence.
She'll have the home and he the high tower,
All ho-dependence – alas-and-all, intercourse

Inducts their polished kids, whose nose-airs
Next smother Romance into gender-quorums.
The yoga ladies gym-siss, as guys, pissed, piss:
Battle-axe of sexes and wealth-insurance forums.

MJM 6/11 SF

494

Switch Hitter at October's End

The *S.F. Giants* win the World Series,
Ninety percent of his mates ecstatic,
The other ten triggered by our disease ~
    Those not buoyed by sport, erratic.

Amid the ten-deep crowd in its throes
Up pulls *Maserati* man and without warn
    Guns his pedal and donuts three "O's"
Flawless on tarmac, *smokin'* wheels shorn.

He peels hot rubber north through a stop
    And the baseball-capped mob cheers!
What a brazen fop! A miracle no cop
Espies him, returns he twice and clears

Gawkers and fans back to the sidewalk!
Through intersection, newly his stadium,
    Wend to unwind drunks *hi-n-lo* for a talk
In a pink room where to drink is as radium.

They'll bitch and moan about drinking,
Intellectuals and haughty girls thinking,
"Sports are just *stupid,* especially on *beers.*"
    He lies, "What comfort meeting with peers,"

When all he wants, sober night, is the treat
    Of three other baseball tricks that are queers.

To Glenn, who prefers hems not hims.
MJM 11/10 SF
'Cum and go Giants:'
    Posey 'n' Panik!

Sworn In

– Dear Messrs. Clinton and Gore,
I admire who you are and what you do.
Herewith, a poem. Should you like it,
it won't make a difference to the world, but a whit.

I beat myself up
In so many ways:
Down the hatch,

Up the ass,
In the heart –
Bullet to yr brain.

From DDT weedy schoolyard days,
When blond and hazel-eyed girls
I'd carry off on a dream steed

Jeered my brown skin
To maniacal nights
Gambled away – Mom

Crashing plates around Dad
& making quaking us
Stand to defend her from

His teeth-baring punches,
To the pulsing daze
Being dubbed a faggot by thugs,

It's no small wonder I lay
Alone on this mattress:
little wig, little wag, little tit, little tad

In my no-nothing business,
Beer on the breath,
Scotch in my stools

Gurgling out to sea.
I've everything
A man could want, save Joy:

My house, my wife, my job,
Gifts from God, a little boy.
While a storm offshore

Threatens other homes
with mudslides,
and a new President,

Just the man I wanted to be,
Takes on idiotic enemies'
Egos and Greed.

Look at Congressmens'
Needs.
So many sheepish,

Sore-abashed faces
Peering to see
If their alpha buds'll stand

A next Ovation, fellate & felled.
It's apparent
We're descended from Apes,

What with their wanking
Troubled troupes
And erstwhile sense of humor

In between screeches
I guess inhered
To keep them swinging.

What a battle from womb
And rattle to bat-and-ball,
Bills and ills,

Wheelchair and cane to the deep.
Isn't there a room, tiny room,
For some power sleep?

I go steep down just to come up high,
Again to tear it down again!
"It's a sham. A scrim,"

You'll hear me cry.
"All's a lie." Yet to die
And leave the baby,

"Daddy, bye-bye,"
Makes me rail, makes
Me set the dial to deal

No matter how false
You, Us,
It, I.

My pain, my jests, my sins
Were set in motion, lullaby
Alibi. And under this steam

Of elocution
I feel I must at least hold on
Until his grad school graduation:

Simple and that ironic.
Doubly moronic:
Daddy, duty, Country, boy.

MJM '92 SF

Sylvia

A girl whorled in world
Pearled Anglo-Saxon
When they played

Around her
What the streets
Had to offer

The mundane shock
Blanched her
Sanguine way.
　　　　She grew grey.

Turning bald eye
To mirror, she
Saw a queen bee.

"World, you fucker!
You maggot receiver,
You wan lax liar!"

The best drama was
She stung herself.
Now nightly

She buzzes
Under lampshades
　　　　into my hollowing.

MJM '83 M.B.

T'ang Horse

Black and tan T'ang horse,
Hi ho, you'll fetch ten million
Bucks – three-feet tall, soon bid
Into a richer rival's stable.

Equine "three colors glaze in
An unusual fashion – saddle a
Solid spinach green set off by
The impeccable brown robe,

White flecks here and there."
Lumens drizzle rays of shine
Down your musculature like
Castle fire light. Do you tense,

Your mouth's ghastly lips t'neigh
Rebellion? Emperor's prize, do
You defame, fume, dare chortle?
Was running wild and naked your

Nastic right? All equine flounces
Flare absurd a male of your
Power. Or that you prop up
A fragile Sire, frip' Pop upon

Your shire? Do you, embroid'r'd
Doll, mainly boast his looms?
Père Force, does it anger you they
Exterior-decorate your hide?

Grand, standing on a Chinese
Mountain, you'd inhale vapors
Blown down upon his kingdom.
As if, were he to saddle you

Amid a company of strangers,
Even a passing Prince might
Blush, 'My Lord! Which be their
Sire?' Betwixt 600 and 800

Anno Domini you were shorn
To bear the Palace Seal
But now parry on the Dynasty.
Artful and feral, Your Grace

Re-races one of *the* Chinese
Dynasties, meant to last an eon –
Your commanding millions upon
Millions, bid now here, at Sotheby's.

MJM 3/11 SF
"Quotation" from Souren Melikian,
Art + Auction, November 2010

Tai Chi

Chinese Tai-Chi
clenches her fists
Then relaxes – going all *lax.*

Hand-swoop of loops:

                         stanchioned!
S l o w lift of leg,
      arms a' *rolling.*

Torsion ~~ fEEt hit turf;
Clomp, clomp.
Withdraw,
Repeat.

MJM 7/14 SF

502

Talulah B.   (66)

Arrived by train from New York, you the papers queried,
"Why would a legend of the Broadway and London stage move out <u>here</u>?"
You panned, "I have come to Hollywood to fuck Gary Cooper."

Sick of craze, you rest benumbed to pity:
Lo, to behold an actress, addict torn
A-mincing all things trimmed in jollity,
Yet trudging hooked, heredity inborn.

On gilded Broadway craftily misplayed,
You eclipsed novices' fame unfabled,
And stayed perfection, trickery displayed
Spot-lit by cocaine's sly boost enabled.

Your guests sit tongue-tied: the audacity
Of your disrobing nude *en fête* for thrill –
Frenzied, *smashed,* you act out, '*Vivacity,*'
Your captive peers beholding captain ill!

Swanked from London stage, you, movie trooper,
Crash L.A. to shambles awed to stupor.

MJM 1/11 SF
After Sonnet 66

Tardeada

Barbra, Latina barfly par *Mexcellence,*
barstool hopping men for drinks, buzzed
camaraderie is all she thinks, ruined and
trading middle-age cunt for half-blunts

And beers. She's high and low, all griz-
zled glow, here and there a bump of men's
Room blow. I had to live a long time to
see someone so blithely broke, her place

With no electricity! Yet tenacious born,
She's gone and plugged an enfilade of
extension cords into her neighbor's out-
door, covered socket ~ power o'pocket!

Her laugh's all coarse and constant
in these dreary, she-makes-'cheery'
in-the-afternoon dives. No homing
pigeon, her leery daughters by many

Pa's must drag her home, come dusky
Dark. She's strident out – all smile and
Pearly whites, save one brown, chip'd
canine, her head always jukebox-

turned around. Like the rank blind

She knows where the front door is
Without looking on! Magnetic present
She, why would these sopt guys put
her down? She's *barrio* clown!

Yet in that *chinolera* way, her phone-
Prone *primas* gossip 'bout her every
day – "What a stray mother, *¡Qué pena,
ella!*" What will the neighbors say,

Say, when they see their light bill?
Lush as she can never have her full
Fill. Pitchers of beer foam and suds
Away the cancer she's chilled to ill.

Barbra for "barbarian." She'll rot-die,
borracha barfly – casket carried in.

MJM 9/15 SF

Teddy

"Mackel, Mackel, Mackel!"

Head a-lope, your face pitched against the southern jetty
In a field of inclining grains, you always wore *Polaroid*
Shades, ripe to ramble, every noon a full moon.
With highways ruffling off your back, you high-wired
Treacherous cliffs clairvoyant made us kindred nomads.

The mountains – giant deceptive brethren – at first held
Your feet fast in their bluffs of powder. You were about
To make a jump when some ice plants broke, slippering your
Step. Now the beach cave is blotched with spores. Deeps
As you, we were omniscient once, still, inhalant cisterns.

MJM '80 Redlands/Laguna
To Susanna, Wiltshire, UK
With us that summer

Tee Vee

– Washington, D.C: 'Hollywood for ugly people.'

Los Angeles TV-media fingerfucks
Your every orifice nightly:
First the eyes go-go taut uptightly
at hardly-anybody-has hardbody good looks.

Then, the nose crinkles; serial bosses smell
Of *mucho dinero* and sex with teenagers by the pool.
At *Real Cops* coke busts, our mouths drool
Third – their big guns and choppers, whizzing helter-skell.

My poor prick limps in fourth, underexposed,
With my hoary ears munched, as if by maggots.
Fifth – that we even have to hear it besots
Us in an English decomposed.

The asshole puckers next in envious tension
Of TV studs out-then-in the closet,
So's rednecks don't cable de-deposit
Over tonight's collusional convention

o'rappers' ho's, delinquent fey elites,
And big stars *qua* philosophe effetes
   because like no one else in town
They read and can talk about wrong.

Holy Toledo, the pokes are finally noted
By Dole, candidate for Prez.
He accuses, and Hollywood sez,
"We only reflect what the public has voted."

I fear our dumbed senses, like pockets with holes,
In letting these twits'
Digits in and
Out are going the way of proles:'

Kinky-pink poodles that jig on the dash
Home entertainment centers, bling flash
Jelly boobs, Senate white-trash
Now a Silicon Valley digital rash!

Stars, stars, stars . . .
A thousand points of light
(to quote less dim George)
Poking holes in the celestina.   *MJM '96 SF*

Teens and Agers

– I'll buy a smartphone when it washes my clothes!

While teenagers thud and levitate down the staircase,
It's odd to be fifty and using a space heater to fend off
Arthritis of the toes, or seeing "Insufficient Funds" notices
Littering my inbox. These wags smoke pot and turn down

Sex with eighteen-year olds, as I sip red wine, starting
An infant start-up online. I deal for painters, yet forswear
My own art, since pictures have a passing chance to score
Big money, but nearly no one reads these tiny B&W poems.

In antique times, I'd say, touch-feel was the master sense,
What with fending off cold, heat, injury, starvation, and
The occasional saber-tooth cat. Comfy-cozy now, the eye's
The fascist ruling our lives, smartphones' over-typing.

The young ones thrive on their screens and www.pages,
Delight in 'fidgets' that won't wash your clothes, and lap-
Tops where once a baby bounced. All I want is to take
Off my duds, and teach a 20-something how to fuck

With style and endurance. I'd send a busy signal to
The World just for a great lick or some awesome head.
Too bad my pain meds tend to impotence, *mais voilà*
I pop the ED cure, while teenagers thud and levitate

Up and down the staircase and turn down sex
With eighteen-year olds. *Aging,* the craftiest hex.

MJM 1/10 SF
1850 Raguna

That and This

Happiness is the lover
Yielding t'ecstasy when over,
Then vanished to another under cover.

Joy, in contrast, is a connection of the soul
To another spirit. Orgasms are not its goal.
With heart work, it is timeless, it is whole.

MJM 12/10 SF

That's Living, Isn't It?

Always carry a flagon of whiskey in case of snakebite
and furthermore always carry a small snake.

– W.C.Fields

Don't know 'bout you, but after several days in hospital
He scrutinizes what he loves about himself and despises.
Let's call it the Louis-B.-Mayer syndrome, which to be fair
Would include that Mr. *MGM* hated movie stars and writers,
And thought of his *pix* as products. But for our hero here
In the ward a-holler with Tagalog, keened by RN mamas,
Who but a guy fronted by a Lion, his name meaning 'bigger'
In Spanish, could yearly gather the ditziest glitziest,
Tuxedoed prigs to posture their lines in English accents?
Fool the audience the world be high class and there
Ain't no Great Depression, neither! The gall of Talulah
Bankhead, cocaine nudist par sexcellence grafted onto
Cary Grant us Peace, Spencer and Hepburn out-weaseling
Each other, as with Roz Russell vs. Joan Crawford –
Though boldered, tough-as-nails Joan, more Nutria
Than Ms. Russell's rather ermine plush – don't ya think?
So it comes down to this: he was born this depassé
Brat, whose alma mater ought to have been *The Algonquin*
Room, not hailed Harvard, or one of Louis' over-budgeted
Sound stages. What would make a serious, sensitive
Man of heart and mind just want a smart bar with a perch
Next to the joint's most fractious wit? That's living, isn't it?

MJM 12/14 SF
'Tipplers' Green!

The Black and White of It

A positive thinker, an optimist
Are unlike others I've known who'll
Freely admit numbness, openly frown.

Their Protestant smiles, weaponry,
Fend off contaminants like me. In
Affluence, they disarm alarm by rote,

Build careers and staffs – their
Swell attitude the appliqué. Living
Death that sombers other men to rage

Dark bottoms of green bottles
Does not reign here. No, "Organism
Life, you hack pluck of random!

"You don't know how bald and fat
The lie life is until you're grown
Up tad enough to stand the smack

"Over and over. Finally you fall."
There's zest in these banker brethren –
Clear bowel, brain, and + charge

Spirit them from here to a high Heaven
Where they order in, sane and content –
Long as the sun slants its given way,

Co-dependent no more than
houseplants.
Will not all of us end the little
Matter of life dry as faded ferns?

Y'all invest your guile. This Other sinks,
Morbid ego drowning even one good day.
We just carry out two ways

Of taking similarly tiny sparks
To an infinitely vast black place
That does not rely on living to be.

MJM '84 Manhattan Beach

The Budding Spaniard

You sport the same goatee your dad did at your age.
It brings out the Spaniard in you; how the two of you
Love *thetas*. You walk around your hip hometown

Leaving school behind you, as your dad once did;
Frustrated by Cambridge scholars and by townies,
He played and stayed in Boston nights at a time.

Both estrangements have in common your strive
For strange, altered places of mind and sex of some
Kind. Now your father re-finds his soul and a con-

Nection to the cosmos, not to mention a righteous
Path. Contrary-wise, you speed and heroin, too,
  And, as when dad was *your* age, you're heady,

Going about stoned, not content in what's true.
Now that Dad has a second life and believes it's
The best of all ways, he has trouble imagining

The trauma to himself of your ever not being here.
Yet it's eerie to plea-bargain with the heavens. He's
Told he must believe in the presented plan. If you
die,

  Shall he man up? Or curse the wretched sky?

MJM 2/11 SF

The Cloisters (33)

Many solitary nights, diminished
By shutters, evil under sovereign eye,
He pissed slow spunk: eye-dazed, porno-nourished,
Surge-rived by diabolic chemistry.

Sluts and jocks, ass-debased by clouds bedside –
His smearing ugly tracks of lust, oil-faced –
His world view, norm-forlorn to lives outside,
Sucked time: magpies to cocktails: soul debased.

Uneven still, the sun also rises
To agitate energy, life in flight.
One shower and prayer at a time, disguises –
Revoked his regions, narrow path, his plight.

Victim's crime: he tunneled in sexy stark.
Now confessed, do cloisters bless rayed or dark?

MJM 4/11 SF
After Sonnet 33

The Confession of Diana

She crashed at *Place de l'Alma*, "soul plaza" in the City of Light
Muslim at her side, tiara and halo of good works to heal a great divide
of class and faith, The Firm – two lads at Balmoral
and the latest digs in *Le Monde*, "The World" –
Up against the Press.

At first,
noble and ordinary, abandoned daughter of a wrecked marriage,
her long lineage from James II, her blond nerve short,
she became the sacrament of Matrimony; and later cornered,
caged, rose to the occasion of Confession. Splitting her world

of heights
into good and evil, she "spit out her bitterness" like Job,
yet in connecting the limbless to the palace, ascended
in her own way to a charity of Holy Mothers like Teresa –
whom God took next week – to censor

the petty jealousies of masses and bourgeoisie alike,
who with enmity of *schadenfreude* – in struggle, middle-
rank and spiteful fascination of the high and mighty –
buy gossip sheets in lines at stores and on telly tune in
to *delicious* muckrakers.

She contained the fact that no king may ride the path
unscathed, nor the fairest audience end with more
than he. For the agony of great *noblesse oblige*
is as the dumbing of the poor, the rat-race in the middle,
and riches' rhymes that pale in the aura of simple mercy.

She finally took mercy on herself; now the World
unshocks its misery to entomb and to re-throne her.
As the Princess of Wales unveiled her labyrinth
of woe and betrayal, the common comfort
of equanimity was she, that even through our

ethered eyes, the sparkle of gems and palaces
never succeeded to outshine her. They say in heaven
there are many mansions prepared for us. How now
Paparazzi by St. Peter f-stopped at heaven's gate,
Spy at *Place de l'Alma* blaspheming, devil's date!

Diana, huntress, your arrows of flint and style
pierced our hearts, even as your own was salved,
stitched and rubbed the last two hours of your life.
Now, the stunned world massages its juggernauts via
CNN, NBC, JFK, Grace of Monaco, Marilyn Monroe;

the Press's flashbulbs banished by HRH with natural light
exquisite, they need re-run venal photos, films and videos
To miss her manifest Soul Bridge arcing to two princess's
Sons. May we know them with unjaded, undivided parts.
Have real Heart. Even as she confessed unselfingly, I Do.

MJM Sun. 8/31/'97 SF
"Let me speak. Let me spit out my bitterness . . ."
– Joni Mitchell, 'Job's Sad Song'

The Day Her Father Died

She cried, "Can't you see?
It came long dingy dingy world
Spreading careless over me,"
Blighted bundle of nerves
Trammeled in Mint City.

"It cuts! No balance to curtsy
And sway, I swill down bilge
To pummel me. Sinking black
Sogs me in this pearled universe

"Of palaces and ether, where minu-
 tiae plague eyeless farmers
Squirming in cars: They say, 'Self,
Go the same nowhere.'" She glooms,
 "Annihilated *me.*"

MJM '84 Santa Monica
– For S. Garfield

The Devil and the Deep Blue Sea

The zoom-&-boom vavoom of fighter jets
here for a weekend of 'entertainment!' –
   above the delicacy of an autumn Bay

   outside the détente of art galleries
is for today what gladiators were to Rome:
a dumbnation of masses crowded, doped

and awed by the power of lords' regimes.
And though bloodshed doesn't show here,
   the drone-&-moan of their engines amps

the birds and cats and gentle lads with fear.
They come every year, these so-called
'Blue Angels.' What sacrilege to allege

the heavens these hateful, eagle machines
whose business is war, now transposed
to a theater of bleachers like some animated

L.A. movie, half horror, half *Pabulum*. Alas,
it was a decade past, an 'Angel' crashed in
   Corpus Christi, torched pilot, gawkers aghast.

Noise, uniformed boys, killer poise.
You can lead a horde to water,
   but you can't make it think.

MJM 10/14 SF

The Ebb of Wince and Whorl

1

In a shooting gallery, all but a few ducks
Have fallen. Leery horizon denizens
They glint like tombstones –
Faces cartooned to insult the dead.
Once they go down – without, one assumes,
An explosive medley of feathers and buckshot –
What? Reset them, wing-dings a'crank?
Daffy, he prays to Mary, then turning tail,
Hires hump.

2

With nothing to depend on
Inevitable vermin over shadowy
Indolence and isolation scramble.
They leave behind the tiniest poison footprints,
Glances askance at marionettes.

3

Nothing divides nothing.
Decapitated eels, grey and black
Bouquet of necks wavering.
From the gallery guillotine,
From the almost unfathomable
Receding chessboard running
Way way back in yr brains distract.
If you're standard, they
Keep you on the move.
If y're not, there's no telling them.
Lobes see-saw.

MJM '84 M.B.

The First Lady

First Lady, laser wit and wiles, compact arrayed,
Holds hands with her husband, digits cresced
And waxen as those from amen-ancient lands.
She leans in, "Not even the Mr. President
Does the 'Impossible.'"

Tête-à-tête, pitched mountains shed snow away,
Ever water melts down marble muscle hills, he
Bows to the sacred un-moveable.

no man does

the undoable.

MJM 8/11 SF
(Revised 11/7/12, Re-election night)

The Houseboy and the Philanthropist

The thimble
Deep inside
The boll within the boy
Hatches, stretches
Out-pitching belly flesh

As Dad studies
To a beam.

           The supports
In there winch – vital glutes cinching
Drum, drum in a tight –
Lidded tunnel –

Learn to loosen. Down under
             Learn love
And curry passage.

The boy stalks analytic
Rhythms, thrums,
Bedizened above and down
By a big buyer
           or two.

Pondering,

He convolutes. Respires.
In time,
      Gains wills,
Property, documents – a complex

Generosity
For all those swoons
Under daddy's
worn ladder.

Newly arbitrageur,
boy heir
      Feels all his adverse
Climates settled
market-fair.

MJM '82 SB

The Met Comes to Boondocks

> "I spend too much, and less than I want."
>
> – Nan Kempner

Behold! The Armida he ached She would be –
Princess in a Rossini opera with a gallant band
Of handsome Christian knights to vie for her –

A Moor. (In his little, racist mind a French
Princess would've been better, *bien sûr,* bone-
Pale skin and celadon eyes.) As it was, he'd

Never heard the name 'Armida' in literature
Or on the news before. He delights to finally find
Mom's exotic name in legend. He loves this

Allusion, wishing it would uplift his family's
Station: blue-collar, red neck, or queer as folk
From Philly to his 'ghetto-'bound Mexican

Cousins. *Here* is a Moorish Princess – those
Same guys as in *real* Spain that one time, (his
'*Accent*' on no *meso*-American-Indian). She

Dresses in stunning costumes in fabled roles.
He's her polished-up-Oliver in this Grand-
Metropolitan Company. He's permitted back-

Stage – 'frilly the kid' – collecting autographs,
And later smug in his center box-seat. Her lover
Rinaldo looks just like Dad, always singing in

World capitals: me wee, Papa's missing-school
Mascot on *who-knows-where-bound* planes.
Delicious attention and supple service oozes

From hot, classy stewardess he craves. *But lo!*
She's a practical gal – tomboy always in jeans.
She hates her exotic name; Dad's b'tombed-away:

Two-pack-a-day-smoker. Not in any center box
Nor backstage at the Met, the little tramp suffers
Major to minor in this miserable desert town.

In the foyer of his little row house, his Dad,
when alive, does the unthinkable – installing
Columns of '*coffee*'-stained cork, alternating

With hideous tiles of gold-veined mirror, hella
'Tacky' all in stripes. He runs to Her closet
To revisit the only glamorous thing she owns,

Not counting the silk sofa he mustn't sit on:
An emerald, Dior-new-look dress, with silk
Twists and heels of file she's dyed to match.

He so wishes her a plenitude of Liz Taylor
Apparel in her closet. And why not several closets?
She'd dazzle him and, social climbing, he could love

Her as an icon. He's never heard this Metropolitan
Armida sing, but he fancies she's exactly as grand as
This Other She can't stand. *He flares*, but She cares not.

MJM 3/11 SF
"F" Street

The Other Biltmore Hotel

His upper-middle class
Victorian's in rehab to sell:
Its paints' and stains' toxic fumes
Repulse him out on his ass

To this dingy Tendernob hotel –
He, youth-hostel hostage if you will.
   Yet pillow-sag, feverish toilet,
Fluorescent bulbs, carpet odor

Attest a senior's Tenderloin
Motel disorder. Has he hit rock
Bottom on sketchy mid-Nob Hill?
How the hell did he end up here?

No fuck-you money to lodge up-
Street, profligacy having drained
   His 401Ks and savings nil.
In the day, cops in New York

Working Hell's Kitchen got extra pay:
Instead of a sandwich to gum,
Tenderloin steak to allay
Each bender-is-the-night-

Tough beat with knife and fork.
As for him, he has a tiny fridge
   That warbles all right ~~
Chock full of beers, cheeses,

And berries that belie his plight;
Fruits and wines on the tallboy –
Oranges, apples, peaches ripe,
A kind of 19th-century comfort saying,

"Do not go gentle into that good night!"
Rage, rage against the dying of elitist light:
Soup-to-nuts, sup damn right
With Bordeaux wine, restore your slight.

But recession's blind-sided
Ex-wife and him, who can't enjoy
The good old life, nor for snotty
Impatience, stand mum lines.

To make matters worse,
He repairs to his dancing bar
To be assaulted by a 210 black,
Who breaks a bottle in his face!

Eyes and bones and brains a-
Throttle, he's in surgery ajar
Some J.C. Superstar, that 'hood-rat'
Farce *Medi-Cal* afar.

It takes him back to last January
Again in hospital, even worse:
   He snapped a leather p-ring
Unwashed around his member:

   Sex toy with the wrong boy,
Got flesh-eating bacteria!
What anti-biomorphic curse,
   Parts south swelled so large:

Hysteria the doc would *little-he*
dismember! Then again, three
Years ago in that same uncivilized club,
A swish of twinks nearly butt him over.

   In ramming back, boy he gets a drub:
Some fleer at the back of this bitches'
Pack cracks small beer atop his head.
Bro' helping him to his car

Steals his phone and money!
   Final fucker, his seeing red . . .
   *The U.S.A. is not like Norway,
Canada, or Sweden* in which each

Canadian, Swede, and Norwegian
Is valued like a *Rare species*,
Cousin of the country's pride.
For Wall Street's and CEOs'

Extreme unction we've traded-in Eden:
   No universal healthcare, but *he* win
Over the country's body Obama,
And every other form of social relief

A long punishment of jumping
   Through dumbshits' hoops,
   And at the end, a petty clerk's
Death knell for pace to melodrama.

   When she finally sells the house,
Eye well, he swears to move to Thailand,
   Where every innocent citizen
Dear to the King near waves a-swell

Swears not for power, guile, or bling,
   But lives in sexy harmony
   With Buddha, *Singha* beer,
And dreamers recreative on sand.

– To D. Brotherston
MJM 4/10 SF

The Sound of Madman

– How, for whom to talk was hyperventilation,
should end a suicide asphyxiation.

So long, farewell
Mr. bipolarity-hilarity
Iconic, manic, comic genius, genie of a generation –
TV to cinema comedy to dramedy
   to tragedy, Oscars and cocaine
   nightly.
The time you shared at the Dry Dock
Me in hock from my last fall from
   sobriety
It's being A.A. and you a man among many
   in our fellowship,
   You seemed embarrassed your whirling
   dervish brain kept boomeranging humor
   in the context of the fatal.
clenching your rubbery face for serious
   but gagging to hilarity
   We became hilarious.
You vainglorious, we uproarious.
Then you did the drag schtick "Mrs. Doubtfire"
   Up the street at the Pac Heights house
   Where of a sudden the neighbors lost their rights
   to peace and quiet – you, the local shit a hit-
   in-Hollywood brought home to roost
   A boost to box-office Hooray El Lay
   And a bust to trust we have in
   anonymity and fans on ceilings
     instead of on lines buying scandal sheets.
A light is off in that house, the sober,
   the sober robber
   the weak a-tweak
   in our house, yours.
"So long, farewell, *auf Wiedersehen,* goodnight.
Adieu, adieu
 To you and you and you.
     Dah-dah-dah-lah
     dun-dun-dun-dun
     dah-dah-dah-lah
     dun-dun."

MJM 8/14 SF
"There are no words . . ." – Crystal and Goldberg

The Team

The team is tense. Picture them on a roof,
Arms stretched up, all hands laid on a smoke-
Stack, an erstwhile Hallelujah Chorus, muted
And black with soot, choking on coughs and coal.
By trade, they'd be inside a dream-like space
Of fine art with windows 'wowing' by the Bay.

Nightmare is, they hide on the roof, dodging
Creditors and clients. Mud druids, they stretch
Up to the boughs of petrified trees, done for,
Finished, *Adiós*, as one used to say to kiss off
Strangers once wealthy. City, state, country,
World have gone broke by this programming

Trader screens for money's Ivy League Mafia.
There's not more to squeeze from the people,
Toothpaste pinched in a regressing, soul-dogging
Recession dunning their budgets. To fill a London
Compact car now costs a hundred pounds, parking
Sixty for two hours. How can folk be lucky with jobs

And businesses, making no money? How did
The children of affluence come to this, raised
On credit, consumption, and risk? The dis-
Economy aborts their upper-middle-class climbs,
Superseded by a new, top troupe of billionaires
& tens-of-millionaires swinging high and haughty

On money they stole via oil, arms, and drugs, plus
Black-shoe trafficking our capital. All their plots
Prove that winners only need screw into places right
Near the spigots of profit. On what they've toiled
Are spoils annexed from the nation, and *sho' enuf*
They walk away free with palms pearled and oiled.

'Bandits' is too folkloric, and 'pirate' much too brave,
'Swindler' too Bohemian. They prefer to be scolded
For 'shenanigans,' as if lo! wild Irish-enabled to play.
Call them shameless exponents for the way they say
Markets work: there's even a demand for thieves on
Wall Street, suckers '*investing*' being the supply!

So this is how the new net works, the grosser left
Behind to pray and fly standby on planes they now
Call 'busses.' Contrast the coked-up CEO, his wife
And kids in several houses, and his hookers lined

Up tonight to lay in line for their lines. That day
in retort to fletched editorials, money boss

Tells *his* team, "We are doing God's work," as if to
Confuse the Almighty with middle-class Adam Smith.
In 'private' jets they make and take calls on peers
Around the planet. Is an extermination of 'losers' next?
Some are quite convinced Wall Street could bank craft
A market demand for murder, the people supplying

The meat. Is that not Mexico's deal these days –
With its posses of pedophile drug-lords next to annexing
Trillions? Not to mention, essential buy-and-sell girls
And 'dry goods' higher-ups sniff on their desks.
As their smart peckers shrink, they can at least snort ego
Via the note in their nostrils, always the hundred buck.
.

They must regret the mint gave up 500's and 1,000's.
Unless, only *they* see them, burrowing inside Treasury.
Either way, they'll throw away snot cash in the trash
For the maid – let her take their bloody bills for scrap.
Up on the roof, that broke band of humanists knows
Too much, and in knowing, may well fall, unknown.

MJM 3/11 SF
(Beach/Geary 1985-'15)

The Vice-President

A son squares the next frame:
He your retort, you his consort,
Tweaks, spins back on the moment,
Jumps and falls: trick he knows.

I search his face for my blemishes,
But Mom's good blood surges his facets
Gendering impermeable patina.
It's not I didn't give my fair share;

I fear I'll transfer my appetites,
Different people all the time needing feed.
Who knows where identity comes from?
Some days I'm the sum of your critiques.

I think he sees me getting disorganized. Yet he
Loves me in that fresh way – with room for fault.
I'm teetering on the brink of being a bad Dad.
Not harm, but for keeping up with his standards.

Then we go to a museum, on a road trip, to resto,
And I see I'm no quack attack, after all.
I do bring home the Napa bacon
And roll with the *bougies,* styling myself

for him a Bit tipped –
       as laughs
       and scribbles
With/in/decent lines of script.

MJM '96 Napa Valley

The Wees *under* Me

The gaps between what I want
and what I get make me fret.

What I *do* do, and what I
Should do

Is not between you and me,
As there *is* no *you,* baby:

   My being solo,
You, a no-show.

Loneliness, we don't pick,
Whereas, isolation is a trick

To get some peace and quiet
From worldly riot.

Still, I wish to spoon
And fall asleep with you,

Especially after sex.
Not making love befuddles

Me and not being cuddled . . .
makes me *Nervous wrex.*

MJM 8/14 SF

Them Again!

Another puerile summer holiday, Friday-to-Monday fiasco fray
of proles on parade – the working wounded, walking in dazes
in the open-air mazes of Fisherman' Wharf: the obese,
the terminally nice – all smiles and gazes, the violent,

the rude, the babies in toddler cry-and-screech fazes. The
chucos and bruthas *trip* on their low-rider crotches, as those
a'bound for Alcatraz eye their phone-watches. The euros
add their mannered touch of lite class, while the blue-collars,

yes, they do, show their cracked asses: Hair o'er tighty-whiteys,
as we roll *our* whites thru our tortoise-shell glasses. We work in
galleries, fest and fed on the rich, the only ones worth hitching
our pitch. So why all plebeians to torture our scouting? –

the ones from Mantēca and Martinez, out loud o'shouting. (Last
I checked *manteca* in Spanish meant 'lard,' and lard-butts
in *caprice* are abundant, let out from backyards!) There are
hippies, spiced Indians, and stoners galore. There are even those

who'll call the gallery a store! It isn't my fault that we can't
serve the poor – our wine and cheese parties fall in Fall
in rapport with our honchos who bid, buy, and collect. But
for now and four days I'll be harassed by nimb-numbs, all

unselect! There'll be churls who demand prices, face-tatted
yells cross the floor, and nitwits who think they pay at front door!
They'll be beach babes with their nose in the air with ten
colors of not-blonde alleged in their hair. We'll have ethnics

and skinheads who'll skulk by the nudes, and one or two
serious collectors, our chosen, the Jews! There'll be Georgia
and Chaumet, hell represented, and families from München
on busses a'rented! They'll be drunks who wanna buy art

on *your* cards, and cards who want us to buy what they
own, as they've earned the rewards of having invested
in art. Eeegads, what retards! They'll be a Svengali from
Turkey who's pierced and an artist, and one from Korea who,

uhh, isn't the smartest. There'll be groups of chill dudes, who
think we're all fags, and those who want just the frame inform-
ation, and those still-stunned by jet lags. And some from Mexico
City, all stylin:' but alas, not Medellín's, coked-up, money bags¡

If the wealthy were numerous then being rich would
mass matter, and if class were spread out my efforts to
flatter would succeed to sell art mid this weekend's cheap
chatter. Alas, I'm a gallerist, a classist, a crank, and I

don't value the demos like a right, good-old Yank. I'd rather
choke on fish eggs than endure this assault. They are broke
and no good to us. Is this my fault? Or could I be a good
Dad and treat as kids, these so-called adults – dolts!

Labor Day "off" should be remembered as this:
Four days on which all art dealers piss!
And if de*hy*drated, then *diss* a dry hiss.
Snoots every one of us, when the rich are a'bliss,

Sailing Mediterranean's azure blue,
And we with a family of *gypsy* Albanians*!*
How rude!

Use to be airplane tickets cost money,
but now they're 'air busses,' my
sunburnt, skin-flakin' sonny-n-hunni . . .

Bubba, your wife-beater tee
is the last thing at work
I wanted to see.

So this is Labor Day!
Uncle Sam set me free.

MJM 9/15 SF

Third Row, Center

> *– Her tail, a swisher,*
> *If she won't move, I'll squish her!*

Aloof on *cour chaises,* Regina Caqui
Nattily selects the perches she prefers,
Changing seats like feline eyes phase:
Throughout the course of a marquise's day . . . .

A gadabout, cat about home rule, she's
Freer than QEII to pick her poses,
No noblesse oblige calendar duty,
Yet not free to stay kaput like a mule

With barrel-chested *me* in Goth tee,
D'gorilla in *Calvin*, black-boxer negligée,
N'er trusty to surrender his seat to a lady!
An old gal – but brat? she's *Skeptical cat.*

MJM 6/13 S.B.

Third-Eye Jail

He meditates on you, alone behind bars.
Hail Mary's, Our Fathers: these prayers
Of youth so wrong, now come to roost.

Tears flow through his eyelids; they always
Well in the moment of the *Divine* present.
Cone fixed, he's ring-pulsed by that vortex;

Or inside the red net; or in the long chute a
Space-fast-train-hyper-flies *to speed of light:*
He sees its back end, time collapsing, as he

Sees the *front car*, too. He used to rebuff
That God knows the sparrow and the lark,
Much less cares. That woman-by-man *He*

Would teach by trial, and test our hearts'
Faith, Hope, and Love."*Of these three, Love's
The greatest beauty.*" Anthony, Godspeed.

MJM 2/11 SF
Martinez

Thoroughly Modern Aunt Millie

My modern Aunt Millie, angular
Aztec face bones, ultra-black hair
Straight-flipped in a pageboy like

Louise Brooks in "Lulu," longed
To travel. Recollecting foreign
Lands, she'd smile like a pepped

Up tad in an *Our Gang* comedy
Snuckt inside a penny candy store.
Flash-bulbs of joy would burst in her

Kodak all full with fountain's splashes
That *crowds* could only glean in the
Glimmering shine of this 'Darla's'

Orbs under eye-sly *brow-n-lashes.*
Voyaging mid-century, when planes
Were frail and to Timbuktu one

Hiked a trail from a rail as to Machu-
Pichu, she'd *collude* as intimate as a
Mandarin, "Would *you believe* there

"Really *is* a Timbuktu? My *goodness*
Gracious, and those *Olmecs!* I'm telling
You, I just dreamt to tuck one of those

Big stone heads in my *itty bitty* purse
For my own backyard!" *"Shrunken head!"*
Her son would cray. Gingerly, she'd

Sip beer from one of her sister's
Stylish '50s glasses, curving up like
A gnu's head and lined thick-to-thin

By silvery chrome leaf, every round
Parallel girt as on Mercator's globe.
It was her lipstick trace on that rim

Of cool pour I peered for – smear'd
Again, true red! *Gosh,* how those gals
Would whip out lip liner and puffs

To pancake foundations to do make-
Up at table! Lawd, I couldn't clip a
Clean fingernail in there without a

'Proper Manners' lecture until a
Neither-here-nor-there *wherefore?*
For Russia, modern Aunt Millie

Garbed in fur *ushanka* – or *shapka*
For those *less*-travelled, and polka dot
Two-piece swim suit for Australia,

"Just like Rita Hayworth's." She'd
Clench her rock-hard teeth, chin and
Slender neck forward with spritely

Commingled smile, irises all mystic
Sparkle that I thought she'd pull out a
Ticket from the *'itty bitty'* for <u>me</u>, *invité!*

Palms to foil, we'd smash a magnum
On the newly minted *Queen Charlotte*
For our wend down the Nile – *she*

All Cleopatra; *my* looking overboard
For baby Moses in his wicker. Alas,
She grew older, but lack of stamina

Sure didn't stop her: *St. Moritz* in
Summer, she no skier, not to mention
Munich and Leningrad before *and* after

Peter! She lived domestic life chided
By charlatan sisters for her poor diet
And not cooking. But *I knew* where

Her thoughts were: skimming a safari
Brochure she'd afford by skimping
On dinner – hers a whole world's table

From goulash to dim sum to *tapas* to
Gator – and then back at our beery
Merry table, *boy-oh-boy* all I'd hear.

MJM 1/11 SF
In memory of Emilia R.
To 'Los Neriachis' kitchen table!

Thou Shalt Not Thou

Why'd no less than Dostoevsky say, "To be a saint you have to be a sinner?"
No garden-variety pimp or thief would he conjure, this author of the criminally
Insane. He means the worst blasphemers, devil psychos who'd sexually molest
A kid on the altar, or a serial murderer discharging cum on the corpses he rapes.

Then he preaches reach of nerve – not unlike great righters in the novels of our lives –
Toward some exotic Ctrl-Alt-Shift, he philosophizes "new-age" ideals, models intellect:
Anarchic, agnostic, free of the shackles of bygone superstition, herd values. Paranoid
Bureaucrats he would replace with his own blank state – men of new fiber, new hew.

Yet no matter how selfless his unrest or Nero-like his bed with magisterial perversion,
How amplified by science, empowered by Tsar or thrill of treason, no matter how fit
To make a killing in *Red Square*, if not on the killing field, amid whatever independence
From history, tradition, common ways "Masters of the Universe" impugn, he who plies

And reapplies brilliance in his own way, in his "own world," no matter what
clairvoyance, art or genius in his zeitgeist or his heist, whatever noble Caesar or lurid
Caligula, golden-flecked whores in hand or a-quarrel with *Duma* for his derangement,
His vision quest finally prevails not, Mr. Roman Feuilleton! When the self flags out

And you, rode off on Bellerophon in your own orbit, plunge mid howling, tears, shrieks
And hospital and prison doors shut, explorers fail, and incendiary men in mighty stations
Flail under the pen of genius. Dostoevsky – Quixote though he be, Shakespeare
Of psychopathy, Galahad of surreal, Merlin of mime, Einstein cubed to the fifth

Degree of novel structure, Mercury at his apogee – *is always coming home to God by page*
One-thousand thirty-three: outwitted to sorcer anything more ontological than yelps
Of ardor to the Lord! I was a badass mutherfucker, and no commandments reigned me.
Now broken, on this Easter Sunday, I go back to Christ and Church like Dostoevsky.

MJM 4/09 SF
In nomine Patris et Filii et Spiritus Sancti, Sancti, Sancti
Во имя Отца и Сына и Святого Духа

Threnody

Garnets sparkle not as sweet
As my heart broods sapphire.
If it glittered down the street
Would stainless you admire?
If first felt love wore a-fray,
What have you felt missing?
My love boy-to-boy astray,
Yours for girls' lips kissing?

Glint your browns, twin evening bars,
Were my little enclaves.
Now you gaze on wife and cars
Finessing not my craves.
Shall I bed the lolling lad,
Push him to my pillow?
Or abstain, romantic nagged,
My soul repressed ill low?

You my heart stiffed; I fled town.
Never think it ceases.
Every other lad I've found
Bar up pawns to pieces.
Were you to come jogging by
Would I let ghosts grieve me?
Let me wonder if I try:
Dashed for, you'd re-leave me?

MJM 1/11 SF
After Mrs. Parker's
You can lead a love to matter, but you can't make it link.

Thug

Bull-cocked, he backpacked such a sacking of dick down
In the lustred butt, palms 'round the ribcage calloused, that the
Boy toy came to insane – his stewed jizz a-splat the pillowed

Boutique throw with ladhood's ejaculate, prick engorged in his
Sunned bum. Hercules-hard, daddy'd-arrow like a lunging steed:
But before he could drop, he tush-crammed that crushed lamb

With extra-trouble bam ram to raid the wracked youth, his Zeus's bolt
Hailed by the kid's neighing, "God, no more!" and flared, cock-ruffed
Like a lion flouncing a deer or an orangutan pound on his full-pile shag rug.

MJM 12/10 SF
To Craig's List!

Tinselitis

– an early El Lay basher

1: Charlie's Angels

Life's a tabloid turner
For bountiful beauties
Clippering down the hill.

When the thrill of leather
Thrusting into fifth
Sputters out, they'll

Rekindle the boss,
Assenting to his rise
Of dough and, fender work over,

Hand in their Porsche
For a hang-glider.

2: West-Side Wonks

Lo! The ladder climber:
Errant angel, slave inelegant
To his eighty-hour work week.

With the 41st barely lapsed,
He panics, but by 79
Excitement swelling

To such a pitch, he exhales
A light soul's magnanimity, heaves
A hearty equanimity.

Downright proud of his ability
To cope, he enters the pub an
Ear-to-ear mug of satisfaction.

But queasy Sunday night,
He'll remember,
Slow's the crawl to junior partner.

3: Idealist Drop-out

You've floated offshore so long
The rip tides finally enwrap
You; now they can't tow you back.

Dredging the bottom yields
No body. They say you lasted
On seaweed ~ food, frolic, float.

After a few weeks, "flux of silver . . .
Finally "ferries him down there."
¿Que piensa la india que vende

Naranjas en la esquina? She's been
Standing in smog so long
One wonders if she's adapting.

4. Venice Ad Guy

If you move to Sin City
Locate near a laundry,
Keep a waxed car & flaxed teeth.

Coming down the hill, do your Industry
Duty – the whole way schmoozing in
'Angelino' your bonny luck to stardom.

– To Fred, Billy, and John at Bentley¡
MJM '85 Santa Monica

Tired, San Bernardino

It's hot. So I *digress.*
Life, liberty, and the pursuit
of nappiness.

MJM 6/13 S.B.

To a Woman

He was faithful,
Lay in your warmth,
Sapling shocked
By snow. How clear

The tingle of wrong
Love can sting,
Mingle in Aurora's
Merging hours

With a rogue's smile
To tame your hollow,
Last speckles
Of a firework finale

Slowly drafting off
A lover no one else's
Passion could conquer.
There's a monkey

At your feet – don't pedal!
Don't abandon the fallen angel.
Administer come-uppance,
One woman's complaint at a time.

Would that he climb
Higher, higher, higher.
In the thin godly air
Be outfaked and reform.

MJM '94 SF

542

To but Voice

To but voice
The ethereal,
Sleep soundly,

Limn like Ariel
Isn't a choice.
And is the rest,

Dimwit, plucking
Out your eyes?
Ever Dalai Lama

Sits down to survival,
Loose a blossom.
Unravel for a rival.

A man, long full
Of sorrow, woke
Up in a festival.

MJM '82 Manhattan Beach

To Want the Pope's Pictures (24)

Here lies Raphael. While he lived
Great Nature feared he might outvie her.
Now, him dead, she fears she too might die.
  – Bembo, Pantheon, Rome

Out-brushed, nature blushed even in skin glow,
And your saintly finish won, less head start.
You framed my youth in fable and by woe,
And limned what only heaven's hands impart.

Within your works the Holy Mother shone;
 In her bosom, rays splayed another's – mine.
As cherubim gay decorate her throne,
Archangel Michael swords, that angels shine.

Muses, crafty, hung worldly pictures forth
Until I mouthed Rembrandt-Velázquez lore,
And deemed you down to decorator's worth:
Authentic paints my idol, I loved more.

Now saved to heaven I repair your might –
What's seen unseen, you drew by cosmic light.

MJM 4/11 SF
After Sonnet 24

¡toothpaste bubble!

brushing my teeth,
i notice
a
small
what's
it,

pinhead
u
 f
o
floating near my cheek –

a bit of feather?
a mothling?
a gnat?

       n
      i g
      c
i see it boun-
mid-
air

to the rhythmic
strokes of my wrist.

with every up
and down of my 'brush
it does a
jig,

as if rigged,
dust-
mote
m
 a
  r
   i   e
o   t
 n t
  e
   t
    t
    e!

I
take
a closer look,
and find
it's
a
tiny
bub-
ble
made by
my *Crest*
with "3-D Whitening"

suds:

a

midget

bubble

no bigger

than

a

smid-

gen!

i blew bubbles
with soap water
and a wand
in
my
childhood,
like you and everyone
else.

but i had
to live a long time
to see
a toothpaste bubble!

o
 r
  b
so
small,
as to be

lilliputian!

though i can barely
see it,
I can
&

the air is an engine
that keeps it bobbing,
            up
and
            down,

. . . when a gnat flies by.

seeming to see it
or sense it,
that gnat changes
course, aiming straight
at the bubble:

as if
a mini,
itty-bitty
teeny-tiny
teen-
sy-
ween-
sy

rocket
pointed at an asteroid →

to blow it up
and save the planet!

They almost collide
when that gnat
changes course,
catching a whiff
of me ~

tiny bubble
a'splat on the milky
lightbulb cover
a-
bove
my head!

Borges wrote,
"There cannot be two
things exactly alike
in the universe."

At
the atomic
level,
he's
right.

But much BIGGER
than that, here is an entire *event*
I bet has never happened
to another person in World History!

a gnat
and a tooth-
paste
bubble

zigging
                              and
                    zagging
in tandem
to the pumped
air
o
 f
  a

good
tooth brushing*!*

mjm 7/15 sf

– to jack, Brahmin

548

Top Drawer

The flock is still religious;
They go to Church on Sunday.
Whereas I, more like a reberal

Go about town, beer-breathed
And exhaling the Good, by way
Of generosity and consideration.

The manners Granny taught me stick
Like Minerva rules, her believing
Evangelicals to be the worst sin.

"It only spreads ill will," she'd say,
To which I'd add, "Spawns a certain
Morbid row always nipt unborn

In courteous circles, who'll avoid
That flap-jack impulse of nasty
Brutes bred on boorish hellfire –

Not a riff ladies and gents smith."
I too remain in the shadows of
Courtliness. Yet, how gerbil-on-wheel

I feel. Do you? The IRS knocks; in a bar fight
I nearly lose my eye; everyone's rude and crass,
"Investment Bank" melt-

Down making outlaws of good peeps.
Everyone says, "MJM just stay an angel.
You were raised on High!" *You punsters.*

The synagogue, the mosque, Buddha,
Hindus, Catholics, cosmos come together:
I loved and sexed. Begat – but *hardly*

Showed off pictures of my kid
To status-mad friends by mail,
As if to establish, "This here

Dillerdom's for Christmas!"
As I feed him his baby food,
On the other hand, I intone,

"We're half-spawn of aliens.
No drugs, no tattoos, wear a condom!"
The last of these, proof we don't settle

For Mother Nature. Confer shaved
Porno balls! Global earth-warming,
Please stop our quest to plastic wrap

Our dumb-ass toys and for packaging
Our everything inside – slobbering lungs
Still left to fend off smog, microbes

And fumes – only now we get to
Watch the hills become the beach!
One does not say these things in church,

Nor would they conscience, "We're only
Half from here." *Well in a way they do,*
But it's not the same story. "You're crazy

Sir, so naturally your discomfit is
Supernatural." Oy. Wouldn't it be just
Like life that such a crock of faith –

Which Greco-Roman I resist – will
Be proved, Martian visions, after
My death? Truth be told, I don't

Believe in flying saucers anymore
Than God. I was trained to await
The One, and the other I dreamt

Up with bad biology and quack
Evolutionary history? But note
That the irony is scientists' reason

For thinking we won't be visited
Like the people in Church do,
Is that all civilizations die or kill

Their planets off before reaching a
Decent travel speed. How mundane!
Also ironic that the churchman's

Truth and the crackpot's outer-space
Invasion theory *both fly*, you might say.
Difference is, my nuttiness notwith-

Standing, egos, evils, the church
And state and monkeyness irk and obsess
Me every day from here to there and

back in
a split
sec.

MJM 2/96 SF

Tornado *tornado*

Self-anointed not to disappoint
In order to make his parents
Violent disorder heel to order –

Crash of glass and plate till the wee
Hours – Mom bombarding her mate:
Addicted gambler, ho-house rambler

Until wee ones shake in terror
In their twin beds – the error of
Dad's a-ways, gaming their last dollar . . .

She, scrimping tips in her coffee-shop
Travail – waitress *suprema,* that small
Stage, her only respite from his shit.

Elder one diverts, dives into school,
All "A"s, until college drinks & drugs
Waste his talents à la dear old Dad to A.A.

Years since Pop's cancer death at 54,
He's not speaking to Ma, her obnoxious
Self-centeredness sheltering her to shut-in, shut up, shut out.

Elder gobsmacks her with sins of the mouth:
"C"-word, "F"-bombs, "You bitchy spic.
You ick, ick, ick," as he licks cocaine

Off a glass darkly – puts his rod in a pot
to pee – family, all peas in a pod. No up,
no out, now these undercover cops, no God.

He's self-unanointed – friends, cousins,
Son, ex-wife wonder aloud – his charmed
Life, wayward strife – and gossip alarmed.

Yet hope is not dead, if he stay out
Of his ravenous head, the bad hood.
Would, should, could – so will, duly?

"He needn't cling to that fear?
It's only that spring will be
A little late . . . this year?"

Stop his tornado. Bolt, a *volta!*

MJM 6/14 SF

Totem Poles

Depends on whom you talk to: his low man up,
Screeching for a squirt, lubed-n-then toweled,
Or the altared saint, tattered, *Bible*-lad – *Word,* bedside.
On his knees: Its incessant, Middle-Eastern threats,
And epistolarians scathing heathens via jacked-up, High-
Command-letters. What of Joy's prayers, semi-daily,
Just cast? Then, struck by gonads' alarm, to conjure
Hellest scenarios – driver-wrassed – Lothario's-arm-
Up-your-ass-to-the elbow, a'helpin' him cum – ab-
Sent love's intense affiliation. He knows the ape's
Quite in there – heir, bumpin' red-boundary crud
By night: but what of the flame-sworded Archangel
He honors? . . . His Blessèd, Virgin Mother?
How did both these ambi-volve to Gemini-stage: –
Almighty, and he with bam-bam in the same cage?

MJM 10/11 SF
Park Merced Towers

Tourists

Here, where red bricks rise as in Boston or in Delft
The tourists take selfie pictures of themselves on ends
of selfie sticks. They see and see, and nothing sticks . . .

Heaven's laid a Bay scape at their feet they admire
but then on double-decker busses, flee in red fleets
as if a fire! Everyone wants to do the same four things:

Alcatraz, Ghirardelli, *Buena Vista* for Irish coffee,
Pier 39 – though why the latter, one must opine:
it's plastic, corny tripe, common to fairs of any stripe.

The Irish coffee, one see's why, since vacation's
a time for being high. They flock to the Golden Bridge –
lately wont to renting bikes and go-carts to take

in everything but the Arts here in the august Gallery.
Seems tourists today are buzzed, athletic creatures
with scant
time for culture preachers. If things don't pick up soon:

I, marooned, bored aswoon, crazy loon, tempted back
to white and spoon, might have to find real work as soon
as change my tune. I a bit depressed, a lonely, loony

Moon on high tonight to mess with heads and hearts,
Illuminate the arts! Let's see if she can't set things right
and make these tourists trade their sites for outta sight.

MJM 8/15 S.F.
Chloe

Towers-of-War in Bologna

> As when one sees the tower called Garisenda
> from underneath its leaning side, and then a cloud
> passes over and it seems to lean the more,
> thus did Antaeus seem to my fixed gaze
> as I watched him bend...
>
> *Divine Comedy*, Inferno, XXXI, 136-140

Luxe, sunny days up in park tower, Skid Row
Behind us. The traffic-rushing-streams
So far away, it sounds like *il Mare*.

Borne back to utensils-and-appliances –
So costly but handy, he recalls buying in-
To their esoteric heft, in defiance

Of the by-laws of Protestant sobriety.
Just he-and-the-mate, now – he has no
Executive Project to missile skyward

For peers to spy from their office windows.
He's-hand-to-mouth, with only two hands.
Poetic justice, as is, he's re-set into this suite-

Of-rooms per his own calendar –
Artful and Old World: "You can't wash
The sass out of a renegade, class."

Taunted by his many shoes, though, he did
Sojourn to the pale: "Crazy cat Big Man suffering
His middle age, seeks Holy Penis Grail."

A legendary knight, he'd charge the stores
To stay the peacock, so breeding fans and fancy
Feathers, frightful fucker, in error of *old* age –

Might yet spill his sexy seed into shoals. He parted
The county, yet, resident there still somehow –
Feels the runt he was on his old block, not that sate,

Date-night rapport of this town, friends all wined
For his floor show – yet sadly, now, Jock-o'holic.
Like a lily, he lay on green water. The skate bugs can't

Scare him, and filth of algae and fish crap,
He fears not – afloat, where the water-and-sky kiss –
Clean away, and 'r' barely bound by gravitas.   *MJM 10/11 SF*

Tractor

In a delusion of sorrow
We walk into your sad tale.
Of each of us, a loved one
Died this year. Then,
In your restaurant tonight
You whisper, "Last night
My sister's husband
Was crushed to death
By a tractor he'd rented
To level his backyard.

   "He leaves a loving wife and
twin sons four-years-old behind."

We sense her anxious
for neighborly advice:
"Can you imagine how
He would have felt
had it been the twins
instead of him?" D's
Picture in fact makes sense,
As I think of the times
I've fantasized me hit by
A bus to save baby Lex.

"I can't believe you said
That. Only minutes before
It happened, he rounded
Up his boys to go inside.
Then went back out to res-
cue their scattered toys."

   "He took it for them!"
I say, nervous patronizing,
Jaded curmudgeonizing,

"That's what you get trying
To save money doing yard
Work. Help should have
  been afforded."

Know-it-all poet, I scribble:

"Your father-in-law, my
Father lost both lungs, as
Your sister bade her tiny
girl to crib death, and I
My *Lampoon* hero . . .

   "The cliff that by the sea
There roiled the sod
That surfed the wave stones'
Flower dusked the veins
Of your destroyer."

   Dinner ends unlike any
Other; toast to: "Duty!
It's our duty. We must
To another – it's our duty,"
*Not to tick a nothing heaven
   Round the stars.*

MJM '00 SF
Fillmore

Trader

They call it 'switching chairs on the *Titanic*' –
overcoming one vice and then entertaining
another. Saw a snarling chihuahua tonight,
actually in the same room with a calm one –
doggy opposites. Do wild animals suffer
vices, domesticated ones? When I see a fat
Golden Retriever, I naturally blame its owner:
"You, madame, overfeed your pet." Drinks
traded in for promiscuity; sex given up for
workaholism; job put on hold for shopping
extravagance; smoking suspended for the
gym until the knees are shot, and one's
diet's all protein, no carbs, no fruit, no yolks.

Dry from drink, he thinks of dry goods.
Sold in the horrid 'hood, they shimmer
in their little baggies, like radio waves
dimly singing of sex addiction's adrenaline
rush and id idols: porn, orgy, edging, a'wank
for four, five nights and days before the
crash into sleep and the next fray's greed
for opiates, beer, a long shower, and some
calories to prop up a twinged skeleton of self.
Those degrading cycles are part of his
pitiful past. Yet in the mind how they last,
and last and last and last. Someone said,
"What we go through, what we've lived

"is the stuff normal people read about in
books and go to the movies to see. Our
travails are their entertainment." So he's
a documentary in all the same ways as
his soulmates. Our suffering rates journalistic
coverage. Same guy, different day, different
vice. Would be nice to settle for a boring,
routine work-week and some mild release
of a weekend. But that's not how he rolls.
Running red lights. Not paying tolls. Dawg
switching highways. Ignoring soul's fight
to the light, then setting up for outta sight.
Powder, pipe, prick, sex hype. Self snipe.

Superego alone with id. No self, like a neigh-
borhood missing a kid.

MJM 8/15 SF

Triolet

Tuck-a-tuck-a-tuck,
Click the castanets
Clamoring for a buck.
Tuck-a-tuck-a-tuck,
My gypsy ran amok
On razored rooster bets!
Tuck-a-tuck-a-tuck,
Click the castanets
Clamoring for a buck.

MJM '79 Cambridge MA
To the memory of L. del Rio,
Prima flamenca assoluta

Trumpet Strumpet

As with the 1850s' "No-Nothing Party," xenophobes with a megaphone,
An obtrusive voice enters the arena, capturing the ears of the masses.
Back then, Protestant men caucused to block immigration's German
And Irish Catholic. As in the dawning of JFK, mobs of scornful men

Impugned their loyalties to the Roman Pope. They would be turned
away at Ellis Island, excluded from jobs and citizen status, shipped back
To Old Countries, that these insouciants stay ensconced. With spec-
Tacular nerve they named themselves "The Native American Party,"

as if landing at Plymouth or upon the shores of the mother colonies
Transcended even the "Indian!" In San Francisco, a Know-Nothing chapter
Was founded in '54 to oppose all Chinese migration; members included
A Supreme Court judge of the state, who ruled no Chinese person

Could testify as witness against a white. A'tort, The Knisms, as they
Were known, battled for offices, governors and mayors and Senate
Seats, unto boards abounding. Some won, even as violent protest
And riot rived communities in their rise and wake. Now, in 2015

A similar rapskallion rides the tide of popularity, a brash burgher
Of New York City, trumpeting the end of American charity, now lost
To the humble Mexican worker, whom he would tall away behind an
Insurmountable wall, dividing the nations. More ambitious than his

Avatars, he'd mock the majesty of China and Russia, unleash his
Hell on the Middle East, dicing diplomacy into deal after deal in dollars,
Arm-wrestling the world to kowtowing to the greatness of the United
States, he sees as having passed, though our influence be unsurpassed

In this our life and moment. He would cut open to surgery every Federal
Bureau and office to the ravages of his raves, demanding fealty as of
Slaves. His cock-sureness to demean the powers of Congress and Court,
As if he, our new Knight might trounce *The Constitution* for his doormat,

The magic 'carpet' that be, trump-trampled to blown to ground. Should
This blound upstart lead the way, portends a nuclear fray. As the globe
Evolves into a stateless whole, we hear unleashed this shrillest prole –
Who *would,* the world, bipole. His money confers no class, nor taste,

Nor international manners of statesmen's grace. He's hate and tantrum,
Ego-maníac, insults evil, abiding under his tongue, and naïveté to *Ignor-
amus ignomin'ous.* President of the U.S.A. – that study in leadership,
Commanding will and lordly deference to be trashed to *cash in on*

The cowardice of opponents, he fancies would fold: the moans of his
Trumpets, political strumpets, whored to the churl, nasty unfurled
In the shouts and insults of his pulpit. Prime Minister to the world,
The one who can press the button, the Father of our minions, hand

Ever tempers cross-bombing opinions among the radiant arrogant
To the facts of pluralism, selfless service under God in His diverse
Ways, Her love of Peace, the ravaged poor, and to us an open door.
Providence-prone, take comfort this louche clown will, surely soon,

be voted out and

down.

MJM 9/15 SF

Turn of Tongue

A love sonnet must contain a *volta*,
A drastic change in plot or temperament,
As when you shred my romantic soul to
Dead, gut and heart bulimic – spirit, rent.

I have no way to ever steer you back.
And so have bull-horned other boys, supine.
Or triaged and romanced girls – all to lack
Breathless, obsessive flush when you were mine.

So, poems to which I turn for therapy,
Shakespearean sonnets writ in vain to you,
Light: I have no love to make me happy,
But loneliness and memories to rue.

I would have put my legs up in the air.
Instead I face down pillows in my lair.

MJM 8/15 SF

Two 'Sons'   (4)

Unthrifty, marriage-less, why did you spend
Reckless on the wretch'd pair you came to be?
Long after Venus shirked, no love to lend,
You craved liquor and cocaine . . . reeling *'free?'*

Mean, the two of you lost your selves to son,
Bounteous, your alls' playing, 'Let 'em eat cake!'
Now you roam, bereft of any union,
And zero sum of sums, reclaim the rake

With but few nickels, poor and left alone.
How the cosmos spins bitter to new sweet
For man bankrupt of trophy-wife – bud's sewn!
You clear to ace: mirth audits glee, heart beat.

When strife and love's denial poison maid,
Champ the willing chet: chad, auspicious trade!

MJM 3/11 SF
After Sonnet 4

SONNET 4

Unthrifty loveliness, why dost thou spend
Upon thyself thy beauty's legacy?
Nature's bequest gives nothing but doth lend,
And being frank she lends to those are free.
Then, beauteous niggard, why dost thou abuse
The bounteous largess given thee to give?
Profitless usurer, why dost thou use
So great a sum of sums, yet canst not live?
For having traffic with thyself alone,
Thou of thyself thy sweet self dost deceive.
Then how, when nature calls thee to be gone,
What acceptable audit canst thou leave?
Thy unused beauty must be tomb'd with thee,
Which, used, lives th' executor to be.

Note: with the ending couplet: *'Thy unused beauty must be tomb'd with thee, which, used, lives th' executor to be,'* SH rather hints that I, his DC, will only complete the homosexual PS, (*'having traffic with thyself alone'*) and that the female PS (*'thy unused beauty'*) will go to my grave, as DC, with me – for SH presupposes his DC exhaustion from having completed the first, homo cycle. Notice how he even absents the "E" from 'the' → *[th']* in the couplet, in order not to conjure the visual cue [t]*he* = 'he,' since it is 'she' that the 'executor' ought/ will next birth into a hetero-PS cycle. SH makes plain that when the homosexual DC are discovered in the DC tomb, the gay series, in turn, *'used, lives th' executor to be'* = 'will, in turn, yield the female PS cycle' that SH will have encoded in the homo PS. (*Cf.* PS 154.) But his DC, dead and buried, SH implication is that a later DC will have to finish the second half of the assignment (the hetero-PS), since, again, the bard imagines his first DC going to his grave, having only completed the homo-PS due to fatigue and, I suppose, outrage at the double-crossing Lord SH.

SH is also wise enough to know that – at least in his own era or close to thereafter – if his DC is ever caught with just the obscene, homosexual PS, then he will be executed for heresy. This imagery is subtle in the SS 4 text: *'Profitless usurer, why dost thou use So great a sum of sums, yet canst not live?'* – wherein, 'profitless' = 'no one can sell a homo-cycle of poetry,' since gay notoriety = a capital crime; and wherein, 'profitless' = 'without issue (children)' + the obvious: 'profitless' = 'prophet-less' = both 'unholy and unspeakable.'

SH is a class-A smart ass, who damn well knows, at the risk of repeating myself, that anybody who finishes the gay PS cycle will be far too exhausted to even contemplate mining a hetero series of 154 PS, all over again: *'Unthrifty loveliness, why dost thou spend/Upon thyself thy beauty's legacy?'* = 'why does his gay DC spend himself upon 'he-selves,' which are only a mirror reflection of 'thy gay self?' *qua* homo PS cycle – the obsession for which the worn-out DC will have 'spent himself,' and – 'sick and tired' – perforce occlude unraveling the 'beauty' of the hetero-PS. Answer? Because, after these three years of DC, I *am* fucking 'spent.' ¡*Joder!*

Two at Tapas

– On "keep-coming-back" birthday

At first our points of view and clamor rico-
Cheted bonking what the other had to say,
Not unlike your wine stem toppling to crash
Your water glass onto our *jamón* Serrano,
Delicate favorite now boggy and sharded.

Your droopy eyes nodding on sniffed pills
Were no match for my *twacked* micro-mannered
Orders, but for the barbarism you've cultivated,
perhaps to hold your own against alpha parents,
Or make macho my over-weaned Restoration
              rafinée.

There was a rancid olive tapenade inedible
At our table whereat the wake-and-bake son
Chides then congratulates his back-to-AA
Daddy with a condescension that only inherent
Drug dependers would reflex to self-deflect.

Obstreperous me and belligerent you drilling,
Knifing wisdom into each other's fool,
The wounds of words and pretzel logic
Of cross-denial arrowed, insidious but for in-
visible armors deigned to drunks and homies.

              Then of a sudden we both go silent
                    Your eyes on mine, mine in yours
So a soft rush of filmic intuition reels
Before the talkies. You touch me; I hold
You. I hold you; you touch me – and by

All the trade winds ever sacred to lost
Sailors and tipping masts, colors of goodwill,
Joy and ransom run and whir up the riggings
By fathers and sons who raised each other right –
Apparent in a spy-scope, not obvious in storms.

MJM 7/17/10 SF

un fleur du mal

the nasty neighbors'
bottlebrush
  clashes color
with their house's
so he plucked it all off
into his perfect vase,
  "fuck off"

MJM '77 SB

Undercover

— Paranoia strikes deep
Into your life it will creep
It starts when you're always afraid
You step out of line, the man come and take you away.
We better stop, hey, what's that sound
Everybody look what's going down – Buffalo Springfield

If I were an undercover cop, which I'm not,
I should think I'd surround the criminal's house
With a giant MRI, psychodomic, as it were,
To read the bad boy's mind. Not just the hospital
Type, but the one the Feds have that can teletype
Your thoughts out, one letter at a time, tick-talk.

Next, I'd hook it up to a lie-detector, inadmissible
In court – but what the hell, *judges* court mistrials.
I'd concertize his mind-map by noise: each schem-
atic assigned its own sound – ambient ones from
the hood, that'd repeat any time he thought that rap.
So, sitting outside in an unmarked SUV, The Man

Can see t/his crime's song. Think cocaine, and three
Finch cheeps go off, signing the cranial colors
Brought on by *that* thought, while robbing a bank
Lights up homey's 'free-money' zone, popping hues
Up like firecrackers in some *in centro, B of A* district
Yonder. They pick up on dog barks and sounds

Round your building: the toilet flushing, the shower,
And then, by vibration, modulate these 'normal'
Noises, via nano-tech in a damning re-vibe, back at ya! –
Hamster, busted, yet without 'legal' evidence. I hide
under the covers, worried their spectroscopy is
Reading the chemical signal of meth in my bath.

(And it doesn't matter whether you have a *Samsung,*
An *Apple,* an *Oracle* or *Bill of Rights* – "You, seen."
The FBI, NSA, CIA screen with scan reveals what's
Obscene. Had they known us at Cabrón in the 1970s,
We'd all be in jail for statutory rape, drug crimes,
And rock-and-roll by these trolls trawling our wholes.)

MJM 11/12 SF

Unshrift!

Once shriven, there's no escaping one's past.
Friends and gossips make of one a kind of luncheon repast.
Everything confessed,
Re-assessed, re-addressed, re-cessed.

Nothing blest by truth, now uncouthly repeated.
   Oneself, re-defeated by their pious 'fears'
and lack of trust. If you must fuck up, don't do as the Lord:
Don't admit it. Submit counter-allegations. Don't legit it.

MJM 10/14 SF

Unsustain Ability

Fixity laxity. Persnickety rickety. Stability. Plasticity. Rigidity spontan-
Eity. You ain't doin what boss wants ya to be. Oy is she. Oy vey is me.
Ai-yai-jai. Jailai-head bing-bang bouncing round the gallery like a poet spree,
Or worse, a hippity musician jamming the grid with half-tones, non-sequitur
Demi-semi quavers. The prolixity of the productive. The self-reliabilty
Of those vain enough their creativity eclipses all audience feedback, author
Of his own illusions, delusions, persuasion gravitation. But like many things
Mortal, the onset of age turns sexy to infirmity and beauty to fragility, little
Errant lines etched in the face like arroyos of the mind others made
Into boulevards famous for reliability and I followed *you* wet dreamer.
But now Peter Pan is an embarrassing old man in tight jeans, green gone
Silver, like an Elvis imitator with hair puffier than original and jowls'
Proclivity to sag not the bones of Roman heroes aquiline nor eroic. Tragedy
Ends disastrously, they teach, and comedy even or upbeat. You dance
To the beat of a drummer alluring to aloof youngsters goofing your
Marcello Mastroianni goggles, black sheen on dashing eyes gone face-lift.
In pity of a youth lost to drugs and drink, I came back addicted to sparkling
Water, wishing to concatenate the years gone by with the here, the hip,
The now. Absurdity ADD. Bi-polar heredity. Son of no one but City. Un-
Suitable for other work, frivolity chafing slave-budget citizenry. The bill
Collector calls for pay or bankruptcy. You fall back on insanity. How you
Could end it all with suicide publicity, showing off disdain, superiority
To those born inclined up but not too steep and beige and grey, as nature
Has selected balance ability. You are poor in discipline. You're a pity
Of extravagance and foiled senility. Angel-heathen of the clinking class
And working man's horse's ass.

MJM 04/08 SF
Kendy

Upper-Middle Class (UMC)

Nothing worse than an upper-middle classer,
Peering down on social inferiors in the flats,
While grasping to penetrate the higher tier.
They shun what's underneath, and crasser
Climb toward an echelon money can't bequeath.

She mistakes facelifts for healthy skin
And he, the income, not the time, he dangles
Fore his kin. Grown fat with age, she's not
Oblivious, tented in fine poncho-wear,
Yet still glides on studded sandals, nose

In the air and wisecracks about losers,
Slacking from the Cheshire corners of her
Dentist-daunted mouth. He mistakes his
Kids' schools for dog-and-pony shows,
Qualifying new fathers for their net worths

At cocktails, where the talk ought be babies.
He's disinterested in his own spawn, until
They're old enough to boss around the lawn,
Catching his hard balls – being told by and by
What college they'll attend and why.

Sandwiched in between the salt-of-the-earth
Blue collar minions and the strata of the well-bred,
          The upper-middle classes ought recede
Like cracks do on asses. The foul odor of their
Snotty pheromones interferes with my whore's moans:

A sound intimately familiar to both aristocrat
And hood-rat, UMCs, iced by frigid other-halfs-n-brats.

MJM 8/13 SF

Van Gogh's Café

Limbs lost in the lather of sizzling ripe days,
Gulls' keening faces, boys screaming on waves,

The rhythmic, hazen cries wooed and crissed
The expiring noon. The tin blue harbor laze,

Sunstroked with sorrow, blanched the edge,
The irony of glare, the rim's dim dazzled daze.

MJM '83 Laguna Beach

Vodka

Denial says it's only 'the shits' & vomits.
But what about this boozy, mucous ooze?

Do you admit it to the boss?
Risk the toss? Get off the sauce?

Or sneak to seek a way to gloss
Over it? Pitiable in a pit.

Some guys are über sick with drink.
You'll hear matinal puking in the sink.

Does a good neighbor intervene? Invalids'
disease – or goad abuse, obtuse obscene?

The sickest candidate didn't eat or mate.
Poor kid, he could have been so great.

Where do we *alt* if what to do
About this unshakeable taboo?

You hack and snot boo-boo after boo-boo.
Dodo. Is there nothing you might do?

Are you trying to die?
Trying to try?

Absenteeism.
Presenteeism.

Two sides of the same lost coin:
As vodka's *ghost* besots your loin.

MJM 3/14 SF
D&D

Vultures   (5)

Those looks you'd drown me in before I'd dive –
More star cast than cinema, flood my nights.
Swoons divided me – by your moons alive,
Your dream boats dreaming pair, twinned mine, my lights.

Beckoning mates, you'd shy rivals off in line.
When closed the door, your scent of clove healed whole,
My bedside being you, we smoothed scars to fine –
Girls on phones let ring, burrowing soul in soul.

How did clinging love become my tyrant?
To that which once was bright, servile I held,
And spied to watch them wear you down, a-pant
That Time won't stand me, vultures unfed, felled.

Love is a flight; if yours could up and go,
These tired birds, over seas of tears, screech low.

MJM 3/11 SF
After Sonnet 5

SONNET 5

Those hours, that with gentle work did frame
The lovely gaze where every eye doth dwell,
Will play the tyrants to the very same
And that unfair which fairly doth excel:
For never-resting time leads summer on
To hideous winter and confounds him there;
Sap check'd with frost and lusty leaves quite gone,
Beauty o'ersnow'd and bareness every where:
Then, were not summer's distillation left,
A liquid prisoner pent in walls of glass,
Beauty's effect with beauty were bereft,
Nor it nor no remembrance what it was:
But flowers distill'd though they with winter meet,
Leese but their show; their substance still lives sweet.

Note: SS 5 gives the first indication in the cycle that SH is setting up his DC for some final prank – a type of cruel *'volta'* that is a feature of all SS, in general. Occurring often in the third quatrain and then restated in the heroic couplet at SS end, this *volta*, or turn of wit, logic, fate, fable, etc. gives the plot, theme, *logos*, action of the SS a twist or turn-about. Think of Hollywood screenplays that keep changing fact and logic through renewed revelations as the movie progresses – twists of plot about the newly true facts of the story *contra* the false ones that the prior storyline seemed to promise, but is now denying. In:

> *Those hours, that with gentle work did frame*
> *The lovely gaze where every eye doth dwell,*
> *Will play the tyrants to the very same*
> *And that unfair which fairly doth excel:*

SH first alludes to the countless hours his 'excelling' DC will spend in deciphering the PS, as well as to his own work-time in creating the 'lovely' SS. But SH next says that other selfsame hours will be spent under the tyranny (of his hints and commands) that the DC will have to obey in order to decipher the PS hidden within the SS. He finally alludes to the unfairness of his joke on the DC – that although the homo-PS were indicated by the bard, he will thereafter in PS 154 command the DC to create a whole, other, hetero-PS cycle, an 'unfair' demand of his 'fair' DC. The obvious encoding = 'un-fairy' and 'fairy,' since *'excel'* = 'take the "L" out of *'fairly,'* while above the word *'unfair'* a 'tyrant' "Y" is SH-commanded down to *suffix* that 'unfair' = 'unfairy.' This 'dropping' of the "Y" to the word beneath is an example of what I will be calling the 'neighborhood' or 'hood' of **letters that surround** a letter or a word in its vicinity. This encoding of adjacent ciphers, commanded by SH to affect a neighboring cipher(s), is an example of his SS-PS dimensionality. One does not only go left to right in reading, one goes up and down and over and across – and finally even backwards through the text! depending on his hints.

As you read on in this book, you will find many examples of SH admitting his tyranny and over-strict control of the DC. He will also repeatedly refer to summer as the season in which homosexual liaisons are more probable, due to London men's access to the 'out-skirting' forests, wherein lewd, homo acts can be performed both in secret and in weather warm enough to allow outdoor nudity. Conversely, winter will become a dicey season in which gay meetings among lovers will be more dangerous – perforce indoors and subject to the scrutiny of neighbors, and even worse, of officials. Thus:

> *For never-resting time leads summer on*
> *To hideous winter and confounds him there;*
> *Sap check'd with frost and lusty leaves quite gone,*
> *Beauty o'ersnow'd and bareness every where:*
> *Then, were not summer's distillation left,*
> *A liquid prisoner pent in walls of glass,*

Of course, the *'walls of glass'* are icy ones – that stop *lust* and *sap* – through which others adjacent might suspect, *see*, or hear homosexual activity, a capital crime in Jacobean England, although reaching up to the monarchy and throughout the nobility and Roman church. If nothing is left of 'summer's distillation" = 'sperm' ← 'sap,' then the winter-bound
homo will become the 'liquid prisoner' = 'masturbator' or 'man alone in his mirror-glass' from the previous SS 3 reference to 'mirror' = 'ice.'

Finally, *'Beauty o'ersnow'd and bareness every where,'* is SH first mention of cocaine ('snow') that will dement the PS players into sexual perversions too horrible to imagine. Through the dis-inhibiting effect of cocaine's base stimulations there will be *'bareness every where.'* On the concrete level of poetry – on which SH will dwell in much of the overall DC – notice how he leaves out the "E" again in *o'ersnow'd* to avoid the visual cue, 'wed' – a state of being only granted heterosexuals, of course. Ironic it is, that 'gay marriage' is now waiting in the wings of today's U.S., gay civil-rights' movement. SH will often reveal his hate of homophobia in the PS.

574

Also of great note is that in today's news (1/29/2013) it is reported that IT and genomic engineers have successfully encoded all of SH-SS into a 'DNA' model, using '0's' and '1's' to describe the SS texts – one assumes that each letter or each consonance/assonance cluster has its own 0/1 code-sequence – to make up DNA strings of code (one for each of the 154 SS). What is revelatory, the scientists say, is that the SS read 'genomically/digitally/numerically' *backwards* in the same order of sequence as *forwards!* You will find me saying, later in this book, but dating from two years ago or just shy of that – that I, as DC, have also had to read the SS backwards, at times when commanded by SH to do so, in order to supplement SH decoding hints and commands given the DC, whilst reading the SS left to right.

Water, Chrism, Then Alcholism

We wake up every morning with monkey in our brain:
The -*ism* in alcohol. So deem ourselves insane.
Restless, irritable, discontent –
Stuck-*atto* thoughts boomeranged from where the party went.

A'walk'd into the sober club, garden-variety zhlub,
He's asked, "How are you?" "I'm fine," which elicits party line:
"Oh! – F.ucked-up, I.ntense, N.ervous, E.xasperated, ey?"
What can he, would he, should he say?

"I'll drink to that?" forgetful brat, or how about,
"Fuck you, I'm a writer. How dare you doubt,
'And authors, too, who once knew better verbs
Now only use four-letter words

Writing prose.'" Not everything goes. I'm fine, you fuck
And your being here just ain't my luck.
Butta bing, butta bang, butta butt, you ain't my buck
And I would say you and your attitude suck

But I'm in the program and so will show you
Benevolence, compassion, and understanding.
The time it's taken for you to read this poem
Is the time it's taken to wipe sleep from my eyes

And the bad vibes in my mind's eye.
I wake up every day like this
With haunts, and lurches, and weird fantasies
Before I even take a piss.

But that is that, and this is this.
I'm off to a meeting now. No rot amiss.
  Word to dismiss.
Nor dis to diss.

Give us this day our daily head.
Unleaven what has been inbred.

MJM 8/14 SF

We Rarely Say the Devil, These Days

Much later, failure hurts like the youthing truth.
Not élan-clean, one lives not to sob, or
Un-sober, annihilate his vertical lot.

Whilst the Lord's elixirs are no low-hanging fruit,
Stoop-down, your 'barely-balls,' harried: it's always
Faults, I, Me, My. We rarely say, "The Devil,"

but why?

MJM 9/11 SF

We Remember World War I

It chills at first:
> Such brain power
> Radiating from old eyes.

To the common world
Far away from Harvard Yard –
Where TV, the cashflow jungle

And mediocre markets
Havoc old-timers
To infantility and stupor –

These fabulous faces contrast.
The wit, the merriment
The Mandarin grins –

Even their bric-a-bracs taste
Echoes self-confidence in life,
Not the normal, dubious

Interior-decorated waste:
Observe the funky sweater,
Pitchfork, the woolen tie!

Diverse old lamps, they a-light,
And share the Great War that
scarred the The World to uncorset.

Here I am, young man
In crime's capital forgetting
The College was these guys!

What dashing elevation.
I seek an alliance!
Then it comes over me:

Do the poor
Or low of IQ
Stand a chance against

The slings and arrows
These jaunty gents do?
If the good die young,

Do only the smart and able
Get to live to be this alive?
Could I, would I go on

Their perilous ambulance drive?
No peace time, war *"over there"*
Inside me bombarding half the time

I see these seers and ask,
"Against the march of Time,
  could we be peers?"

MJM '93 NYC
Cf. <u>Harvard Magazine</u>, Nov.-Dec. '93

We Want Art Jobs!   (44)

If the dull, work world as my dreams were art,
Rebellious romance would my part not staunch.
In spite of trading 'stuff,' I could compart
Each labored canvas with a lover's launch.

No matter pinstripes be garb for thieving,
That ilk would be laid off, all earth re-limned.
Nimble, art feeds hearts full, cash relieving –
As well as any stock or bond, soul-dimmed!

But ah! work kills that Muses spark no crops,
Nor clothes, nor shelters as bull markets do –
All that, taste to want, dollars start and stop.
So, art's chased only after rich accrue.

　　Nought art bought, bohemians cannot but show
　　Empty bank, *badges of each other's woe.*

MJM 3/11 SF
After Sonnet 44

Weak Bladder

What fresh misery is this?
Every time I turn in bed, I have to piss!
What strange bed is this?
90-Day *'Progress Program's'* for the mentally ill . . ?
  Instead of drinks, I take pills.

House-fevered, how did boy joy succeed
only to destroy? Has the drunk
lasted so long, been so severe
  you'd guess he'd end up here?
Third floor of a gritty, city 'home,' midst techie rehabs?

Pity my hopes I cannot see.
God be good to you and me.
  Beware alcohol awash you from your City.
It stands white on hills: thrills, frills,
But beware the bridge-wrecked ones it kills.

As you grow old, don't let the skills
  of jobs outpace you.
Even God may erase you.
  Even if to be a'raised

MJM 3/15 SF

West Coast Nor'wester

*The City is where sirens make white streaks of sound in the sky
and foghorns speak in dark grays.*
>   – Herb Caen

Winds unfurl drizzly vapors, blanching thru black
tree boughs and condensing inside plastic newspaper
wrappers. The leaves shimmer and flap in your gusts,
tiny droplets in mists clammy on the gate-hinge that rusts.

Helios, yesterday hot yellow and sunny, can't break
through your brume's blockade in the Heights, until
the skies seem fluoresced over your gray southeast light.
You inhale – a veil dry, then exhale – and another

Wet-front arcs by. Our people ensconced in the gelid
house 'cross the street, mumble and grumble 'bout
New England sleet, comparing this San Francisco
scud torrent to Boston's frozen rain, student-abhorrent.

Some of us grow achy depressed, Seasonal Affect
Disorder the psychiatrists' guess. One day sweating
in sunrays meant for L.A., the next day heads hung
in that glum Eeyore way. Mind and mood awhirl

In your clouds, we drift off wishing bed-bound in warm
blanket sheet shrouds. Depression couldn't touch us,
as long as there light, but now we inhibit uptake to fight
the good fight: pops-a-pill hoping to o'ercome the *chill*.

It's said my people have overly sensitive senses,
Hard to see, just now, through my fog-billow'd lenses.

MJM 9/15 SF

> *"It's snowing still," said Eeyore gloomily.*
> *"So it is."*
> *"And freezing."*
> *"Is it?"*
> *"Yes," said Eeyore. "However," he said, brightening up a little, "we haven't had an earthquake lately."*

What You Don't Need   (6)

Then don't let drinkers' jolly face erase
Wise take-aways, so youths won't die self-killed:
They, lost villains to walking dead someplace,
When sages' measures break them to God-stilled.

Man's end is not self-centered gain. Betoll
What's given you and pay the willing done:
That from despair you seed another soul,
And ten times happier, why not ten from one?

Ten *times* yourself is happier than *you* are,
Yet, ten *His* ten times you snickered *over,*
As death you conjured night to morning star;
Your posterity, the *vial* lover.

Be not self-willed, for you to madness dare.
Be *His* page, and re-sheaf that others fare.

MJM 2/11 SF
After Sonnet 6

SONNET 6

Then let not winter's ragged hand deface
In thee thy summer, ere thou be distill'd:
Make sweet some vial; treasure thou some place
With beauty's treasure, ere it be self-kill'd.
That use is not forbidden usury,
Which happies those that pay the willing loan;
That's for thyself to breed another thee,
Or ten times happier, be it ten for one;
Ten times thyself were happier than thou art,
If ten of thine ten times refigured thee:
Then what could death do, if thou shouldst depart,
Leaving thee living in posterity?
Be not self-will'd, for thou art much too fair,
To be death's conquest and make worms thine heir.

Note: The SH of my long-held imagining is a man obsessed by his own genius, wit, punstering, and intellectual superiority over every other mortal in England, if not all of Europe or the world. He is also an amazingly erudite student of etymologies across many languages, and he is cock-sure in showing off his once-in-a-millennium linguistic endowment. This arrogant, smart-ass profile is requited throughout the upcoming PS: indeed, SH comes off to the reader of the imminent pages as a sneaky, double-talker, who is out to fool even his own DC! Early on in the actual PS-DC – the sequence of which will follow this initial sequence of MJM-OR – I, as DC, come to predict that SH will eventually play a textual trick on me: that he will try to shrug responsibility for the obscene nature of the PS, and put the blame on the DC's own (my own) sick imagination. And yet, this is *not* what happens. Reading further, you will find SH repeatedly chiding the reader to *believe* the insight of his DC and to accept his-my DC-PS as an accurate incarnation of what SH intended to be mined from his 'insipid' SS. But what a fool am I, when in PS 154 SH demands I re-commence the entire DC project, by finding a hetero- or female-PS cycle buried within the homo-PS cycle!

In the *ibid* SS 6, the 'thee/thyself/thy/thine' person to whom the speaker is addressing is *me* – the DC himself, whom SH knows is a homosexual/bi-sexual, for he queries the reader later, "Who else would know the filthy language and practices of sex-obsessed catamites, but one of our own kind?" Such gay knowledge, *ipso facto*, would be required to detect SH hints and commands onward toward the PS, borne of the 'whitewashed' SS. In the SS 6 text, *'winter's ragged hand'* = DC hand, **defaces** the SS beauty. More important – by stopping at the end of his homo-PS cycle and being satisfied with that gargantuan (*'ten times ten'*) task – wherein, 'ten' is both the number of syllables in a SS line, and the length in inches that SH claims his cock to be in the PS text – the DC will end up dead ['executed'], and only *'living in posterity,'* = the 'anal' quarters of the homosexual body. If the DC is *'self-willed,'* as SH warns him/me not to be, then he is gay with a homo/self-*erection*, indicated by the conflation of the double "L" in 'wi**ll**ed,' and the nesting of the name 'Will' within that word. A double "L," as occurs in *'willed'* (also = 'Will led') is, concretely, a pair of parallel lines that stand erect on the page, as in 'll.' This is SH code for the SS-PS as running parallel to each other, from SS/PS 1 – SS/PS 154. (Keep in mind that in geometry parallel lines never cross but are infinitely long in geometric space.) SH further puns on the 'will' of a deceased person, that is, the *noun* 'will' that gives instructions to the authorities on how to disperse of a dead one's wealth among family, charities, etc. I argue that the noun is also suggested in a 'will/Will/will' (verb-Name-noun) triple-speak, which also = 'Will will will, *to his DC*, the project of dis-encoding the SS into the homo-PS.' But what will come as the lynchpin surprise of a SH giant trick on his DC, is that in homo-PS 154, SH will call for an entire new, or third, sequence based upon the [female] 'beauty,' quoted above in SS 6. *'That's for thyself to breed another thee,'* = 'You, my DC, are commanded to dis-encode the SS into the PS, which because it will be homocentric, is another 'thee,' or 'I' – wherein SH, the author of the SS is the first 'I' and his DC, dis-encoder for the PS, the *second* 'I' = second 'eye.' The concreteness of 'eye' is next conjured, in that, given the word 'eye,' the two "E"s stand for one's two eyes, and the "Y," the nose between them: eye.

But the final SH command is:

> *Be not self-will'd, for thou art much too fair,*
> *To be death's conquest and make worms thine heir,*

wherein *self-will'd* = 'the gay DC in league with the gay SH,' for 'self-willed' alludes to the gay man looking at his own reflection in a mirror, as if a first 'I' sees a second 'l.' In order *not* to make *'worms'* (= 'penises' = 'll') *'thine heir,'* SH commands that a third sets of sonnets – the hetero-PS – be the DC final legacy, and the homo-PS, be but his penultimate work. The tripling of 'Will's will wills,' is echoed in the SS/homo-PS/hetero-PS trio. Furthermore, for SH *'heir'* often = 'Herr' ('Mr.') in German. So as not to *only* be remembered as the 'heir' of *'hind-quarters* of one's *posterior,'* SH advances his encoded hints to the DC = 'take the "I" out of 'heir' = 'her,' wherein "I" stands for the homosexual in league with himself or with those of his same gender (the "I" gender,) made all the more 'gay' by the concrete pun on 'll' = two gay guys, or an erect penis or two, two "I"s, two eyes, etc. This concrete letter play becomes very important later in the DC because SH thoroughly hints that the 'starter dough' for a particular PS-DC are those lines in an original SS containing "I"s = SH = the DC =

584

'double "I"s, eyes, 'll's. Starter dough, therefore, that is to seed the DC of a homo-PS will not be 14-lines long = 'too long to dis-encode' – but will only be as long as the number of lines containing the SS "I"s. In all cases the maximum number of "I" lines will = 2, 3, or 4, but no more, thereby making the homo-PS/DC easier to surmise and execute. Finally, SH-the-punster causes *'thine heir'* – the last two words of the heroic couplet to = '[t]hine ('stag') or 'hind' ('derrière'), also 'hiney', since the front verts of the final SS 6 couplet = 'Be not "T" = 'make "T" not exist' → '[t]hine' and also, surprisingly → 'bear' ← 'heir,' wherein the "H" is silent in both 'thine' and 'heir,' as in prior examples, and a *"B"* not a *"T"* is conversely commanded onto 'heir' by the opposite of *'Be not,'* which is equally evident in the front verts = "B[e]" → [h]eir + "B" = 'bear,' the term SH will constantly use to suggest burly, gay men in the overall action of the forthcoming PS.

Whether Six, Nineteen or Twenty-One, L. Diller Gets All A's from His Daddy, OK?

When it comes to mathematics,
I got static in the attic,
No, Sir, nothing's clear.
— Joni Mitchell

There is a secret to this poem I write from a hotel to you for your
Birthday

Since I saw a photo of you and me on Varon's couch Mom gave me again
Today.

You're a squirming, cutie smugger who's glad he has a fun fatty daddy and
a cra-

zy friend making a fuss he's your Jewish uncle from New York and likes Mom to
boot! *"Hey,"*

behind the camera, *"Who's that Catholic guy claims to be your dad? Let's do a D
NA!"*

If you knew, Lex, the bachelor and married-men sins committed on that sofa,
Oy vey,

I'm sure you'd hop out of the photo right now at six and go screaming down the
Hallway,

Calling Mom or a cab on your Ninja-Turtle cell phone making a break for
Broadway –

What a little kid *would not have known to do*, being *"innocent* at that age,"
They say.

Gift from God, you had the power it would seem from my unfazed smile in the pic
To sway.

Back then to make even me forget what a den of iniquity it was:
The way,

Wonderful children change the room-scape for the clearer, cleaner, and the dearer.
¡Olé!

– Love from Dad on your 19th. Wish I were all there for you, but am in heart, as always.
MJM 7/10/10 SF

White Scratches

He faces, all brain, two white scratches
defacing fake wood grain of this pseudo
cabinet, (it has *no doors,* lest a patient
slam his fingers) – that describe the longer
parameters of a parallelogram – long
lines of cocaine, not the hot-pink slashes
on his wrists, nose-close.

The phlebotomists request, "Make a fist,"
Heart wilting in morbid compliance – his
reliance on salvation from exes – loved
ones with whom his binary soul didn't click,
   full of drugged lust to jerk a mushroom
into a pole. O the chary distance
between lone-sex, long – brief love:

   Gay uncle and macho dad –
two fathers,
one son from
lad to had it, had –
parallel scratches –
No Miss Matches
or Mister Sister in the closet.

MJM 5/15 Los Gatos
For nurse John

Whose Bad Idea Was Working for a Living?

Fabu he on steed-back! "Oy, *jodido*" elite hooves and hind hocks
Kerplunk too, kerplunk too, kerplunk too . . .

MJM '09 SF

Widow's Widower   (9)

Is it that I reared up, you widow me,
And leave me consumed, sinned to take a wife?
Your ghost is issueless, and I may flee
Beyond you, swoon to widowed afterlife.

Your world will be my widower to weep.
Love took back, when you had me cleft behind,
Then fronted with broad wife, a son to keep:
Children's eyes change what husbands seek to find.

Look what a spendthrift on our pair I spent.
Then you shift place, in common house to sit;
But bachelors' waste *was love* for jilted gent,
Now unused, abusers free destroy it.

    Loathe to love, I push angels from my seat,
    Heaven not sent, who murders love complete.

MJM 3/11 SF
DC of Sonnet 9

SONNET 9

Is it for fear to wet a widow's eye
That thou consumest thyself in single life?
Ah! if thou issueless shalt hap to die,
The world will wail thee, like a makeless wife;
The world will be thy widow and still weep
That thou no form of thee hast left behind,
When every private widow well may keep
By children's eyes her husband's shape in mind.
Look what an unthrift in the world doth spend
Shifts but his place, for still the world enjoys it;
But beauty's waste hath in the world an end,
And kept unused, the user so destroys it.
No love toward others in that bosom sits
That on himself such murderous shame commits.

Wife

I'm in this sink
And what you retort is
You'd rather be alone
Than suffer my drama.

That I haven't said
Ten words in ten days.
That you don't disport
 Well in pathos.

Am I not whom you married?
High-volt enough to whip up
Frisky 8 p.m. conversation,
Recollect beloved dog Binky,

Dice up how dinner's so suave?
The phone rings. It's my good
Doctor friend from college.
You could fall in love with him

Now that I've gone fallow.
That's how sprightly I see
You click into receiver
One bright girl on the line

With another what-the-heck soul.
He seems to ring away desolation
 Your husband hammers home.
 I haven't touched you

In quite awhile, though I'm
Longing and yet afraid to stay put
Here in DaDa's decorated rooms
And you. Dad, who in his careless

Pain forgets to manage himself,
Embrace your Judaic calm,
 Aloof warmth, forged
To a pragmatic bent of mind.

You'd never name the world
A bed of roses, yet to flower
 Not sticker, you might evict me,
Leaving me wandering childless

As soon as take another call?
As you chin-cradle the handset,
You lamp it out like smoke signals
  If in anguish I won't

Straighten up and fly right,
Hand in this knifing conscience.

MJM 3/92 SF
Steve, Campari, Ricky, Marco,
Josh, and Jake

Will of the Whisperer

– Hetty Green would have seemed less a miser,
Had her headdress not been a green cellophane visor.

He's letting go – laissez-faire, lazy fairy.
On the one hand, bruised by money,
On the other, land of milk and honey.

He lets buzz sangria *fría* up-an'-down
His spineless spine, fuzzy allergies
At his temples, ear-down, glands.

He can only conjure foreign lands.
The ice in his wine glass ought cool
This moribund idiot to sang-froid.

Swirl his blood with cold fear, "Your
Guts murmuring mold, the end is near."
Nothing come of art, guillotines, cocks-n-locks

Who'll plume poetic heart? Dash, jab, dart!
Pirate's fizzl'd apart; his miserly mother's
Miserable million, marooned

In his brother's bank. The pain of her
Zero, followed by all those zeroes:
He – *Herr* bankrupt Roman Paris Nero.

MJM 6/13 S.B.

Wiki: "Hetty Green (née Robinson), nicknamed "The Witch of Wall Street" (November 21, 1834 – July 3, 1916), was an American businesswoman, remarkable for her frugality during the Gilded Age, as well as for being the first American woman to make a substantial impact on Wall Street. There are many tales of various degrees of accuracy about Green's stinginess: She never turned on the heat, nor used hot water. She did not wash her hands, and rode around in an old carriage. She wore one, old black dress and undergarments that she changed only after they had worn out. She ate mostly pies that cost fifteen cents. One tale claims that she spent half a night searching her decrepit carriage for a lost stamp worth two cents. Another asserts that she instructed her laundress to wash only the dirtiest parts of her dresses (the hems) to save money on soap." *Whatevah, ma.*

willie

every now and then, I just wanna do heroin with billie holiday . . .

MJM 8/11 SF

Winehouse

The throat, with bearpaws around it ~ stoned, mumbled, reverberant
tossed you into the devil's light of paparazzi flash bulbs! – an assault
of UFO flying saucers beaming hostile radiation, sickening as X-rays
never turned off blaze the DNA with bombardments of toxic waves,
frequency tight and shrill, your opposite, to metastasize cells, 'flate fame.

Recipe for disaster, your being young, innocent, a'crave to love,
and the fallen angel world, avaricious schadenfreude, first raised
on high in plastic ceremonies beamed worldwide, then joked about
and snarled after on the late-night shows by so-called comedians,
the crowds, financiers of the kill, laughing in their pathetic anonymity,

Pathetic fame and wealth, your lot, and how opposites attract.
Then the pot, the wine, the beer, the booze, the coke, the needle and foil –
locked inside, against multitudinous stalkers, to have something to do
to undo the real, the soiled, the wronged, the wretched taking of body
and soul, so poisoned, doctors astonished and God damned, you in a bodybag.

The trashcan of treasure: Elvis, Marilyn, Janis, Michael, Billie, Whitney, et alia
Amy . . .
Better Winehouse to have been real estate in Vienna than the organ of sotto voce
in stadia. The best jazz singer of the 21st century, gone by '11. Inherit the wind!

Corrina Corrina
Do you have to go
Corrina Corrina
Tell me why do you have to go
Just made me come to love you girl
Now you pack your things and go

MJM 8/15 SF

Without Prayer

Fanned out to some farther cosmic truth,
Our airy dreams ring on death.

MJM '04 SF

Women Are from Venus

Mars! Where are you Mars!
I search the stars!
O there you are.

Nowadays, Venus, I see double.
Cop trouble and the AA
Clinic funnel. Don't you see

This wife with whom I work
Stirs up trouble, as only
A colleague could inside

Our artsy bubble to out-
Do mated me *vis-à-vis?*
So this is what refined

Capitalism brings us to:
Chiaroscuro *(I clear, she obscure)*
Cataclysms of mis-reading

Every night what fresh hell
Transpired today on-site.
My hard-ons go unnoticed,

Even as my trading politics
Make it into minor media,
Or give St. Vitas' dance

To this Vivien Leigh
I married. What to do?
I am very married too.

MJM Mars/97 SF

World Series 2014

The Giants seize their Third in Five!
This Day of the Dead, so good to be alive!
As thrives The City, so thrive our
Boys of summer. Now, autumnal
Orange-and-black describe Her
Queer confluence of Halloween o'play
and Double-Decker Cavalcade. Im-
mortal Holiday and *batty* history, wed!

MJM 11/14 SF

Worries

Catastrophes malign his week. Scant business,
Overdrawn accounts, a car he can't move since
The street-sweeper brushed up his car keys dropped
On the ground, driver's side, the night before. Igno-

miniously, he finds his steely key ring mangled,
Spit out by that rotary monster and a key to his art
Gallery, for which many spares dangle in a closet.
Gutter gone: key to his SUV and its remote, *three-*

Hundred dollars for the lot! Not to mention the $55
Ticket he got, and the one for seventy-five just paid,
When this same car got towed last week: lo! four tows
In four months to the tune of two-thousand paid to

The once-loved city, now a rapist. *'Why me?'* Micro-
Chip and security set, the pair cannot be replaced
Without a tow to the dealership! Panicked, he joins
$70-AAA to wait 48 hours for his 1st tow, free.

Already, his debit card is drawing on funds he'll only
Have in a few days: Gods willing, soon may his gallery
Vend. Even worse, next Tuesday, all his worldly
Goods arrive at a new storage place, closer to home

Than the prior, so he can switch out clothes and shoes
As the seasons change in summer. The container
Contract, stringent and brusque, wracked his nerves.
He fears his next paycheck, if late or elusive, won't

Cover the first month due! Inside, are to be stored
Trappings of his once-baroque life in Pacific Heights,
And the scads of clothes he bought, shopping every day
Of the year he went bipolar. He had declined a mood

Stabilizer, not willing to gain any weight, so is now
Saddled and charged by the manic weight of huge debt
He's run from, ever since the market crashed: he, laid-
off from his art-world job, to 'well fare' after farewell.

Then his task today bursts back, a focus on *real crisis.*
A younger friend, only twenty-eight, faces a judge next
Week, a warrant for his arrest now a month old for his
Fourth DUI. Suddenly, his luxury problems seem like

Patter play. The young man has since sobered up
in AA, and now they're trying to find a free lawyer.
The youth's parents cannot help, not savvy around
The law, and themselves broke and just surviving.

Calls don't work. So he tries *Google* before they try him:
Alcohol-and-drug-addict bonds, alone, a grim trial.

For Anthony
MJM 2/11 SF

Wraith

It is inexorably sad
To concede Leo dead.

Kitchen magician, connoisseur
Koala keeper – about town

Collecting eucalyptus,
He was welcome at every site.

I imagine he works a strange
Trance on me, as if he

Saw himself die as well
Never believing it either.

These roses' dark, red, ruffled eyes
He grew betoken lifespan sinisterly

And poke on the room's reality.
I owe Leo fidelity. Can I believe

In ghosts, my love? My chance
At *Who's that* in the *distance?*

MJM during that terrible plague SF
– to Fred . . .

600

Wranglo-Saxon

Loth Lex, manipulator par excellence,
Tells lies that omit, a-latent.
A hundred for honey, hang out and dine?
Be money for sneakers to buy, then re-broker.
Had he hoisted me up, 'A hundred for shoes?'
Pops o'said, "¡No – ai, yai, yai!"
Worded *his* way, little wanker
Gets the goods! God knows he always
Does. Darn my destiny, father
To this unshy, shyster. Shyte!
If it's not me he maunders, it's Mom.
Fool afar, beware the foot-
Wear my Lex wheedle you wear.
Anon, to another dinner with chicks.
Lord Larceny L, a-will!

MJM 8/14 SF

<u>*Anglo-Saxon*</u> *verse =*
4 stresses per line
three alliteratives per line
a caesura in each line
general avoidance of Latinates

XXX

If one doesn't write a poem to xylophones,
One's index doesn't have an "X" – my favorite
Letter, in both matters of sex and my ex.

Now xylophones at the symphony seem
Rare, and considering their glittering tones,
This seems prejudicially unfair. I think some

Snobs fear that the instrument, African in origin
And played outdoors, is rather "oompah"
For lofty stratospheres of classic and romantic

Art. Lord knows it was always played on
The Lawrence Welk Show, that pitiful parade
Of saccharine serenade. Now if you call a

Xylophone 'marimba,' you instantly make it
Cooler, but obviously don't *remembah* they
Are not one in the same. Xylophones have

A drier timbre. Speaking of wood, it's what
One would have made a xylophone out of.
Until they came out with ones for kids, not

Authentically real and made of chintzy steel.
As I finish this reel, I invite you to henceforth
View the xylophone as folkishly genteel.

And if you yourself have a poem that starts
with "X," then perhaps we can take a look
At it and ex this one out. Unless you've

Already·X·also exxed out this whole sexy book.
And now that I think of it, indexes come
At *The End.* I meant 'Table of Contents' –

All your stuff up front. My ex-poetry
Teacher, being a fastidious friend.

MJM 10/15 SF
To Lex-i
-con,
conservative

Yellow Pages

A ghoul on the bus, hunched over in a hoody,
Face invisible to us, stipples a capped pen
Over a *Yellow Pages* he's just done some
Random graffiti on: glyphs, tags, patterns,

Like an old-time editor tapping copy with
Red pencil. Suddenly, he starts to shiver,
Shaking – a heroin addict, bent at the waist,
Dope ill. Is this pen-and-ink exercise his

Desperate way of keeping his mind off a fix?
The closed ink-pen telegraphs *'metaphor for*
The needle he doesn't have:' blunt, capped,
No medicine inside for his hurting human,

Humanity-sapped. I begin merciful prayers
To the Lord and Our Lady, when of a sudden
The bus overloads. People sit down, notice,
Then dart to stand up – or to move in disgust.

They have their own problems, heaven knows.
And don't care to which parts of Hell he goes.

MJM 1/15 SF

Yo, My Afro-Grammarican!

I been seen't it.
I done saw'll it.
I done saw'll it.
I been seen't it.

I been seen't it.
I done saw'll it.
I done saw'll it.
I been seen't it.

I been seen't it.
I done saw'll it.

Lawd ha' mercy.
Chriss ha' mercy.
Chriss ha' mercy.
Lawd ha' mercy.

Lawd ha' mercy.
Chriss ha' mercy.
Lawd ha' mercy.
G-rant us peece!

– To L.
MJM 8/10 Santa Barbara
"al Colegio Draive"
"I stayed been seen't it."

604

You Can't Live with Him and You Can't

Of spoilation and travail, these decades later,
I find it scarcely worth the cab fare to have got
Here in the first place.

Every bless and torment striven after, jail
Of self, valley-stuck PTSD, have/have not
Lines etched in haste on fate upon ego

Race: the switch from pony mail
To on-line: seamless as not, distraught
Me that the generations redo then erase.

Did God almost die a long time ago? Still I fail
The nerve not to believe Him as taught,
Like a Pascal wager's trace

In between every brain-fold, sail
Up – will, down. Please know that he
Fought and fought not to lose face.

MJM 1/08 SF

You Don't Have a Prayer, Pop

> *Puny pugnacious, pious pompous*
> *politithrope?*
>
> – Carol Z.

It's nights like these I'm glad I don't have a gun.
I could so easily pick it up off the noir table
And blow my brains out.

Right there next to my innocent wife:
Black hair wrapped around her eyes
To keep out the light – a lady who snores!

It's humiliating being alive –
The embarrassment of this runaway project Mankind.
You'd be surprised how many prairie folk

Might agree. What with AIDS, plutonium,
Quakes and UV, I keep looking around for a Statesman
Only to find these seedy, excellent poet-in-garrett types

Skirting my windshield vs.
Captains of industry all greased up on TV.
They tend to duties with the Press in their faces

Holding on to self-worth,
Caucasoid patriarchs dodging jail for bad kingmanship.
Hell, they're Federal evidence, *some of them Feds!*

II

Here's the list I wanted to save me:
  One. You're physically fit and sexy, sexy, sexy
  In your toney, tone, tone.

Two. You donate time to worthy charities and foundations.
Three. You love the working
Life of an artist expressing humankind's soul.

Four. You get to toy with jetset society
At brilliant dinner parties where everyone
Is elevated, enlightened, and enthralling.

Rebuttal:

1) You hate exercise.
2) You're too insecure about your
   Place in the world to share.
3) You may lack what Art exacts of great Musers?
4) You believe in trust funds and coats-of-arms
   At this late date; still you conjure

Dynastic ancestors and
"Be in the best set,"
Even if there isn't one left.

Anyways,
Young people of quality these days
Just don't think that way.

Then again,

I know what I'm hooked on;
That Jesus is coming any minute
To save us from degradation!

So why can't an alien like ET
Do it for him? I keep waiting.
Some spaceship has just got to crash.

They'll splice genes with us.
Teach us to zap through the universe
Fast to find our Immortality!

III

I have this weird notion
Certain Medea members of my family
Have been genetically encoded
To carry out this Awful Pride.

Not the escort of self-esteem,
A job well done or *carpe diem*,
But psycho-eyed monster pride:
Smothering, singeing, spiteful

Egos devouring little worthies writhing against hope in a pit!
It can never be sated. In fact, it covets
The elevated station of, say, a Princess Diana
For me, myself, and I from which I could

Wave and stare out at little you
With her theme-endowed melancholy
Crying on the inside (like I do now anyway)
But with that savory tension of the spotlight.

My brain was born for elevated things
To happen in and around it – I, trapped in this dowdy dinge
Ancestral house that keeps smoking
& drinking hale members to death.

How they chomp up that mouthbit!
Winos, lunatics, slaves!
There is no patriarch *alla Romano*
Who, seeking the gods, opens Olympus for the rest of us.

Truly
A great grandfather.
A noble Pop.
I could have withstood one.

IV

This much we have in common:
As this shit, *merde alors*, sludges
Through me, it does through you too;
Hazardous waste of great society
Treacling to the elements.

I would say we're a bunch of head-ticked apes.
All this construction! All this chatter!
It's almost enough to make you want to join
The Optimists' Club over there on Embarcadero Street,
Scratch, scratch.

  Well, why am I so blank? No shame shocks me.
That's a lot of cheap thrills gone over the edge
I can't whorl in anymore; I'm hip to the studs!
No level of great dazzles me teenwise.
  Look what became of Napoleon.

That mythic rock, I refuse to push
For some very rational reasons of contempt for hard work.
I was brainstormed that with adulthood
Would come integrity and independence.
  That in old age I'd be pushed up closer

Higher toward the Godhead – that Blake Old Man,
His White Beard! But it's only clouds,
Yer carpet of vapor.
As for ET:
I portend the contrary, motherfucker!

I would never hand over my baby son Lex in terror
(Over my dead armed body)
To those bastard aliens
With their c approaches mc^2 flying saucers and telepathy.
They're child abusers, just like down here!

Not expanders of the universe! God decoders.
Nor least of all Immortal! They're hot to cop a fondle of innocence
Just like you and me, man, on the way
To making certain their line carries on.
And they're fast-fading, immuno-deficient!

They need our babies' blood-parts just to survive.
Like we in our petty wars.
Like the Yakuza in the sex trade,
They'll import a little girl in a monkey cage
Down to their compound

                                Then have the heart
To fall in love with the little thing and want children with her –
And then have the gall to call it an Immaculate Conception,
Should scandal hit TV
Or the Pentagon bring out bigger guns.

       ***

The life of a creature among "fixed" stars
Is living humiliation.
  Do you survive it at any cost?
File Chapter 11? *Gone with the Gun?*

  Somehow, I'm glad I don't have one
Handy.
  My son will need me in the morning.
He'll want his bottle just like Dada!

  Half-conscious, I'll go bounding in there,
Big bundle of joy! Boy o' boy.
  I decorated this nursery just for you!
Can you believe it?

MJM '95 SF

You Funny Daddy

The only traces of evil I leave
are my stench and maggots
drilling me to soil, tomb-wise.

Brilliantine, I ought to have died
  Adventurous, like a Lex's *X-man*.
  Had "all A's" not evaded me,

I might have gone down
Old and hale and dramaturgic,
  but my "C"s made tragedy

The other guy's novella:
Up then down-down-down,
So random, has ways

  To pick one out &
Grandstanding, an M.D. friend
  could later say,

"But you did *live like that."*
 Who knew better, letters of
Law, Board-Certified craw?

There was my beloved Jew
With a debt of sorrow due her.
Germans in work mode off

The deep end. Britons in decline,
And Frogs forgotten
By my son's Italian TV guys

Ruling slick and shiny,
  me already gone.

Jhinja, jhinja tertelles
  me already gone.

MJM '09 SF

Your Allure

In her yesterday's allure, he stirs again today.
As if continuity were, at last, his gain again in lovers' play.

For days now, her flirtation echoes an after-mirage.
Worried about potency, he'll make a pilgrimage

To the pharmacy to pump up his confidence. She's
A known man-eater, full of 'Give me *more my babies!*'

Her flawless face marbles forth philosophy and soul,
While her body hides lush secrets, manic to bipole.

Will she concede her body to beneath him, and licks
Where lovers do? Or will she set down rules, his prick's

Sergeant-at-arms; or lay off ordering traffic up, down,
Over? He craves his reckless rambunction's renown,

Admired by others, lead her to, "Wow! You're the *best lover.*"
Or will she boss him and shrink him back under cover?

He so believes a girl should let him climb, climb, climb,
And kiss, and suck, and dirty talk – she the pantomime

Lost to speech for her, *'Oh my gods'* and 'moans.' If
She lets him steer the car, she'll orgasm. He'll stay stiff.

Thus, mounting tension finally melts for good. He'll seek,
Not to dominate, but lord their next play at her peak, to meek.

MJM 2/11 SF

Your Dick Again

Ninety-four's over –
So I channel surf
These *Years-in-Review*

To hear declared
There was no such thing
    as Decades till lately:

Alas, classic cats were
Roman-numeral blind –
As if time had facets.

Now outside, their chanting
And howls to the numbers –
Seem as blades dicing time

Or Big Apple to pie in the sky!
Right guys, squawk it down
With your bleat tooters!

Take off the 1st! "Feast
    of the Circumcision."
That *"feast"* does not quite

Serve good taste
In this particular case
is a foregone

Pound of my flesh.
That the Church,
like body-bound *Homo sapiens*,

Would carve out the first
Day of the year for penis
Points to mortal sin from Venus!

We should have left Christmas
in Spring, when His Birth
we opine happened anyway –

New lamb, fresh life, the light, cocksure –
Instead of moving it to the 25th,
When we are forced to deal with prick

Right from the start, one week
after a Jewish birth being
the obligatory bris-cut party:

25 + 7 =
The first
Clocked dick.

There are moths impaled on pins.
Our Lord nailed to the Cross.
A bat for every ball.

But there is no axis through the earth.
Nor time, nor day, nor month to start
No year. Anyone in the cosmic light

Of God knows that.
It ain't brain surgery,
and you don't have to be Einstein.

Nonetheless, with their Roman candles,
This headless flock's all fired up again!
And it's pissing me off – *but just a wee bit.*

MJM 12/31/94 NYC

Zodiacal

Would that the Lord put moon and stars
In place to give us some kind of trace

On what we might expect to go on
From on-high, up there down here.

There is no scientific reason to believe
The position of heavenly bodies

Has a whit to do with us,
Our fears' and tears' calculus,

Any more than Jesus' passion, Buddha's,
Or Mohammed's, or Moses's mission.

MJM 9/10 SF

Zoo Sea

Out at land's end where the Martha's Vineyard-like dunes
And hillocks rise bunkered up, all silicon and calcium grit,
By gale and moon that jet sea to wet the sand in plains,
Then ebbing surrender grains to parch in sun and wind to
Somersaults' brush a-spin that piles spits underfoot at rest.

Down yonder street the zoo that tends the wild and exotic
In our care to eat the hay and fruit and meat and seed
We grew afar and far from salt enliven our kids to gaze
Toy totems of their books and screens they've come to
Love but not seen flesh inspire their awe and wonder.

I note splays of sandy plants that root in chills on shif-
ting rills gravely plain like fervent heads' balded pates'
Clumped tufts of hair above the ears of men sad aware of
Their fragile brains curious and furious to fare to oracle
Storms chafing sands from the ocean floors as eons of

Antique life that plied afloat to roam the waters sank in
Zillions till dinosaur epochs and *Mammoth mammalia*
Not in the zoo but in this ground around my feet that
Walk my life and smelled when cells as on the sands
Rotted dead to blow to the sea before my skull grind to

Calcite shards, my spirit as stout as bone to outstrip a span
Of an age's Jurassic fossils, now filed in the earth and torpid
Graves that tell the story of seas and chemicals which flashed
Fiery 'first' cause on unfurled, hurled rife rock to transmogrify
Sand and soil and water with life that compounded in seas

To build identity that stayed or crawled again to dry land,
Begot anew and lived and died, re-rose that I not yet in zoo
Align my mankind's soul with skull in full to sky to
    Hand-over, marveled, or marbled.

MJM 11/11 SF
At Land's End to celebrate
superstitiously 11/11/11

"On the rough wet grass of the backyard
my father and mother have spread quilts. We all lie there,
my mother, my father, my uncle, my aunt,
and I too am lying there. They are not talking much,
and the talk is quiet, of nothing in particular,
of nothing at all in particular, of nothing at all.
The stars are wide and alive, they seem each like a smile
of great sweetness, and they seem very near.
All my people are larger bodies than mine . . .
with voices gentle and meaningless
like the voices of sleeping birds . . .
We are talking now of summer evenings
in Knoxville, Tennessee in the time that I had lived there,
so successfully disguised to myself as a child."

– James Agee
Knoxville: Summer of 1915

I say that one must be a seer, make oneself a seer. The poet makes himself a seer by a long, prodigious, and rational disordering of all the senses. Every form of love, of suffering, of madness; he searches himself, he consumes all the poisons in him, and keeps only their quintessences. This is an unspeakable torture during which he needs all his faith and superhuman strength, and during which he becomes the great patient, the great criminal, the great accursed—and the great learned one!—among men.—For he arrives at the unknown! Because he has cultivated his own soul—which was rich to begin with – more than any other man! He reaches the unknown; and even if, crazed, he ends up by losing the understanding of his visions, at least he has seen them! Let him die charging through those unutterable, unnameable things: other horrible workers will come; they will begin from the horizons where he has succumbed!

– Arthur Rimbaud

. . . these would-be gentlemen who leave Harvard "as **great Blockheads as ever***,*
only more proud and self-conceited."

– Ben Franklin

. . . and I basked

In the art-felt knowledge that Uncle A. was dancing flamenco
For Her Serene Highness that very day at a party thrown at *Fox.*
Thence back in L.A, we all choked with laughter one playful day
When our *Carol* tagged me and José the Harvard Mexicans!

– MJM "Mexican Ivy"

Some fucks like me 'cause I'm classy
Others, 'cause I'm sassy
Some fucks think I'm funny
Others, I got money
Some tell me "Daddy . . .
Bro'flake, you're built for speed."
Now if you put that all together
'S everything a good wo/man needs

– after Billie Holiday

finis

MJM 2017 SF

Acknowledgements

The author wishes to acknowledge the marvelous mitzvah
That is S.-F. Strang, this book's publication editor.
Zenith of perfection, he knows the value of a space and the
Do-or-die of a line break, neither faulted by eye nor by hand.
Tough customer, he took a liking to my work. Of that I am proud.

The author also wishes to acknowledge the enduring attentions
Of his closest readers M. Wornick, art collector, and S. Kurzfeld,
Screenwriter. What they did not say was as invaluable as
What they did, for silence comes with pointers. I will always
Treasure their encouragement and apt critiques. Best ears I know.

Practical thanks are due to Vlad B. (aka Uncle Val!) for his
Help underwriting the costs of book production. <u>Очень спасибо</u>.

MJM 10/17 SF

This book has been printed in 10 and 11 point Chaparral Pro.

Made in the USA
San Bernardino, CA
14 April 2019